CRIMINOLOGY AS A MORAL SCIENCE

This book proposes an explicit recognition of criminology as a moral science – that is, an empirically rigorous social science that takes full account of the presence and role of values in people's reasoning and motivation. This endeavour requires input from both criminologists and moral philosophers, and careful dialogue between them, so the book contains chapters by scholars from both disciplines.

Several social sciences – notably social anthropology – have in recent decades experienced a 'moral turn', leading them to focus research more fully and explicitly on ethical issues. Criminology is now experiencing a similar movement, and the central aim of this volume is to extend and enhance this welcome development.

Theoretically, the book explicates inadequacies and implausible elements of social scientific positivism and suggests directions for a more illuminating conception of the role of valuative considerations in social science. It also clarifies key theoretical issues such as the so-called 'fact-value distinction'. Empirically, analyses are offered of the moral dimensions of important criminological topics, as illustrations of a moral science approach. These analyses focus on whistleblowing in police services; the moral dilemmas faced by mothers of children whose fathers have been imprisoned; analyses of offenders' shame and guilt; and ethical aspects of attempts to desist from crime.

Studies in Penal Theory and Ethics: Volume 9

Studies in Penal Theory and Ethics

A Series Published for
the Centre for Penal Theory and Ethics
Institute of Criminology, University of Cambridge

FOUNDING EDITOR: ANDREAS VON HIRSCH

GENERAL EDITOR:
LEO ZAIBERT

The Series publishes cutting-edge work on penal theory and ethics – both broadly construed – and on their intersections. The Series is particularly open to approaches belonging to different intellectual traditions – whether analytical, comparative, or historical – and to interdisciplinary approaches. While the Series's emphasis is theoretical, it is hoped that many of its volumes will highlight some of the ways in which theoretical work relates to practical concerns.

Previous volumes in the series:

Ethical and Social Perspectives on Situational Crime Prevention
edited by Andrew von Hirsch, David Garland and Alison Wakefield

Restorative Justice and Criminal Justice: Competing or Reconcilable Paradigms?
edited by Andrew von Hirsch, Julian Roberts, Anthony E Bottoms, Kent Roach and Mara Schiff

Incivilities: Regulating Offensive Behaviour
edited by A P Simester and Andreas Von Hirsch

Previous Convictions at Sentencing: Theoretical and Applied Perspectives
edited by Julian V Roberts and Andrew von Hirsch

Setting the Watch: Privacy and the Ethics of CCTV Surveillance
Beatrice von Silva-Tarouca Larsen

Criminal Law and the Authority of the State
edited by Antje du Bois-Pedain, Magnus Ulväng and Petter Asp

Penal Censure: Engagements Within and Beyond Desert Theory
edited by Antje du Bois-Pedain and Anthony E Bottoms

Re-Reading Beccaria: On the Contemporary Significance of a Penal Classic
edited by Antje du Bois-Pedain and Shachar Eldar

Criminology as a Moral Science
edited by Anthony Bottoms and Jonathan Jacobs

Criminology as a Moral Science

Edited by
Anthony Bottoms
and
Jonathan Jacobs

•HART•
OXFORD • LONDON • NEW YORK • NEW DELHI • SYDNEY

HART PUBLISHING
Bloomsbury Publishing Plc
Kemp House, Chawley Park, Cumnor Hill, Oxford, OX2 9PH, UK
1385 Broadway, New York, NY 10018, USA
29 Earlsfort Terrace, Dublin 2, Ireland

HART PUBLISHING, the Hart/Stag logo, BLOOMSBURY and the Diana logo are trademarks of Bloomsbury Publishing Plc

First published in Great Britain 2023

A catalogue record for this book is available from the British Library.

Library of Congress Cataloging-in-Publication data

Names: Bottoms, Anthony E., 1939- editor. | Jacobs, Jonathan A., editor.

Title: Criminology as a moral science / edited by Anthony Bottoms and Jonathan Jacobs.

Description: Oxford ; New York : Hart Publishing, 2023. | Series: Studies in penal theory and penal ethics ; volume 9 | Includes bibliographical references and index. | Summary: "This book proposes an explicit recognition of criminology as a moral science: a philosophically textured appreciation of the presence and role of values in people's reasoning and motivation, set within an empirically rigorous social-scientific account"—Provided by publisher.

Identifiers: LCCN 2023014742 | ISBN 9781509965328 (hardback) | ISBN 9781509965373 (paperback) | ISBN 9781509965359 (pdf) | ISBN 9781509965342 (Epub)

Subjects: LCSH: Criminology—Moral and ethical aspects.

Classification: LCC HV6018 .C738 2023 | DDC 364—dc23/eng/20230524

LC record available at https://lccn.loc.gov/2023014742

ISBN: HB: 978-1-50996-532-8
ePDF: 978-1-50996-535-9
ePub: 978-1-50996-534-2

Typeset by Compuscript Ltd, Shannon

Preface

THE TWO EDITORS of this volume – one a criminologist, one a moral philosopher – have for a number of years been in conversation about the relations between their two disciplines. Arising from their early dialogue, they jointly organised a workshop on this topic, held in September 2018 at the Institute of Criminology, University of Cambridge, and sponsored jointly by the Centre for Penal Theory and Ethics, University of Cambridge and the Institute for Criminal Justice Ethics, John Jay College, City University of New York.

The 2018 workshop followed the format developed by the founder of the Cambridge Centre for Penal Theory and Ethics, Professor Andreas von Hirsch, for Centre-based workshops. The number of participants was limited, and papers by criminologists and by moral and political philosophers were delivered and debated in plenary sessions. These papers and discussions focused in particular on two broad questions: how can empirical research in criminology best capture the moral dimensions of the topics that it seeks to address; and how can social scientific investigations help to clarify philosophical discussions concerning morality? Several different views, from diverse avenues of approach, were presented.

This volume would not have been possible without the 2018 workshop, but it is not a 'book of the conference'. There are two main reasons for this. First, several contributors to the workshop were not able to work up their initial presentations into chapters for the volume. Second and more importantly, in the continuing dialogue between the editors it became clear that while the workshop had opened up some fundamentally important issues, there was significant scope for further development of these issues. The most obvious example of this is that the concept of 'Criminology as a Moral Science' has been developed entirely in post-workshop discussions.

While, therefore, some of the chapters in this volume owe their origin to presentations at the workshop, in all but one instance these have been significantly developed for inclusion here. In addition, some chapters have been freshly commissioned by the editors, in order to produce what we hope is a balanced and stimulating volume. As editors, we would like to express our considerable gratitude to all the contributors for their willingness to engage in detailed discussions with us about the content of their chapters, and for their patience in preparing fresh drafts following these discussions. We hope, of course, that the published book will encourage other scholars to take up the issues that motivated both the workshop and this set of chapters, so that the dialogue between criminology and moral and political philosophy will be further enhanced.

This book is Volume 9 in the 'Studies in Penal Theory and Ethics' published for the Centre for Penal Theory and Ethics, University of Cambridge by Hart/Bloomsbury. We are pleased to be joining this distinguished series, and we are most grateful to Hart/Bloomsbury for their support of the Series, and their support for us in developing this volume.

Finally, we would like to express sincere gratitude to the Centre for Penal Theory and Ethics and the Institute for Criminal Justice Ethics for their financial support of the 2018 workshop. More personally, our warmest thanks also to Ailie Rennie, a PhD student at the Cambridge Institute of Criminology, for her invaluable and much-appreciated help in preparing the manuscript of this book for publication. In addition, Jonathan Jacobs would like to thank the American Philosophical Society for support for research that is reflected in this volume, and the Hayek Fund for Scholars programme of the Institute for Humane Studies for funding that supported his research and travel.

Figure 1 on page 25 is reproduced by permission of the copyright holder, Cambridge University Press.

Anthony Bottoms
Jonathan Jacobs

Table of Contents

PART IV
DESISTANCE FROM CRIME: ANALYSES IN POSITIVE AND CRITICAL MORALITY

Contributors

Jennifer Barton-Crosby is a Research Director in the Crime and Justice Programme, NatCen Social Research, London.

Anthony Bottoms is Emeritus Wolfson Professor of Criminology, University of Cambridge and Honorary Professor of Criminology, University of Sheffield. He is also a Fellow of the British Academy and a former Director of the Institute of Criminology, University of Cambridge.

Sophie-Grace Chappell is Professor of Philosophy at The Open University, and Honorary Research Fellow in the School of Philosophy and Anthropology, University of St Andrews.

Sophie Ellis, a former psychologist in the Prison Service of England and Wales, is now a PhD student at the Institute of Criminology, University of Cambridge.

Alice Ievins is a Lecturer in Criminology, University of Liverpool.

Jonathan Jacobs is Professor of Philosophy and Director of the Institute for Criminal Justice Ethics, John Jay College of Criminal Justice, City University of New York.

Caroline Lanskey is Associate Professor of Criminology and Criminal Justice, University of Cambridge.

Friedrich Lösel is Emeritus Professor of Psychology, University of Erlangen-Nuremburg, and a former Director of the Institute of Criminology, University of Cambridge.

Lucy Markson is an Associate Forensic Psychologist, Tully Forensic Psychology, and Visiting Scholar at the Institute of Criminology, University of Cambridge.

Matt Matravers is Professor of Law and Director of the Morrell Centre for Toleration, University of York.

Karen Souza is Senior Research Associate at the United States Sentencing Commission.

Christine Swanton is retired from the Philosophy Department, University of Auckland. Her recent publications include *The Virtue Ethics of Hume and Nietzsche* (Wiley Blackwell, 2015) and *Target Centred Virtue Ethics* (Oxford University Press 2021).

Justice Tankebe is Associate Professor of Criminology, University of Cambridge.

Ryan Williams is Senior Lecturer in Studies in Religion, University of Queensland.

Introduction: The Nature and Scope of a Moral Science

ANTHONY BOTTOMS AND JONATHAN JACOBS

THE TITLE OF this volume – *Criminology as a Moral Science* – makes two assumptions, which we should acknowledge at the outset. First, it assumes that the subject matter of criminology is inextricably concerned with moral issues. Second, it assumes that these moral issues can be appropriately discussed without detracting from the nature of criminology as a *social science.*

The first of these assumptions is not hard to defend. A classic summary of the scope of criminology was offered in a well-known textbook by Sutherland and Cressey (1960: 3):

> Criminology is the body of knowledge regarding crime as a social phenomenon. It includes within its scope the [study][1] of making laws, of breaking laws, and of reacting towards the breaking of laws.

Although this definition is now 60 years old, it has more recently been described by Loader and Sparks (2011: 13) as 'still hard to beat', and it has also been endorsed by Lawrence Sherman (2010), who places particular emphasis on the need for criminologists to address all three of the substantive areas mentioned by Sutherland and Cressey, rather than (as many have done) ignoring the first ('making laws'). Sherman is surely right in taking this stance, and careful reflection on this aspect of criminology will soon reveal that the prohibitions enshrined in a country's criminal statutes will be 'always and inevitably expressive … of a prevailing social morality adopted and enforced' by those with power in that state (MacCormick 2007: 211).[2] Equally, those who research aspects of 'breaking laws' and 'reacting towards the breaking of laws' – the other two main fields in Sutherland and Cressey's definition – will inevitably, and on numerous

[1] The original word in the definition was 'process', but that has on occasion led to the misunderstanding that Sutherland and Cressey were concerned only with process and not substance. We have therefore substituted 'study'.

[2] This is so even in colonial states, where – as Tamanaha (2001) pointedly noted – the formal legal system is usually imposed by the colonists and may have little connection with the norms of the indigenous people. In such situations, the enforcement of the law can be not only difficult but often unjust; but it will still be expressive of the social morality of those in power.

occasions, find themselves studying people who are making moral choices of various kinds. While there are differences between law and morality, and there are important debates about how they are interrelated, perhaps especially in liberal democracies, there is no question that there are morally significant aspects of making laws, breaking laws and reacting to the breaking of laws.

Our second assumption raises the more complex issue of what constitutes a 'social science', a question that leads inexorably to what WG Runciman (1983: 1) described as the 200-year-old 'debate between those who affirm and those who deny that there is a fundamental difference in kind between the sciences of nature and the sciences of [humankind]'. Runciman adds, helpfully, that despite their differences, those on opposite sides of this debate agree that the debate arises 'because the study of self-conscious human behaviour is itself self-conscious human behaviour'; so the dispute concerns 'the conclusions which [the two sides] hold to follow, or not follow, from that fact' (1983: 2). We acknowledge the continued relevance of this age-old debate within contemporary criminology, and we will return to it later. For now, it is sufficient to say that we agree with those who consider that social science is, because of the existence of 'self-conscious human behaviour', in certain respects (but not in all respects) importantly different from natural science. However, we also want to affirm, with Runciman (1983: 4), that there is a difference between science (both natural and social) and non-science; hence 'there is a difference between science and metaphysics, or science and art'. Within this framework, our use of the term 'moral science' is simply a way of emphasising that social life (and 'self-conscious human behaviour') always and everywhere includes moral elements, so 'social science' inevitably includes 'moral science'.

The term 'moral science' is, however, not one that we have invented; it has a history, and that is part of the reason we have adopted it in our title. That history began in the seventeenth and eighteenth centuries, and it is connected with the work of the so-called 'British Moralists' such as Hutcheson, Reid, Shaftesbury and – most famously – David Hume and Adam Smith.[3] One of us has recently suggested, drawing on this background, that the work of some contemporary empirical criminologists has some affinities with British Moralism (Jacobs 2022a), and he has also written an article with the subtitle 'Recovering the Moral Sciences through Criminology' (Jacobs 2022b). In that second paper, he identifies 'moral science', in a contemporary context, as a social-scientific approach that 'includes a philosophically textured appreciation of the presence and role of values in people's reasoning, judgements and motivations, while striving to make that appreciation part of an empirically rigorous account of the topics studied'. He adds that, within such an approach, 'considerations of value and agency are vitally important' (Jacobs 2022b: 80). If that characterisation is

[3] An example of the use of the term 'moral science' is that in the nineteenth century Cambridge University created an undergraduate honours course in 'the Moral Sciences of Psychology, Philosophy and Political Economy'. This lasted until 1969, by which time its scope was restricted to philosophy, because the economists and psychologists had set up their own, separate, honours courses.

correct, the optimal development of contemporary 'moral science' will require careful cross-disciplinary dialogue between moral philosophers and social scientists. This is because social-scientific expertise will be necessary in order to deliver 'empirically rigorous accounts', while input from moral philosophy will be required to make accounts of values and agency appropriately 'philosophically textured'. It is a central hope of the editors that this volume will act as a catalyst for the better development of this kind of moral science.

Before proceeding further, it will be useful to introduce a distinction, originally drawn by the legal philosopher HLA Hart (1963: 20), between 'positive morality' and 'critical morality'. In this framework, 'positive morality' is the observed moral behaviour or moral attitudes of a given social group or individual, while 'critical morality' consists of evaluative statements (positive or negative) about moral claims or moral behaviour. As we shall see, what we are calling 'moral science' can include both positive morality and critical morality, but it will always be important to be clear which is in play, because one is descriptive/explanatory and the other is evaluative.

THE ENLIGHTENMENT BACKGROUND

We begin with an introduction to the work of the 'British Moralists'. The late seventeenth and eighteenth centuries are sometimes described as the period of 'The Enlightenment' – a set of developments that affected 'many levels of [European] society and politics' and extended also to 'other parts of the world touched by European influence' (Outram 2019: 9). With a background of the Reformation and the Wars of Religion, as well as European discoveries in the Western hemisphere, and some revolutionary developments in the natural sciences and in epistemology (Descartes), this was a time of re-examination of fundamental principles in several areas of thought, including political legitimacy and political obligation. It was, therefore, a period during which some aspects of what is often described as the 'modern world' were developing. This was the social context within which the British Moralists wrote.

Any theory of morality (or ethics – we are using the two terms interchangeably) needs to account for at least three things: first, the locus and nature of moral value (where in the world are values?; are they subjective or objective?); second, the basis of moral judgement (what is involved in apprehending value?); and third, the character of moral motivation (how is a person moved to do what morality requires?). A key general feature of the writings of the British Moralists was that they provided accounts of moral value, moral judgement and moral motivation that were innovatory in that they offered alternatives to *moral rationalism* and *moral intuitionism*.[4]

[4] A few of the British Moralists, such as Ralph Cudworth, were rationalists, but the greatest impact of the tradition has been through critics of such views.

By 'moral rationalism', we mean any theory that maintains that reason *alone* is a source of moral knowledge, or that the exercise of rationality can ascertain what is morally right and morally wrong, or that moral facts entail moral reasons to act. There were several different forms of moral rationalism but the key point is that, for each of them, the operation of reason was seen as the basis or foundation of moral judgement and/or moral motivation. On this view, it is reason that enables us to ascertain what we morally ought to do, and it is reason that motivates us to do what we ought.[5]

As for 'intuitionism', in philosophy this generally refers to any view which maintains that there is a kind of knowledge that is uninferred, unmediated and direct. Even if it is knowledge that one attains after having certain kinds of experience and engaging in certain kinds of thought, intuition is itself *direct knowledge*. Plato is an excellent example of intuitionism, as is Descartes (1641/1998), who held that each of us has intuitive knowledge of our own existence as a thinking being ('*cogito ergo sum*'). Another example is Aristotle's view of our knowledge of the first principles of the sciences. We only come to know them after enquiry and reflection, but the first principles, the axioms of scientific knowledge, are intuited. The principle of non-contradiction, that an entity cannot both have and not have the same property in the same respect at the same time, is an illustration. Such principles *do not follow* from something else; there is nothing more basic from which they are inferred. Moral Intuitionists believe that there is intuitive knowledge of moral properties such as *right* and *wrong*, or *prohibited* and *obligatory*. This is not a feeling, a hunch, a somewhat undeveloped idea. What is intuited is known, grasped, understood directly. Unsurprisingly, some rationalists were intuitionists.

Those of the British Moralists who rejected moral rationalism and intuitionism tried to show that an adequate account of morality can be given in broadly *naturalistic* terms, ie, in terms of faculties, modes of experience, forms of receptivity and sensibility that are elements of human nature, with no direct role for rationalism or divine revelation.[6]

It might be thought that scepticism regarding moral rationalism would undermine the foundations of morality, but most critics of rationalism were keen to show that neither the genuineness nor the authority of moral considerations is undermined by the critique of rationalism. Of course, people committed to rationalism and to divine law (and revelation) as a source of morality regarded these 'moral sense' thinkers as sceptics, but in general they did not see themselves in that way. Rather, they tried to explicate those features of human nature

[5] As different as their philosophies were, Plato and Descartes were both rationalists regarding knowledge. Each held that reason, and reason alone, is the source of genuine knowledge. The senses are a source of various perceptions and ideas, but knowledge is attained only by reason. Moral rationalists held a similar view with respect to moral judgement and moral motivation.

[6] Many of these thinkers were Christians, but there is little theological content in their moral theories.

crucial to the kinds of relations, responses and concerns that are integral to moral life, and thus to provide accounts of moral value, moral judgement, and moral motivation while avoiding what they saw as excessive and unsupportable rationalist claims. Indeed, Hume (1739–40/2000), in the Introduction to his youthful masterpiece *A Treatise on Human Nature*, explicitly argued for a *science* of human nature. As David Fate Norton (2000: 14–15) explains, Hume thought that:

> Moral philosophy … will be able to move beyond fruitless debate only if we change its focus. Instead of turning directly to particular issues currently debated in, say, metaphysics or ethics or politics, we should first focus our attention on the 'science of human nature', on, that is, the one branch of learning on which other branches … depend … Hume also suggests that recent successes in natural [science] have given us an important clue about how to proceed in our efforts to develop this foundational science … [He thus] attempts in the *Treatise* to articulate a new kind of philosophy, an experience-based science of human nature.

It is, of course, the 'experience-based' nature of the moral philosophy of the British Moralists that makes their work of potential interest to contemporary social scientists. In developing their views, they gave prominence to the concepts of *sensibility* and *sociability*, and we will return to their discussion of these matters later in this Introduction.

MORALITY IN CONTEMPORARY SOCIAL SCIENCE

In recent decades, several social sciences have experienced what is often described as a 'moral turn'. This has involved, first, a widespread acceptance within a particular discipline that the way in which research in that discipline has been conducted has, generally speaking, underplayed the importance of moral issues; and second, attempts to rectify that situation by developing new kinds of research.

Perhaps the most prominent of these 'moral turns' has taken place in the field of social (or cultural) anthropology. In an important encyclopedia entry summarising this development, the Cambridge social anthropologist James Laidlaw (2017: 1) has written that 'the academic discipline of anthropology has been centrally concerned with morality or ethics … throughout its whole history … [but until recently] there was nothing that could reasonably be called the anthropology of ethics'. Within anthropology, early understandings of morality were particularly focused on 'problems of social control and enculturation' (Laidlaw 2017: 4–5). However, that situation changed at about the turn of the millennium, when a range of questions became pressing – for example:

> How do we understand what happens when people doubt or question the dominant values of their social milieu? And what about when they face irreconcilable conflicts of values … Can people's sense of responsibility and freedom in relation to their own

character and conduct really be written off, with a causal story about how, generally speaking, they come to do what society (or their culture or their class) requires of them? (Laidlaw 2017: 4).

In response to such questions, Laidlaw continues, social anthropologists have begun to develop work that 'engages systematically with [wider] intellectual traditions, often in other disciplines … in an effort to develop a [better] conceptual vocabulary for anthropology and to advance a general understanding of the nature of ethical life'. As a result, several 'established topics of anthropological research … have been materially enriched by being subject to "the ethical turn"'.[7] The main intellectual traditions that have been thus newly considered are 'virtue ethics, ordinary language philosophy and Michel Foucault's "genealogy of ethics"' (Laidlaw 2017: 5).[8]

Also since about the turn of the millennium, the discipline of sociology has experienced its own more muted 'ethical turn', although apparently (and strangely) this has occurred largely in isolation from the developments in social anthropology. Concurrently with this development, sociology has also seen the rapid rise of what is called 'relational sociology', which has, in the words of one relational sociologist, 'sought to find new ways to move beyond seeing individuals as either determined subjects of social structure or as atomised subjects' (Abbott 2020: 1). Owen Abbott's important book, while noting that 'sociologists still approach any sort of questions of morality with an air of trepidation', aims to bring together relational sociology and the sociology of morality, in order to 'explain how people become able to engage morally with practice in the ways that they do' (at 5).

These developments in social anthropology and in sociology are referred to, explicitly or implicitly, in several chapters in this volume. Our advocacy of 'criminology as a moral science' is, of course, an effort to accelerate some similar developments in criminology. We fully acknowledge, as was said in a Presidential Address of the American Society of Criminology a decade ago, that there is already at least 'a glimmer of a moral awakening in criminology' (Messner 2012: 7) – and probably now more than a glimmer. In our view, however, there remains significant work to do before criminology can claim to be dealing well with the ethical issues that are pervasive within the topics that criminologists study.

Laidlaw (2017, 2014) has identified moral relativism as a particular intellectual barrier that anthropologists have needed to overcome in order to develop an adequate anthropology of ethics, though this had its difficulties because traditionally relativism was seen as 'a sort of disciplinary membership badge' for anthropologists (Laidlaw 2014: 23). Analogously, in our view a necessary step

[7] As an example of this, see the re-evaluation by Robbins (2018) of the concept of 'values' in light of the kinds of questions raised in the quotation from Laidlaw, above.

[8] For important works that give a flavour of the 'ethical turn' in social anthropology, see Fassin and Lézé (2014); Laidlaw (2014); Mattingly (2014); and Lambek et al (2015).

in the development of 'criminology as a moral science' will be to address some of the legacies of positivism, given the traditional dominance of positivism in 'mainstream' criminology. In later sections, we shall deal more fully with the challenges of positivism and relativism, but first we shall offer some (necessarily rather brief) observations on how, historically, criminology has dealt, or not dealt, with moral issues.

Such a history has to begin with positivism, because, as Radzinowicz and Hood (1986: 5) have rightly said, '[t]he birth of criminology as a separate discipline will forever be associated with [the] names and writings' of the Italian positivists Cesare Lombroso, Enrico Ferri and Raffaele Garofalo. These scholars attempted 'to construct a bold new conception of criminal law and penal policy based on the negation of free will' (Radzinowicz and Hood (1986: 3), a fully determinist stance that they deemed essential in order to develop criminology as a science. In consequence, they proposed (in the case of 'natural crimes')[9] to abolish those aspects of criminal justice that were based on moral rather than scientific principles. This was a very radical proposal, because it involved doing away with concepts such as (i) moral responsibility (or mens rea) as a requirement of criminal liability, and (ii) the severity of punishment being related to the (moral) seriousness of the offence. For the positivists, once it had been shown that a person had committed a 'natural crime' (with or without mens rea), the aim would be to 'effect the cessation of the criminal's harmfulness to society' (Garofalo 1914: 406) by the most effective means – a process that was described as 'social defence'. As the Italian positivists were well aware, this approach differed fundamentally from that of the earlier 'classical school' of jurists such as Beccaria (1764/1995; see also du Bois-Pedain and Eldar 2022) because, in a word, what was proposed was that the main focus of attention should shift from the *crime* to the *criminal*. Hence the famous epigram of the Dutch jurist GA van Hamel that: 'Former lawyers bade men study justice, but Lombroso bids justice study men' (quoted in Radzinowicz and Hood 1986: 17). That epigram was still being widely quoted with approval when one of the present authors (AEB) began his criminological studies in the 1960s.[10]

[9] Garofalo, in his proposed 'principles … for an international penal code', explicitly restricted the scope of the Code to 'natural crimes', defined as 'such acts as offend the sentiment of humanity or violate the rules of conduct exacted by the common or average probity of present-day civilized peoples' (Garofalo 1914: 405; see further his ch 1, *passim*). The categories of 'natural criminals' were said to be 'murderers; violent criminals; criminals deficient in probity; and lascivious criminals' (at 406). Garofalo conceded that all breaches of law should 'beyond question … be attended with a penal sanction' (at 34), but by no means all of such acts were, in his view, 'natural crimes'. Among offences excluded were some intra-family and some political offences (at 35–40), as well as breaches of the public peace, carrying unlawful arms, criminal trespass, assisting prisoners to escape and smuggling (at 42).

[10] Interestingly, also, at that time no one quoted the wise remark of the Cambridge criminal lawyer Courtney Kenny that 'each precept is good [but] better still is the combination of the two' (cited in Radzinowicz and Hood 1986: 17).

Although the Italian positivists never succeeded in getting their policy proposals enacted in full in any state, they were very successful in influencing the future foundations of criminological study, and partially successful in influencing policies for the treatment of offenders.[11] This was true even in the United States, despite the much greater influence of sociology on American as opposed to European criminology.

A cogent and influential criticism of aspects of US criminology was published in the 1960s by David Matza in his *Delinquency and Drift* (1964). Matza argued that American criminology, although 'increasingly integrated into sociology, ... was and still is a separate field with its own traditions and preconceptions', derived from positivism (at 3). He identified three fundamental assumptions made by positivism (at 3), each of which he called into question. One was what he called its 'hard determinism'. Its second and 'most explicit' assumption was (echoing van Hamel's epigram) 'the primacy of the criminal actor rather than the criminal law as the major point of departure in the construction of etiological theories' (at 3). This, he argued, meant that positivists completely missed the dimension of *infraction* necessarily present in offending; and more broadly it entailed an absence of attention to 'the complex relationships between delinquents and legal institutions' (at 4). Matza's third assumption, implicit in the first two, was that of essentialism: 'the delinquent was [seen as] fundamentally different from the law-abiding' (at 11).

Matza's substantive focus was adolescent male delinquency. At the time he wrote, there were several competing explanatory accounts of what were described as 'delinquent subcultures' among male adolescents, and central to each of these theories was the notion of 'commitment ... to deviant ideas and practices' (at 25). One of Matza's strongest criticisms of subcultural theory was that, like 'biological or personality theor[ies] of delinquency' (at 25), it 'accounts for too much delinquency' (at 21). This was because if people really held strong and enduring commitments to deviant norms, the well-known reduction in rates of criminality in the third and fourth decades of life would not occur. This error had, Matza concluded, been generated by positivistic essentialism.

We need not follow here the intricacies of Matza's own theory, but two points should be noted. First, central to his theory were two concepts that he had previously developed in joint articles with his mentor Gresham Sykes (both now reprinted in Blomberg et al 2018: chs 3 and 5): namely, 'neutralisation' and 'subterranean values'. Second, the final chapter of *Delinquency and Drift*

[11] Hence, as Roger Hood (1974: 1) expressed the matter, while in most jurisdictions most of the time the judge retained the function of fixing the maximum period of penal custody according to the seriousness of the offence, in many places (especially in the US) it became a commonly accepted 'doctrine' that 'the actual period of a custodial sentence served should be fixed by review boards of various kinds advised, in the main, by the penal authorities who [had] been responsible for containing and "training" the offender'. Hood's important paper challenged this 'doctrine', and was one of several influential neo-classical critiques that were developed in the 1970s.

explicitly introduces the concept of the 'will'. Thus, although this point is only apparent with hindsight, Matza's theory prefigured a moral science approach, given that within moral science 'considerations of value and agency are vitally important' (Jacobs 2022b: 80). It is therefore of great interest that in 2018 there appeared a book (Blomberg et al 2018) honouring David Matza's brief but stellar criminological career. In the preface to this book, Francis Cullen writes that even if we do not fully endorse them, Matza's claims are 'powerful ideas that merit our continued attention', because they 'continue to question persistent disciplinary assumptions, they make us pay attention to realities we have blissfully ignored, and they inspire us to theorise more innovatively than otherwise would have been the case' (Blomberg et al 2018: xiii, x).

It seems likely that, at least since about 2005, a main factor generating fresh interest in Matza's work has been growing attention within criminology to the concept of human agency. Thus, in the first substantive chapter in the volume honouring Matza, Travis Pratt (2018), who started his doctoral studies in 1996, states that '*Delinquency and Drift* was not a staple in the reading lists of criminologists of my generation'. However, he began to notice that 'terms like "human agency" and "maturational reform" were being kicked around the discipline with increasing frequency … [and] whenever they were mentioned it was done with a strong link to *Delinquency and Drift*' (at 13). So eventually, Pratt read this book. When he did, he concluded that it had many merits, not least because 'much … contemporary criminological theory remains rooted firmly within the very form of positive criminology that Matza warned us against' (at 14). Hence, he argued that – despite some inevitable weaknesses – *Delinquency and Drift* deserved to be added to a short list of criminological classics that all graduate students should read (at 23).

But what had triggered the increasing criminological salience of 'human agency' that Pratt had noticed? Tracing exact origins is difficult, but it seems that one important factor was the explicit use of this concept in a major research study in the field of developmental criminology by Laub and Sampson (2003). This book was a successor to earlier research by the same authors that had re-analysed data on the criminal careers (to age 32) of a classic longitudinal cohort of male repeat juvenile offenders (Sampson and Laub 1993). The 2003 volume provided an update on the known offending of this cohort, but more importantly it contained data derived from fresh retrospective life-history interviews with a subsample of 52 of the men, then in their sixties. These interviews were included because the authors – both major figures in American criminology – had taken seriously a review of their earlier work which claimed that it had not been 'adept at discerning the inner logic of lives' (Modell 1994: 1391). For Laub and Sampson (2003: 8–10) the life-history interviews, by offering a 'person-based approach' to complement their previous 'variables-based approach', had allowed them 'to develop a richer and more comprehensive picture' of criminal careers and their cessation. Their final conclusion was, therefore, that while there were multiple pathways to desistance from crime, desistance 'is facilitated by self-described "turning points" – changes in situational and structural life circumstances like a good marriage or a stable job – *in combination with individual actions (that is, personal agency)*' (Laub and Sampson 2003: 278, emphasis added).

Arguably, Laub and Sampson's discussion of agency was underdeveloped (Bottoms 2006), but the innovative and explicit use of this concept within a major contribution to criminological scholarship certainly generated interest in 'human agency'. That interest has continued, and is well exemplified in a recent series of articles in the *Journal of Developmental and Life-Course Criminology*, beginning with a paper by the late Ray Paternoster (2017), and concluding with a review of the debate by Alex Piquero (2021). In his final paragraph, Piquero – a leading scholar in developmental criminology – concludes that '[t]here is a place for agency, a place for causation, a place for both in our thinking about crime ... [A]gency and causation are not mutually exclusive. The key for us is to understand how they intermix to affect behavior' (at 719). This is, perhaps, a summary of a new consensus in mainstream theoretical criminology. If that is so, it is very encouraging for the project of 'criminology as a moral science', which has no difficulty in accepting this set of propositions.

But although acceptance of agency is a necessary condition for a moral science project, it is not in itself sufficient. This is so for two reasons: first, because we need a clear understanding of the characteristics of agency in order to develop such a project; and second, because agency, in itself, says nothing about morality. We shall return to the first issue later; but before that it will be helpful to review some ways in which 'morality' has been and is being discussed in criminology as the previously strong grip of positivism has been loosened.

Challenges to criminological positivism (and to 'mainstream criminology' more generally) go back at least to the 1970s, and they include 'critical criminology', 'feminist criminology', 'green criminology' and (more recently) 'decolonising criminology'. Any open-minded scholar will conclude that each of these schools has raised important issues for the discipline of criminology, and they have usually done so using moral concepts. In general, however, it would be fair to say that their main purpose has lain in what Hart (1963) described as 'critical morality' rather than 'positive morality': that is, in criticising the moral frameworks of mainstream criminology and offering alternative (or at least additional) moral frameworks. Sometimes such movements have also suggested new approaches to the study of 'positive morality', and a good example of this is feminist criminologists' use of Carol Gilligan's (1982) 'ethic of care' (which has a central place in the chapter by Caroline Lanskey and colleagues in this volume). However, this has been the exception rather than the rule.

Nevertheless, a number of recent criminological publications have undoubtedly contributed to the study of 'positive morality' (in Hart's sense). By way of illustration (and certainly with no claim that this is an exclusive list) we offer three examples here. They are of varying types: two refer explicitly to morality, one more implicitly so; two are empirical, one is theoretical; two concern criminal justice, one the explanation of criminality.

The first example stays with the field of criminal career research, to which Laub and Sampson had contributed so much (see above). Per-Olof Wikström has developed a theory of crime causation (Situational Action Theory, or SAT) and has subsequently tested and confirmed it empirically with a mixed-gender population cohort in Peterborough, UK ('The Peterborough Study': Wikström et al 2012). Unlike positivist theories (see above), SAT explicitly focuses on *infractions* rather than *actions* as the variable to be explained. This is because it argues that crimes are *breaches of rules of conduct*, and that to explain 'why a person performs an action that breaches a rule of conduct (eg, drives at 100mph on a road with a 70mph speed limit)' is not the same as to explain why the same person performs a similar action where there is no rule of conduct prohibiting it (in this example, drives at 100mph) (Wikström et al 2012: 13). In tackling its explanatory task, 'SAT maintains that crimes are best explained as *moral actions*, that is actions guided by *moral rules*' (Wikström et al 2012: 12, emphasis added). Breaking a moral rule (eg, knowingly committing an act defined as criminal) is seen as a *choice* (described as a 'perception-choice process'), and it therefore involves agency. However, in SAT the 'perception-choice process' is not untrammelled; rather, it is 'initiated and guided by the *causal interaction of … propensity and … exposure*' (Wikström et al 2012: 17, emphasis added). A causally relevant factor in the explanation of action is defined in SAT as 'a factor that when manipulated will change the relevant input into the perception-choice process and, hence, influence a person's (automated or deliberate) choice of crime' (Wikström et al 2012: 17). In published work on SAT to date, significantly more attention has been paid to the proposed 'causally relevant factors' (ie, 'propensity' and 'exposure') than to the perception-choice process. However, and importantly for present purposes, both 'propensity' and 'exposure' contain explicitly moral elements.[12] The Peterborough Study therefore pays much more attention to issues of morality than does any other major longitudinal study of criminal careers. It has not, to date, focused attention on the kinds of questions raised by Laidlaw (2017) when describing the 'moral turn' in social anthropology (see above), but the character of its theorisation has certainly meant that some important criminological issues now need to be seen in a fresh light.[13] (For a further innovative deployment of SAT, see Justice Tankebe's chapter in this volume.)

[12] Thus, in the Peterborough Study 'exposure' refers to the moral context of social settings, measured by the amount of time spent in 'unstructured peer-oriented activities' in places with a higher than average crime rate (Wikström et al 2012: 147). The more personal variable of 'propensity' is comprised of two elements, namely 'Morality' and 'Ability to Exercise Self-Control'. Of these, 'morality' is primary, since it is seen as the 'basic personal factor' (at 16). Morality is principally measured by answers to questionnaire items concerning the wrongness or otherwise of various acts such as 'hit another young person who makes a rude comment' (at 134).

[13] eg, social disadvantage is often thought of as generating criminality. In Peterborough, however, a combined index of family and neighbourhood disadvantage explained only 4% of the variance in the frequency of crimes committed by adolescents; by contrast, the combined dimensions of propensity and exposure to criminogenic settings (the two key causal concepts within SAT), explained 56% of this variance (Wikström and Treiber 2016).

The focus of SAT is on individuals ('propensity') and on the immediate settings in which their actions take place ('exposure'). In sociological language, its focus is therefore on micro-level and meso-level issues. But macro-level moral contexts can also strongly influence action at both the meso and the micro levels – as reflection on, for example, how people live in atypical political regimes, such as that in the former apartheid South Africa, will quickly reveal. The Dutch scholar Hans Boutellier (2019) is a theoretical criminologist who focuses largely on macro-level issues in his book *A Criminology of Moral Order*. Boutellier is concerned to trace some of the criminological consequences of major recent changes in West European societies, including technological change and the growth of the 'network society'; greater individualisation; globalisation (and related migrations); and secularisation. Together, he suggests, these changes have led to a decline in the salience of meta-narratives of social order, such as those offered by religion or movements such as socialism; and this has led to a more uncertain, and sometimes contested, moral order. A main consequence of this for criminal justice has been, he argues, the development of what he calls 'victimalisation'. It is now 'hard to get consensus about a positive ideal on what it is to be a community' (Boutellier 2019: 60), but much easier to agree on what is *not* acceptable. Morality thus becomes identified 'through the lens of victimhood' (at 61), and the criminal justice system moves from the periphery of society to become 'a central institution of moral order' (at 59), because it is 'awareness of one another's vulnerability [that] supplies the emotional building blocks for an empathetic morality' (at 61). As these brief quotations suggest, there is much of great interest in Boutellier's bold work, and there are certainly possibilities of developing it further. However, empirically the theorisation is heavily focused upon criminal justice in the West European context, and studies in comparative penology have taught us that states – even apparently similar states – can differ significantly in their criminal justice practices. We therefore need to be cautious in generalising from one society to another.

These thoughts lead naturally to our third example, that of comparative penology. State punishment is, of course, an ethically relevant topic of study, and there is an extensive philosophical literature that focuses upon it. The sociology of punishment has developed more recently, and comparative penology even more recently, so as David Garland (2018: 14) has commented 'this field of enquiry is still at an early stage'. There have also been complexities in its development, but hopefully a brief sketch will be sufficient here. The focus of attention is necessarily large-scale – how can we explain differences in the manner and extent of punishment practices across different legal jurisdictions? Early works (eg, Cavadino and Dignan 2006; Lacey 2008) focused on broad socio-economic categories – hence, Cavadino and Dignan compared states categorised as 'neoliberal', 'conservative corporatist', 'social democratic corporatist' and 'oriental corporatist'. As Garland (2013) has commented, such analyses provided

> our first cuts into the dense thickets of causation … [T]hey provided empirical support for causal claims that had previously rested on logic and impressionistic

> observation ... But even [the] more sophisticated studies [of this type] leave us with something of a black box when it comes to demonstrating how penal laws and policies are shaped and how penal decisions are made (2013: 490, 492).

This missing dimension Garland described as 'the institutions and processes of *the penal state*' (Garland 2013: 492, emphasis original). He defined the 'penal state' as 'those aspects of the state that determine penal law and direct the deployment of the power to punish' (at 495) – namely, those that comprise the main institutions of government (legislature, executive and judiciary) and the leadership of penal services such as prisons and probation. Garland saw David Downes' (1988) study of 'contrasts in tolerance' between the Netherlands and England as a good example of a comparative empirical study of the operations of 'penal states'.

Most recently, Louise Brangan (2023) has argued for attention also being given, in comparative penology, to what she calls 'political culture', which she sees as arising through an interplay between 'cultural sensibilities' and 'political dispositions' (at 6). Brangan explicitly references earlier work by Garland (1990) on the cultural dimensions of punishment, and says that she hopes to 'return the importance of punishments' cultural resonances' to the toolkits of comparative penologists. Drawing further on Garland, she argues that what she calls 'cultural sensibilities' are configurations of value, meaning and emotion that give punishment its expressive functions and its cultural force (Brangan 2023: 6). These can, in a given culture, become embedded as a form of 'practical consciousness' (at 1),[14] and so become 'the taken-for granted ideas' in different jurisdictions that are 'a critical but untapped source of cross-national penal differences' (at 16). She then seeks to apply this conceptual framework to the case of penal developments in Scotland[15] and the Republic of Ireland.

Two points are perhaps of special interest about these studies in comparative penology. First, scholars have provided us with good reasons why, when searching for explanations of varied penal developments in different jurisdictions, three matters are likely to be relevant, namely: (i) macro-level socio-economic contexts; (ii) decisions made within the 'penal state'; and (iii) the influence of local 'cultural sensibilities' on individuals making decisions within the system. Second, the inclusion in the above list of the concept of 'cultural sensibility' is fascinating, because as briefly mentioned above, and elaborated later, 'sensibility' was a key term in the thinking of the eighteenth-century British Moralists.

We hope that these three examples give a reasonable flavour of some varied analyses of positive morality in contemporary criminology (although

[14] 'Practical consciousness' has been well described by Giddens (1984: xxiii) as consisting of 'all the things that actors know tacitly about how to "go on" in the contexts of human life without being able to give them direct discursive expression'. See also Giddens (1984: 375) for a more formal definition.

[15] Within the United Kingdom, there are three separate criminal justice systems: those of Scotland; Northern Ireland; and England and Wales.

as previously stated we make no claim to completeness of coverage, and in a later section on methodology we shall consider some further examples). Taken together, we believe that the examples show that, as in other social sciences, there is at least the beginnings of an 'ethical turn' in criminological scholarship.

Before turning to the positive case for further developing criminology as a moral science, we now need to consider two important challenges to such a development – those of positivism and relativism.

CHALLENGES TO THE IDEA OF A MORAL SCIENCE: I: POSITIVISM

The notion of a moral science diminished in importance in the nineteenth and certainly the twentieth century. Economics, psychology, sociology, anthropology, politics and other specific disciplines developed in recognisably modern form, emulating the natural sciences. The impressive developments of the latter motivated many thinkers to commit to the view that there is a unity of scientific method, and it is the method of the natural sciences. That, of course, is an oversimplification, but the central point is valid; namely, that many social scientists wished to emulate the natural sciences in regard to method, rigour and the overall character of theorising and explaining. The broadly humanistic and morally inflected character of moral science was largely replaced or displaced by social scientific disciplines increasingly distanced from moral concerns and moral considerations. There was a shift of emphasis away from a broadly humanistic conception of moral science (even though it included much more than the morality of right, wrong, obligation and prohibition) towards a more scientific study of human behaviour, relations, practices and institutions.

Sources of positivist social science can be found in thinkers such as Comte, and in criminology in the work of the Italian positivists, but the main focus of interest here is the positivism influenced by the philosophical school of Logical Positivism and its implications for the understanding of the relations between facts and values. While philosophical positivism had some roots in Humean empiricism, its more immediate origins were found in the work of German and Austrian philosophers such as Schlick, Carnap and Neurath, who elaborated the approach known as Logical Positivism and its criterion of cognitive meaningfulness. Logical Positivism sought to supply a clear *verification criterion* of meaningfulness, and that became an important project for many defenders of philosophical positivism in the first half of the twentieth century. Logical Positivism developed as a formidable intellectual movement, especially after several of those shaping it fled Europe for the Anglophone world. (Some of its main commitments and claims became known to many Anglophone philosophy students through Ayer's [1936/2001] *Language, Truth and Logic*.) Applying the rigorous methods of logical analysis in conjunction with empiricist epistemological claims seemed to many to promise conclusive resolutions to various philosophical questions. Among them was the relation between facts and values.

The philosophical positivists' conception of a criterion of cognitive meaningfulness seemed to render the fact/value distinction clear, unambiguous and solidly supported. If only what can be empirically verified (or what is tautological) can have cognitive meaning then, according to philosophical positivism, moral claims have no truth-value (they are neither true nor false) and they are not cognitively meaningful. They do not report verifiable facts. Thus the meaning that moral discourse and judgements have is *expressive* meaning. Positivists recognised that moral judgements can influence behaviour and they saw that, in that respect, moral judgements can have considerable practical significance. But these judgements do not report anything.

On this view, to regard something as morally wrong reflects one's feeling of disapproval or repugnance. It is not a factual report about the act, or character, or situation, or policy being judged. It is not even a factual report about the speaker's feelings, because it is couched in valuative language. There is an important difference between 'Kidnapping is always morally wrong' and 'I find kidnapping repugnant'; the latter is a factual statement about the speaker's psychological state. Finding kidnapping morally wrong is not a cognitive judgement, a factual report of any kind according to positivism. That view maintains that there are no moral facts.

In chapter one of this volume, Jonathan Jacobs mentions David Wiggins' (1998: ch 3) distinction between a moral judgement in the sense of a moral *evaluation* of something (an action, a practice, an institution) and a moral judgement in the sense of an *action-guiding, deliberative judgement*. Hume had argued (without Wiggins' language in making the distinction) that neither kind of moral judgement follows from facts. He did not believe that facts were irrelevant; that would be an amazingly implausible position to take. Of course facts are relevant to what we think right and what we think wrong, and what we think we must do or must not do. But Hume was explicit in denying that there is a *rational* connection – a matter of logical derivability – of either type of judgement from facts.

This view had an impressively broad influence on social scientific positivism, and many social scientists seem to assume that the matter was decided, ie, value-judgements are non-cognitive and accordingly, neither true nor false. There is no question of deriving the correct moral judgement from facts: no such derivation is possible. That did not necessarily mean that there is no point in studying people's moral beliefs and practices; for some social science positivists, there can be explanatory purposes for which we might want to acquire factual knowledge about people's moral views (ie, Hart's 'positive morality' – see above). Positivist social scientific investigators can also make judgements regarding those values, but if they do they must acknowledge that there are no criteria to decide whether those judgements are correct or not. Thus, positivists might find a positive morality to be objectionable in various ways, or they might wish to endorse some of its core values. But that is not itself an explanatory project and the 'verdicts' will have no cognitive or moral authority. One can undertake a detailed description of a positive morality without claiming or even suggesting that such a description enlarges or deepens moral understanding. It might enlarge and deepen our social scientific understanding of the moralities of various groups (as, for example, when criminologists study the values of youth subcultures), but that is 'ordinary' empirical knowledge, not moral knowledge.

Some social scientific positivists have been so resolute about excluding values and norms that they even reject the view that it can be useful to acquire factual knowledge about people's moral views, because such data do not, in themselves, explain anything. For example, one of us has previously reported an occasion when he was upbraided by a very senior American criminologist (Bottoms 2022: 35, 38–39): the alleged error was to have, in part, explained the high offender rate in a particular housing area with reference to the 'non-mainstream moral values' held by a group of families in one part of the area, and transmitted to their children. That critic was a radical (Skinnerian) behaviourist,[16] but other social scientists have also claimed that there are no valuative or normative facts, and thus that neither values nor norms have explanatory significance. For example, a 2006 book on norms and developmental psychology (DP) begins with the trenchant statement that 'the question "Can developmental psychology deal with normativity?" has a standard answer "No"' (Smith 2006: 1). The author, who is critical of this position, goes on to explain why it is widely held:

> If DP is an empirical science [engaged in a] search for natural laws and their explanation through causal theories, norms would be absent from its domain of investigation. This is because facts and norms are independent of each other ((Smith 2006: 8).

We can call this view – acceptance of a clean break between facts and values, such that values cannot be part of the scientific endeavour, even descriptively – normative *eliminativism*. It seems to us to be a very implausible position to adopt regarding norms and values. Even if one maintains that moral values are not objective, or that moral considerations are merely expressive, it seems undeniable that: (i) people frequently make moral choices; (ii) people very often regard moral matters as highly important; and (iii) moral decisions, responses and behaviour are pervasive features of everyday social life. The claim that moral considerations and norms cannot have a role in the sciences of human behaviour is, therefore, the sort of claim one could hold only if one is hostage to a theory, and in this case, a theory that is not congruent with features of nearly everyone's lives. Eliminativism, in short, is a more radical denial of morality in social scientific investigation than is denial that there are objective norms and values, or claims that norms and values are not objects of scientific enquiry in the way that factual matters are.

Within the natural sciences, some theorists are physicalist reductionists. They maintain that biological phenomena, for example, can be completely

[16] On the various strands of behaviourism, see Graham (2019).

assimilated (reduced) to physical phenomena and they deny that biological properties and processes have any explanatorily independent status or significance. All phenomena are physical phenomena and there is a single, fundamental level of description of what-there-is, what properties it has, and the causality that explains phenomena in the world of living things (as in every other world). They regard the reduction as eliminativist; ultimately, there is no need for biological concepts and processes in our theorising and explanations. Biological concepts and accounts might provide a helpful shorthand in some contexts or the complete precision of a strictly physicalist presentation of phenomena might not be needed in various contexts. Still, the language and concepts of biology can be eliminated because everything that needs to be said can be said in physicalist terms. Eliminativism with regard to values and norms is analogous to this view.

One might be led to eliminativism by a mistake: the mistake of supposing that if there are no *moral facts* or *objective moral values*, then there just is not any moral reality, as it were, of which an account is needed. What is mistaken about this view is the notion that morality exists only if there are objective moral values or moral facts. That just is not the case. Things could morally matter to people; making moral judgements could be an important part of our lives; and we could think it of the first importance to have certain moral characteristics *even if* there are not objective values. 'Mattering' does not depend wholly on what kinds of entities there are. If a toddler falls down a staircase and is injured and in pain it would be crazy for someone who could help to think, 'In the absence of objective values there is no basis for morally criticising my behaviour or my character for regarding the matter as morally vacuous'. The point is not that any decent person would have a sympathetic response to the injury and distress of the child – though that is probably a fair observation. The main point is that moral judgements and moral concern need not somehow attach to *entities* – to items we encounter in sense perception – in order to have a meaningful and important role in our lives. These issues are further discussed in chapters one and two, by Jacobs and by Swanton.

CHALLENGES TO THE IDEA OF A MORAL SCIENCE: II: MORAL RELATIVISM

A second challenge to the idea of a moral science comes from the notion of *moral relativism*. There are numerous types of relativism, for example, conceptual relativism, moral relativism, cultural relativism, alethic relativism (relativism in regard to truth) and other types. In general, the claim of relativism is that judgements (whether moral, scientific, or otherwise) are to be assessed in relation to some non-objective, non-universal framework or set of norms. Thus, moral relativism regards moral judgements as correct or mistaken only *relative to the values and principles of a particular group, society or culture*, and it therefore denies that any moral view can have universal or objective validity. (Thus, even if everyone, everywhere agreed on a moral matter the relativist would insist that this universality is only a contingent matter; universal agreement has no justificatory significance.) On this view, therefore, there is no basis for making objective or authoritative judgements of different moralities. We might perhaps find that we cannot help doing that; but if so, we need to always remind ourselves that doing it does not have compelling justificatory grounds.

Moral relativism is a stance that, within the social sciences, has historically been particularly adopted by social and cultural anthropologists, whose early ethnographic studies of non-Western, small-scale communities uncovered a widely divergent range of customs and values. Unlike eliminativists, anthropologists were happy to report such differences as important data; but as social scientists seeking to be objective, they were reluctant to make any ethical judgements about the cultures and values that they studied. Anthropologists found attractive the avoidance, in moral relativism, of claims to objective or universal validity: this stance seemed to them to be a good way to express a toleration of difference and an absence of judgementalism. In a world in which many colonial power structures have been dismantled, where there is increasing acknowledgement of (sometimes horrifying) historical abuses of people and cultures, and where many different groups are pursuing aspirations of self-determination, relativism can seem to be attractive as a way to show that claims to moral superiority are never based on any objective or universal measure, and are perhaps more likely to reflect the power of one culture or nation over others – a kind of power that does not reflect legitimate authority.

But there are complications. This is because, if one is a true relativist, one must deny that there are objective reasons for others also to endorse these commitments to toleration, equality, respect for difference and other related values. This point has been sharply made by Laidlaw (2014: 28), who notes that 'assertions of the cultural relativity of moral values are typically made [by anthropologists] in the furtherance of values – self-determination, tolerance, diversity, racial equality, anti-imperialism, etc – that they hold absolutely'; yet, as he points out, for a relativist to hold a value absolutely is a 'performative contradiction' (at 29). He adds that this logically confused commitment to toleration[17] is often accompanied by sharp criticism of 'Western' values as hegemonic and part of a colonial mentality – a position which 'depends, of course, on moral relativism being not only untrue, but palpably untrue' (at 29). To this we might add that because, for relativists, there are no intrinsic constraints on what values to endorse, one can (in principle at least) be a relativist and at the same time a ferociously ethno-nationalist, racist, patriarchal devotee of thuggish violence.

[17] The confusion is between a particular moral commitment (namely, not being judgemental, or being tolerant of moral diversity) and a metaethical commitment (namely, that moral values are relative in the way indicated in the text).

Of course one can argue that, in practice, the prevailing norms of one's society or one's group are likely to have authority, so most people are habituated in certain moral views and values; moral relativism is, therefore, not a person-relative free-for-all. Indeed, relativism is compatible with enduring social traditions and long-held, stable values, and practices that transmit them along with rationales for them. Accordingly, as an empirical matter it is not clear that acceptance of relativism would result in a great deal of flux in moral views and instability of values, at least in societies that are relatively distinct. However, as Boutellier (2019) has emphasised (see previous discussion), more recent social and technological developments mean that alternative moral views are now omnipresent in many societies, and this creates a difficulty because there is no specific, systematic way of identifying the contexts to which moralities are relative. The principles and norms to which a morality is relative could be those of a political community, a cultural group, an ethnic group, a professional organisation, a political party, a religious tradition, or some other group. Moreover, a great many individuals (especially in liberal democracies with diverse, dynamic civil societies) are members of many groups and might choose to identify themselves and their valuative commitments in a variety of ways. That there is not some authoritative articulation of groups to which moral values are relative might not trouble the relativist. However, it can make a for a pragmatically perplexing state of affairs, with the mapping of the moral terrain subject to continuously shifting borders.

As a final point, we should note that relativism has a serious difficulty in dealing theoretically with the concept of a moral conflict. This is because, as Stephen Lukes (2008: 16) has pointed out:

> [R]elativism removes the sense of *conflict* between apparently conflicting moral judgements by suggesting that since they are relative to different standards, they do not really conflict. When we are internally torn by conflicting moral intuitions, it really is hard to believe that our sense that there is a conflict is an illusion (emphasis original).

Thus, moral conflict and the difficulty of finding a single standard for resolving all such conflicts are not special difficulties counting against objectivity; actually, they make sense *only* on the supposition of moral objectivity.

In the final paragraph of his book on moral relativism, Lukes nicely summarises what he describes as the 'surviving truth' resulting from the debates about relativism: namely, that there are indeed multiple morally appropriate ways for human beings to live. But, he rightly claims, acceptance of this point 'can be combined with making moral judgements and thus recognising the authority of moral standards and the reality of moral disagreements'. Ending with a criminologically-relevant example, he adds that while many ways of life will pass tests of moral appropriateness, 'wife-battering certainly will not' (2008: 142).

DEVELOPING A MORAL SCIENCE APPROACH

It is a mistake to suppose that the empirical study of moral considerations allows only for the possibilities offered by positivism (including eliminativism) or moral relativism. There is a further possibility, one that is defended here. What we are calling *moral science* differs from eliminativism in treating morals as something that is properly within the scope of social-scientific investigation, and it differs from both positivism and moral relativism in holding that moral views can have more than expressive or relative validity. This approach therefore has some important affinities with the eighteenth-century moral science tradition, in which moral theorising was closely connected with understandings of social life, attitudes, modes of interaction and forms of mutual regard as essential elements of moral life.

Theorists such as Hume and Smith sought to understand morality and moral judgement in the context of the social world (as well as general, naturalistic features of human beings) rather than giving an account of moral value in a priori terms, or in terms of a putative state of nature or a social contract concerning fundamental principles of a political order. They took into account, as relevant to morality, some highly general features of human beings and their circumstances. These included the facts that benevolence is a regular feature of human life and relationships, but it is not present in infinite supply; that different persons will contribute in different ways to the provision of subsistence; that all human lives are precarious in certain respects; and that the vulnerability of human beings makes for an important form of equality. Their approaches were more naturalistic than social contract theories or approaches based upon hypothetical starting points, and that is the basis of much of their appeal: they elaborated accounts of morality that are broadly empirical, but not scientistic. They avoided both a priorism and reductionism, so – for example – they did not argue that normative considerations, including moral values, are *nothing but* natural events or occurrences and to be explained in just the same way as chemical, biological, or physical events and phenomena.

Of course, these authors wrote before the many critically important developments in modern natural science and social science, so a simple replication of their approach is no longer appropriate. In addition, we have a much increased (and increasing) understanding of relations between physiological, chemical and neurological phenomena and behaviour. (Though it would be an unjustified leap to assert that eventually all of mental life and all modes of behaviour will be explicable in such terms.) The chapters in this volume by Jacobs and Swanton go into more detail regarding some of the main philosophical debates concerning the relation of facts and values and also regarding the ways in which moral considerations can be involved in explanations of behaviour and practices. Moral life and moral experience (aspects of which are discussed in depth in various chapters in the volume) are complex; they draw from and are reflected in many aspects of our lives and the contexts of them. While it is possible to assert a number of high-level generalisations about morality, we would be wise to expect that our understanding of it will be enlarged as social scientific studies increasingly reveal, and as moral philosophy increasingly connects with, a complex variety of findings about human beings and social life.

As previously noted, in recent years criminologists have increasingly recognised the appropriateness and the importance of explicating the moral features of the issues they study, and they have done so in a variety of ways. We make no claim here that our case for moral science is uniquely pathfinding. However, what is perhaps distinctive of it is that it seeks to emphasise and to illuminate how it is that *normativity is integral to the issues studied by criminologists*. In a moral science approach, normativity is not a laminate projected onto the empirical issues by investigators; it is always present, and needs to be investigated.

To develop this point, we need now to take a closer look at the concepts of *sensibility* and *sociability*, which according to the British Moralists hold a key place in explicating the moral aspects of social phenomena.

Sensibility has a special meaning in philosophy, which was identified in the classic *Oxford English Dictionary* as a 'power or faculty of feeling, capacity of sensations and emotions as distinct from cognition and will'. More recently and more fully, the *Oxford Companion to Philosophy* defines it as 'a set of individual or collective dispositions to emotions, attitudes and feelings. As such, sensibility is relevant especially to value theory, including ethics, aesthetics and politics' (Sankowski 2005). Emotions and values can, however, be expressed in various ways. When thinkers such as Hume and Smith wrote about sensibility they did not confine it to thoughtless, spontaneous emotion, feeling or preference. They had much more complex and interesting views of sensibility, and the often subtle importance of attitudes and feelings in daily interactions, including those with moral content. It is also a mistake to attribute to them the view that the role of sensibility must be as a distinct moral sense, a perceptual faculty that enables us to detect the presence of moral properties. We can imagine someone arguing that in addition to the familiar five senses we also have a distinct 'moral sense', a perceptual faculty with which we can perceive the rightness or wrongness of actions or the moral goodness or badness of situations; but even those thinkers within British Moralism who are commonly called 'moral sense theorists' rarely held such a view.

Sensibility, then, comprises the role of attitudes, forms of concern, commitment and receptivity, and the ways that notions of worth, appeal, repugnance and other responses and perspectives figure in experience, judgement and motivation. These matters are not best understood (only or primarily) as occurrent mental episodes, though feelings and responses might sometimes have that as part of their phenomenology. Instead, they have a more *dispositional* presence in a person and in that person's ways of responding to, and judging acts, persons and situations. Also, sensibility is not cut off from cognition by a clean break: a person can work at revising and refining many of their sentiments on the basis of reflecting on experience and giving thought to their values. RJ Wallace (1994), for example, argues that reactive emotions have a central role in judgements of responsibility. He notes that emotions can be backward-looking as responses to actions that people have performed, yet they are also often responses to ways in which people have violated moral expectations that we hold, as a matter of disposition (Wallace 1994: 67). Thus, in his view, 'To hold a person to moral obligations one accepts, in this dispositional sense, is to view the person as the sort of agent whose violation of moral obligations one accepts would render reactive emotions appropriate' (at 70). Thus, distinctions between censuring or merely scolding, or whether we are merely disappointed or believe that we have been wronged and treated unfairly, depend on judgements about what we take the facts to be and what we think are the relevant norms. Beliefs, commitments and judgements of actions and agents are related to feelings and emotions in numerous and often complex ways. The chief point here is not whether to accept Wallace's conception of moral responsibility, but to see his view as an example of the way in which sensibility can have a role in moral experience, judgement and motivation that goes well beyond simply being *felt*.

For the British Moralists, sensibility was closely connected to *sociability*, within which the concept of *sympathy* played a key role, notably in their accounts of moral experience, moral judgement and moral motivation. However, 'sympathy' was not limited to feelings for another's suffering or plight. As Adam Smith (1759/1982: part I, section 1, ch 1, 5) noted:[18]

> Pity and compassion are words appropriated to signify our fellow-feeling with the sorrow of others. Sympathy, though its meaning was, perhaps, originally the same, may now, however, without much impropriety, be made use of to denote our fellow-feeling with any passion whatever.

A contemporary moral philosopher, Michael Slote, has pointed out that 'empathy' is the term that we would now most often use in contexts where seventeenth and eighteenth-century British writers speak of 'sympathy' – but this word 'didn't exist in English till the early twentieth century, when it was introduced as a translation of the German word *Einfuehlung*' (Slote 2010: 15). Slote himself defends a moral sentimentalism, a view in which 'empathy is a crucial source and sustainer of altruistic concern or caring about (the wellbeing or welfare of) others' (at 20).

The British Moralists contrasted 'sympathy' (or empathy) with egoism – the view that all human action is motivated by self-interest. If human beings have naturally sociable propensities, then moral motivation does not have to somehow meet and defeat egoism; instead, natural sociability exists, and needs to be extended, guided and strengthened, which is itself a social project. Many in the British tradition argued that egoism simply does not have the empirical

[18] Hume also elaborated a quite complex account of sympathy. It overlaps to some extent with Smith's view but has its own distinguishing elements.

evidence on its side. People are often selfish, callous, or unconcerned for others, but that is not because egoism is the 'natural', default motivational drive of human beings. Protecting one's interest is a priority for people, but that is not the same as egoism.

Returning to the broader concept of sociability, for the British Moralists this is not only a natural(istic) feature of human life; it also obviates the need for reason to be a sufficient source of motivation, a matter that had long been a philosophical difficulty (ie, how could cognition be motivationally efficacious)? They claimed that empathy, benevolence and a general responsiveness to the wellbeing and suffering of others can provide practical (or motivational) 'energy', where reason or cognition could not. Consider some of the forms of sensibility and the attitudes that are very prominent in human lives: such things as admiration, resentment, empathy, contempt, respect, a concern for fairness, and gratitude for example. These, among many others, involve awareness of others and ways of relating or responding to them. These are ways of relating to others that are *felt* (though they are not merely feelings) and at a fundamental level what unites human beings in a common moral world is sociability.

In summary, therefore, in the British Moralist tradition there was an important relation between sensibility and sociability, though different thinkers articulated these concepts, and the relationship between them, in diverse ways. Both elements were crucial to developing naturalistic conceptions of morality, making it possible to both (i) draw on empirical considerations in explaining morality and justifying moral claims, and (ii) giving a role to moral considerations in the explanation of human action. Moral value, moral judgement and moral motivation were thus reconceived. This way of thinking resonates with many thinkers in our time because of its naturalistic character; and of course its naturalism is a potential point of connection with empirical social science.

Recent criminological publications that have focused on morality rarely use the terms 'sensibility' or 'sociability' (although some do – see the discussion of Brangan 2023, above). However, careful reading of such studies shows that, in what is being described, sensibility and sociability often have pronounced importance. How people regard each other, how their attitudes are formed and reflected in their actions, and the ways in which sensibility shapes motivation, deliberation and judgement are vitally important in this kind of criminology, as are discussions of various aspects of social order. Whether this was intended or not, to a moral philosopher work of this kind has significant resonance with that of thinkers such as Smith and Hume. It is as though some of the main currents of thought in the tradition of the British Moralists are being retrieved and developed in contemporary work in social science. This is not a matter of 'applying' Hume's moral theory or Smith's moral theory. Rather, it is a matter of recognising the texture and significance of a complex fabric of attitudes, responses, passions, concerns, needs and forms of acknowledgment and regard constitutive of the relations between human beings, and the basis for much of how we act and what we decide to do. In order to be both illuminating and plausible, the approach does not require fully elaborating a moral theory and then applying it to empirical results of investigation.

How then might a moral science approach of the kind sketched above be relevant with regard to the distinction drawn by Hart (1963) between positive and critical morality (see above)? We believe that, in summary, the answer to this question, in a criminological context, is threefold.

First, criminological researchers, in carrying out their rigorous empirical research studies, should take appropriate account of people's ethical understandings and behaviour (ie, studying 'positive morality'). This is on the basis that – as noted above – normativity is an integral feature of social life, and not a laminate projected onto empirical studies by researchers. Such studies should be conducted with a commitment to objectivity by the researchers – they should be trying to understand the morality of the research subjects, saying little about their own moral commitments.

Second, criminologists can and should take account of the results of relevant empirical studies when thinking about policies and practices in the field of criminal justice (ie, when developing 'critical morality'). However, they also need to recognise that critical morality is not just a way of asserting one's own views or indicating one's own moral commitments. It can be critical in a more robust and disciplined way, reflecting on the moral phenomena encountered and considering their coherence, their mutual consistency, their presuppositions and implications. In addition to attaining clarity about that 'vertical' dimension of morals, it can also consider connections between the moral views that have been empirically disclosed and other beliefs, attitudes and perspectives so that a fuller picture of the moral phenomena is achieved. It is not as though there is one, isolable set of norms that constitute morality, or that there is some single valuative dimension to which critical moral judgement needs to be alert. In this volume, the chapter by Matt Matravers exemplifies this kind of careful, empirically sensitive approach to an issue of critical morality.

Third, it can sometimes be appropriate, when carrying out social science research, to inject an element of 'critical morality' into an empirical analysis. An example of this can be found in the work of Alison Liebling (2011), where she drew a distinction between 'good' and 'right' staff–prisoner relationships. A 'good relationship' was simply one in which the parties got on well, but – Liebling proposed – a 'right relationship' meant that the parties got on well within a morally appropriate context for staff–prisoner relationships. Accordingly, a relationship within which a prisoner bribed an officer to import drugs into the prison might be 'good', but it could not be 'right'. The example therefore illustrates the point that in practical situations there can sometimes be a complex relationship between 'positive' and 'critical' morality. We return to this issue in our next section.

METHODOLOGY

At the beginning of this Introduction, we indicated our view that the methodology of the social sciences must, to some degree, differ from that of the natural sciences. This is because, unlike the natural sciences, an important element in social science is the study of 'self-conscious human behaviour'. We can now say a little more about the issues involved in taking that position.

In his penetrating book on the philosophy of social science, the late Martin Hollis (2002) presented his readers with two central dichotomies. The first is the division between 'Explanation' and 'Understanding' (at 16), where:

> *Explanation* is a methodological approach which takes the view that 'since human beings and societies belong to the natural order, a single method, broadly defined, will serve for all sciences'; while *Understanding* aims at 'an "interpretive" or "hermeneutic"... social science', the central proposition of which is that 'the social world must be understood from within, rather than explained from without'.

The second dichotomy focuses on the ways in which social structures (economies, political and ideological systems, etc) and individual actions are understood. Here the distinction is between 'Holism' and 'Individualism'(Hollis 2002: 5):

> *Holism* 'attempts to account for ... action by reference to ... an encompassing social structure, and thus proceeds, so to speak, "top down"'; while *Individualism* 'takes the actions of individuals to be the stuff of history and regards structures as the outcome of previous actions ... here the direction is "bottom up"'.

Hollis then cross-cuts these two dichotomies in a simple diagram (shown here as Figure 1), with the four features of 'systems', 'games', 'agents' and 'actors'.

Figure 1 Martin Hollis' Framework of Approaches in the Philosophy of Social Science

	Explanation	Understanding
Holism	Systems	'Games'
Individualism	Agents	Actors

Source: Hollis (2002) Figure 1.2, 19. (Copyright, Cambridge University Press).

At the end of his book he summarises some conclusions by working anticlockwise through the four cells of the Figure (Hollis 2002: 248–49). To focus solely on 'systems' (top left), he claims, would seem to leave us 'grossly blind to the scope for human manoeuvre'. So we move to the bottom left quadrant, where 'the "Agents" of Rational Choice theory and Game Theory make the action and perhaps even the structure too ... [b]ut these agents are [perhaps] oddly mechanical'. If we think so, we move to the bottom right quadrant, 'where

"Actors" live a more richly textured existence and their actions have subjective meaning'. However, when we try to understand these meanings, 'we become aware that there are schemes of meaning-rules and normative expectations external to each actor'; so we are propelled into the top right quadrant, where we find an 'intersubjective social order' which is 'woven from constitutive rules and regulative rules'.

This perceptive summary leaves us – as Hollis intends it to leave us – with the feeling that we will need to combine some or all of these four elements if our methodology is to be adequate to answer research questions in complex social situations. The present authors find this suggestion congenial; indeed one of us has gone on record as being not only 'open to the insights offered by many theories', but also 'an unrepentant advocate of serious attempts at synthesis' in social science (Bottoms 2008: 82). Good synthesis, however, requires careful attention to the theoretical underpinnings of different approaches, with linkages being made only when this is theoretically justifiable. In that spirit, Hollis' final chapter is devoted to a consideration of possible meldings between Systems, Agents, Actors and 'Games'. A key issue for present purposes is that this exploration yields, for him, a 'stubborn contrast … between Explanation and Understanding, with naturalism and hermeneutics still in dispute over ontology, methodology and epistemology' (Hollis 2002: 257). He then briefly explores these philosophical issues, but he reaches no firm conclusion, only four 'summarising questions' (at 259–60).

Philosophically, therefore, clear answers to these complex questions might be elusive. But this will very probably not satisfy those social scientists who have been persuaded (in our view rightly) that moral values, moral judgements and moral motivations are part of the stuff of everyday life, and therefore need to be studied. Yes, such scholars might say, ethical issues are real, but so are the social contexts within which they occur. Such scholars will certainly want to focus on what Hollis describes as the 'richly textured … social meanings' of Actors (where moral judgements and moral motivation are often to be found) and how these relate to the 'Games' of intersubjective norms (which will include social values). If they are appropriately open-minded, however, they will want to allow these Actors the freedom to be, sometimes, 'Rational Choice Agents'; and they will also want to recognise that the structural 'Systems' within which actors are placed will often shape and indeed constrain their freedom to act. Above all, such scholars will want to insist that, just because they choose to study actors' moral motivations and intersubjective moral values, this should not preclude them from seeking *explanations* (as well as understandings) of social action in various specific circumstances. In other words, it should be possible to include both 'subjective understanding' and 'explanation' within a coherent practice of social science.

Is this in fact possible? An analysis by the sociologist WG Runciman suggests that it can be. With regard to the long-standing debates concerning the similarity or dissimilarity of the methodologies of natural science and social science

Runciman (1983: 2) notes, with regret, the apparently 'persistent compulsion of one side to reject all of the recommendations of the other'. He further suggests that the few scholars who have made a lasting contribution to this discussion 'have for the most part done so, as Max Weber did … by occupying and holding a limited area of the middle ground against attacks directed from either front'. Such a 'middle ground' position will, in particular, attempt to hold together the traditions of causal explanation and 'agentic understanding' (*verstehen*).[19]

Runciman (1983: 56) is aware of the complex philosophical debates in this area, but he believes that practising social scientists can reasonably 'bypass those disputes without damage to their substantive research … [and] without further misgivings about … vulnerability to methodological criticism'. This can be achieved, he proposes, by adopting a threefold characterisation of what social science research projects usually need to include. These are: 'reportage'; 'appreciative description'; and 'explanation'.[20] Runciman further proposes, crucially, that 'the logic of explanation' does not differ as between the natural and the social sciences (at 15). Instead, he suggests that the special difference between natural and social science is the presence in the latter of 'appreciative description' (the description of subjective meaning), which he illustrates by quoting the words of a French historian who had been in the army at the time of the defeat of France in 1940:

> Did I truly know, in the full sense of that word, did I know from within, before I myself had suffered the terrible, sickening reality, what it meant for an army to be encircled, what it meant for a people to meet defeat? (Bloch 1954: 44, quoted in Runciman 1983: 17).

An implication of Runciman's account is that some social science research can be adequately conducted without including an element of appreciative description, but that such an element is usually helpful, and sometimes essential, in order to obtain a full account of the situation. Moreover, appreciative description can (*pace* Hollis) play an important part in the explanation.

While these three concepts (reportage; appreciative description; and explanation) are clear, the boundaries between them (especially 'reportage' and 'appreciative description') are not fully watertight (see Bull 1991). But, as Runciman (1983: 19) himself suggests, the general point of differentiating these different aspects of social scientific research is plain enough, and can be indicated by some simple questions: 'what is/has been happening?' (reportage); 'what is/was it like?' (appreciative description: how do/did people perceive and

[19] Runciman's (1983) proposals are therefore broadly Weberian, building on his previously published critique of Weber's methodological writings (Runciman 1972).

[20] Runciman uses the term 'understanding' as a generic concept to embrace all three of these matters, but to avoid confusion with Hollis' different definition of this term (see above) we have not followed Runciman in this respect. We have also expanded the name of Runciman's 'description' to 'appreciative description', in order to give a fuller sense of what was intended.

understand these events?); and 'why matters turned out as they did' (explanation). We agree with this view, and we believe that this conceptualisation is helpful as a way of thinking about social science research underpinned by a commitment to the project of moral science. As we shall shortly show, ethical matters can feature in answers to any of Runciman's three questions.

We turn now to some more practical methodological issues concerning how ethical matters might be handled in empirical criminological research. One possibility is for criminologists to use a particular approach within ethical theory as a framework for reporting empirical findings. A paper by Bottoms and Shapland (2014) exemplifies this approach: they utilised the recently revived tradition of 'virtue ethics'[21] in order to theorise some of the findings from their Sheffield-based study of processes of attempted desistance from crime among a sample of male young adult recidivists. Virtue ethicists argue that one of the chief merits of this approach is that 'its focus is on moral agents and their lives, rather than on discrete actions' (Crisp and Slote 1997: 3). It therefore pays relatively less attention to act-focused ethical concepts such as *right* and *wrong*, and relatively more to personal and character-focused valuations such as *kindness*, *courage* and *integrity*. Empirical research has shown that desistance from crime is often a gradual process, characterised by Bottoms and Shapland (2014: 326) – for their habitual offending sample – as 'a process of learning to live a non-criminal life when one has been living a largely criminal life'. Such a process usually involves significant changes in everyday routines; and it was the evidence about people trying gradually to change that led these researchers to their interest in virtue ethics (Bottoms and Shapland (2014: 320).[22]

There is, however, an interesting sequel to this story within the present volume. In her chapter, the philosopher Christine Swanton (a leading writer on virtue ethics: see most recently Swanton 2021) offers a number of criticisms of moral philosophy as it is generally practised within the analytic tradition. One of these criticisms concerns what Swanton calls the 'excessive abstraction' of the dominant theories in normative ethics, including virtue ethics. It follows that, for her, virtue ethics *simpliciter* is an 'overly simple abstract theoretic framework' for the usage to which Bottoms and Shapland (2014) had applied it. In relation to desistance, Swanton therefore proposes the adoption of an 'expanded notion' of

[21] Virtue ethics has a long history, going back at least to Aristotle. In the Anglophone world, however, the dominant theories in normative ethics in the nineteenth and early twentieth century were utilitarianism and deontology. Virtue ethics then began to be revived, so Crisp and Slote (1997: 1) refer to their edited book on this subject as offering 'a detailed map of some highly significant changes which have been taking place in the landscape of moral philosophy in the second half of the twentieth century'.

[22] As noted in Laidlaw's (2017) encyclopedia essay, virtue ethics was also one of the intellectual traditions that social anthropologists turned to in developing the 'new anthropology of ethics' (see especially, Mattingly 2014). However, when writing their 2014 paper, Bottoms and Shapland were not yet aware of the 'moral turn' in social anthropology, so these were parallel rather than connected developments.

the concept of 'burdened virtue' first suggested by Tessman (2005). In a further chapter in this volume, Bottoms and Lanskey accept Swanton's proposal and work with it in relation to some cases in the Sheffield sample.

More generally, Swanton argues in her chapter that, to avoid excessive abstraction, 'philosophical ethics needs to deploy the resources of the social sciences to enrich the landscape of ethics and understand fully the forms of life in which ethics is immanent'. It follows from this, of course, that moral philosophers, as well as criminologists, would benefit from a more sustained and careful dialogue between their disciplines – a view with which we fully concur. But acceptance of such a view has a further important implication, namely that both social science and moral philosophy can be enriched by empirical studies that, while including ethically relevant data, make only limited reference to formal ethical theories.

A good illustration of this point is to be found in the extensive research oeuvre of the prisons scholar Alison Liebling. In a very brief summary of some of her main findings, she wrote:

> [I]n order to feel able to develop their potential ... prisoners need to feel that they are safe; that they are treated with humanity; that they understand the way that the prison system, including [its] release procedures, works; and that they are in a well-organised and professional prison where staff have enough experience and expertise to deal with the issues that matter to them, and where staff use both ... formal and informal means of authority (including relationships with prisoners) ... to maintain order. This is not a 'heavy' version of authority. Staff in better prisons ... are fair, competent, clear and responsive. Not many prisons reach these standards (Liebling 2015: 21).

Notice that this paragraph, which summarises more than a decade of empirical research, is studded with evaluative terms (eg, 'safe'; 'treated with humanity'; 'professional'; 'fair'; 'responsive'). All these terms are used to describe prisoners' expressed 'positive morality' of the factors that they see as constituting a 'good prison'.[23] However, Liebling's main concern is not moral theory, but high quality description. Discussing the role of prisons researchers as ethnographers, she argues that their main purpose must be to 'get the description right'. This requires not only 'courage and skill', but also the development of 'I–Thou relations with our participants: that is, an orientation towards an experiencing subject, not an experienced object (Buber 2010: vii)' (Liebling 2015: 18; see further Liebling 2021). Only such relationships, she adds, will allow trust to develop between researchers and research participants, encouraging participants to speak freely about what matters to them in the complex and sometimes fraught environment of a prison. Without that trust, true 'positive morality' cannot be expressed by research participants, nor understood by researchers.

[23] To develop her findings, Liebling used a methodological approach known as 'Appreciative Inquiry', in which prisoners were asked to identify occasions when they experienced an institution most positively (eg, when they had felt 'most human') and to articulate as clearly as possible what made those occasions positive experiences for them.

As the reference to Buber attests, Liebling is aware of and uses some relevant philosophical sources, but these are deployed mainly to orient her strong primary focus on social-scientific description (which is essentially an amalgam of Runciman's 'appreciative description' and 'reportage', with the former as primary). What is of special importance in the present context is that a focus of this kind in no way limits the moral insights that can be gleaned from her work, notably about aspects of sociability in the prisons context.[24]

Liebling (2015: 18–19) also states that her in-depth, 'I–Thou' ethnographic methodology 'stands in methodological and theoretical opposition' to that of some other criminologists, particularly those who favour methodologies modelled closely on the natural sciences. This is true and important, but it raises two linked further questions, namely: can what Runciman calls 'reportage' (as opposed to 'appreciative description') realistically be used as a method of studying ethical matters, or is it too crude for that, especially if the research is quantitative? The answers to these questions are, respectively, 'yes' and 'no', as is shown by Justice Tankebe's chapter in this volume. Using a quantitative questionnaire-based methodology, and with a theoretical underpinning of Situational Action Theory (see above), Tankebe highlights some important differences between the ethical intentions and the actual behaviour of his sample of police officers – results that would have been difficult to demonstrate so clearly using ethnographic methods (although ethnography would certainly be useful as a follow-up to some of his findings). Thus, in 'moral science' as in social science more generally, it is valuable to consider a variety of research methods in the search for truth (Bottoms 2008).[25]

As a final point relating to 'reportage' and 'appreciative description', we need to return to the issue raised in the previous section about injecting an element of 'critical morality' into a report/description of 'positive morality'. As shown by the prisons-based example previously given, this possibility is sometimes methodologically appropriate. However, there are some obvious potential problems with it, notably that it will be over-used by an investigator, and/or that focusing upon its use will detract from the observer's full understanding of the positive morality he or she is attempting to research. Awareness of these problems has been sharpened through critiques rightly made by the 'decolonising' movement in various social sciences. These critiques suggest that the research mode in

[24] To take just one example, note the primacy of safety in Liebling's summary of her findings, quoted above. This is highly congruent with Bernard Williams' (2005: 3) identification of order and safety as the 'first political question', 'because solving it is the condition of solving, indeed posing' any other political issues. Prisons can be dangerous places, and most prisoners care very much about keeping safe.

[25] Liebling's work also demonstrates this point. She has used her ethnographically derived research findings on 'good prisons' (see above) to develop a now widely used quantitative instrument known as 'Measuring the Quality of Prison Life' (MQPL) to assess the social climates of individual prisons. She describes this instrument as a form of 'ethnography-led measurement'. For an example of research using this method, see Liebling et al (2019).

question (injecting critical morality into a positive morality description) needs to be used sparingly, and when it is used it should be explicitly flagged in the research report. This will require significant self-awareness, and awareness of the complexities of the fieldwork situation, on the part of the researcher.

We turn lastly to the third of Runciman's dimensions of social science research (in addition to reportage and appreciative description), namely *explanation*. Despite Hollis' philosophical reservations, experience suggests that explanation can indeed be derived from data concerning the subjective meaning of phenomena (Runciman's 'appreciative description'). An example of this can again be found in Liebling's work. In the late 1990s, she led a government-commissioned research project to assess the working of a new system of incentives that was introduced into English prisons. This policy was based on principles of rational choice, and it was anticipated by the government that the system would lead to improved behaviour by prisoners. The research showed that this was not the case, to the government's dismay and puzzlement. However, the 'appreciative description' element of the research provided compelling evidence of the reasons for this result. Prisoners supported the concept of incentives in principle, but they judged that several aspects of the way that the new system was being administered were fundamentally *unfair*, so they chose not to engage with it (Liebling et al 1999; Bottoms 2003). This was, therefore, a morality-based explanation of the limitations of a social policy initiative.

AGENCY AND VALUES

At the beginning of this Introduction, we mentioned Jonathan Jacobs' (2022b: 80) comment that, within a moral science approach, 'considerations of value and agency are vitally important'. In concluding our substantive discussion, we therefore return to this issue.

In our discussion (above) of Hollis' distinctions between explanation and understanding on the one hand and holism and individualism on the other, we suggested that an exclusive focus on any of them, or on only one pair, is likely to needlessly diminish the conceptual resources we can employ in criminological investigation. Why decide a priori what are the only permissible strategies of accounting for what we investigate? The complexity and character of the phenomena might be impediments to a single, exhaustive, methodologically homogeneous approach. It is possible to attain coherence without an exclusive measure of homogeneity.

One of the main, disputed issues regarding social scientific explanation is the question of whether there is one, univocal sense of causality (namely, event-causality) or two senses, event-causality and agency. Positivists tend to regard agency as mysterious and unscientific. How could it possibly be explanatory (one might insist) if we assert that an agent performed a particular action and we claim that there was nothing that caused the agent to perform it? It sounds like a kind of personalised power for creation *ex nihilo*. However, that is a much too swift dismissal of agency. While what follows is not a presentation of a theory of agency, it is meant to encourage at least some consideration of the ways in which conceptions of agency can be important elements in criminological explanation.

Issues concerning the nature and explanation of human action are notoriously stubborn, and the stubbornness is due in part to the complexity of the issues. Certainly the question of causation is central, but it is connected with issues concerning the respective roles of reasons and desires; what sorts of distinctions to recognise between motives, intentions and volitions; the question of how to understand weakness of will; the role of values; the role of states of character in action, and numerous other matters. Even just focusing on desire is a complex matter. Some desires are episodic and are felt, as is the desire for a cold drink when one is hot and thirsty. Other desires are temporally extended and do not involve a characteristic feel: the desire to have an academic career is an example. Some desires are accompanied by the sense that it would not be a good idea to act on them. Suppose someone feels a desire to embarrass another person; he might acknowledge that this is an objectionable desire and might fail to act on it for that reason. Another, but not altogether different sort of case, is when one has a desire one wishes not to have, as when someone who is trying to quit smoking has a desire to smoke.

There are also desires with regard to long-term concerns, such as the desire to live without debt or to pass on at least a modest estate to one's children. Or, for a person who is struggling to make ends meet, the desire to free oneself from the need to borrow money might be an example. So, too, is the desire to marry a co-religionist and have religious observance and practice as part of family life; or one might desire to eliminate religion from family life. There is a sense in which one can have *reasons* for (at least some of) one's desires; they do not just occur inexplicably. There are good reasons to want to fulfil one's responsibilities in a more reliable, less selfish way. Yet, some desires do seem to occur inexplicably; the desire to throw a rock out onto the ice on a frozen pond, just to see if the ice breaks, might be an example. Desires, therefore, occur in different modes, are felt in different ways (though some do not have a distinctive phenomenology) and figure in practical reasoning and judgement in diverse ways.

When we say that 'Desire D caused the individual to do A' it is not as though that has a single, universally applicable meaning in all action explanations. What is meant by 'Desire D' and perhaps even what is meant by 'caused' might need careful explication, given the many modes of desire and the ways that desires are connected with actions. Someone might decide to perform a particular action in the future, and when the time comes, does it; and it would be right to say he or she did it because they desired to, but whether there was an occurrent desire at the time of action, and how it is related to the earlier decision is not obvious. There is a trivial sense in which all actions might be said to be a matter of persons doing what they want to do; namely, having done X that indicates that X is what the person wanted to do. But that does not actually imply that there was an antecedent desire to do X, or even that the agent desired to do it. The agent might have done it with nearly despairing regret, but feeling that she had no other option with any greater appeal.

Moreover, the way in which an action is described can make an important difference to whether and how it is regarded as caused. What we regard as a particular action, or as someone Ø-ing, depends on *how the behaviour is described*, and many different descriptions are possible. One might insist that there is some single, privileged description, the one that tells us what the act is in the most fundamental, or most accurate, or relevant sense. But that is likely to depend on a view about what is the most explanatorily relevant context. That might be the context in which the actors take themselves to be; or it could be the context of a particular theory of what motivates people; or it could depend on the particular interests of the investigator. The point is not that we inevitably suffer from action-description vertigo and there is no basis for choosing from alternative descriptions of behaviour. But we do need to be alert to the relevance of presuppositions and the kinds of considerations that best serve the sort of explanation we are seeking to formulate. Considering only economic factors, or explaining exclusively in terms of macro-level social structures can have important purposes but they are not necessarily the most authoritative, adequate and complete with respect to explanation. Different descriptions, different levels of theorising, explanations formulated in the idioms of different sciences; these and other matters point to the difficulty of proposing any single description as uniquely primary in an indisputable sense.

Some of the differences between descriptions depend on where we take an act to begin and end, and there can be many different ways of doing that. Is she lashing out at him because he has hurtfully insulted her, or is her action an expression of long-simmering anger over having been treated in condescending and disrespectful ways by men in the past? Or, is this another instance of how this person pays little attention to circumstances and to what is appropriate, and lets her emotions get the better of her even in settings where that is inadvisable? Or was the insult so uncalled-for and gratuitously mean that *of course* she lashed out – anyone with self-respect would react that way? There are several different ways that the act can be individuated, each involving a different description. There are multiple angles of approach, depending in part on what considerations are of greatest interest to the investigator. We might feel tempted to ask: 'But what is the person *really* or *actually* doing?' However, there can be multiple, factually correct descriptions without just one of them being primary in all explanatory contexts.

The discussion of the work of Hollis and Runciman (above) indicates that we are persuaded that the terms of explanation are not to be formulated and fixed in advance of what is found to be illuminating and constructive in the project of investigation. Explanation that is responsive to the complexity of the phenomena might require conceptions and insights that do not all come from a single source. In addition, taking valuative considerations seriously in empirical investigation and explanation suggests that there is a role for agency understood in a much more complex manner than explanations of action in terms of lawlike (or probabilistic) statements of event-causality. Value figures in action in as complex and multiform a way as desire. Indeed, there are relations between them in the sense that what persons value often shapes their desires, and what persons desire can have a considerable impact on what they value. Just as desires can have a temporally extended, dispositional significance, so too can a person's values.

Speaking of 'a person's values' risks reifying them somewhat; in many contexts it would be less misleading to speak of 'what a person values' and the diverse ways in which those considerations figure in the person's behaviour. What a person values is reflected in their patterns of practical reasoning, their responses and attitudes, and their judgements of what is important, necessary, or indicative of worth and significance. Rather than treating values in an exclusively expressive sense we would do well to acknowledge the ways that values often underwrite reasons, and through that, have a crucial role in a great deal of human action. Their role cannot be assimilated to a covering-law model of explanation, and acknowledging that values have a significant place in the explanation of action helps us see that agency (in contrast to event-causality as the only form of the explanation of action) is neither mysterious nor somehow an offence against rigorous empirical standards. It is not as though the only alternative to event-causality is a ghost in the machine or some form of mysterious metaphysics. There are ways in which *the capacity to act for reasons* is best described and understood as involving exercises of agency. Valuative considerations are often among a person's reasons and the ways that they figure in action are not confined to what is allowable in positivist terms. A valuatively vacuous strategy of explanation is bound to miss a great deal of the criminological reality. For example, Justice Tankebe's chapter in this volume discusses what he describes as 'the choices made by individual police officers when they are confronted with unethical actions by their colleagues'. He employs Situational Action Theory, which maintains (among other things) that the moral context of a given social setting constitutes an immediate normative order or social environment within which action takes place. Tankebe's study is empirical, but it is one in which persons' valuative propensities and patterns of valuative judgement are recognised as having considerable explanatory significance. Among the conclusions to which his study led him is that 'officers who believe it is right to act against misconduct are more likely to do so if they witness, or believe, that other officers do act against misconduct'. This is not a matter of bringing one particular moral theory to bear, and using it to 'process' the facts in order to identify their ethical significance. It is a matter of accepting that moral considerations can have a genuine explanatory role, but not in a causally mechanical manner.

All of the chapters in this volume – and not just those that are explicitly philosophical – help make that point. There are various ways in which moral concepts need to be employed in many projects of empirical explanation, and that involves engaging in moral thought. This is not a way of judging what is studied, but of more fully understanding it. As the discussion of 'appreciative description' has highlighted, morally illuminating thought is often a matter of articulating what it is that needs to be described rather than 'adding' a valuative accessory to a value-neutral description.

The chief issue regarding the debate over agency is how to answer the question, 'What sorts of concepts are required for the most adequate, explanatory account of human action?' From several different angles of approach the chapters in this volume suggest that the concepts that form a positivist account of human action are not adequate and there are good reasons for taking agency seriously in criminological investigation and explanation. One of the main reasons is this: whereas positivist accounts of behaviour focus on events in lawlike relations,[26] the concept of agency is open to include notions of capability, of valuative commitments, and of practical rationality that are not limited to means-end reasoning. Much of the practical reasoning that people do concerns the specification of their ends, and the ordering of commitments and aims according to notions of priority and importance. Even desires are often the objects of reflection and our own criticism. As mentioned above, we sometimes have desires we wish we did not have, or a desire needs to be made more clear, specific and elaborated in a way that makes acting on it feasible. For example, simply wanting to desist from criminal activity is not likely to be efficacious. The person needs to form that desire into a course of possible action, involving a way forward and then continual assessment of one's efforts and circumstances, as well as resolution to do what is required.

Thus, there are normative considerations, as well as deliberative efforts, woven throughout human actions. 'Agency' refers to a complex ensemble of human capacities (including cognition, reasoning, affect and judgement) that become reflected in practical activities such as deliberation, choice and voluntary action.[27] Often, the explanation of action will (appropriately) focus on a

[26] ie, such that positive instances confirm a relation between events that is explanatory – one stronger than coincidence or accidental generalisation.

[27] As this description suggests, 'agency' is not a single or simple concept, of the kind that Pratt (2018) was apparently searching for in his thoughtful and positive reappraisal of Matza's work. 'The lack of an agreed-upon definition' of agency by criminologists, Pratt argued, 'means that [it] can go unmeasured in empirical studies and nobody seems to raise an eyebrow about it ... But [this is not] good enough' (at 22–23). However, if agency is defined as in the text above, then it is clear that we cannot meaningfully use, in empirical research, a single concept such as 'the degree of agency exercised by research subjects'. We can, however, certainly employ quantitative measures of *aspects* of agency, as criminologists routinely do when they ask questions about future intentions. We can also sometimes measure the results of agentic choices, as shown for example in the study by Liebling et al (1999) of a prison incentives policy (see discussion above), where prisoners' perceptions of unfairness overrode considerations of rational choice. Subtle aspects of agency can also be richly described in qualitative criminological studies using what Runciman (1983) called 'appreciative description'; this is illustrated in, eg, the chapters by Williams (ch 7) and by Lanskey and colleagues (ch 4) in this volume.

particular desire, a particular felt concern, or other identifiable events. But a vast amount of human behaviour needs to be understood in the context of agency, as characterised here, and the explanation of it is not best expressed in lawlike statements relating events as causes and effects. A great many *doings*, things done by human beings, involve elements that are connected in ways that are not captured and expressed entirely in terms of antecedent conditions (causes) and determined consequences (effects). Certainly, there are necessary conditions for anything a person does. That is obvious and unavoidable, but not trivial. Still, it is not a sign that identifying a few additional conditions or circumstances will yield causally necessitating conditions confirmable as lawlike.

Can norms and values figure in action explanations? Of course they can; the practical rationality exercised by human beings unavoidably involves such considerations. Practical rationality is not limited to instrumental exercises of reason and there is a complex fabric of concerns, commitments, aspirations, excitement, fears, ideals, forms of purposefulness, resoluteness, indecision and so forth that is intelligible only through normativity and valuative considerations. There is a connection between the debate about the relation between facts and values on the one hand, and the debate about event-causality and agency on the other. The ways in which values are empirically significant and have a place in the explanation of action point to the plausibility of agency as a meaningful, illuminating concept. This is not simply a matter of, 'if there are values, there is agency' or 'if there is agency, there are values'. The connections between them need to be spelled out in more conceptually specific and empirically informative ways. But we have tried here to suggest some of the main reasons in favour of there being a good case for understanding human beings as agents for whom values and norms are integral features (for better or for worse) of a great deal of their behaviour. A crucial part of seeing a way to move on from positivist strictures regarding the terms of explanation is recognising the importance of including norms and values in empirical enquiry. They have earned that importance by making possible explanations that are more fully responsive to the actual complexity of the phenomena studied. In the chapters in this volume the reader can see that even in many places where arguments for the inclusion of values, or for a more than positivist-causal explanation are not explicitly presented they are strongly relevant aspects of what is being asserted. In his chapter Justice Tankebe notes that:

> Social scientists do not, in general, seek to resolve … moral dilemmas. They ask a different set of questions, including the following: what knowledge do officers have about the set of behaviours that constitute misconduct? How often do they encounter whistleblowing opportunities? What moral beliefs do they hold about whistleblowing?

And he concludes that paragraph by saying: 'As a social scientist, my main concern in this chapter is with explanatory questions of this kind about whistleblowing by police officers'. Though he is therefore explicit in distancing his discussion from directly addressing moral problems, and the Situational Action

Theory that is central to his discussion is a social-scientific rather than an ethical theory, it is clear that ethical/moral considerations are as fully a part of the explanatory endeavour as are other facts about propensities or circumstances. That point, and the way that moral considerations and the concept of agency are interrelated, are among the most important claims made by the various chapters in this volume.

THE CHAPTERS IN THIS VOLUME

In turning finally to consider the chapters in this volume, we must first emphasise that while all the contributors share the goal of promoting a better dialogue between criminologists and moral philosophers, the specific arguments of this Introduction are our own, and they are not necessarily shared by the other authors. That said, attentive readers will quickly discover that each of the chapters by criminologists attempts to explicate a variety of moral considerations that they find inseparable from the empirical issues that they study. Likewise, all the chapters by philosophers regard empirical considerations as integral to the study of morality, and they connect with specific criminological issues at numerous points. Hopefully, therefore, the overall effect will be to persuade readers that the prospects for criminology as a moral science are substantial and important.

The chapters are divided into four parts, which we will discuss separately.

Orientations

Part I consists of two chapters by philosophers that develop some of the points raised in this Introduction. In chapter one, Jonathan Jacobs argues that as a result of a robust, multifaceted critique of Logical Positivism the fact/value distinction as understood by positivists is no longer regarded as philosophically defensible. This is important because that distinction has had considerable influence in the social sciences, and continues to be endorsed by many social scientists. However, one of the most important developments of recent decades is that there is now an understanding of important elements of Hume's philosophy in naturalistic terms rather than narrowly positivist terms. This reorientation helps us to understand how Hume could be both a critic of rationalist morality and a moral theorist who elaborated what has become a highly influential conception of morality. Moreover, post-positivist empiricism is much more open than is positivism to extensive connections between philosophy and various empirical sciences. Again, Hume is important here because he held that the understanding of morality needs to be undertaken as an empirical rather than an a priori project. While this chapter is not a straightforward defence of Humean theses regarding the understanding of morality, it is a sympathetic explication of how the naturalistic reading of Hume on morality shows us how any putative clean break between facts and values is actually very implausible, and Hume's philosophy contains valuable resources for exploring relations between moral philosophy and empirical criminology. Indeed, Hume (and others of the British Moralists, such as Hutcheson and Smith) provide some important conceptual resources for pursuing a broadly empirical study of morality of just the kind to which criminology is especially well placed to make important contributions.

Chapter two, by Christine Swanton, begins by identifying some significant ways in which twentieth-century philosophical ethics put impediments in the way of the 'moral turn' that some social sciences are now attempting, and in the way of empirical investigations that can inform moral philosophy more fully. While some broadly similar claims have been discussed by philosophers in recent decades, Swanton's chapter is distinctive in addressing directly the significance of overcoming these impediments in order to develop a better interrelation between moral philosophy and social scientific research. That interrelation is further encouraged by Swanton's critique of moral philosophy as practised – especially in Anglophone philosophy – through most of the twentieth century. During that century much moral philosophy was focused not directly on moral issues, but on metaethical ones (ie, issues concerning the epistemology, metaphysics and semantics of moral judgement and discourse). Metaethical issues are indeed important, but for too long they, and a small number of highly abstract approaches to moral theory (chiefly Utilitarianism and Kantian deontology) so completely dominated Anglophone moral philosophy that the complex reality of concrete, lived moral experience was largely neglected. Drawing on work by Heidegger, Durkheim, Bernard Williams and others, Swanton exposes some of the most significant deficiencies of much recent moral philosophy and directs attention to avenues that would enable it to connect more adequately with empirical studies – for example, in elaborating a conception of virtue that is responsive to the complexity and the challenges of moral reality. In particular, she highlights and develops the work of Tessman (2005) on ways in which paths towards virtue can be 'burdened', and she applies the concept of 'burdened virtue' to empirical work on desistance from crime by Bottoms and Shapland (2014).

Criminal Justice-Related Ethical Dilemmas

In what can be read as a response to Swanton's plea for studies of 'moral reality', Part II of the volume focuses attention on two sharp moral dilemmas that can and do confront some people in criminal justice-related contexts, usually in circumstances not of their own choosing.

The first of these dilemmas, discussed in chapter three, concerns police officers' reactions when they encounter ethical misconduct by a police colleague.

Here the dilemma concerns whether the misconduct should be reported (as official guidance decrees that it should) or whether the ties of colleagueship and comradeship between the two officers are deemed by the observing officer to override the official code of conduct. These issues were empirically studied by Justice Tankebe, using quantitative survey methods with a sample of Ghanaian police officers. The theoretical framework for the study is Situational Action Theory (SAT), as described earlier in this Introduction. SAT has previously been empirically tested solely in relation to the explanation of acts of crime, but its author (Per-Olof Wikström) has claimed that 'explaining acts of crime is not different from explaining why people breach moral rules more generally' (Wikström et al 2012: 12), and Tankebe's study is the first to test SAT in relation to non-criminal moral rules. The results of the study differ somewhat from SAT-based crime studies, which have shown that the frequency of individuals' acts of crime is best explained through an interactive effect between (primarily) moral beliefs and the moral context of social settings. In the Ghana police study, there were no significant interactions; instead, moral beliefs were dominant in the explanation of intentions to report misconduct, but the moral context of the officer's work environment (ie, the extent to which reporting occurred in his or her team) was dominant in explaining actual reporting by officers. As Tankebe notes, this result raises questions about the strength of character traits, since officers had ethical dispositions but frequently did not follow through on their beliefs in group situations where reporting was not favoured.

Chapter four, by Caroline Lanskey and colleagues, examines a different set of dilemmas, namely the moral choices faced by women with children whose fathers are or were imprisoned. These mothers are confronted by unavoidable and deeply important issues concerning how to guide their children, and whether (and if so, how best) to sustain a commitment to their partner – both in prison and after discharge. The accounts given in this chapter – based on qualitative research in England – are not of women who abandon their partners, but instead of those who seek ways of providing stability and healthy parenting as mothers, while also maintaining a degree of commitment to the children's fathers. The authors focus particularly on Carol Gilligan's (1982) 'ethic of care' as providing an appropriate theoretical framework to capture the deep emotional commitment of the mothers to their children's welfare. That ethic informed the mothers' approach to resolving the moral tensions linked to the father's offence and prison sentence: for example, concerning what to tell the children and how best to protect them from stigmatisation or hostility from others. The focus of the authors' analysis is very much on how the moral dilemmas of the mothers are understood not through abstract, principle-based ethical approaches, but through the sensibilities within their understanding of parenting. Perhaps more than any other chapter in the volume, this analysis connects empirically with the British Moralists' emphasis on sensibility.

Moral Emotions

In Part III, attention turns to the important topic of moral emotions, and in particular to the emotions of shame and guilt, which have an obvious relevance for criminologists. Here we pair a philosophical and a criminological contribution.

In chapter five, the philosopher Sophie-Grace Chappell examines the moral psychology of guilt and shame, the latter having become a prominent topic in criminology through the work of John Braithwaite (1989). Influential philosophers such as Philippa Foot and Bernard Williams have in recent decades written on guilt and shame as part of the retrieval of rich moral-psychological reflections, following the diminished influence in philosophy of emotivism and prescriptivism. Chappell looks into the ways in which shame and guilt – like other attitudes and aspects of sensibility – need to be understood not simply as feelings but in a rational-explanatory context. Just as pride can only be felt properly with regard to certain matters, and resentment or admiration are appropriate only respecting certain types of action or characteristic, guilt and shame also have proper objects. (One cannot take pride in the earth being larger than the moon, or resent the fact that the Pacific Ocean is deeper in places than the Black Sea.) Chappell is especially interested in the ways in which shame and guilt have different and important roles in moral life. They are not just painful or disagreeable feelings; each has a place in a well-formed moral personality. In addition to shame and guilt there is a rich phenomenology of related notions and responses to consider: these include agent-regret; remorse; embarrassment; and humiliation. Chappell's discussion lays out some of the key lines of analysis of shame and guilt with specific reference to the criminological context. As her title ('A Plea for Guilt') emphasises, she also notes a recent tendency in both philosophy and criminology to prioritise shame over guilt, and she argues that it would be a mistake to neglect or sideline the significance of guilt as a moral emotion.

Chapter six, by Alice Ievins, examines shame and guilt as they have been issues for recent empirical research in criminology. She notes, among other things, that there have been two contradictory narratives in this literature: one suggests that guilt and shame prompt desistance from crime, and the other suggests that they threaten it. In an attempt to resolve this issue, she suggests that it is helpful to think about desistance as a process with stages, each of which has different emotional accompaniments. She argues that, empirically, one of the chief differences between shame and guilt is that the latter is often the form that shame takes after it has been cognitively processed and distanced from the self. Thus, guilt is generally not an effective motive for desistance, given that it tends to follow it. If a person has managed to transition to a (largely) non-criminal life, it is then that guilt is more likely to emerge as an aspect of a change in the person's conception of their own identity. Ievins also relates this literature to the issue of whether there is a role for repentance in punishment, and whether motivating repentance should be an aim of the criminal sanction.

Here, a key suggestion is that, empirically, it is not necessary for punishment to aim at 'deep' repentance for such repentance to be achieved. Feelings of shame and guilt about past offending can emerge autonomously in certain conditions, and thus a potential goal for state intervention would be to aim to create these conditions, or at least to avoid working against them.

Desistance from Crime: Analyses in Positive and Critical Morality

In this final part of the volume, we turn to the topic of desistance from crime. As we noted when discussing Matza's (1964) challenge to positivist criminology (above), the widespread reduction and cessation of criminal careers in people's twenties and thirties constitutes a significant problem of explanation for criminological theory. Since the seminal work of Laub and Sampson (2003), the explanation of 'desistance' has attracted much attention from criminologists, but – despite the change in moral behaviour necessarily involved in true desistance – little of this work has been explicitly linked to ethical analysis. The first two chapters in Part IV add to this empirical literature with differing analyses of the 'positive morality' of desistance journeys; the final chapter then offers an analysis in 'critical morality' linked to this topic.

Chapter seven, by Ryan Williams, explores some of the challenges faced by prisoners for whom their Muslim faith was an important centre of gravity while they were in prison. Williams highlights a 'problem of moral consistency' encountered by those prisoners: namely, how to maintain the requirements of their faith when, on release, they need to deal with some of the complexities of the social world outside the prison. The author draws on a distinction made by Bernard Williams (1985/2006: ch 10) and others between a 'morality system' (in this case, a religious-deontological one) and a more flexible virtue-centred context of 'ethics'. This contrast is used as a way of bringing out the conceptual anatomy of the challenge of navigating the social world when guided by a religious commitment; the contrast helps to clarify the character of the challenge of responding to two sources of obligation when the transition to free society after having been imprisoned complicates the lives of these men and leads them to various reflections on what they should regard as morally most important. As a prelude to this discussion, the chapter begins with the sharply contrasting practices of two Muslim probation officers, one of whom recommends to his supervisees an approach to desistance based on the 'rule-following' of Islamic precepts, while the other recommends an approach based on Islamic learning and practice. After considering his empirical case studies, Williams suggests that a combination of these two approaches perhaps 'offers a way of supporting Muslims in a way that can meaningfully bring their behaviours into alignment with Islamic precepts that cohere with socio-legal norms'. This is a study of desistance in an important context that has not yet garnered the attention it merits.

Chapter eight, by Anthony Bottoms and Caroline Lanskey, is entitled 'Ethical Aspects of Journeys Towards Desistance by Male Young Adult Recidivists'. It combines theoretical analysis with an in-depth look at three cases from the Sheffield Desistance Study (SDS). Like Bottoms and Shapland (2014), the authors adopt a virtue ethical approach, but following the advice by Christine Swanton (see above), they frame this in terms of 'burdened virtue' – a very appropriate term in light of the extensive criminal histories, poor schooling, lack of qualifications, and weak employment records of these young men (initially aged between 19 and 22). Despite these very disadvantageous backgrounds, many of the men made serious attempts to desist from crime, although almost always in a gradual manner (ie, reducing the frequency of offending, rather than stopping completely), and in contexts that often made their attempts vulnerable to unexpected events. The authors utilise the traditional sociological categories of 'structure' and 'agency', but also more recent work in 'relational sociology' (as previously described in this Introduction), and the case studies demonstrate the great importance of relationships (particularly with girlfriends, mothers and male peers) in influencing the success or otherwise of attempts to desist. The chapter also draws on philosophical sources, in particular: (i) Charles Taylor's (1989) concept of a person's 'moral framework' (perhaps including contrasting values), which helpfully illuminates some of the changes in the priority of individuals' values in the case studies; and (ii) Richard Holton's (2003; 2009) discussion of 'strength of will', given the research subjects' need for such an attribute in order to maintain their resolutions to desist, and their frequent resort to tactics of 'diachronic self-control' in order to avoid places or people where or with whom they might easily be tempted to reoffend.

The author of the final chapter (chapter nine) is Matt Matravers, a political philosopher. This is the only chapter in the volume that explicitly addresses an issue in what Hart called 'critical morality', and the approach taken by Matravers fully exemplifies what we as editors regard as an appropriately 'moral science' approach to critical morality (see discussion at the end of the section on 'developing a moral science approach', above), including attention to empirical research findings relevant to the discussion. In his chapter, Matravers addresses the issue of what are the state's obligations in regard to helping citizens to live non-criminal lives. This is part of a conception of a just political order, though the question has been considered much less frequently than other questions concerning justice. The view that there are numerous conditions that rules must satisfy in order to be valid as law (and therefore prompt compliance) has been much discussed, but this chapter is distinctive in addressing the question of whether there are ways in which the state can be expected to intervene to assist those trying to *desist from* criminal behaviour, and to help persons to be reliably law-abiding. Does the legitimacy of the state's power and the validity of the rule of law include an obligation to assist offenders striving to abandon criminal careers? This is considered as a normative concern of political theory, not just an instrumental matter of policy. Matravers' discussion is an especially suitable concluding chapter for the volume, articulating some fundamental matters of moral and political value that are motivated by questions concerning desistance.

APPENDIX: JAMES Q WILSON'S *THE MORAL SENSE*

We are not the first to suggest that modern criminology can benefit from some reconsideration of the work of the British Moralists. The late James Q Wilson, a major contributor to American criminology, explicitly described his book *The Moral Sense* as 'a continuation of work begun by certain eighteenth-century English and Scottish thinkers, notably Joseph Butler, Francis Hutcheson, David Hume, and Adam Smith'. Wilson emphasised, however, that he was not a philosopher, so what he hoped to add to the work of the British Moralists was 'knowledge of what the biological and social sciences have since learned about what they were the first to call the moral sense' (Wilson 1993: xiii). In a later interview Wilson described *The Moral Sense* as 'the most important book I've ever written' (Newton 2007). However, despite Wilson's prominence in criminology, the book has received little attention from criminologists.

In his text, Wilson argued that a properly developed human being acquires a moral sense, defined as 'an intuitive or directly felt belief about how one ought to act when one is free to act voluntarily (that is, not under duress)' (Wilson 1993: xii). He identified four 'sensibilities' that he saw as important examples of our moral sense: they are sympathy, fairness, self-control and duty (at xiii and chs 2–5). The origins of these 'sensibilities' are natural: 'they are to some degree innate, and they appear spontaneously amid the routine intimacies of family life' (at 229). But because they have 'a common origin in our natural sociability', and people grow up in different social contexts, 'gender and culture will profoundly influence' which of the four sensibilities 'are most valued' by any particular individual or group (at 229). Developing this point, part of Wilson's thesis is that the Enlightenment left succeeding generations with an 'ambiguous legacy' (at 244). It produced a 'great gain for humanity' by promoting the sensibilities of sympathy and fairness (leading, for example, to the abolition of slavery); but unfortunately, at least in its 'modern formulation', its 'radicalized individualism' posed important challenges to the other two sensibilities discussed in *The Moral Sense*, those of self-control and duty (at 245). Then, on the penultimate page of his book, although without specifying which thinkers he has in mind, Wilson criticises the 'fatally flawed assumption of many Enlightenment thinkers … that autonomous individuals can freely choose, or will, their moral life' (at 250). Moreover, because they have believed that

> individuals are everything, rights are trumps and morality is relative to time and place, such thinkers have been led to design laws, practices and institutions that leave nothing between the state and the individual save choices, contracts and entitlements.

Like Wilson, we see our project as having an affinity with those moral philosophers for whom moral sentiments and sensibility are critically important, and strongly shaped by sociability. However, unlike him, in this volume we are not making a case for any substantive conception of a morally well-ordered individual, nor are we offering any overall assessment of the present moral state of Western societies. Of course, any moral view presupposes notions concerning human good or flourishing, or what is repugnant and what is imperative, and so on. But our main concern in this volume is to show that empirical criminology can, with advantage, include the study of moral considerations, including an explanatory role for them, without violating the integrity of empirical science. Wilson's claims are much more specific regarding first, what is involved in sound moral judgements and morally well-ordered habits, and second, about the condition of Western morality.

We do of course concur with Wilson in rejecting the propositions that 'individuals are everything … and morality is relative'. As we hope to have shown, however, the British Moralists also rejected such claims, and in our view such a rejection is a necessary feature of the case for a moral science.

REFERENCES

Abbott, O (2020) *The Self, Relational Sociology and Morality in Practice* (Cham, Palgrave Macmillan).

Ayer, AJ (1936/2001) *Language, Truth and Logic* (London, Penguin).

Beccaria, C (1764/1995) *On Crimes and Punishments and Other Writings*, ed R Bellamy (Cambridge, Cambridge University Press).

Bloch, M (1954) *The Historian's Craft* (trans P Putnam) (Manchester, Manchester University Press).

Blomberg, TG, Cullen, FT, Carlsson, C and Jonson, CL (eds) (2018) *Delinquency and Drift Revisited: The Criminology of David Matza and Beyond* (London, Routledge).

Bottoms, AE (2003) 'Theoretical Reflections on the Evaluation of a Penal Policy Initiative' in L Zedner and A Ashworth (eds), *The Criminological Foundations of Penal Policy: Essays in Honour of Roger Hood* (Oxford, Oxford University Press).

——(2006) 'Desistance, Social Bonds and Human Agency' in P-O Wikström and RJ Sampson (eds), *The Explanation of Crime: Context, Mechanisms and Development* (Cambridge, Cambridge University Press).

——(2008) 'The Relationship between Theory and Empirical Observations in Criminology' in RD King and E Wincup (eds), *Doing Research on Crime and Justice*, 2nd edn (Oxford, Oxford University Press).

——(2022) 'Criminology and "Positive Morality"' in A Liebling, J Shapland, R Sparks and J Tankebe (eds), *Crime, Justice and Social Order* (Oxford, Oxford University Press).

Bottoms, A and Shapland, J (2014) 'Can Persistent Offenders Acquire Virtue?' 27 *Studies in Christian Ethics* 318.

Boutellier, H (2019) *A Criminology of Moral Order* (Bristol, Bristol University Press).

Braithwaite, J (1989) *Crime, Shame and Reintegration* (Cambridge, Cambridge University Press).

Brangan, L (2023) 'Making Sense of Penal Difference: Political Cultures and Comparative Penology' *Punishment & Society* (forthcoming).
Buber, M (2010) *I and Thou* (trans RG Smith) (Eastford, CT, Martino Publishing).
Bull, M (1991) 'Selective Naturalization: WG Runciman's Social Theory' 22 *Journal of the Anthropological Society of Oxford* 235.
Cavadino, M and Dignan, J (2006) *Penal Systems: A Comparative Approach* (London, Sage).
Crisp, R and Slote, M (eds) (1997) *Virtue Ethics* (Oxford, Oxford University Press).
Descartes, R (1641/1998) 'Meditations on First Philosophy' in J Cottingham (ed), *Descartes: Selected Philosophical Writings* (trans J Cottingham and R Stoothoff) (Cambridge, Cambridge University Press).
Downes, D (1988) *Contrasts in Tolerance* (Oxford, Oxford University Press).
Du Bois-Pedain, A and Eldar, S (eds) (2022) *Re-Reading Beccaria: On the Contemporary Significance of a Penal Classic* (Oxford, Hart Publishing).
Fassin, D and Lézé, S (eds) (2014) *Moral Anthropology: A Critical Reader* (London, Routledge).
Garland, D (1990) *Punishment and Modern Society: A Study in Social Theory* (Oxford, Oxford University Press).
——(2013) 'Penality and the Penal State' 51 *Criminology* 475.
——(2018) 'Theoretical Advances and Problems in the Sociology of Punishment' 20 *Punishment & Society* 8.
Garofalo, R (1914) *Criminology* (trans RW Millar) (Boston, MA, Little, Brown and Company).
Giddens, A (1984) *The Constitution of Society* (Cambridge, Polity Press).
Gilligan, C (1982) *In a Different Voice: Psychological Theory and Women's Development* (Cambridge, MA, Harvard University Press).
Graham, G (2019) 'Behaviorism' in EN Zalta (ed), *Stanford Encyclopedia of Philosophy* (Spring 2019 edn), available at: plato.stanford.edu/entries/behaviorism/.
Hart, HLA (1963) *Law, Liberty and Morality* (London, Oxford University Press).
Hollis, M (2002) *The Philosophy of Social Science*, rev edn (Cambridge, Cambridge University Press).
Holton, R (2003) 'How is Strength of Will Possible?' in S Stroud and C Tappolet (eds), *Weakness of Will and Practical Irrationality* (Oxford, Clarendon Press).
——(2009) *Willing, Wanting, Waiting* (Oxford, Oxford University Press).
Hood, R (1974) *Tolerance and the Tariff: Some Reflections on Fixing the Time Prisoners Serve in Custody* (London, National Association for the Care and Resettlement of Offenders).
Hume, D (1739–40/2000) *A Treatise of Human Nature*, eds DF Norton and MJ Norton (Oxford, Oxford University Press).
Jacobs, J (2022a) *Criminology and Moral Philosophy: Empirical Methods and the Study of Values* (London, Routledge).
——(2022b) 'In Dialogue through Philosophy: Recovering the Moral Sciences through Criminology' in A Liebling, J Shapland, R Sparks and J Tankebe (eds), *Crime, Justice and Social Order* (Oxford, Oxford University Press).
Lacey, N (2008) *The Prisoner's Dilemma: Political Economy and Punishment in Contemporary Democracies* (Cambridge, Cambridge University Press).
Laidlaw, J (2014) *The Subject of Virtue: An Anthropology of Ethics and Freedom* (Cambridge, Cambridge University Press).

——(2017) 'Ethics/Morality' in F Stein, S Lazar, M Candea, H Diemberger, J Robbins, A Sanchez and R Stash (eds), *The Cambridge Encyclopedia of Anthropology*, available at: www.anthroencyclopedia.com/entry/ethics-morality.

Lambek, M, Das, V, Fassin, D and Keane, W (2015) *Four Lectures in Ethics: Anthropological Perspectives* (Chicago, IL, HAU Books).

Laub, JH and Sampson, RJ (2003) *Shared Beginnings, Divergent Lives: Delinquent Boys to Age 70* (Cambridge, MA, Harvard University Press).

Liebling, A (2011) 'Distinctions and Distinctiveness in the Work of Prison Officers: Legitimacy and Authority Revisited' 8 *European Journal of Criminology* 484.

——(2015) 'Description at the Edge? *I-It – I-Thou* Relations and Action in Prisons Research' 4 *International Journal for Crime, Justice and Social Democracy* 18.

——(2021) 'What is Philosophy in Prison? George Eliot and the Search for Moral Insight' 7 *Journal of Prison Education & Reentry* 104.

Liebling, A, Laws, B, Lieber, E, Auty, K, Schmidt, BE, Crewe, B, Gardom, J, Kant, D and Morey, M (2019) 'Are Hope and Possibility Achievable in Prison?' 58 *Howard Journal of Crime and Justice* 104.

Liebling, A, Muir, G, Rose, G and Bottoms, AE (1999) *Incentives and Earned Privileges for Prisoners: An Evaluation,* Home Office Research Findings No 87 (London, Home Office).

Loader, I and Sparks, R (2011) *Public Criminology?* (Abingdon, Routledge).

Lukes, S (2008) *Moral Relativism* (London, Profile Books).

MacCormick, N (2007) *Institutions of Law: An Essay in Legal Theory* (Oxford, Oxford University Press).

Mattingly, C (2014) *Moral Laboratories: Family Peril and the Struggle for a Good Life* (Oakland, CA, University of California Press).

Matza, D (1964) *Delinquency and Drift* (New York, John Wiley and Sons).

Messner, SF (2012) 'Morality, Markets and the ASC: 2011 Presidential Address to the American Society of Criminology' 50 *Criminology* 5.

Modell, J (1994) 'Book Review of *Crime in the Making*' 99 *American Journal of Sociology* 1389.

Newton, J (2007) 'James Q Wilson: The Power of His Written Word' *Los Angeles Times* (3 June 2007).

Norton, DF (2000) 'Editor's Introduction' in D Hume, *A Treatise of Human Nature*, eds DF Norton and MJ Norton (Oxford, Oxford University Press).

Outram, D (2019) *The Enlightenment*, 4th edn (Cambridge, Cambridge University Press).

Paternoster, R (2017) 'Happenings, Acts and Actions: Articulating the Meaning and Implications of Human Agency for Criminology' 3 *Journal of Developmental and Life-Course Criminology* 350.

Piquero, AR (2021) 'Reflections on Choice and Agency in Context: A Reply' 7 *Journal of Developmental and Life-Course Criminology* 711.

Pratt, TC (2018) 'Delinquency and Drift: Challenging Criminology Then and Now' in TG Blomberg, FT Cullen, C Carlsson and CL Jonson (eds), *Delinquency and Drift Revisited: The Criminology of David Matza and Beyond* (London, Routledge).

Radzinowicz, L and Hood, R (1986) *A History of English Criminal Law and its Administration from 1750*, vol 5 (London, Stevens and Sons).

Robbins, J (2018) 'Where in the World are Values? Exemplarity and Moral Motivation' in C Mattingly, R Dyring, M Louw and T Schwarz Wentzer (eds), *Moral Engines: Exploring the Ethical Drives in Human Life* (New York, Berghahn Books).

Runciman, WG (1972) *A Critique of Max Weber's Philosophy of Social Science* (Cambridge, Cambridge University Press).

——(1983) *A Treatise on Social Theory, vol 1, The Methodology of Social Theory* (Cambridge, Cambridge University Press).

Sampson, RJ and Laub, JH (1993) *Crime in the Making: Pathways and Turning Points through Life* (Cambridge, MA, Harvard University Press).

Sankowski, ET (2005) 'Sensibility' in T Honderich (ed), *The Oxford Companion to Philosophy* (Oxford, Oxford University Press).

Sherman, LW (2010) 'Defiance, Compliance and Consilience: A General Theory of Criminology' in E McLaughlin and T Newburn (eds), *The Sage Handbook of Criminological Theory* (London, Sage Publications).

Slote, M (2010) *Moral Sentimentalism* (Oxford, Oxford University Press).

Smith, A (1759/1982) *The Theory of Moral Sentiments*, ed K Haakonssen (Cambridge, Cambridge University Press).

Smith, L (2006) 'Introduction' in L Smith and J Vonèche (eds), *Norms in Human Development* (Cambridge, Cambridge University Press).

Sutherland, EH and Cressey, DR (1960) *Principles of Criminology*, 6th edn (Chicago, IL, Lippincott).

Swanton, C (2021) *Target Centred Virtue Ethics* (Oxford, Oxford University Press).

Tamanaha, BZ (2001) *A General Jurisprudence of Law and Society* (Oxford, Oxford University Press).

Taylor, C (1989) *Sources of the Self: The Making of the Modern Identity* (Cambridge, Cambridge University Press).

Tessman, L (2005) *Burdened Virtues: Virtue Ethics for Liberatory Struggles* (Oxford, Oxford University Press).

Wallace, RJ (1994) *Responsibility and the Moral Sentiments* (Cambridge, MA, Harvard University Press).

Wiggins, D (1998) *Needs, Values, Truth: Essays in the Philosophy of Value*, 3rd edn (Oxford, Clarendon Press).

Wikström, P-O, Oberwittler, D, Treiber, KH and Hardie, B (2012) *Breaking Rules: The Social and Situational Dynamics of Young People's Urban Crime* (Oxford, Oxford University Press).

Wikström, P-O and Treiber, K (2016) 'Social Disadvantage and Crime: A Criminological Puzzle' 60 *American Behavioral Scientist* 1232.

Williams, B (1985/2006) *Ethics and the Limits of Philosophy*, with commentary by AW Moore (London, Routledge) (originally published by Fontana 1985).

——(2005) *In the Beginning Was the Deed: Realism and Moralism in Political Argument*, ed G Hawthorn (Princeton, NJ, Princeton University Press).

Wilson, JQ (1993) *The Moral Sense* (New York, Free Press).

Part I

Orientations

1

Criminology and Moral Philosophy: Prospects for Fuller Engagement

JONATHAN JACOBS

IN THIS CHAPTER I present a case for two interrelated main claims. The first is that one of the most influential ways in which the significance of the putative fact/value distinction is understood is dubious and the way that the understanding is often attributed to David Hume overlooks some key elements of Hume's philosophy. This problematic interpretation has been a central part of a great deal of positivist social science and social scientists' reluctance to involve moral considerations in their investigations and explanations. The second main claim is that amongst some criminologists that reluctance has been overcome and they are working their way to showing how and why moral considerations have an important role in criminological investigations and explanations. It is becoming increasingly clear that philosophical and empirical studies of morality can fruitfully inform each other. That points to significant possibilities that had been doctrinally ruled out by positivist social science. There is a way of understanding Hume that does not exclude moral considerations from empirical social science. He argued that morality loses none of its genuineness or authority when interpreted in empirical (in contrast to rationalist) terms, and that is often overlooked when appealing to Hume as a crucial source of a fact/value distinction.

THE BASIC CONTOURS OF THE ISSUE

Hume (along with other early modern and modern British Moralists) is an especially important contributor to what is called 'moral science', an empirically informed explication of moral judgement, moral motivation and moral experience.[1] Until recognisably modern distinctions between specific social

[1] In the *Treatise*, Hume wrote, 'There is no question of importance whose decision is not comprised in the science of man … [and] the only solid foundation we can give to this science … must be laid on experience and observation' (Hume Treatise: 4). And later he wrote, 'Men are now cured of their passion for hypotheses and systems in natural philosophy and will hearken to no

sciences developed, what we would call social science (or the study of human beings) and society was referred to as a 'moral science', in contrast, say, to mathematics. As discussed in the Introduction to this volume, there is a distinguished British tradition of moral science that goes back at least as far as the seventeenth century and includes figures such as Hutcheson, Hume, Smith, up to Bentham and Mill in the nineteenth century. These were not thinkers for whom epistemological considerations placed morality on the 'disqualified' list of matters to be explored empirically. Several were sharply critical of rationalist and intuitionist conceptions of moral value, and they denied that values are among the items to be encountered directly in sense-perception, but they did not deny what we can call the genuineness of moral judgement and the authority of moral considerations. The tradition of moral science was basically a tradition of multidisciplinary empirical study of human beings and the social world and what makes for well-led human lives.

One result of regarding twentieth-century philosophical positivism (Logical Positivism or Logical Empiricism) as providing strong theoretical bases for social scientific positivism was the view that morality is not a proper object of scientific investigation and there are no objective moral considerations. Many social scientists held that social scientific theorising and explanation could be as fully scientific as physical sciences, but that involved a clean break between facts and values, the latter not being objects of scientific enquiry.

To many people the semantics and epistemology of Logical Positivism appeared to make a conclusive case for denying that moral discourse could be fact-stating and that moral judgement is a form of cognitive judgement. This view held that there are no moral facts, there is no factual basis for moral claims, and moral discourse should be interpreted as expressive rather than assertoric. It does not say anything about what there is and what its properties are, and positivism denies that there is such a thing as moral understanding and that moral values could be part of the factual, empirical explanation of human action. The moral science of earlier times might seem to lack the philosophical rigour and clarity of twentieth-century Logical Positivism, but the moral scientists generally held that morality does not fall outside the boundaries of empirical enquiry. In some respects, the approach of some contemporary criminologists is a retrieval of moral science insights and perspectives refined and responsive to developments in philosophy following what has been a very thorough critique of Logical Positivism.

The entire positivist project has undergone extensive critique, including close attention from philosophers committed to empiricism.[2] Several elements of the

arguments but those which are derived from experience. It is full time they should attempt a like reformation in all moral disquisitions; and reject every system of ethics, however subtle or ingenious, which is not founded on fact and observation' (Hume EPM: 77).

[2] The positivism of a great deal of the social sciences is not exactly the same as the Logical Positivism of the philosophers. The former have not been as focused on the analysis of semantic

project are widely regarded (by philosophers) as just not tenable. Granted, it has some contemporary defenders and they address objections to it, and positivism has been instrumental in the critique of many other philosophical views. Yet, several reasons have emerged for doubting the positivist understanding of the relation between facts and values. Hume's philosophy has been reconsidered in ways that recognise it as including a broadly naturalistic conception of morality rather than dismissing morality as beyond the limits of empirical science. The exclusion of moral considerations from social scientific enquiry leaves us with a seriously incomplete – and potentially quite distorted – view of a great deal that is integral to and important in human beings' lives, especially their social lives. If morally relevant features of human action, motivation, practices, relations and so forth are objects of empirical enquiry, then social scientific investigation can extend to significant, substantive aspects of human action and relations, making possible considerable illumination where before nothing explanatory could be said.

The other chapters by philosophers in this volume provide clear evidence of the depth and diversity of considerations about human beings and human actions that are now regarded as elements of illuminating accounts of action and value. The resources of positivism limited the significance of moral discourse, the depth of moral judgements, and the explanatory possibilities of moral considerations themselves apart from influencing people's attitudes or emotions. (That is important, certainly; but it still left moral considerations without cognitive content.)

Explaining moral features of human behaviour and relations involves understanding values through their connections with numerous other matters. The ways in which moral considerations figure in human beings' lives is not a stand-alone matter but is thickly connected to aspects of sensibility, to sociability, self-conceptions and attitudes towards others. For example, work undertaken to explain desistance from crime could connect in illuminating ways with investigations of how attitudes of trust and respect are reinforced, how persons might be able to revise their states of character, and the roles of character and situations in moral judgement and practical reasoning. Also, normativity of various types pervades the human context and moral normativity is one of the most important forms of it. The critique of positivism – and the employment of conceptions that have been elaborated in place of positivist views – opens the door to a large-scale revision of the conceptual infrastructure through which the human acts and relations are intelligible, and normativity is a key element of that infrastructure.

considerations as the latter, for whom accounts of cognitive (and other forms of) meaning has been centrally important. But there is a broad likeness between the positivism of the two contexts, in regard to distinguishing factual statement from valuative discourse and in denying that there are objective moral values, moral facts, or a cognitive basis for moral judgements.

To say that there are ways of studying morality empirically does not imply that criminologists should see themselves as moral experts or as engaged primarily in a project of moral explanation. Rather, the point is that the scientific character of social scientific investigation does not require excluding the discussion of moral phenomena in moral terms, and there can be a role for moral considerations themselves being explanatory. The study of aspects of prison life, and how those aspects impact motivation, aspiration and attitudes could be illuminating with regard to what sorts of habits and attitudes are required for reintegrating in civil society successfully. Such a study need not be prejudiced from the outset by an enquirer's conception of the primary aim of sanction. Instead, the empirical results of the enquiry can help guide our thinking about what the aim should be.

Investigators firmly committed to positivism and a fact/value distinction typically regard those commitments as essential to a scientific understanding of human action and relations. They are also likely to maintain that people's moral attitudes, perspectives, judgements and motives are devoid of cognitive content. Morality and moral values could still *matter* to people, even in the positivist's view; however, they could not be regarded as reflecting factual understanding (or ignorance) and they could have no role in fact-grounded explanations of behaviour. But for moral values to have a role in explanation they do not need to be entities, items in the world in a manner comparable to how there are oak trees, marble quarries, and birds, bees, cigars and folding chairs in the world. The commitment to science should take the form of commitment to what is required for the most adequate, illuminating and supportable empirical account of the object of investigation. The cost of an a priori exclusion of moral considerations is enormous. It removes (on non-empirical grounds) from the human world numerous aspects of action, reactive attitudes, forms of affect and concern, notions of worth and significance, and conceptions of self and others. Positivist commitments can render explanatorily silent a host of considerations that we can see actually are empirically ascertainable if not excluded antecedently to seeing how they might genuinely figure in explanation. This is not 'science going subjectivist'; this is 'normativity being explicable empirically'.

The works of numerous contemporary criminologists illustrate and confirm the notion that traffic between criminology and moral philosophy can have a constructive impact on both. This is true of works by Anthony Bottoms, Alison Liebling, Richard Sparks, Ian Loader, Nicola Lacey, John Braithwaite, Shadd Maruna and others. Of course, there are significant difficulties. What – if any – role should the investigator's own moral commitments have? What is the proper role of moral critique of the morality of the subjects being studied? What interaction should there be between morally illuminating results and the formulation of policy? In what ways (if any) should moral theory be brought to bear on empirical enquiry? I do not underestimate the difficulty of such matters. We cannot discuss everything within the compass of one chapter, but we can make some highly general points about the relation between facts and values, and Hume's thought and its legacy provide an especially apt starting point.

The discussion proceeds with a summary of key points concerning the significance and role of Hume's thought regarding the relation between facts and values. Hume was a fierce critic of moral rationalism, but not in a way that undermines morality. Some of the distinctive features of positivism are discussed, as well as some of the chief difficulties it has encountered and how those difficulties have motivated an understanding of Hume that is less beholden to certain positivist commitments. The discussion then focuses on the way Hume understood sensibility and attitudes as providing a basis for distinguishing between sound and unsound moral judgements. It also discusses whether norms and normativity can be objects of empirical investigation rather than being simply expressive. The final part of the chapter addresses criminology more directly, discussing implications for the relation between criminology and moral philosophy. The overall upshot is that: (i) moral considerations *can* be included in empirically rigorous criminology; (ii) empirically rigorous criminology can help illuminate and explicate important moral issues; and (iii) moral theorising can contribute to the clarification of key concepts employed in criminological investigation, especially concerning the explanation of human action, action-guiding considerations, and how values figure in persons' self-conceptions and regard for others.

HUME'S EMPIRICISM AND MORALITY

Hume is rightly regarded as a key figure in modern empiricism. In addition, his claim in the *Treatise*[3] that he had never seen a satisfactory demonstration of a conclusion about *what one ought to do* drawn from premises stating *what is the case* has been enormously influential. It is one of a handful of nearly iconic insights and arguments that have shaped metaethics during the last two and a half centuries. Hume wrote:

> In every system of morality, which I have hitherto met with, I have always remark'd, that the author proceeds for some time in the ordinary way of reasoning, and establishes the being of a God, or makes observations concerning human affairs; when of a sudden I am surpriz'd to find, that instead of the usual copulations of propositions, *is*, and *is not*, I meet with no proposition that is not connected with an *ought* or an *ought not*. This change is imperceptible; but is, however, of the last consequence. For as this *ought*, or ought not, expresses some new relation or affirmation,' tis necessary that it shou'd be observ'd and explain'd; and at the same time that a reason should be

[3] The *Treatise of Human Nature* is a very long work that Hume wrote as a young man. In it he elaborated the main elements of his philosophy in considerable detail, addressing a large number of significant issues. It sold poorly and was not read widely. Hume later wrote the *Enquiry Concerning Human Understanding* (EHU) and the *Enquiry Concerning the Principles of Morals* (EPM), each of which was meant to present in a more compact, accessible form the main claims from major sections of the *Treatise*. The *Enquiries* were both successful and influential. They are much more readable than the *Treatise*.

> given, for what seems altogether inconceivable, how this new relation can be a deduction from others, which are entirely different from it (Treatise: 302).[4]

Only one page before that celebrated passage Hume made another point equally important to his moral philosophy. He asks whether virtue and vice are matters of fact, the presence of which is inferable by reason. He writes:

> Take any action allow'd to be vicious: Wilful murder, for instance. Examine it in all lights, and see if you can find that matter of fact, or real existence, which you call *vice*. In which-ever way you take it, you find only certain passions, motives, volitions and thoughts. There is no other matter of fact in the case. The vice entirely escapes you, as a long as you consider the object (Hume Treatise 301).

Nor do we see – in the sense of directly perceive – the oddness of the number seven but for that case Hume would argue that its being odd is provable via relations of ideas that involve no reference to matters of fact or existence. (It is, as many would say, an *analytic* truth.) With respect to morality, Hume was making two fundamentally important claims in the passages quoted. One is that there is an insuperable difficulty for any claim that reason can prove an *ought* to follow from premises stating what *is* the case. The other is that the moral features of an action are not present and observable in the manner of non-moral features. We can see the knife being thrust into the victim; we see the victim slump to the ground bleeding; we hear the laugh of the assailant as he picks the victim's pocket; and we see the assailant hop onto his bicycle and ride away. Among the facts about stabbing, bleeding, expiring and robbing we do not also find a fact of *viciousness* or *vice* present as a matter of fact. Hume has formulated what he takes to be a crucial issue regarding prescriptivity, and also a crucial issue regarding what constitutes moral reality, the two being related in that (Hume insists) no matter of fact or grasp of a matter of fact has prescriptive significance in its own right, and the 'presence' of moral value is not a matter of fact. He explains valuative judgement (whether moral or aesthetic) in terms of sensibility. That is not to say that he believed that 'everyone has their own morals'; he certainly did not believe that. Rather, he denied that moral values are factual constituents of the world or that they are directly perceived.

There have been several versions of a dualism of fact and value, facts and norms, or descriptive content and prescriptive force, or matters of fact versus normativity. In the early twentieth century Moore's (1903/1993) identification of the putative 'naturalistic fallacy' was another especially important formulation. Also, Kant's (1785/1981: sections II and III) distinction between laws of causality and a law of reason marks another relevant dichotomy. This is not to say that there is broad agreement among the authors of these philosophical claims; they remain far apart in regard to many of the relevant issues. However, each

[4] In his writings, Hume uses italics freely. In this and subsequent quotations from Hume, the italics are always in the original.

elaborated a conception of how moral value is to be understood and how it is related to non-moral facts. The positivist formulation of a fact/value distinction has been especially significant with regard to empiricism, though there are other forms of the distinction.[5]

Hume's thought continued to have an impact in the twentieth century in part, due to the ascendant position of Logical Positivism. Given its semantic and epistemological elements, Emotivist and then Prescriptivist views were developed in regard to the moral context. Hume's thought remains influential though the character of its influence has changed in some ways. The powerful philosophical critique of positivism during the middle and second half of the twentieth century has helped motivate new interpretations of Hume. At least in regard to ethics, someone who, in 1930, claimed to be endorsing a Humean view might have in mind something different from someone in 1990 or 2020 claiming to endorse a Humean view. One way to characterise the difference is in terms of Hume being understood first as having a positivist conception of moral value and moral judgements, and then later, being understood as having a more naturalistic conception. The conception of empiricism in post-positivist analytic philosophy differs from positivist empiricism. That difference makes a difference.[6]

[5] The sorts of fundamental contrasts mentioned are very nearly unavoidable in philosophy. They indicate some of the most basic and indispensable categories of the intelligibility of the world, including human thought and action. Philosophers have focused on the distinction from a number. of different approaches, some highlighting the distinction between factual considerations and normative considerations, others focusing on the distinction between causal relations and rational relations. When GE Moore introduced the expression 'naturalistic fallacy' he meant it in the following way: 'It may be true that all things which are good are *also* something else, just as it is true that all things which are yellow produce a certain kind of vibration in the light. And it is a fact, that Ethics aims at discovering what are those other properties belonging to all things which are good. But far too many philosophers have thought that when they named those other properties they were actually defining good; that these properties, in fact, were simply not "other"' but absolutely and entirely the same with goodness. This view I propose to call the "naturalistic fallacy" and of it I shall now endeavour to dispose' (Moore 1903/1993: 62). Moore regarded 'good' as simple, undefinable and unanalysable, and thus any attempt to articulate its (putative) elements is doomed to fail. Good (the basic object of ethical thought) is not constituted by something else. It is a reality in its own right. Many other philosophers have meant by 'the naturalistic fallacy' the attempt to derive what ought to be from what is. In any case, what is at stake has to do with fundamental categories of world and thought. Both Hume and Moore were interested in the relation of the non-moral to the moral, but the forms they gave that interest were different and certainly the conclusions they reached are quite different.

[6] There are numerous conceptions of naturalism and there can be serious disagreement over whether this or that philosopher's views are naturalistic; eg, Aristotle's ethics can be interpreted as naturalistic, especially in contrast to Plato's, but it is also plausible to insist that naturalism does not extend to include Aristotle. In very general terms naturalism is the view that only natural entities and properties and processes exist. There are no beings or agents or properties that transcend nature, and the study of the world is to be undertaken by the methods of the sciences plus ordinary observation. In that respect naturalism is a view about what there is. The notion sometimes is interpreted to also involve the claim that the methods of the sciences and the way that sciences explain phenomena account for the full range of whatever knowledge we can attain. Empiricism is a primarily epistemological position, one committed to the claim – with respect to some body of knowledge – that all knowledge has its basic source in sense experience and we do not have innate knowledge or substantive a priori knowledge, and reason on its own is not a source of knowledge.

What we might call a 'positivist' interpretation of Hume includes the claims that: (i) Hume rejected moral rationalism and moral intuitionism; (ii) Hume maintained that moral values are not objective; (iii) Hume also maintained that prescriptive conclusions cannot be drawn from premises containing only descriptions of matters of fact; and (iv) Hume regarded moral judgements as non-cognitive, merely expressive and thus, there are no empirical grounds for moral judgements; and (v) accordingly, Hume's view shows that there cannot be scientific study of moral values. Moral values just are not among the matters of fact that can be investigated scientifically.

A centrepiece of positivism was the search for an empiricist criterion of cognitive meaning that could be expressed as a principle of verifiability. Numerous important claims about the scope and form of possible knowledge were connected to that principle. Positivism disqualified any putative rational (a priori) knowledge purporting to be substantive. Rather, all a priori knowledge is analytic (formal) and says nothing about – as Hume puts it – 'any real existence and matter of fact' (EHU: 108)). We will not pursue here the specific issues involved in formulating an empiricist criterion of cognitive meaning and the several iterations of the attempt. What is most important for our purposes is that positivism endorsed a conception of empiricism according to which there are no objective moral values and there is no moral knowledge. In a well-known statement of part of the positivist view AJ Ayer (1952: 104) wrote: 'What we are interested in is the possibility of reducing the whole sphere of ethical terms to non-ethical terms. We are enquiring whether statements of ethical value can be translated into statements of empirical fact' (at 107). He goes on to argue that ethical concepts are unanalysable; they *cannot* be translated into statements of empirical fact. However, in his view, this is because 'they are mere pseudo-concepts. The presence of an ethical symbol in a proposition adds nothing to its factual content'. According to Ayer, in making ethical statements we are 'merely expressing certain moral sentiments' (at 107).

Of course, even a social scientist committed to positivism can study a society's moral attitudes and practices; it is not as though moral life would be altogether off-limits, as it were. Moral attitudes and responses can help explain various practices of a society inasmuch as people are often motivated to act in certain

Of course, reason has vitally important functions regarding inference, consistency and other formal and logical matters. But our concepts have their ultimate sources in sense experience and accordingly so does our knowledge. There are relations between naturalism and empiricism and defenders of naturalism tend to be epistemological empiricists. But that is a not an ironclad, logical connection. Empiricism is an epistemological view, and the notion of 'empirical' methods is a bit less formal and specific. It often refers to methodological considerations concerning the significance of observation, the formulation of testable hypotheses, confirmation and replication (when feasible). Empirical investigation need not be exclusively quantitative. Also, one can undertake empirical investigation without a commitment to empiricism. One might be permitting the inclusion of concepts that do not satisfy empiricist criteria but still have a meaningful bearing on what sorts of considerations are regarded as explanatory.

ways by sensibility, affect and attitude. But there would be no question of exploring whether the society has a plausible understanding of moral facts, since there are none; and there would be no question of moral facts explaining behaviour. Moreover, what count as virtues and vices could easily be regarded as coming under the umbrella of relativism, given that there are no objective considerations by which to evaluate moral features (or actions, dispositions, responses, etc) of persons. We discussed relativism and some of its most problematic features in the Introduction and below we note that Hume was no relativist.

Despite more and more revisions and qualifications, by the mid-twentieth century the positivist project began to break down under the weight of objections it could not answer.[7] Numerous philosophers sought other avenues besides positivism to reach the conclusion that there are no objective moral considerations or moral facts. One might argue that there is no role for them – for moral facts – in *explaining* anything, and they are thus, superfluous, not needed, and this is independent of positivist commitments. One might try to show that everything about a person's moral experience and moral life can be explained without reference to any moral facts. What is explanatorily needless has not earned a place in our 'inventory' of what kinds of facts, entities and properties there are.

I have used the formulation 'moral considerations' several times and will continue to do so. We should note, though, that there is a difference between a moral judgement in the sense of a moral *evaluation* of something (an action, a practice, an institution) and a moral judgement in the sense of an *action-guiding, deliberative judgement* (see Wiggins 1991). When one claims, 'It is wrong to tell lies meant to damage a person's standing' that is a moral evaluation. When one says, 'in this situation fairness requires that you return the items' or 'I really must make sure to express my gratitude' those are action-guiding judgements. I am using 'moral considerations' in a manner meant to be applicable to either context.

Hume's arguments concerning moral value address both evaluation and action-guiding judgement. Positivism typically claims that there are no objective moral considerations for either evaluation or deliberation. There is no moral cognition, there are no moral facts to be cognised, and thus, no objective basis for moral normativity. In Hume's view while there might be facts about people's morality, and about their attitudes, desires and passions there are no moral facts or objective values or (cognitive) moral beliefs.

According to positivist social science, investigators might be able to help policymakers by showing – empirically – what are the probable social and economic

[7] These critiques were chiefly of interest to philosophers and were not directly relevant to the somewhat broader notion of positivism that shaped a good deal of social science. That is not to say the critiques were irrelevant to the way that non-valuative, empirical social science was understood. After all, the philosophical issues concerned the details of the relevant semantics and epistemology. However, the empirical methods of positivist social science and its rejection of objective valuative considerations remained largely intact though they, too, were subjected to numerous critical approaches and challenges, often reflecting developments in philosophy.

outcomes of *this* legislation or policy in contrast to *that* legislation or policy. They might have considerable causal, explanatory knowledge at hand regarding how former prisoners or some other relevant group responds to certain initiatives, or what sort of impact on the public's attitudes is to be expected from redeploying scarce resources in a specific way. One could maintain a positivist view of morality as expressive but also argue for evidence-based policy. The view would claim it is the job of *policymakers* to determine what is to be done and perhaps also to articulate what they take to be the moral relevance of the issues. According to positivism there is no moral expertise, no moral wisdom. According to positivism if we admire someone for their moral wisdom that is just a (misleading) way of praising them for making moral judgements or taking actions we approve of. That could lead one to wonder what the virtues are of evidence-based policy; is it mainly just a way of shifting responsibility?

Actually, many social scientists are strongly committed to bringing about positive change in policy and increasing social welfare. Many criminologists are engaged in social scientific investigation because of their concern to play some part in the complex project of reform of criminal justice. What would be inconsistent is insisting on a fact/value distinction *and* claiming that the valuative claims one makes are more fully supported by the facts than any other valuative position on the issues in question. Or, as noted in the Introduction, social scientists might embrace relativism, denying that there are objective grounds for moral judgement but nonetheless being committed to specific moral judgements.

What is often not recognised in attributing the fact/value distinction to Hume is that he himself argued that acquiring factual knowledge makes a difference to our moral judgements. For example, suppose I regard someone as selfish and inconsiderate for arriving late and in a messy state at a long-planned celebration of someone's lifetime achievement. I think to myself, 'that figures; he'll always find a way to spoil someone else's occasion'. I then learn that the late arrival was because the person stopped to help at the scene of a road accident and actually ran three miles through the woods to find the nearest physician. My evaluation of the person and his action change so readily that it is almost as if logical or rational necessity brought about the change. An example such as this illustrates Hume's point that even though logical necessity has no role in the change, our views often change with changes in factual knowledge or reconsideration of the facts leading to a changed perspective.

The influence of facts on moral judgement works through sensibility rather than logical derivation – but the influence is real. Our values shape our concerns and the ways we believe we should act, while factual beliefs have an impact on valuative stances and judgements. Indeed, if factual considerations were thought to be distinct from valuative considerations in a way that included mutual irrelevance the change in my view of the late arrival at the party would be no better than any other judgement I might have come to upon learning the new facts. But it surely is morally intelligible and morally appropriate. Hume's point was that rational necessity is not the only kind of relevance bearing on the intelligibility of moral judgements.

Thus, even if moral judgements are grounded in sensibility and largely shaped by attitude, they are not cut off from factual beliefs and so personally subjective that we cannot argue about which judgements are morally plausible.

HUME AND MORAL NATURALISM

The second half of the twentieth century was a period during which various forms of post-positivist analytic philosophy developed. A combination of the critique of positivism, increased interest in the history of philosophy, along with the impact of the later thought of Wittgenstein (and several other thinkers) led to the development of influential forms of post-positivist empiricism, among numerous other developments. Wittgenstein's influence has been very diverse and thinkers with strikingly different views plausibly claim to be influenced by Wittgenstein.[8] Hume remains centrally important, but his thought is understood somewhat differently now. Reading him now, in ways that are shaped by the critique of positivism and growing interest in naturalism with regard to many philosophical issues, we are likely to place the emphasis differently. In recent decades philosophers have engaged much more extensively with empirical investigations and the relevance of naturalistic considerations is more fully acknowledged.

Moreover, a strict positivist reading leaves it somewhat of a mystery why Hume developed a moral theory to the very considerable extent we find in the *Treatise of Human Nature* and in the *Enquiry Concerning the Principles of Morals*. As noted in the Introduction to this volume a key point that positivists and ethical relativists often overlook is that Hume presented a sceptical case against moral rationalism and intuitionism, not against *morality*. He held that morality retains the genuineness and authority we generally take it to have. His view was not 'If we take our epistemology seriously and grasp its implications, we will see that what we regard as morality is nothing more than attitudinising and expressing non-cognitive feelings in ways that undermine morality's significance'. Rather, his view was that 'Even if we take our epistemology seriously and grasp its implications, we will see that morality is undisturbed and no less genuine than it needs to be in order to have all the significance and authority we take it to have'. That includes making distinctions between sound and unsound moral judgements, recognising differences between shallow and sophisticated judgement, and even differences between informed and uninformed judgement. One can argue that Hume was mistaken; however, that was his view.

[8] Wittgenstein's thought has had a wide range of influence and his thought is interpreted in several quite different ways. He is regarded as a linguistic idealist by some philosophers and as endorsing a form of naturalism by others. He has influenced the development of various forms of relativism, behaviourism and scepticism, while other interpreters regard him as primarily concerned to do away with familiar philosophical ' – isms' as ways of being 'bewitched by language'. While I refer to Wittgenstein in the present discussion, I am not taking an interpretive stance regarding his thought.

Hume adopted a broadly similar view towards numerous fundamental philosophical issues. They include: (i) whether we have knowledge of the external world – of a public order of objects independent of our mental states; (ii) whether the self is an enduring entity – a substance or entity with some other form of identity through changes in mental states; and (iii) whether there is objective causal necessity – the question of what 'holds the world together' and how things in it are related to each other. What makes the world a coherent, integrated, intelligible order of things that come to be, undergo change and then cease to exist? With respect to each of these Hume elaborated what he called a 'sceptical solution' to doubt.[9] The source of doubt is, in Hume's view, that there is no rational demonstration of the existence of an external world, or an enduring substantial self, or of objective causal necessity. What beliefs could be more basic than the ones indicated? Yet, we are not able to provide rational justification for any of them. However, that is not a disaster for our beliefs about the world and ourselves. We will continue, Hume argued, to believe that there is a public world of objects, that there are causally necessary relations, and that each of us has an identity that persists through time and change. Rational demonstration of these beliefs, fully adequate justification of them, is not forthcoming but *neither is it needed* for us to maintain the beliefs in question.

Hume was not saying that we can believe whatever we like, and these basic beliefs are among the ones we choose to hang on to. His chief point was that where reason fails us, nature provides. As he put it, 'Nature will always maintain her rights, and prevail in the end over any abstract reasoning whatsoever' (Hume EHU: 120). That is, we unavoidably believe that there is a public, external world of objects, that the self persists as the same individual through experience and through changes in mental states, and that events are not just one thing after another in no coherent order, but they occur in regular, and often predictable patterns. Given our natural constitution, our psychology and our propensities, we cannot help but have those beliefs, and our experience seems to provide steady reinforcement of those habits of mind. (There is no point reached at which the accumulation of experience somehow becomes a basis for rational justification in the sense of objective necessity. The ten-thousandth time we watch uncooked eggs roll off the counter and splatter on the floor gives us no more insight into supposed causal necessity between striking the floor and splattering than the first observation of the conjunction of events of those kinds. We do not perceive some necessary connection we did not observe the first few times.)

Still, Hume held that even in the absence of rational proof we distinguish between reasonable and unreasonable beliefs, plausible versus implausible hypotheses, and causal explanations in contrast to mere correlation or coincidence. We do not *choose* to believe there is an external world. We do not *choose*

[9] Section V of Hume's *Enquiry Concerning Human Understanding* is called 'Sceptical Solution of these Doubts'.

to believe that our identity is maintained through time and change. We do not *choose* to believe that events are causally related. We could not think or have coherent experience at all in the absence of such beliefs, and in Hume's view, we have natural propensities to have such beliefs. In regard to morality, the absence of rational demonstration of moral judgements does not result in a collapse of moral commitments or distinctions. Hume wrote, 'Those who have denied the reality of moral distinctions, may be ranked among the disingenuous disputants; nor is it conceivable, that any human creature could ever seriously believe, that all characters and actions were alike entitled to the affection and regard of everyone' (EPM: 73).

Moral judgements are not *derivable* from factual beliefs, but they do not *need* to be derivable from them to have a coherent relation to the facts. Hume wrote:

> But though reason, when fully assisted and improved, be sufficient to instruct us in the pernicious or useful tendency of qualities and actions; it is not alone sufficient to produce any moral blame or approbation … It is requisite a *sentiment* should here display itself, in order to give a preference to the useful above the pernicious tendencies … Here therefore *reason* instructs us in the several tendencies of actions, and *humanity* makes a distinction in favour of those which are useful and beneficial (EPM: 158).

For example, in Hume's view justice is ultimately grounded on the utility accruing from people abiding by a set of rules that applies to all of them in conditions in which benevolence and resources are limited, but in neither case does desperate shortage make the situation hopeless. It is the broad equality of human beings (in a world with finite resources) that makes mutual forbearance and mutual regard so important. If there was such desperate scarcity of resources or benevolence that the rules of property and justice were useless they would never be established; they do not have a rational justification independent of the human condition. He regarded property as fundamental to justice and held that 'in order to establish laws for the regulation of property, we must be acquainted with the nature and situation of man; must reject appearances, which may be false, though specious; and must search for those rules, which are, on the whole, most *useful* and *beneficial*' (Hume EPM: 91).

As he put it in the *Enquiry Concerning the Principles of Morals*, 'every quality of the mind, which is *useful* or *agreeable* to the *person himself* or to *others*, communicates a pleasure to the spectator, engages his esteem, and is admitted under the honourable denomination of virtue or merit' (Hume EPM: 151). Those positive responses have a key role, but they are responses to matters of fact. There are no moral facts, but there are facts relevant to moral judgements. Hume's view is the view of someone who believes that reason *on its own* can neither ascertain what is morally right nor motivate us to do what is morally right, though facts about what is useful and beneficial have an important bearing on moral judgement.

Hume also held that in making moral judgements we adopt a universal standpoint and are not merely expressing whatever person-relative affect happens to feel most pronounced. Hume regarded morality as consisting of judgements made on the basis of propensities that are shared by people universally. He wrote:

> But the sentiments, which arise from humanity, are not only the same in all human creatures, and produce the same approbation or censure; but they also comprehend all human creatures; nor is there any one whose conduct or character is not, by their means, an object to every one of censure or approbation (Hume EPM: 148).

He may have been overstating the case, given what we know (and what he probably knew, as well) of the diversity of cultures and societies' different values when he wrote:

> Would you know the sentiments, inclinations, and course of life of the Greeks and Romans? Study well the temper and actions of the French and English: You cannot be much mistaken in transferring to the former *most* of the observations which you have made with regard to the latter. Mankind are so much the same, in all times and places, that history informs us of nothing new or strange in this particular. Its chief use is only to discover the constant and universal principles of human nature, by showing men in all varieties of circumstances and situations, and furnishing us with materials from which we may form our observations, and become acquainted with the regular springs of human action and behaviour (Hume EHU: 150).

Even if that claims too much it is important that he took moral judgement to reflect *human* sensibility and not just person-relative affect. Hume (EPM: 148), speaking of the moral agent, wrote: 'He must here, therefore, depart from his private and particular situation, and must choose a point of view common to him with others; he must move some universal principle of the human frame, and touch a string to which all mankind have an accord, and symphony'. And:

> When [one] bestows on any man the epithets of *vicious* or *odious* or *depraved* he then speaks another language [than that of self-love] and expresses sentiments in which, he expects, all his audience are to concur with him ... If he mean, therefore, to express that this man possesses qualities whose tendency is pernicious to society, he has chosen this common point of view, and has touched the principle of humanity, in which every man, in some degree, concurs (Hume EPM: 148).

It is clear that Hume was anxious to preserve the features and the force of moral experience and moral judgement. His sceptical arguments do not explain them away or expose them as illusory. In the way that he understood the fact/value distinction morality is undisturbed, so to speak, by the distinction between facts and values.[10]

[10] David Wiggins (1995: 310) remarked that Hume was sufficiently confident that there are common sentiments across mankind and that those sentiments are a basis for agreement in moral judgements even across considerable distances of space and time, that 'not even the phenomenology of moral obligation need contradict' those claims regarding sentiments. That is, Hume regarded sentiment as an adequate ground for being morally obligated. He did not interpret his own view as supporting only 'morality-lite'.

In the course of defending what he takes to be a basically Humean projectivist account[11] of moral value, Simon Blackburn has claimed that from the first-order perspective – from the perspective of being an engaged participant in morality – it seems to us that moral values are objective. In saying, 'Causing people needless suffering just for one's own pleasure is wrong' we take ourselves to be talking about the wrongness of that sort of pleasure-taking, rather than talking about our attitudes. Blackburn argues that *of course* the objects of our attitudes and feelings are the objects of concern. In moral judgements we are judging acts, situations and people's characteristics; we are not talking about our feelings. Blackburn (1993: 176) puts it this way:

> From the inside, the objects of our passions are their immediate objects: it is the death, the loved one, the sunset, that matters to us. It is not our own state of satisfaction or pleasure. Must projectivism struggle with this fact, or disown it? Is it that we projectivists, at the crucial moment when we are about to save the child, throw ourselves on the grenade, walk out in the snow, will think, 'Oh, it's only me and my desires or other conative pressures – forget it'?

Blackburn regards his projectivism as a Humean view. Reflection and analysis show that sensibility projects responses and it is really affective responsiveness that is the basis of values. However, the view is that projective values are *all that moral values need to be in order to be genuine*. We do not come to a point where we conclude that values are not real; we reflectively discover that the only reality they need is projective. As Blackburn (1993: 172) says, 'It is because of our responses that we say that cruelty is wrong, but it is not because of them that it is so' and '[what] makes cruelty abhorrent is not that it offends us, but all those hideous things that make it do so'. His view is that 'there is only one proper way to take the question 'On what does the wrongness of cruelty depend?': as a moral question, with an answer in which no mention of our actual responses properly figures' (Blackburn 1993: 173). It is important to the case for projectivism that while sensibility is the basis of moral value it is not a matter of the *actual* responses that this or that individual has. 'I happen to feel *this* way' is not a remark that carries moral weight.

Blackburn (1993: 178) argues that projectivism has in its favour 'the possibility of identifying the [moral] commitment in a way that contrasts it usefully with belief, and a "neat, natural account" of why the state that it is should exist'.

[11] It is perhaps helpful to think of a property that is projected as contrasting with a property that is detected. The moral realist claims there are moral properties that are features of actions, practices and agents and that recognition of them is no more mysterious than recognition that whales are mammals or that copper has atomic no 29. They are not directly observable in the way that the sour taste of a ripe lemon or the red of a post box is observable. But they are no less real features of actions and agents than being mammalian is a feature of whales and being composed of amino acids is a feature of proteins. By 'projectivism' Blackburn means that moral properties reflect sensibility, affect, attitude though the way that is experienced is as if moral properties are present, to be found in the object of moral judgement.

Naturalism holds sway in a two-fold way. First, it accounts for how there came to be creatures with the sensibility and conative capacities that make moralising part of their lives. Second, it explains the states of mind involved in moralising as non-representational. No rational account of the basis for ethics is needed apart from the naturalistic account of how the sensibility underlying ethics came into the world.

David Wiggins, who disagrees with Blackburn over the question of how exactly to explicate the role of sensibility in moral judgement wrote:

> Hume's interest in morality was that of a moral scientist or as one would now say moral psychologist. His first question is not the question of the vindication of duty (that question can arise later), but the question of how natural beings such as ourselves can have arrived at the point where we can even think the refined and complex thoughts we do think about morality and its requirements (1995: 300).

Despite the disagreement between Wiggins and Blackburn, a broadly naturalistic interpretation of Hume helps us appreciate the depth of Hume's insights and the significance of his arguments. It enables us to see that there are ways of understanding the relation between facts and values that are not limited by positivism's strictures. The naturalistic interpretation opens the way for much more extensive connections between moral philosophy and empirical investigations. We can see how Hume's distinction between facts and values opens up an approach to morality that situates moral distinctions within a naturalistic context, one that can be investigated by the methods of empirical sciences.

CRIMINOLOGY, NORMATIVITY AND MORAL SCIENCE

Analytic philosophy is no less rigorous than it was when Logical Positivism was 'in charge' but it is much more open to diverse sources of insight and the complex semantic and conceptual texture of various forms of experience and enquiry. It does not portray the philosophical project as an a priori audit of propositions and beliefs, all being measured by a universally applicable, fully and fixedly defined criterion of cognitive meaning. Again, the philosophical chapters in this volume illustrate that very effectively. Rigour and clarity remain of the first importance but philosophy is not limited to auditing the language of science in an effort to maintain its purity.

The question of how to understand normativity is one of the main philosophical challenges. One reason is that normativity is pervasive; it is found in all or nearly all contexts of human activity and thought. Of course, in a statistical sense it is found in non-human contexts as well. It is everywhere. However, in the present discussion rule-governed normativity is the focus of interest. Practices, institutions, standards, judgements – all of these and numerous other matters are informed by norms. In some cases, norms are explicit and agents are aware of their application, while in many other cases, there is normativity without conscious awareness. In the Introduction we mentioned MacCormick's example of people queuing. He wrote, 'People know how to queue, and can tell cases of queue-jumping, and protest about them, even if they have never articulated exactly what their governing norm is' (MacCormick 2007: 15).

Normativity has a crucial role in several 'layers' relevant to criminal justice. At a highly general level, there is the normativity of a political order; for better or worse, any political order reflects a certain conception of normativity. One level down, there is the normativity of how the rule of law is understood, and the normativity of particular laws. At a more concrete level normativity shapes the practices of criminal proceedings and law enforcement. There are norms shaping sanction and forms of post-sanction monitoring. There are norms shaping very routine matters as well as highly significant ones, and there are non-moral norms as well as moral norms. Wherever there are questions concerning legitimacy or validity, norms are relevant. Wherever there is an issue of whether a particular instance fulfils the criteria for being an X, the norms determinative of being such a thing are relevant. One might object that in such a case we are discussing criteria, not norms. However, the criteria have normative significance.

The notion of a rule figured centrally in Fuller's treatment of the 'inner morality' required for legality. Fuller (1964: 96) said that law is 'the enterprise of subjecting human conduct to the governance of rules'. Even if one challenges Fuller's specific requirements for a rule to count as a law the general point is clear, namely, a law must be intelligible as a guide to the conduct of rational agents. That imposes a number of requirements concerning matters such as promulgation, not requiring what is impossible, coherence, and absence of contradiction, being relatively stable rather than constantly in flux, and other conditions as well. A regime could try to impose requirements that do not satisfy those conditions but for a regime to have any recognisably legitimate authority it cannot ignore fundamental conditions concerning what can count as law, and laws are a class of norms.

If we are interested primarily in broadly liberal-democratic or social-democratic political orders then the norms will reflect values specific to that kind of order. Antony Duff (2011: 138) writes:

> A conception of criminal law as a law for citizens depends on a democratic political theory, to argue that a legitimate criminal law requires a political community whose members share the status of citizen; citizenship being understood roughly as equal, mutually respectful participation in the civic enterprise.

The values of the public sphere in such a polity include 'norms about how citizens should treat each other, which gives us a basis for an idea of public wrongs – of wrongdoing that violates the polity's defining values; and this then gives us a basis for an idea of criminal law as a formal way of identifying and responding to such wrongs' (Duff 2011: 139). Laws are especially important in the political context because,

> What the law's institutions can do is that which moral deliberation cannot itself achieve. They can lay down a common rule in relatively determinate terms, and where the rule first enunciated is insufficiently clear, there are legal practices of

> reasoning and interpretation that can further clarify, further determine, the law (MacCormick 2007: 253).

Bottoms (2002: 24), in the course of arguing that, 'if they are to be true to their calling, all criminologists have to be interested in morality', quotes anthropologist Meyer Fortes who wrote:

> The capacity and the need to have, to make, to follow and to enforce rules are of cardinal importance for human social existence ... For without rules there can be neither society nor culture; and what I am arguing is that it was the emergence of the capacity to make, enforce, and, by corollary, to break rules that made human society possible (1983: 6).

Bottoms (2002: 25) went on to remark that 'the rules (including the prohibitions) in any given emerging group or society will be based on the developing social norms (or positive morality) of the group in question'. In the article quoted, Bottoms was focusing on compliance and the relevance of normative considerations to compliance, and he distinguished between habitual compliance, prudential compliance and normative compliance. He noted though that even 'habitual compliance may also contain a valuable latent normative content' (Bottoms 2002: 34). Also, 'good socialisation may have valuable long-term effects in producing normative compliance, even though the norms may not, for much of the time, be consciously articulated by those who have been subject to such socialisation' (Bottoms, 2002: 34).

If we insist that norms are not proper objects of empirical enquiry we will be limiting our explanatory conceptions to a kind of actuarial, statistical representation of behaviour and cutting ourselves off from a potentially much fuller grasp of the intelligibility of what is studied. In the present discussion our primary concern is moral normativity. In the last couple of decades several criminologists have been willing to address normativity and moral matters and have argued that criminology cannot afford to continue regarding them as off-limits or unintelligible by empirical investigative methods. A great deal of human behaviour is recognised and identified as behaviour of specific types through our grasp of the norms that inform the behaviour. And, often, among the relevant norms are moral considerations.

Numerous criminologists have developed positions on the *relation between normative theory* and *explanatory conception*, arguing that considerable intelligibility is sacrificed if we fail to understand that relation. Anthony Bottoms, Richard Sparks, Ian Loader, Nicola Lacey, John Braithwaite, Philip Pettit and Alison Liebling for instance, have pursued that question in depth in recent years. Bottoms (2002: 22), commenting on the powerful influence of the fact/value distinction as understood by many positivists, writes: 'That difficulty can be simply stated: it concerns the question of how, if at all, from a positivist perspective one can give any serious weight to moral judgements'. Bottoms follows Hart in distinguishing between 'positive morality' and 'critical morality' (a distinction discussed in the Introduction to this volume), and he goes on to say of the work of Sir Leon Radzinowicz: 'A clear implication of Radzinowicz's analysis is that criminologists interested in morality must – if their work is to be comprehensive – consider questions both of positive and critical morality' (Bottoms 2002: 24).

Norms of various types are crucial to the intelligibility of human action, and the role of moral beliefs and judgements in many of the contexts studied by criminologists makes the study of them crucial to understanding many criminal justice issues. We noted above that there are several layers or levels of normativity in the human social world, and whether they are distinguished explicitly or not, numerous layers can be crucial to a particular action, decision or response. Often, it is important to have a grasp of how the various layers of normativity are interrelated.

As Loader and Sparks (2011: 127–28) note:

> Anthony Bottoms has, in somewhat cognate vein, combined patient, multi-method empirical enquiry into criminal behaviour and crime patterns in urban contexts and the operation of criminal justice institutions and prevention programmes, with an explanatory ambition that links criminological and social theory ... He has also developed in various ways that idea that criminology is a moral enterprise ... as well as being able to think in policy terms about the import of his work.

In an essay on 'the relationship between theory and empirical observations in criminology' Bottoms (2008: 92) remarks (on the basis of a good deal of argumentation) 'Doing criminology, in short, necessarily entails some engagement with normative issues, and it is for that reason that a brief discussion of normative theory is included later in this chapter'. Indeed, later in the article, following detailed discussion of several aspects of theorising and methodology in criminology he writes:

> In short, normative analysis in criminology is emphatically not the unintellectual pursuit that positivism made it out to be. It can involve extremely intricate philosophical analysis, and this analysis can intersect with, and be illuminated by, empirical research at many points ... Normative analysis has not often been included in previous discussions of the theory/research relationship in criminology; in the future it needs to be more centrally located in such discussions (Bottoms 2008: 106).

From a somewhat different angle of approach Braithwaite and Pettit (2000: 145) also have argued for an important relation between a normative conception and an explanatory account. They write: 'any normative proposal should be subjected to the test of seeing whether it points us towards a plausible explanatory category'. And,

> any explanatory category – or at least any that is based in a story about human psychology – should be subjected to the corresponding test of seeing whether it directs us towards a plausible normative ideal: to an ideal that people can be brought, on reflection, to find significantly attractive.

In their view, arriving at a clear, illuminating conception of normative considerations is part of the point of social scientific investigation. There is the task of explicating (and perhaps, evaluating) the norms governing the behaviour that is studied, there can be normative considerations concerning the project of enquiry, and there are the valuative commitments of the investigator. Being clear about the relations between those can be a very demanding challenge.

Braithwaite and Pettit wanted to show 'how the normative argument that republicanism provides is buttressed or likely to be buttressed by an argument that derives from the explanatory significance of the republican ideal of non-domination' (2000: 153). They argued that 'in doing social theory we should look for an adjustment between normative and explanatory categories of analysis and that, if we do so, we are likely to reach a higher level of performance on both fronts'. 'Normative theory without explanatory theory is empty; explanatory theory without normative theory is blind, often dangerously so' (Braithwaite and Pettit 2000: 161). Whether or not one agrees with that claim and their overall conception of the relation between normativity and explanation, it is crucial to minimise confusion and strive for clarity regarding the various involvements of normativity. The chief concern is not actually a fact/value distinction but that there are multiple ways for valuative considerations to be involved in social scientific investigation and explanation.

Sometimes defenders of a fact/value distinction claim that it is necessary to an aspiration to objectivity. Keeping values out of the investigation is a way to guard against the investigator's values influencing explanations and a way to guard against the values of the persons studied infiltrating the (objective, scientific) explanation of their behaviour. However, it would need to be shown that values have no explanatory efficacy; that eliminating them from the scientific project is costless in regard to the conceptual resources available to us. Is there a good argument for concluding that values could not have any explanatory role? An empirically open-minded, informed conception of human behaviour seems to point in the opposite direction. Consider how much of human action is motivated by, responsive to, and reflective of people's values – again, for better or worse.

Suppose there is substantial evidence indicating that a domestic situation including a stable relationship with a partner in a household including members of different generations is strongly correlated with gradual but successful desistance, even if the offender had not chosen that domestic situation for that reason. Further suppose that such circumstances, in conjunction with breaking away from one's drinking buddies, often lead to job-seeking and, when successful, managing to remain employed. What scientific virtue is protected by refusing to accept values among the explanatory factors? Is it not it possible that the offender now recognises and responds to values that formerly had little or no resonance? Suppose it is found that a requirement to assist the eldest member of the household and also help with the youngest are part of a domestic regime of responsibilities that seem to help the person become more responsible in general. (The outcome might have been different. The offender might have resented the expectations and decided to move out.) We might find that there is indeed an explanatory relation between the circumstances, expectations and impact on the offender but what would be unscientific about understanding the explanatory relation to have moral aspects? Suppose the head of the household was insistent about members of it assisting with looking after others. Suppose a condition for staying was that household expenses must be fully paid before anyone can spend money on drink. Suppose the offender has grown tired of being arrested, jailed and substituting theft for honest toil. Would we not be leaving out something real and explanatorily significant if we refuse to ascribe any moral significance to the facts and how the desisting person regards them? Could it not it be the case that trust, respect, self-respect, gratitude and other morally inflected considerations have a genuine role in explaining the behaviour being investigated? And the absence of those might very well be found in a situation that develops in a much less positive way. The clearer we are about the valuative considerations involved and the ways that various norms have causal significance, the more fully we will understand the facts. The point is not that the moral features of similar situations will be exactly the same, but that the moral features are aspects of the situation.

To explore and explain the moral aspects of an action or a practice does not require having a fully elaborated moral theory and then 'applying' it (whatever that might mean) to the phenomena. It is more realistic and more illuminating to think about moral aspects in a different way. For example, in Liebling's (2004) work on the moral performance of prisons she studied aspects of prison life such as trust, and unofficial, spontaneous conversational interaction between staff and inmates, willingness to be responsive to prisoners' requests and concerns. Thus, '[b]y moral performance we mean those aspects of a prisoner's mainly interpersonal and material treatment that render a term of imprisonment more or less dehumanising and/or painful' (Liebling 2004: 473). She noted that the virtues that matter so centrally in prisons' moral performance – virtues such as respect, fairness, showing concern for others, being helpful and so forth – are among 'the foundation of our social life' and are virtues 'that human beings need' (Liebling 2004: 470). This is very much in the intellectual/moral tradition of the British Moralists. The emphasis on aspects of sociability and on the role of sensibility resonates with some of the long-standing values of that tradition. The same can be said for Tony Bottoms' recent work on desistance, and numerous other works by contemporary criminologists.

Instead of bringing a moral theory to the object of study, in Liebling's work she employs concepts and categories of moral life and experience that are recognisably relevant, without the aid of elaborating a specific moral theory. Granted, there can be important disputes about how to understand fairness, for example. However, there are also paradigmatic examples of fairness and unfairness, and the same holds regarding a large number of moral categories, such as trust, good faith, generosity, unconcern and many others. Many of the questions of fairness in a prison do not require first, articulating an account of a just political order and society overall. It is true that there are important connections between the prison and the political order overall; the latter is indeed a relevant level of normativity and assumptions regarding it can be very important. But one need not theorise about everything in order to make significant claims about something. Also, there can be important disagreements about how exactly trust should be interpreted, or about the degrees of privacy and autonomy prisoners should have. I do not mean that the moral features are obvious. But neither are they mysterious or altogether inaccessible. The more we know about the non-moral aspects of prison life (or desistance, or many other issues) the better positioned we are to consider the moral aspects. They are not something applied to what we find. They are among what we find.

CONCLUSION

It seems clear that there are reasons to reconsider the relation between facts and values, and the motivations to do so have origins in both philosophy and in the social sciences. Developments in criminology and in philosophy suggest that there could be considerable benefits to both from greater interaction. Some of the important recent work in criminology looks to philosophy for help in articulating conceptions of agency, moral value, character, virtue, and forms of mutual regard, responsibility and self-conceptions. At the same time, the empirical theorising and explanations provided by criminologists can help refine and clarify the work of philosophers in which those conceptions are centrally important, and they can help philosophers engage with empirical issues in ways that are constructive for philosophers and non-philosophers. The overall community of scholars can arrive at a fuller, multidimensional understanding of the issues and phenomena studied.

Criminological studies of incarceration, desistance, how offenders manage different forms of probation, societal attitudes toward offenders, and so forth can be very helpful to philosophers' attempts to illuminate important issues of moral psychology and their relations to practical reasoning and the explanation of action. There is certainly much to investigate regarding what sorts of attitudes are important to sustaining trust in political institutions and the rule of law in a liberal democracy. Criminological investigations of topics such as regret, conscience, resolve, aspiration and numerous others can and should inform philosophical analyses of agency, action, character and will. This interaction is being pursued in ways that might not have made sense to criminologists or philosophers at a time when there was a confident compartmentalisation of facts and values. But now there are criminologists connecting with the tradition of moral science in ways that involve continuity with the past while showing a way forward for empirically rigorous and morally substantive criminology.

REFERENCES

References to the works of David Hume are given in the form (Hume Treatise), (Hume EHU) or (Hume EPM). These refer to, respectively:

Hume, D (1739–40/2000) *A Treatise of Human Nature*, eds DF Norton and MJ Norton (Oxford, Oxford University Press).
Hume, D (1748/1999) *An Enquiry Concerning Human Understanding*, ed TL Beauchamp (Oxford, Oxford University Press).
Hume, D (1751/1998) *An Enquiry Concerning the Principles of Morals*, ed TL Beauchamp (Oxford, Oxford University Press).

Ayer, AJ (1952) *Language, Truth and Logic* (New York, Dover Publications).
Blackburn, S (1993) *Essays in Quasi-Realism* (New York, Oxford University Press).
Bottoms, A (2002) 'Morality, Crime, Compliance and Public Policy' in A Bottoms and M Tonry (eds), *Ideology, Crime and Criminal Justice: A Symposium in Honour of Sir Leon Radzinowicz* (Cullompton, Willan Publishing).
——(2008) 'The Relationship between Theory and Empirical Observations in Criminology' in R King and E Wincup (eds), *Doing Research on Crime and Justice*, 2nd edn (Oxford, Oxford University Press).
Braithwaite, J and Pettit, P (2000) 'Republicanism and Restorative Justice: An Explanatory and Normative Connection' in H Strang and J Braithwaite (eds), *Restorative Justice: Philosophy to Practice* (Aldershot, Ashgate Publishing).
Duff, RA (2011) 'Responsibility, Citizenship and Criminal Law' in RA Duff and SP Green (eds), *Philosophical Foundations of the Criminal Law* (Oxford, Oxford University Press).
Fortes, M (1983) *Rules and the Emergence of Society*, Royal Anthropological Institute of Great Britain and Ireland Occasional Paper no 39 (London, Royal Anthropological Institute).
Fuller, L (1964) *The Morality of Law* (New Haven, CT, Yale University Press).
Kant, I (1785/1981) *Grounding for the Metaphysics of Morals* (trans JW Ellington) (Indianapolis, IN, Hackett Publishing).
Liebling, A assisted by Arnold, H (2004) *Prisons and Their Moral Performance: A Study of Values, Quality, and Prison Life* (Oxford, Oxford University Press).
Loader, I and Sparks, R (2011) *Public Criminology?* (Abingdon, Routledge).
MacCormick, N (2007) *Institutions of Law: An Essay in Legal Theory* (Oxford, Oxford University Press).
Moore, GE (1903/1993) *Principia Ethica*, rev edn, ed T Baldwin (Cambridge, Cambridge University Press).
Wiggins, D (1991) 'Truth, Invention, and the Meaning of Life' in D Wiggins, *Needs, Values, Truth: Essays in the Philosophy of Value*, 2nd edn (Oxford, Blackwell).
——(1995) 'Categorical Requirements: Kant and Hume on the Idea of Duty' in R Hursthouse, G Lawrence and W Quinn (eds), *Virtues and Reasons: Philippa Foot and Moral Theory* (New York, Oxford University Press).

2

Implementing the 'Moral Turn' in the Social Sciences: Three Obstacles and Three Solutions

CHRISTINE SWANTON

In the abstract to his 'Moral Philosophy and the "Ethical Turn" in Anthropology' the philosopher Michael Klenk (2019) claims that:

> Moral philosophy continues to be enriched by an ongoing empirical turn, mainly through contributions from neuroscience, biology, and psychology. Thus far, cultural anthropology has largely been missing. A recent and rapidly growing 'ethical turn' within cultural anthropology now explicitly and systematically studies morality.

The nature of this recent 'ethical (or moral) turn' in anthropology is fleshed out by the anthropologist James Laidlaw (2017). Ethical features have begun to be appreciated by anthropologists as an irreducible part of everyday life, and not reducible to concepts (such as power, solidarity, social control and enculturation, self-interest) understood in a non-evaluative way. For Laidlaw, ethics is pervasive in human action as such and ethical qualities are not mysterious phenomena that are somehow attached to actions wholly understood within the framework of supposedly non-evaluative sciences. There is also a corollary to the thesis of the 'moral turn': anthropologists are now taking moral theoretic stances towards the ethical phenomena. And what is fascinating to me is that these stances are inspired by philosophy that is far from the dominant strains of ethics in the analytic tradition: namely virtue ethics (particularly MacIntyre); the later Wittgenstein, Austin and Cavell; phenomenology; Foucault. In the analytic tradition these contributions are characteristically marginalised, misunderstood, ignored, forgotten or downright denigrated. The deployment of these intellectual resources is an excellent development, and here I contribute to that development.

Specifically, I discuss how three dominant features of analytic philosophical ethics present obstacles to implementing the moral turn. These are:

1. The parlous state of the metaphysics of ethics in the analytic tradition.
2. The thinness and narrowness of our moral/ethical concepts both in that tradition and in public discourse in the West.

3. The excessive abstraction of moral theories developed in the analytic tradition.

All of these features have damaged the ability of ethics to be empirically informed and the social sciences to take a 'moral turn'. In relation to each of these obstacles I will first describe the problem and then offer a solution. Most attention will be paid to the third of these obstacles where I claim that virtue ethics, endorsed by Bottoms and Shapland (2014: 327) as a superior ethical framework for assisting 'the social-scientific quest for a deeper understanding of desistance processes', still has an overly simple abstract theoretic framework for this task. The last two sections contribute to showing how virtue ethics can overcome this deficiency, primarily in relation to desistance.

HERMENEUTIC ONTOLOGY

Consider now the first obstacle: the parlous state of the metaphysics of ethics in the analytic tradition, at least since GE Moore (1903). This state has contributed to the disastrous fact/value dichotomy. That in turn has created a positivism in the social sciences which has so damaged the possibility of a moral turn. To illustrate the problem, I quote a well-known passage from Hume (1739–40/2000: 301):

> Take any action allow'd to be vicious: Wilful murder, for instance. Examine it in all lights, and see if you can find that matter of fact, or real existence, which you call *vice*. In which-ever way you take it, you find only certain passions, motives, volitions and thoughts. There is no matter of fact in the case. The vice entirely escapes you, as long as you consider the object. You never can find it, till you turn your reflection into your own breast, and find a sentiment of disapprobation, which arises in you, towards this action.

It is standardly thought that this passage poses a dilemma for understanding the ontology of ethics, the two horns of which are as follows:

(1) If ethical properties are objective they can't be found by ordinary means, and they must be queer.
(2) To avoid the queerness problem[1] they must be understood in a subjective way (we must 'turn [our] reflexion into [our] own breast').

Hume is standardly read as resolving the dilemma by going down the subjectivist route that is, endorsing (2). On my interpretation of Hume however, the dilemma does not arise (see Swanton 2015). The thought that the dilemma is genuine is driven by a tendency to assume something Hume rejects: that the nature of ethical properties, if objective, should be understood on the model

[1] See the famous 'argument from queerness' in Mackie (1977).

of science and 'matters of fact' understood according to that model. On this *rejected* model, ethical properties are assumed to be queer unless in some way reduced to scientific properties. To show how the dilemma can be avoided we need to develop a new or rather unfamiliar (in the analytic tradition) metaphysics of ethics.

In short Hume rejects (1), so is not forced into (2). As we shall see on the favoured understanding of the ontology of ethics turning one's attention to one's breast should not be understood in a subjectivist way.

To show how it should be understood, and how (1) (the first horn of the dilemma) can be rejected we need to turn to Heidegger's (1962) hermeneutic ontology. Indeed this proposed solution is suggested by one of Laidlaw's (2017) intellectual traditions animating the moral turn in anthropology, namely phenomenology.

The essential idea of hermeneutic ontology is that truth and knowledge presuppose a context of meaningfulness through which we understand the nature of entities. Meaning for Heidegger 'involves the holistic way in which something can become intelligible *as* something in a web of relations' (Hoy 2006). The ontology of entities presupposes that we have intentional access to them through what Charles Taylor (2006) calls the background of understanding constituting '*engaged* agency'. Hence, to understand the nature of entities we need to understand the manner in which human beings engage with the world. Heidegger fought against traditional spectator metaphysics dominated by perceptual models of cognition, arguing that our fundamental orientation towards the world is practical. This is well understood by anthropologists if not philosophers, with the later Wittgenstein (2009) a notable exception.

We may summarise Heidegger's view in terms of a number of key theses which I have elaborated elsewhere (see Swanton 2021):

1. For an entity to exist as something we can talk about, it must have a certain *mode* of existence; it must have 'being'. For example it exists as a piece of equipment, or as an art work, or as an object of scientific observation.
   'Being is that in virtue of which entities are entities' (Macquarrie and Robinson 1962: xiv).
2. For an entity to have being and thereby an ontology, we must be able to intend it. We must have intentional access to that entity in order to make sense of them (They are no longer 'queer'.) Hence there is two-way ontological dependence.
   'Being is entities making sense (to us) as entities' (Macquarrie and Robinson 1962: xiv).
3. Intentional access to entities (intending entities) is gained through frameworks of significance constituting forms of '*engaged* agency'. There are several such frameworks that are not reducible to the scientific or to any other privileged framework. Notably, the frameworks of the natural sciences do not provide what Heidegger calls 'THE theory of the Real'.

Let us now return to the problem exposed by the quoted passage from Hume. Hume is saying that if we have the wrong framework we cannot intend, make sense of, an entity in a relevant way. We cannot intend the action of killing as *vicious* if we try to intend the action through a representational metaphysics dominated by a perceptual model of cognition suitable for the natural scientific disclosure of the world. Rather you have to 'turn your attention to your breast' to appreciate the framework necessary for making *ethical* properties intelligible. To describe this framework would require another chapter, but here at least is my view of Hume in a nutshell. We have to turn our attention to our breast to make the world of ethics intelligible, for what is necessary for that structure is (amongst many other things) an emotional familiarity with the world of ethics. This is what Hume calls the moral sense, and its emotional conditions and psychological mechanisms, benevolence and extensive sympathy tempered by self-love. On a conceptual and practical level for Hume (as well as for virtue ethics in general) we need the thick virtue and vice concepts and their associated practices, emotions, and so forth which together, in all their richness, give us familiarity with the worldhood of ethics.

It is not just ethical theory that benefits from Heidegger's hermeneutic ontology. Sociology also benefits, in particular by providing the correct view of the ontology of Durkheim's social facts. Durkheim's conception of social facts as the object of sociological study was treated with suspicion and criticised from two opposite poles: one from a reductivist direction which wanted to reduce the objects of sociological study to, for example, the levels of individual psychology, biology or the 'economic substratum'; and the other from an idealist direction in which such facts could not be regarded as 'things' as Durkheim insisted (Thompson 2004: 1–2). For him, in short, social facts are 'things' as opposed to 'ideas' (Durkheim 1901/2013: 7). They should be seen as part of the causal order, for example, according to Durkheim (1902/2013: 293) they can cause evil, and they are external to individuals and their psychology. They come in two main categories, social 'currents', for example, the pressure to learn to drive, and own and use a smart phone; or are in some way institutional such as gift giving practices in various cultures, professional roles and so forth. As such they are both normative and to varying degrees coercive for Durkheim.[2] However, he claims, 'we do not say that social facts are material things, but that they are things just as are material things, although in a different way' (Durkheim (1901/2013: 7). This is exactly Heidegger's picture.

THE NOTION OF THE MORAL AND THE THICK CONCEPTS

I turn now to the second obstacle to implementing the moral turn, the thinness and narrowness of the notion of the moral through which our conception of ethics is characteristically understood in the analytic tradition.

[2] Thus role obligations, for example, constitute an objective reality for Durkheim (1901/2013: 20).

In his book *Ethics and the Limits of Philosophy* Bernard Williams (1985) has a chapter entitled 'Morality, the Peculiar Institution'. Here he suggests that the chief culprit for the narrowness of our moral concepts and the excessive focus on the so-called 'thin' moral concepts, notably obligation,[3] rather than on the so-called 'thick' concepts such as generosity, kindness, patience, courage, amiability, brutality, cruelty, is the notion of the moral itself. That notion is said to have a special sense, indeed a special force that marks it off from other common or garden practical evaluative concepts. Both Williams (1985: 174) and Anscombe (1958) advocate jettisoning the special sense of the moral in favour of what Williams calls the ethical – a broad notion embracing a huge range of evaluative thick concepts.[4]

Fortunately anthropologists have brought ethics down to earth with their conceptions of 'ordinary ethics' (see, eg, Lambek 2010; Das 2015; Zigon 2014). By stark contrast to the narrow domain of the 'peculiar institution', the field of ethics studied by anthropologists in the 'moral turn' is very broad. Ethics is not seen by anthropologists as an object or as an isolatable domain of theory but as an orientation to the world that is ubiquitous and pervasive through life in general. For Lambek there is an 'ethical dimension of living' by which he means

> living with others and over time', and includes 'everything from minute acts of daily greeting and our tone of voice, the quality of how we engage with others and with the world, through keeping immediate and long term commitments and callings, and from the language by which we describe our immediate conduct ... to momentous, disruptive, spontaneous, and unique acts of physical or political courage (2015: 6).

According to Bernard Williams, 'the morality system itself with its emphasis on the "purely moral" and personal sentiments of guilt and self-reproach, actually conceals the dimension in which ethical life lies outside the individual' (1985: 191). This includes 'the forms of social organization within which they [the thick evaluative concepts that map out the dimensions of our ethical life] work' (1985: 131).

Why is the recommendation that the 'special sense' of the moral be jettisoned important for the social sciences? If one thinks that there is a special transcendent notion of the moral having 'mesmeric force' (to use Anscombe's (1958) language), that notion becomes 'queer': a concept impervious to and outside the studies of the social sciences. This predicament has encouraged positivism in those sciences, and a scepticism towards ethically important social

[3] Says Williams (1985: 180): 'It is a mistake of morality to try to make everything into obligations'. Further, morality 'misunderstands ethical practical necessity, thinking it peculiar to obligations' (at 196), and in the case of ethical conflict 'encourages the idea, *only an obligation can beat an obligation*' (at 180).

[4] Note however that I have ignored the taxonomic issue of what demarcates the ethical thick concepts from say the aesthetic (Williams 1985: 135), but a major point of Williams is to downgrade the importance of those distinctions within the broadly practical or normative and to deny that they have clear boundaries (at 6–7).

facts such as roles (with their associated obligations) (in sociology) and character (whether strong or weak, good or bad) (in psychology). By contrast the thick concepts have an empirical or descriptive component entwined with the evaluative, and are susceptible to all sorts of interesting study, for example (in psychology) Peterson and Seligman's (2004) *Character Strengths*.

But how is ethics embedded in our language and ethical sensibilities? How can it be part and parcel of our ordinary lives and character formation? And given that under any conception of ethics, narrow or broad, ethics requires standards how are these provided and how do these connect to the empirical world? Importantly what kind of ethics overcomes the three obstacles to the 'moral turn' described above? I show how a development of virtue ethics, the first of the intellectual traditions inspiring the 'moral turn' described by Laidlaw (2017), answers these questions.

First, what is virtue ethics? I have argued elsewhere (Swanton 2003, 2013) that virtue ethics is a family of theories having several genera and species (such as species of eudaimonistic and target-centred virtue ethics). What are the essential features of virtue ethics understood as a family? As claimed elsewhere, there are two main theses.[5]

Thick Concept Centralism (TCC)

Within the network of concepts denoting features that are reasons and relations of fittingness (only some of which constitute obligations) relatively non-evaluative features such as helping, giving pleasure, satisfying preferences, benefiting (broadly reasons of beneficence) need to be further conceptualised by a large range of thick evaluative concepts such as kind, just, callous, generous, humiliating, manipulative, for their reason-giving status to be properly assessed. The same point applies to broad reasons of respect, and other general classes of reasons. Specifically, TCC claims that the general concepts of right and ought are not logically prior to and independent of reason-giving thick concepts that favour or disfavour responses (such as action).

The Centrality of Virtuousness (CV)

According to CV, rightness and/or excellence are understood through the virtue/vice notions. TCC does not entail CV for one basic reason: though the thick concepts provide evaluative shape to non-evaluative reality and thus demarcate an evaluative reality, they do not in themselves connote excellence or even *pro tanto* rightness. Even honorific concepts such as patient, loyal, courageous,

[5] See Swanton (2021), where these theses are elaborated, especially in the Introduction and ch 2.

are not themselves strictly virtue terms: one can have the courage of a thief where the courage is put to bad ends, an assassin may display extreme patience while stalking his highly virtuous target, one's loyalty may be blind, extreme, or misguided, one's love foolish or destructive. What is needed to yield reasons and relations of fittingness, features which make actions right, and feelings appropriate, is the virtuousness of the loyalty, patience, love and so forth.

Notice that TCC combined with CV (henceforth TCC/CV) does not make concepts denoting virtues of character *alone* central; rather what is central are the thick concepts in general combined with notions of rightness and/or excellence. These concepts can be applied not only to virtues of character but to actions, for example, a (virtuously) generous or loyal act; the targets of the virtues at which virtuous agents aim.

Though the analytic tradition in moral theory has been slow to follow the advice of philosophers such as Williams (1985) and broaden the field of ethics in a way which makes ethics more amenable to the insights of the social sciences, there have been interesting developments within those sciences. The work of Jonathan Haidt (2013) on 'moral foundations' is premised on broadening the foundations of ethics in several ways (see further Swanton 2021: ch 2). The foundations are identified by means of a robust knowledge of human needs and interests as a social animal living in a certain kind of world. They have empirical credentials. For example, the fairness/cheating foundation 'evolved in response to the adaptive challenge of reaping the rewards of cooperation without getting exploited' and institutions and virtues of justice serve that foundation, providing their evaluative point (Haidt 2013: 178). The care/harm foundation 'evolved in response to the adaptive challenge of caring for vulnerable children. It makes us sensitive to signs of suffering and need; it makes us despise cruelty'. Hence, the points of dispositions of caring, benevolence and non-maleficence. The loyalty/betrayal foundation evolved in response to the need to form and maintain coalitions making us sensitive to people who are or are not 'team players' (Haidt 2013: 178). The authority/subversion foundation reflects our need for social hierarchy within institutions, and roles within those institutions. The love/hate foundation, omitted by Haidt – a serious omission in my view – has as its biological basis 'an inborn attachment behaviour system that functions to enhance survival by regulating proximity to a caregiver' (Peterson and Seligman 2004: 315).[6] We are creatures that have a basic need for bonding with others.

Four important points must be made about the ethical foundations.

First, the foundations are considerably more pluralistic than the foundations of traditional concepts of morality. As Haidt (2013: 109) claims 'there is more to

[6] According to Peterson and Seligman (2004: 315) attachments to attachment figures 'can be distinguished from other types of social relationships in terms of four defining features … seeking to stay near to or in contact with (*proximity maintenance*) turning to for comfort or reassurance (*safe haven*), being upset by unexpected or prolonged separations (*separation distress*), and using the attachment figure as a base of security from which to explore and operate in the world (*secure base*)'.

morality than harm and fairness' (see also Hoffman et al 2014). Indeed on my view Haidt does not have enough foundations: the work of Hume, for example, provides material to add more, but that is a story for another day. Furthermore, especially given the rise of conspiracy theories and widespread misinformation, the knowledge foundation reflecting our need to acquire knowledge to solve problems, with its associated large array of the epistemic virtues, should be added to the list.

Second and most importantly, the foundations provide evaluative point to the thick concepts. They undergird TCC by providing a link between the evaluative domain of ethics as understood through the thick concepts and knowledge of the world gained through the social sciences. By reference to the foundations we can understand the evaluative points of thick concepts such as loyalty, courage, compassion, and thereby conceptualise a myriad of disparate shapeless natural facts such as running away, hurting someone, supporting someone, through the evaluative lens of those concepts.

Third, the foundations undergird CV. Via the conceptual apparatus of the thick concepts associated with the various foundations, and empirically informed ideas of what it is to do well in relation to the foundations gleaned from the social and other sciences, we can form educated conceptions of virtue and vice associated with those foundations. For example, the epistemic virtues enable us to do well in the face of the overwhelming misinformation online and elsewhere. Knowledge of psychology through studies of the many forms of pathological altruism allows us to understand the difference between virtuous and non-virtuous forms of compassion or pity for example. In relation to the loyalty foundation, studies of tribal behaviour and attitudes enable us to distinguish between non-virtuous forms of loyalty revealed in studies of implicit bias and more virtuous forms. Love may exhibit disordered attachment (studied in attachment theory) and manifest in a non-virtuous way.

Fourth, the foundations are not mysterious; they do not rest on some metaphysically obscure notion of the moral. Rather they are understood through important features essential for characteristic human functioning in a social context. The nature and demands of those contexts can be investigated and debated through the social sciences. This gives concrete expression to Williams' (1985) claim that morality/ethics does not need special materials. The thick concepts associated with the foundations destroy the fact/value dichotomy which has so blighted the social sciences, at least in the past. For example, the early twentieth-century view of the psychologist Gordon Allport that character was the subject matter of philosophy, and not psychology, reflected the positivism sweeping social science at this time and its rigid distinction between fact and value (Peterson and Seligman 2004: 55).

EXCESSIVE ABSTRACTION AND DIFFERENTIATED VIRTUE

The third obstacle to implementing the moral turn in the social sciences is the excessive abstraction of the dominant ethical theories in the analytic tradition including virtue ethics.

In his 'D'Ou Venons-Nous … Que Sommes Nous … Ou Allons-Nous?' Elijah Millgram sums up the problem of excessive abstraction with a 'lesson' of Bernard Williams' contribution to moral philosophy (2009: xx):

> [T]he unintended lesson of Williams' work is that we have made an astonishing mistake about who we are. The philosophical common sense of the past half-century has been suitable for impossible simple minded creatures, creatures competent to live only in impossibly simple environments. Consequently, the descriptive metaphysics and ethics that have been spun out of it are useless to us.

Philosophical ethics needs to deploy the resources of the social sciences to enrich the landscape of ethics and understand fully the forms of life in which ethics is immanent. As the moral anthropologist Michael Lambek (2015: 19) states:

> Persons, as social beings, are constituted through their relations with others. This is partly an intersubjective process, beginning with the mother–infant bond, but it is mediated by what society objectifies as the identities people are given (names and statuses), tasks expected of them (roles), positions they are given to occupy (offices), and programs they come to identify with (callings), as well as the structures of relations in which statuses, roles, offices and callings are manifest.

There are two main manifestations of the excessive abstraction of philosophical ethics. First is the fact that virtue is not relativised to central aspects of human life such as roles, the trajectory of human development, and what Shapland and Bottoms (2011: 275–77) call 'the obstacle-strewn society'. Virtue itself is conceptualised in a way which is too abstract. Second is the insulation of ethics from the social sciences as noted above, and the correlative suspicion with which moral philosophers have held those disciplines. In the remainder of this chapter we discuss the first of these manifestations. This section shows how to conceptualise the idea that virtue needs to be relativised to such pervasive features of our lives as the roles we inhabit. The last section, 'Burdened Virtue and Desistance' focuses on the aspect of relativisation most important to the problem of desistance: 'the obstacle-strewn society'.

It may be thought that virtue ethics with its apparent attention to the richness of our moral lives and language is immune to the charge of excessive abstraction. Not so. All too often 'the' or 'a' virtuous agent carries an impossible theoretical weight: a weight that can be borne only by idealisations. In that case the close connection between virtue ethics as an ethical theory and its applicability in the real world is weakened. What is needed, as both Bernard Williams and Alasdair MacIntyre saw, is attention to culture, history, burdens, difference of perspective due to, for example, age, roles, gender and the narrative shape of an individual life in which 'projects' have personal significance. 'The' virtuous agent is seen simply as someone possessing what I shall call basic virtue, generosity, courage, honesty and so forth. But such a conception of virtue must be refined. We need to think of generosity as a CEO; loyalty as a defence lawyer; the differences between a virtue as manfested in old age as opposed to one manifested as a youth. The notion of basic virtue *simpliciter* must be supplemented by a notion of basic virtue *differentiated* according to such things as cultural location and roles if it is to apply to the real world. What I call basic virtue such as generosity is differentiated by such factors as role requirements, narrative permissions, cultural demands.

It is illegitimate to think one can gain objectivity in ethics by abstracting away virtue from its relativity to such factors as history, culture and roles within that culture. This relativity gives rise to what I call ethical differentiation, and in the context of virtue, differentiated virtue.

There are several forms of ethical differentiation:

1. Cultural features.
2. Historical features.
3. The narrative particularities of an individual's life, including her relationships.
4. 'Burdened' or oppressive settings.
5. Stage of life.
6. Roles.

Other possible forms of potential differentiation are controversial: for example, are there gender differentiated virtues?

We now ask: what are basic and differentiated virtues and what is the relation between them? What I call basic virtue such as generosity is differentiated by such factors as role requirements, narrative permissions, cultural demands.

By 'basic virtue' is meant virtue understood at a high level of generality (kindness *qua* human being) or abstraction (kindness *simpliciter*) as opposed to the kindness of a lawyer or a doctor *qua* doctor or lawyer. Kindness for example as a basic virtue is an abstraction only: what kindness demands or permits cannot be resolved until there is further specification in terms of, for example, roles (such as kindness *qua* doctor, *qua* parent of young child, or *qua* friend), the narrative shape of one's life, or the nature of one's culture.

Importantly, debates about, for example, whether the kindness of a doctor requires empathy with or detached concern for her patient,[7] and how precisely we are to understand these possible requirements, are undetermined or at least underdetermined by appeal to basic virtue. Similarly, resolution of debates about what, on various views about social responsibility, is required by justice in business executives is left open. These are issues of role ethics (eg, business

[7] For this distinction, and a sophisticated psychologically and medically informed discussion of it, see Jodi Halpern (2001).

ethics, medical ethics) on which virtue ethics in general is silent. Hence a theory of differentiated virtue in relation to role requirements of a doctor say brings ethics down to earth in a way that attention to basic virtue alone cannot. Again, sensitivity is differentiated to form the virtue of cultural sensitivity, an excellence that is more specific than sensitivity in general. A sensitive person, if ignorant of culture, will not be culturally sensitive.

Differentiated virtues then are character traits associated with ethical differentiation. More specifically basic virtues such as generosity are differentiated by such factors as role requirements, narrative permissions, cultural demands to yield types of differentiated virtue. Until a basic virtue is 'contoured' by contextual features, such as a person's role, historical and cultural situatedness, we characteristically cannot form an accurate conception of the target of that virtue in a particular context. Once such a contouring of a basic virtue has taken place, we have an account of what I call a *differentiated virtue*, such as a role-differentiated virtue of generosity in a CEO, and a role-differentiated virtue of loyalty (to client) in a defence lawyer – a disposition of virtuous zealousness in advocacy.[8]

What is the relation between basic and differentiated virtue? First, basic virtue constrains differentiated virtue. Though accounts of basic virtues abstract away from role differentiation for example, they are not empty. Basic virtues provide anchors for our moral thought even when contoured by role demands, narrative integrity, cultural imperatives. In this way, they provide constraints on the unfettered pursuit of goals associated with ethical differentiation, such as cultural goals, personal goals consistent with the narrative shape of one's life, and institutional goals served by institutional roles. Basic virtue alerts us to possibilities of excess and other forms of wrongness when determining the scope of differentiated virtue. For example, zealous advocacy in a defence lawyer will be distinguished from what has been called hyper- zeal;[9] narrative integrity and pursuit of one's creative goals may permit differentiation of a basic virtue such as caring (for one's family say) in a talented artist but not to the point of total neglect and abandonment; the hospitality required in a culture will not permit lavishness to the point of endangering the welfare of the young. Such anchors are deeply embedded dispositions which provide constraints on contouring action in line with, say, role demands.

Second, the nature of a differentiated virtue of type X such as a role differentiated virtue is determined not just by the relevant basic virtue but by relevant social facts of type X. For example, social facts of cultural beliefs and

[8] For an early discussion of differentiated virtue, from which some of this section is adapted, see Swanton (2007); and see further Swanton (2021).

[9] For the distinction between 'mere zeal' and 'hyper-zeal' see Dare (2000). Unlike Dare, however, I would describe 'mere zeal' as a role differentiated virtue of zeal in advocacy constrained by basic virtue.

institutional role obligations respectively constrain how the basic virtue of generosity operates as a culturally differentiated virtue of generosity, and the permitted latitude of generosity of a CEO in relation to the firm's funds. But recall that basic virtue constrains differentiated virtue: hence, for example, cultural relativism is avoided. Not all sets of cultural beliefs pass the test of basic virtue. Again some roles may be vicious and any institutional requirements of those roles as *social* facts would not be or generate genuine *ethical* requirements. Differentiated virtue is still virtue.

BURDENED VIRTUE AND DESISTANCE

In this section I apply the idea of differentiated virtue to the problem of the 'obstacle-strewn society' in relation to desistance. To this end I introduce an expanded concept of burdened virtue owed originally to Tessman (2005) to show how, with the help of the concept of differentiated virtue introduced in the previous section, the notion of burdened virtue contributes to the ethical understanding of desistance. In short, one of the forms of ethical differentiation is the 'obstacle-strewn society' in which social facts such as 'the pull of still criminal friends' and the 'general difficulties of social reintegration' (Bottoms and Shapland 2014: 320) constrain in a systematic way basic virtues in burden-differentiated virtue (burdened virtue). To understand the role of virtue ethics in desistance I argue that we need an expanded notion of burdened virtue. This expanded notion I call burdened (2) to differentiate it from Tessman's notion (burdened (1)).

Tessman's notion of burdened virtue is defined by her as follows:

> [*B*]*urdened virtues* include all those traits that make a contribution to human flourishing – if they succeed in doing so at all – *only* because they enable survival of or resistance to oppression … while in other ways they detract from their bearer's well-being (2005: 95).

An agent is burdened (1) in respect of virtue in Tessman's sense if and only if:

(i) she possesses the virtue, and
(ii) in exercising the virtue she is 'burdened': the very exercise of the virtue detracts from her well- being.

For our purposes I wish to broaden the definition of burdened virtue so that it can be burdensome to an agent not only to exercise the virtue but to acquire and maintain the virtue.

An agent is burdened (2) in respect of virtue, then, if:

(iii) it is burdensome (very costly, or difficult) to acquire the virtue and/or
(iv) it is burdensome (very costly or difficult) to maintain the virtue.

Burdened virtue is a form of differentiated virtue. A differentiated virtue, recall, is a character trait associated with a form of ethical differentiation, such as burdensomeness. In the case of burdened virtue a basic virtue such as courage has characteristics which are appropriate to the burdened quality of an agent's life. A basic virtue is differentiated by the nature of its burden to its possessor (such as political resistance in the face of oppression). That burden may arise in relation to the acquisition, maintenance or exercise of that virtue. Tessman gives an example of a burdened virtue of courage in a resistance fighter in relation to burdened (1). The political resister, says Tessman (2005: 108), is in a 'position of perpetual struggles, with a constant demand for the virtues of resistance'. That is to say the courage of the political resister takes the form of resistance, a resistance which involves perpetual struggle.

Of course there can be rival views about the nature of burden-differentiated virtue: for example, about the role of anger as a motivational spring in oppressive contexts, but let us turn now to the relation between burdened virtue and desistance. How is the idea of burdened (2) virtue relevant to criminology and desistance in particular?

We are used to hearing that poverty seeds crime. However, it is also true that virtue, sufficiently entrenched in an agent, 'silences' reasons that may tempt one or drive one towards criminal behaviour even in the face of poverty. Although the notion of silencing (owed to McDowell 1998) has been misunderstood and criticised, the basic idea is simply a point about the relative robustness of virtuous dispositions of character in the face of the lure of supposed reasons in favour of vicious acts. Silencing is defined thus by Denise Vigani (2019) in her defence of the concept. It is a phenomenon where for a virtuous agent 'considerations in favor of acting contrary to virtue are not outweighed or overridden, but rather silenced altogether; in other words, they fail to operate as reasons at all' (Vigani 2019: 229). One source of confusion surrounds the notion of 'operate as reasons'. It is not that something that is or could be a reason ceases to be a reason because a virtuous agent makes it so. Rather a feature such as the value of a vase is not a reason to steal it at all, and that is recognised by a virtuous agent for whom it is *not* the case that that feature (the value of the vase) is a reason for stealing but is overridden. Rather that feature is silenced as a possible reason. Silencing is a psychological phenomenon analogous to perception, where virtuous agents see features in a distinctive way. Features are silenced by virtuous agents in the process of *reasoning*.

In the Great Depression for many people, strong dispositions of honesty, industriousness, self-help/non-parasitism, resilience, silenced putative reasons to act contrary to virtue notwithstanding considerable poverty. Unfortunately, where virtue is burdened (2) these traits are either weakened so that desistance is less probable, or vice may silence reasons of desistance altogether.

What factors make for the existence of burdened (2) virtue? In particular, how do we understand the part played by culture, such as gang culture, business culture, corrupt institutions, in the maintenance and acquisition of virtue? How is it that these constitute burdens such that factors which are apparent reasons for crime are not silenced?

To address these questions we note a useful distinction of Bottoms and Shapland (2014: 323) between normative and habitual compliance. The process of acquiring virtue (leading to habitual compliance) in a burdened context may begin with an act of normative compliance owed to a highly significant or dramatic event (eg, an intervention by a pastor). Eventually religious conversion as a result of a series of such interventions with repeated encouragement, support and determination can result in habitual compliance.[10] As Aristotle (1975: Book 2, iv) reminds us, excellence is a habit gained through repeated virtuous actions (actions conforming to virtue) which gradually become actions from a state of virtue.

Frequently the social facts constituting the burdensomeness of burdened virtue (2) are very difficult to overcome as the result of the interaction between culturally differentiated *vice* and burdensomeness. For example, the criminal gang culture of the Mongrel Mob (a criminal gang in New Zealand) is legitimised within the culture of the gang. According to Tuhoe Isaac (2007: 2) 'in my era there were no rules except the 'law of lawlessness' … If it was considered evil, bad and lawless we embraced it as good'. The reason for this was that 'we felt all levels of society hated us … so we just reflected that hatred back at them' (at 1), hence '[W]e created a new society based on hatred' (at 2).

Furthermore the opportunities to break out of the culture are highly limited for two main reasons: coercion and extreme insularity – the epitome of the closed society. Says Isaac: 'All family ties are severed when you join the Mob' (2007: 3) and 'If you weren't a Mobster you weren't worth knowing' (at 2). It was also difficult to leave: 'there was no escape from the Mob; prospects that absconded were always forcibly returned and severely bashed for their disobedience' (at 5).

CONCLUSION

A major impediment to the 'moral turn' in the social sciences is the extreme abstraction of philosophical ethics, including virtue ethics. To remedy this within virtue ethics we need a distinction between basic and differentiated virtue. This distinction cannot be usefully deployed without an understanding of the social facts relevant to forms of differentiation. Of particular importance in desistance is the recognition that basic virtue is differentiated by various forms of burdensomeness.

The 'moral turn', as Laidlaw (2017) recognises, must go both ways. Not only must there be awareness of the pervasiveness of ethics as part of our daily lives and that ethics is thus a proper study within anthropology, but philosophical ethics including virtue ethics must also be more sensitive to social facts.

[10] For examples see Cruz (1968) and Isaac (2007).

Otherwise the moral turn will be distorted by false moral theory. This is true at a fundamental level if philosophical ethics is based on false metaphysics, a metaphysics which readily leads to forms of scientism and positivism, or forms of subjectivism in ethics.

REFERENCES

Anscombe, GEM (1958) 'Modern Moral Philosophy' 33 *Journal of the Royal Institute of Philosophy* 1.

Aristotle (1975) *Nicomachean Ethics* (trans JAK Thomson) (Harmondsworth, Penguin Books).

Bottoms, A and Shapland, J (2014) 'Can Persistent Offenders Acquire Virtue?' 27 *Studies in Christian Ethics* 318.

Cruz, M (1968) *Run Baby Run* (London, Hodder & Stoughton).

Dare, T (2000) 'The Role of Law and the Role of Lawyers' in T Campbell and JD Goldsworthy (eds), *Judicial Power, Democracy and Legal Positivism* (Aldershot, Ashgate Dartmouth).

Das, V (2015) 'What Does Ordinary Ethics Look Like?' in M Lambek, V Das, D Fassin and W Keane (eds), *Four Lectures on Ethics: Anthropological Perspectives* (Chicago, IL, Hau Books).

Durkheim, E (1901/2013) *The Rules of Sociological Method and Selected Texts on Sociology and its Method*, 2nd edn, ed S Lukes (trans WD Halls) (Basingstoke, Palgrave Macmillan).

——(1902/2013) *The Division of Labour in Society*, 2nd edn, ed S Lukes (trans WD Halls) (Basingstoke, Palgrave Macmillan).

Haidt, J (2013) *The Righteous Mind: Why Good People are Divided by Politics and Religion* (London, Penguin Books).

Halpern, J (2001) *From Detached Concern to Empathy: Humanizing Medical Practice* (Oxford, Oxford University Press).

Heidegger, M (1962) *Being and Time* (trans J Macquarrie and E Robinson) (New York, Harper).

Hoffman, W, Wisneski, DC, Brandt, MJ and Skitka, LJ (2014) 'Morality in everyday life' 345 *Science* 1340.

Hoy, DC (2006) 'Heidegger and the Hermeneutic Turn' in CB Guignon (ed), *The Cambridge Companion to Heidegger*, 2nd edn (Cambridge, Cambridge University Press).

Hume, D (1739–40/2000) *A Treatise of Human Nature* (eds DF Norton and MJ Norton) (Oxford, Oxford University Press).

Isaac, T (2007) *True Red* (New Zealand, Wild Side Publishing).

Klenk, M (2019) 'Moral Philosophy and the "Ethical Turn" in Anthropology' 2 *Zeitschrift für Ethik und Moralphilosophie* 331.

Laidlaw, J (2017) 'Ethics/Morality' in F Stein, S Lazar, M Candea, H Diemberger, J Robbins, A Sanchez and R Stash (eds), *Cambridge Encyclopedia of Anthropology* (Cambridge, Cambridge University Press).

Lambek, M (2010) *Ordinary Ethics: Anthropology, Language, and Action* (New York, Fordham University Press).

——(2015) *The Ethical Condition: Essays on Action, Person & Value* (Chicago, IL, University of Chicago Press).
Mackie, JL (1977) *Ethics: Inventing Right and Wrong* (London, Penguin Group).
Macquarrie, J and Robinson, E (1962) 'Translator's Preface' in M Heidegger, *Being and Time* (trans J Macquarrie and E Robinson) (New York, Harper).
McDowell, JH (1998) *Mind, Value, and Reality* (Cambridge, MA, Harvard University Press).
Millgram, E (2009) *Hard Truths* (New Jersey, Wiley-Blackwell).
Moore, GE (1903) *Principia Ethica* (Cambridge, Cambridge University Press).
Peterson C and Seligman, MEP (2004) *Character Strengths and Virtues: A Handbook and Classification* (Oxford, Oxford University Press).
Shapland, J and Bottoms, AE (2011) 'Reflections on Social Values, Offending and Desistance among Young Adult Recidivists' 13 *Punishment & Society* 256.
Swanton, C (2003) *Virtue Ethics: A Pluralistic View* (Oxford, Oxford University Press).
——(2007) 'Virtue Ethics, Role Ethics, and Business Ethics' in RL Walker and PJ Ivanhoe (eds), *Working Virtue: Virtue Ethics and Contemporary Moral Problems* (Oxford, Clarendon Press).
——(2013) 'The Definition of Virtue Ethics' in DC Russell (ed), *The Cambridge Companion to Virtue Ethics* (Cambridge, Cambridge University Press).
——(2015) *The Virtue Ethics of Hume and Nietzsche* (Chichester, Wiley Blackwell).
——(2021) *Target Centred Virtue Ethics* (Oxford, Oxford University Press).
Taylor, C (2006) 'Engaged Agency and Background in Heidegger' in CB Guignon (ed), *The Cambridge Companion to Heidegger*, 2nd edn (Cambridge, Cambridge University Press).
Tessman, L (2005) *Burdened Virtues: Virtue Ethics for Liberatory Struggles* (Oxford, Oxford University Press).
Thompson K (2004) 'Introduction' in K Thompson (ed), *Readings from Emile Durkheim*, rev edn (trans M Thompson) (London, Routledge).
Vigani, D (2019) 'Virtuous Construal: In Defense of Silencing' 5 *Journal of the American Philosophical Association* 229.
Williams, B (1985) *Ethics and the Limits of Philosophy* (London, Fontana).
Wittgenstein, L (2009) *Philosophical Investigations*, 4th edn (trans GEM Anscombe, PMS Hacker and J Schulte) (Chichester, Wiley-Blackwell).
Zigon, J (2014) 'An Ethics of Dwelling and a Politics of World Building: A Critical Response to Ordinary Ethics' 20 *Journal of the Royal Anthropological Institute* 746.

Part II

Criminal Justice-Related Ethical Dilemmas

3

Whistleblowing: An Ethical Analysis of Police Officers' Reporting of Misconduct by Colleagues

JUSTICE TANKEBE*

INTRODUCTION

POLICE OFFICERS OCCUPY a special position in society. They have been described as 'the state made flesh' (Laurie 1970) because their everyday conduct represents a concrete manifestation of the abstract principles that underpin the state. In a liberal democracy, these principles include equality before the law, freedom of expression and association, and protection from harm. Given this role, Bayley (2005) argues that the true test of democratic governance is the quality of policing: a state cannot claim to be democratic if its police officers regularly abuse their powers. However, globally, the public police face two important ethical problems, of which the first is the problem of police misconduct. By misconduct I mean police misuse of their authority – through omissions or commissions – for their private interests or to advance organisational or sectional interests (Kleinig 1996). For example, in September 2021, an officer of the London Metropolitan Police Service was sentenced to life imprisonment for the murder of Sarah Everard. Earlier in the same year, an officer of the Minneapolis Police Department (USA) was convicted for the murder of George Floyd, an African American man. In Ghana, the police administration dismissed 28 police officers for unlawful detention of civilians, misuse of firearms, and being drunk on duty between January and August 2020 (Ghana News Agency 2020). An important function for the police is to support the rule of law; they are expected to do this through

* For helpful comments, I am grateful to Tony Bottoms, Jonathan Jacobs, P-O Wikström and Roz Spinks. A draft of the chapter was presented at a colloquium series at the Institute for Law, Politics and Philosophy, University College London. I am grateful to the participants for their feedback. I also thank Alberta Kwei for fieldwork assistance.

their own exemplary conduct and by ensuring rule-violators are held accountable. Hence, police officers who break the law violate the rule of law.

The second ethical problem in policing concerns the choices made by individual police officers when they are confronted with unethical actions by their colleagues. For example, an aspect of the killing of George Floyd was that officers who were with the offending officer did not intervene to stop him from breaking organisational rules about the use of force. Their inaction contrasts sharply with that of Cariol Horne, an officer with the New York Police Department. She intervened to stop a colleague White officer from using a chokehold tactic against a young African American man: 'she forcibly removed the white officer and began to trade blows with him' (*New York Times* 2021). Arguably, how individual police officers – and by extension the police organisation – react to misconduct is the most fundamental ethical problem in policing. It is the most fundamental ethical problem because effective accountability, the rule of law, unfettered access to justice, confidence in democratic governance, and preventing police capture by corrupt political elites or organised crime depends on a solution to that problem.

Globally, police officers are expected, even required, to blow the whistle on colleagues engaged in suspected misconduct. However, officers are known to renege on this duty (see Wood 1997). The question of police obligations to obey rules and regulations can be approached from different disciplinary perspectives. For moral philosophers, the questions that arise might include the following: can we elucidate general principles that ground police whistleblowing duties? Are there moral reasons that warrant obedience to this duty or that can permit its repudiation? What is the exact nature of these reasons and how persuasive are they? Are these reasons universal or are there situations that compel a temporary suspension of police whistleblowing obligations? For example, might threats to the life of an officer count as a compelling moral justification for not blowing the whistle on misconduct? Within a consequentialist framework, should misconduct go unreported if that will achieve a greater good for society? What if the police operate in a repressive state such that 'whistleblowing' has the effect of protecting unjust systems of power that threaten the wellbeing of citizens, and 'misconduct' might seek to undo such power arrangements?

Social scientists do not, in general, seek to resolve such moral dilemmas. They ask a different set of questions, including the following: what knowledge do officers have about the set of behaviours that constitute misconduct? How often do they encounter whistleblowing opportunities? What moral beliefs do they hold about whistleblowing? Do these beliefs change over time? What might account for such changes? Do they believe all forms of misconduct should be reported or are they more discriminating, and differentiate between misconduct types in terms of their whistleblowing worthiness? What is the basis for any such differentiation? How can researchers explain differences between officers in whistleblowing intentions and acts? What interventions might prove effective in encouraging whistleblowing among officers? As a social scientist, my main concern in this chapter is with explanatory questions of this kind about whistleblowing by police officers.

Studies of this phenomenon have identified two main reasons why police officers do not blow the whistle on misconduct: first, an officer sub-culture that discourages misconduct reporting and, second, experiences of organisational injustice[1] (Wolfe and Piquero 2011; Long et al 2013; Kutnjak Ivković et al 2022). Thus, the explanatory emphasis is placed on the institutional environments of policing as opposed to individual choices. However, the question of the relationship between institutional pressures and personal factors in shaping ethical decisions by individual officers remains largely unexplored. Another feature of previous research is its focus on measuring the reporting *intentions* of police officers rather than *actions*. However, intentions might not always translate into actions (Elster 2007). An officer might express a readiness to report misconduct, yet resile from the intention when confronted with the opportunity to do so. Nor is it known whether the factors that explain police officers' reporting intentions are the same as those that explain actions.

This chapter addresses these theoretical and empirical issues. It does so by drawing on survey data from a convenience sample of Ghanaian police officers to examine the applicability of Wikström's 'Situational Action Theory' (SAT) to our understanding of why individual police officers choose to resolve the ethical problem of whistleblowing the way they do. SAT proposes that moral actions are the outcome of interactions between a person's individual moral propensity and the moral features of the setting in which he or she is currently placed. The theory has so far been applied almost exclusively to explain criminal acts, for example: youth delinquency (Wikström et al 2012; Hirtenlehner and Hardie 2016; Kokkalera, Marshall and Marshall 2020); political violence (Schils and Pauwels 2014); white-collar crime (Jordanoska 2018); and terrorism (Wikström and Bouhana 2017). It has also been applied to police officers' self-reported use of force (Noppe 2018). With limited exceptions, empirical tests provide support for the theory's key propositions (see Pauwels, Svensson and Hirtenlehner 2018).

Although Situational Action Theory has to date been applied mainly to criminal acts, the theory has an inherent flexibility that allows for its application in non-criminal contexts. According to Wikström et al, 'a theory of crime causation is a special case of a general theory of moral action. Explaining acts

[1] Organisational injustice here refers to officers' experiences and perceptions of being treated unjustly by the police department. This injustice can manifest itself in a multiplicity of ways. It can be procedural such as when officers feel the department shows little care for their wellbeing, treats them with disrespect and does not actively seek their views when making decisions that affect them as police officers. Injustice can also be distributive such as when officers experience unequal or discriminatory treatment – eg, they are more likely to be investigated for misconduct, or to be assigned to certain duties, or not be considered for promotion – on account of their rank, religious beliefs, race or gender. Organisational injustice matters not only for whistleblowing but also for the commitment of officers to the rule of law, to fair treatment of citizens, and to obeying departmental rules (see Bradford and Quinton 2014; Tankebe 2014; Tyler, Callahan and Frost 2007).

of crime is not different from explaining why people breach moral rules more generally' (2012: 12). This implies that criminal acts do not exhaust the moral actions within its purview. Whistleblowing – that is, disclosing unethical or illegal actions by one's co-employees or organisation (Near and Miceli 1985: 4) – is an example of moral acts not so far considered in SAT research. Yet, in both 'criminal acts' and 'whistleblowing', there are moral rules specifying what potential actors ought to do or not do. In the former, the moral act of breaking rules can threaten the social order and the wellbeing of its citizens; in the latter, the action can have the effect of protecting citizens from the consequences of unlawful individual conduct or from unjust systems of power. Consequently, in applying Situational Action Theory to the intentions and actions of police officers to blow or not blow the whistle on unethical behaviours by their colleagues, I adopt the (probably uncontroversial) view that such behaviours constitute moral actions. As moral actions, they are potentially explicable in terms of the *person–environment* configurations of Situational Action Theory.

The chapter is organised as follows: first, I provide an overview of the key arguments made by Situational Action Theory. Second, I outline the methods used in testing the theory using survey data from a sample of police officers from Ghana. Third, I present findings from the data. Contrary to SAT propositions, misconduct reporting *actions* are shown to be the outcome of a perception-choice process in which the moral features of the setting are much more dominant than individual propensities. In the case of misconduct reporting *intentions*, the opposite was true: propensity dominates the influence of moral context. Finally, I reflect on the implications of these findings for our understanding of ethical intentions and actions of individual police officers.

SITUATIONAL ACTION THEORY

Situational Action Theory (SAT) is a theory of moral action. Moral actions are defined as 'actions which are guided by value-based rules of conduct specifying what is the right or wrong thing to do (or not do) in response to particular motivations in particular circumstances' (Wikström and Bouhana 2017: 178). In a key publication, *Breaking Rules* (Wikström et al 2012), a criminal act is proposed as one of many such moral actions, leaving open the possibility of application to other moral actions. However, Situational Action Theory has developed as a theory of crime causation (Wikström and Treiber 2016). Its starting point is that societies or groups have rules which some people choose to break. The task of the criminologist is to explain such acts of rule-breaking. However, any explanations, the theory claims, cannot be sought solely in the personal characteristics of actors or in the social environments in which they are located. On the contrary, what is required are explanations that bring these two variables together to set out the mechanisms through which they relate to each other to explain the acts of rule-breaking. The major claim of Situational

Action Theory is that 'human actions, such as acts of crime, are the outcome of a perception-choice process initiated and guided by the *causal interaction* of (crime) propensity and (criminogenic) exposure' (Wikström et al 2012: 17, emphasis original).

Propensity

Propensity is a personal characteristic. In an everyday sense, the *Oxford English Dictionary* defines it as a 'predisposition or inclination *to*, *towards*, or *for* a particular action, habit, quality, etc; a tendency *to* do something' (emphasis original). Its use in Situational Action Theory is consistent with this ordinary usage: propensity is theorised as a predisposition to *see* and to *choose* crime as a 'viable action alternative' (Wikström et al 2012: 15).

According to Situational Action Theory, a person's propensity depends on two factors: morality and the ability to exercise self-control. Morality refers to 'a code of conduct that guides behaviour' (Bicchieri 2017: 31). In this sense, it covers the domain of 'oughtness', of a person's sense of what is 'right' or 'wrong', 'good' or 'bad' in particular settings (MacCormick 2007). People differ in terms of how strongly they feel they should obey certain moral codes; a person may feel obliged to obey some moral codes but not others. This helps us to understand why some people sometimes break certain moral codes, but others do not (Hirschi 1969; Wikström et al 2012). Moral rules have meaning only in specific behaviour contexts. When X says she believes it is right or wrong to obey rules, such a declaration might not tell us much about how she would act when confronted with opportunities for bribery or breaking Covid-19 rules. A distinctive feature of Situational Action Theory is that it is concerned not with the generality of moral beliefs but with what it calls 'action relevant moral rules; that is, the specific moral beliefs that are relevant to actions in particular situations (Wikström et al 2012: 16).

The SAT view that morality is crucial to action comports with Charles Taylor's work on 'moral frameworks'. According to Taylor (1989), people regularly have to choose between different commitments and courses of action; some of these commitments and actions they might consider right or wrong, good or bad, dignified or undignified. What allows them to make these choices are their moral frameworks. Ruth Abbey (2000: 34) observes that, for Taylor, these frameworks are moral maps that

> orient people in moral space … individuals feel themselves to exist within a space of moral questions about what is the right thing to do, what goods should be pursued and what is the right direction for their lives to take. Moral frameworks help them to answer these questions. Just as individuals orient themselves in physical space and find it hard to function if disorientated, so we orient ourselves in moral space: we usually have a sense of where we stand on moral questions and we feel ourselves as either moving towards or failing to move towards the goods in our lives.

Will an individual break the rules against bribe-taking? Will an offender decide to move away from a life of crime? Will an officer, confronted with evidence of suspected misconduct by a colleague, report the alleged conduct? Based on Taylor's arguments, people's moral frameworks will shape the answers they give to these questions, and, therefore, the actions that follow. Without the resource of moral frameworks, meaningful action is highly unlikely. Consequently, Situational Action Theory sees morality as 'the basic personal factor' in attempts to understand people's predispositions to rules (Wikström et al 2012). This primary role assigned to morality implies that propensity is always to be viewed as a deeply moral concept.

However, it is often the case that people encounter normative orders that conflict with their personal moral beliefs. Indeed, the idea of moral frameworks presupposes this conflictual situation; that is, situations in which what people want to do, or what people are inclined to do, conflicts with that they morally ought to do. Situational Action Theory proposes that the more people's moral beliefs correspond with the demands of a given normative order, the less likely they are to break its rules (Wikström and Treiber 2016). Let us take the hypothetical case of officer Betty: she has strong moral convictions about the propriety of reporting misconduct. She believes misconduct violates a fundamental commitment and it is her responsibility to help prevent it by reporting those who engage in it. Betty finds herself in the company of peers who seek to dissuade her from acting out her moral beliefs. She must choose whether to give in to peer pressure or act in accordance with her deeply held moral beliefs. How she chooses to act, according to Situational Action Theory, will depend on her ability to exercise self-control, the second element of propensity.

In their well-known *General Theory of Crime*, Gottfredson and Hirschi (1990) conceptualise self-control as a stable personal trait. According to them, ineffective childhood socialisation leads people to develop low self-control. To have low self-control is to be impulsive, insensitive to the plight of others, risk-taking and given to the immediate gratification of pleasure. These qualities make people vulnerable to the 'temptations of the moment', and thus more likely to act on criminal opportunities. In Situational Action Theory, self-control is different: it is a person's 'ability to withstand external pressure to act against their own personal morals' (Wikström and Treiber 2016: 431; see also Wikström and Treiber 2007). It is therefore relevant to behaviour only when there is a conflict between a person's moral beliefs and the moral features of the social environment. In those conflict situations, action will depend on the strength of one's self-control. If fictional officer Betty has high self-control, she is more likely to resist the situational pressures to act against her beliefs in the rightness of blowing the whistle on misconduct; if, however, her self-control is weak, she will succumb to such pressures, making misconduct reporting unlikely. Consequently, Situational Action Theory argues that a person's propensity can be understood as the outcome of an interaction between personal morality and the ability to exercise self-control (Wikström et al 2012; Wikström and Treiber

2016). Put differently, propensity to act morally entails strong moral beliefs about a particular act and the self-control to fend off temptations to deviate from those beliefs.

Exposure

Propensity, as discussed above, concerns people's predispositions, not their actions. Having a predisposition to act ethically such as reporting misconduct does not amount to acting ethically. Propensity requires a trigger, and this trigger, in Situational Action Theory, is the moral features of a person's social settings. Settings are important for action because they present 'different moral contexts, that is, different *moral norms* and *levels of enforcement*' (Wikström et al 2012: 16, emphasis original). The theory claims that settings do not always mirror or align with prevailing social rules. On the contrary, there is sometimes friction between what particular rules require of individuals and what the settings demand of them (see Tamanaha 2001). In the context of criminal actions, the phrase *criminogenic settings* is used to describe those settings that encourage rule-breaking actions (Wikström et al 2012).

Central to SAT's notion of exposure are potentially conflicting normative orders. Of particular relevance here is the conflict between the normative order of state law and the prevailing normative consciousness of actors within a specific context (MacCormick 2007). In the context of policing, researchers have drawn attention to the normative order of so-called 'police culture' with its distinctive logics and values that shape how police officers approach their work and how they orient themselves to the formal rules governing what they do. The main features of this normative order include cynicism, masculinity, suspicion, pessimism, a sense of social isolation, and solidarity among officers (Bowling, Reiner and Sheptycki 2019). The emphasis on solidarity breeds among officers a 'code of silence' which sometimes justifies both the breaking of rules and the refusal to report misconduct. The conclusions of the Royal Commission which investigated corruption within the New South Wales police underscored the power of the code of silence among police officers:

> Almost without exception officers approached by the Commission initially denied ever witnessing or engaging in any form of corrupt activity. Even with an undertaking that police would not be disciplined for failing to report certain forms of corruption, the offer of amnesty and the availability of protection against self-incrimination, officer after officer maintained this stand until presented with irrefutable evidence to the contrary. Each knew the truth, yet the strength of the code, and the blind hope that no one would break it, prevailed (Wood 1997: 155).

Accordingly, it is reasonable to imagine a continuum between *unethical settings* and *ethical settings* of policing. In predominantly unethical settings, the code of silence will form the dominant moral context for officers. Even though officers witness misconduct, they will find in their everyday experiences that misconduct is not reported. What they might find is that ridicule, reprisals, exclusion and loss of esteem await officers who report misconduct by colleagues. Based on the claims made by Situational Action Theory, this lack of exposure to misconduct reporting in unethical settings will inhibit the willingness of officers to act otherwise. Thus, analysing data from a survey of 604 police officers in the United States, Kutnjak Ivković, Haberfeld and Peacock (2018) found that officers expressed a willingness to report misconduct if they believed other officers would do so. In predominantly ethical settings, on the other hand, exposure to misconduct will be low but reporting will be high; misconduct reporting is encouraged, experienced and rewarded.

In conclusion, Situational Action Theory is a theory of moral action. Central to such actions are people's propensities – that is, personal morality and an ability to exercise self-control – and how propensities interact with the settings or the moral contexts in which they operate. The aim of this chapter is to apply the theory to ethical actions and intentions by police officers. In doing so, I postulate that misconduct reporting is also a moral act likely to be shaped by similar personal and situational variables.

POLICING AND POLICE MISCONDUCT IN GHANA

Ghana is a country of 30 million people located in West Africa. It was a British colony until political independence in 1957, under the leadership of Kwame Nkrumah. The police as a professional entity were the brainchild of Governor George Maclean, the colonial governor of the Gold Coast (as Ghana was formerly known) between 1830 and 1844. British colonialism was a predatory economic enterprise with its own social order needs. The object of colonial law was to establish, facilitate and protect the extraction of resources from the Gold Coast (Tankebe 2008, 2013). The colonial police were created to enforce this new order and to protect its administrators. As Killingray (1991: 123) argues, colonial policing in Ghana 'had little to do with serving the community and everything to do with upholding the authority of the colonial state'. This colonialist logic of protecting property and the propertied classes has persisted throughout the post-colonial period. Policing continues to be characterised by selective enforcement and subservience to political elites (Tankebe 2013).

A recurrent feature of police–public interactions is misconduct by police officers. Among public institutions, Ghanaians consistently rate the police as the most corrupt. In a national public survey in 2019, 60.9 per cent of 2,260 Ghanaians perceived 'most' or 'all' of police officers to be corrupt (Afrobarometer 2021). Out of 1,036 people who answered a question on payment of bribes to 'avoid problem with police', 42.8 per cent responded in the affirmative. In 2021, a survey of 14,843 Ghanaians by the United Nations Office on Drugs and Crime reported that 53.2 per cent of those who had contact with police officers had paid a bribe (UNODC 2022). This was the highest among all the institutions covered. Beyond these surveys, media reports document cases of police extortion. In May 2021, five police officers were detained on allegations of extorting money from civilians during night patrols (Citinews.com 2021). These actions contravene the formal rules of the police service that forbid officers from abusing their authority. As a result of perceptions and experiences of police corruption, confidence in the police is low, which, in turn, has spawned animosity between police officers and the public.

Regulations governing police conduct in Ghana stipulate that 'police officers must not engage in acts of torture, ill treatment and violence on citizens in order to solve a problem or case' (Ghana Police Service 2019). Yet, in practice, violence characterises aspects of Ghanaian policing. Some of the violence arises from police response to public concerns about violent crime (Tankebe 2013). Analysis of police records shows a steady increase in the rates of violent robberies since 2017. In that year, the country recorded 6.1 robberies per 100,000 population; this rose by nearly 10 per cent in two years to 6.6 in 2019 (Boakye and Tankebe 2020).

A feature of the police response to violent crime has been extrajudicial killings of suspected offenders. When these killings happen, the police issue a press statement presenting their version of the circumstances. This typically involves a claim of a shoot-out between officers and these suspects, which resulted in the killings. In the estimation of the police administration, these press statements constitute accountability. An unquestioning media and civil society, coupled with the absence of independent institutions, has allowed vacuous accountability gestures and police misconduct to persist. In exceptional cases where public pressure has occasioned an investigation, the police accounts have proven to be false. For example, in July 2018, police officers killed seven young men whom they said were armed robbers. An official committee of inquiry contradicted the police version of events and recommended the interdiction of the police involved (Citinews.com 2018).

Police accountability in Ghana lacks credible and independent actors. In England and Wales, there are two external bodies that seek to hold the police to account: the Independent Office of Police Conduct, which investigates complaints against individual police officers, and His Majesty's Inspectorate of Constabulary which conducts regular inspections of police forces to improve performance. In Ghana, by contrast, accountability is mainly internal:[2] members of the public must lodge complaints at their local police stations or directly with the national headquarters for investigations by a unit called the Police Professional Standards Bureau. The Ghana Police Service, which is a

[2] The Commission on Human Rights and Administrative Justice occasionally visits police stations to inspect the conditions of police cells. However, this is not a core mandate of the Commission. The Parliamentary Committee on Defence and Interior represents another layer of accountability. However, this aspect of its mandate remains opaque. Moreover, it is accountability to political elites rather than to local communities.

centralised police organisation, say their 40,282 police officers 'shall rigorously oppose and combat all [acts of corruption or abuse of power]' (2019).[3] However, as the Bureau does not routinely publish reports on the sources of complaints received and the outcomes of its investigations, there is no information on the proportion of cases generated by officers who might be concerned about the conduct of their colleagues.

In a survey of 36 officers in Accra, Boateng and his colleagues (2019) found that the behaviours most considered to be unethical were corruption (47.2 per cent), excessive use of force (16.7 per cent), and drinking and sleeping on duty (11.2 per cent). When asked about the behaviours they believed their colleagues engaged in, the officers mentioned bribe-taking, nepotistic decision-making, and acceptance of favours. In another survey, Kwakye-Nuako et al (forthcoming) presented a series of scenarios to 88 police inspectors and superintendents and asked for their views on whether the misconduct depicted violated official policy and warranted reporting. One of the scenarios involved a failure by a supervisor to stop violence against a suspect.[4] The authors found that 86.1 per cent of inspectors and 77.8 per cent of superintendents believed the conduct violated organisational policy. When asked if they would report such behaviour, 78.4 per cent of inspectors and 77.8 per cent of superintendents said they would.

METHODS

The current study used cross-sectional survey data from a convenience sample of police officers in Accra, Ghana's national capital. The surveys were administered between July and August 2019 at three police stations. A research assistant visited a convenience sample of police stations across three police divisions: Nima, Madina and Adenta. Officers on duty were approached, the nature of the study explained to them, and they were asked if they would like to take part. If they agreed, the questionnaires were placed in an envelope and handed over to them. They completed and returned them to the local police station in a sealed envelope for collection. Some officers worked in the night shift and insisted on handing the questionnaires directly to the research assistant rather than leaving them at the station for collection the next day. The research assistant obliged them, retrieving some questionnaires as late as 9 pm. In all, 350 police officers

[3] The 40,282 represent the personnel strength of the Ghana Police Service as of July 2021, obtained by the author from the police. It comprises 28,611 males (71%) and 11,671 females (29%).

[4] The scenario read as follows: 'A police sergeant, without intervening, watches officers under his supervision repeatedly strike and kick a man arrested for child abuse. The man has previous child abuse arrests' (Kutnjak Ivković et al 2022: 8).

were invited to take part in the study; of these, 208 completed and returned their questionnaires, resulting in a response rate of 59.4 per cent. The experience of the officers ranged from one to 40 years, with a median of 13 years. Two-thirds were male and one-third female. In terms of rank, 73 per cent were junior officers (constables, corporals and sergeants) while 27 per cent were senior ranks (inspectors and superintendents).

Given that the data came from a convenience sample in three police divisions, it is difficult to say whether the views, experiences, decisions and actions of the 208 officers are representative of the population of Ghanaian police officers. For a representative sample, future studies would need to randomly select officers from a list of all officers, a near-impossible feat. Another important caveat is the fact that the samples come from an urban setting. The social worlds of rural officers in Ghana are likely to be different from those of their urban counterparts. Notwithstanding these data limitations, the study offers a unique opportunity to explore the relationship between personal and environmental factors in shaping the ethical behaviours of police officers.

Dependent Variables

I measured misconduct reporting in two ways. First, *whistleblowing actions* were measured with 10 items. The research participants were asked to indicate whether, within the 12 months preceding the study, they had reported a fellow officer for engaging in any of the following acts of misconduct: (i) always sleeping on duty; (ii) coming to work drunk; (iii) taking bribes; (iv) dropping a case because of 'connections'; (v) kicking, punching or slapping a suspect; (vi) refusing to record a case; (vii) insulting a victim of crime; (viii) refusing to arrest a suspect because the suspect is a friend or family member; (ix) detaining someone unlawfully; and (x) forcing a suspect to confess to a crime she or he did not commit. Each was measured on a binary response set (1 = no; 2 = yes). The variable 'Misconduct Reporting Actions' is a summation score of responses to the 10 items (Cronbach's alpha = .832, mean [*M*] = 1.093, standard deviation [*SD*] = .189).[5] However, the data were positively skewed (skewness = 2.153, standard error = .170). I therefore performed a log transformation, which reduced the skewness considerably (skewness = 1.166).

[5] When multiple items are used to measure a construct (such as the use of 10 items to measure 'Whistleblowing Actions'), it is important to establish that they are interconnected and do consistently reflect the construct being measured (Schmitt 1996). This is described as the reliability of a scale, and the Cronbach alpha is an index of this scale reliability. Its values range from 0.0 and 1.0. Although 'there is no sacred level of acceptable or unacceptable level of alpha' (Schmitt 1996: 353), a threshold of 0.7 is commonly used.

The second dependent variable measured *intentions* to report misconduct. I presented research participants with four scenarios on misconduct: (i) planting of evidence on a robbery suspect; (ii) forced confessions in a kidnapping case; (iii) a robbery case in which bribes were collected to terminate an investigation ('close a docket'); and (iv) another robbery case in which bribes were collected to enter a verdict of 'no further action' (colloquially, render the alleged robbery a 'foolish case'). Details of these scenarios are reproduced in Appendix A. Each scenario was followed by a single question, except in the second scenario where two questions were asked because it was designed to measure assault of suspects and forcible extraction of confessions. The response categories ranged from 0 = not likely at all to 3 = very likely. The variable 'Misconduct Reporting Intentions' is a summation score of responses to the five questions (Cronbach's alpha = .845, *M* = 2.259, *SD* = 1.030), with higher scores indicating a greater willingness to report misconduct.

Independent Variables

Propensity

Propensity is one of the two key concepts in Situational Action Theory. It combines two sub-scales: morality and self-control. To measure *morality*, or an officer's approval of misconduct reporting, officers were asked how 'good or proper' it was to report a colleague officer for engaging in the 10 misconduct instances previously indicated in 'Whistleblowing Actions'. Each item was measured with response categories ranging from 0 = Not good at all to 3 = Very good. The variable 'Morality' is a summation score of responses to the 10 questions (Cronbach's alpha = .912, *M* = 1.732, *SD* = .813), with higher scores indicating a greater approval of the morality of reporting misconduct.

Self-control was measured with the same eight items as used in empirical analyses of Situational Action Theory (see Wikström et al 2012). In those prior analyses, the responses had been coded to measure low self-control. In this study, I adopted the opposite approach by measuring high self-control, which has been linked to ethical actions among police officers (see Donner, Maskaly and Thompson 2018). Each item was measured with response categories ranging from 0 = strongly disagree to 3 = strongly agree. The variable 'Self-control' is a summation of responses to the eight items (Cronbach's alpha = .68, *M* = .848, *SD* = .418), with higher scores indicating ability to exercise greater self-control.

Exposure

Exposure is the second of the key concepts in Situational Action Theory. In SAT studies of criminal acts, a variety of measures is used to operationalise exposure, including peer criminal involvement.[6] Given my interest in the prosocial acts of misconduct reporting, I measured exposure to peer misconduct reporting. I asked the research participants whether they personally knew of cases in which any of their colleagues – specifically, officers they often spent time with on duty and worked with at their local station – had reported other officers for misconduct. They were asked to indicate how often, in total, that happened in the 10 misconduct instances previously indicated. Each item was measured with response categories ranging from 0 = no, never to 3 = yes, very often. The variable 'Misconduct reporting exposure' is a summation score of responses to the ten questions (Cronbach's alpha = .916, $M = 1.033$, $SD = .619$), with higher scores indicating more frequent misconduct reporting exposure.

BASIC FINDINGS

Extent of Whistleblowing Actions

The first question is the proportion of police officers who reported acts of misconduct to the authorities. An important cautionary note is required at the outset. Criminologists often say 'opportunity makes the criminal'; similarly, an exploration of the prevalence of misconduct reporting requires information on experiences of peer misconduct. If officers are not exposed to misconduct behaviours by their colleagues, there are no grounds for their morality to be activated or for them to report anything. This study was unable to capture this information. Consequently, the data presented in Table 1 should be viewed against the backdrop of this informational ignorance.

The data in Table 1 show variations in reporting prevalence across types of misconduct. Misconduct reporting happened least for acts of corruption – that is, those situations in which officers exercise their authority for private or organisational advantage (Kleinig 1996). Forcibly extracting confessions from suspects is a form of corruption sometimes described as 'noble cause corruption', and only 3.4 per cent indicated they had reported officers who engaged in such conduct. The officers also reported few cases of bribery and nepotistic decision-making (both 5.9 per cent). By contrast, misconduct relating to performance was relatively more often reported. Thus, 14.2 per cent indicated they had reported fellow officers who came to work drunk. Similarly, 16.2 per cent reported officers who refused to record cases brought to their attention. I also found that 14.8 per cent indicated they had reported officers for unlawful detention of civilians, while 13.2 per cent acted against police violence directed at suspects.

[6] For a review of the different ways exposure is operationalised in Situational Action Theory, see Pauwels, Svensson and Hirtenlehner (2018).

Table 1 Prevalence of Whistleblowing Actions (%)

Misconduct	Percentage
1. Not recording crimes (*n* = 204)	16.2
2. Unlawful detention (*n* = 203)	14.8
3. Drunkenness (*n* = 204)	14.2
4. Violence against suspects (*n* = 204)	13.2
5. Sleeping on duty (*n* = 202)	9.9
6. Victim abuse (*n* = 204)	8.8
7. Nepotistic nonarrest (*n* = 204)	7.8
8. Nepotistic case termination (*n* = 204)	5.9
9. Bribery (*n* = 204)	5.9
10. Forced confessions (*n* = 204)	3.4

The analyses have established the whistleblowing rates among the officers across a plurality of misconduct situations. What I have not determined yet is the extent to which officers react randomly or consistently across different misconduct situations. For example, does an officer report violence against suspects but not abuse of victims, or report bribery but not false confessions? To answer this question, I computed Cramer's V, a statistic which tests the strength of association between variables with two categories (McHugh 2018). The overall average strength of the associations for the 10 misconduct situations was .339. This can be expressed in percentage terms by taking the square of the value Cramer's V (ie, $.339^2$) which yields a result of .109 (or, 10.9 per cent). What this means is that a police supervisor's knowledge that fictional officer Betty blew the whistle in a given misconduct situation can only allow that supervisor to predict 10.9 per cent of her whistleblowing in another misconduct situation. I will return to this finding and its implications for the so-called situationist perspective of virtue ethics in moral philosophy.

Whistleblowing Intentions

I also sought to examine the commitment of the research participants to ethical policing by asking them to indicate their willingness to report misconduct. Table 2 presents descriptive statistics on this question across five unethical situations. Three clusters emerged based on a rank ordering of the responses to those situations, reflecting *high*, *medium* and *low* misconduct reporting cases. Reporting intentions were highest in bribe-taking: 61.1 per cent would report officers who took bribes to terminate investigations and 63.5 per cent would do the same if the reason for the bribery was to free criminal suspects. Police violence – whether in the form of the forcible extraction of 'evidence' from suspects or physical assault of suspects – was least likely to be reported. The proportion of officers who stated they would report such misconduct was 40 per cent and 47.2 per cent, respectively. Situated between the high and low reporting poles is planting of evidence: 50.5 per cent of the officers indicated they would report colleagues who engage in such conduct.

Pairwise t-test analyses showed the reporting differences between the three clusters were each statistically significant. Thus, officers were statistically more inclined to report bribery than they were to report violence against suspects or the planting of evidence on criminal suspects. The average reporting intention was also statistically greater in the case of planting of evidence than in violence against suspects. What I have established are differences between clusters. But how large are the differences? To answer that question, I computed Cohen's *d* (see Cohen 1988). The results showed the difference between high versus low clusters was substantial (.63) while the high versus medium clusters (.25) and medium versus low clusters (.30) differences were small. Overall, the analyses show variations in reporting intentions across different misconduct situations. I will return to explore potential explanations for this variability.

Table 2 Intentions to Blow the Whistle (%)

	Very unlikely	Unlikely	Unsure	Likely	Very likely
High Reporting					
Bribery to close case file (n = 203)	11.3	12.8	14.8	29.1	32.0
Bribery to free suspect (n = 195)	7.4	9.9	19.2	25.1	38.4
Medium Reporting					
Planting of evidence (n = 202)	16.3	15.8	17.3	22.3	28.2
Low Reporting					
Forced confessions (n = 195)	15.4	26.2	18.5	25.1	14.9
Assault of suspects (n = 203)	17.3	23.3	22.3	23.3	13.9

I have so far explored the proportion of officers who reported misconduct by their colleagues and those who resolved to do so. A bivariate analysis examined a possible association between reporting intentions and actions. The results were not statistically significant ($r = .11$, $p > .05$), implying that the two were not related. A multiple regression analysis, controlling for job experience and gender, confirmed the results of the bivariate analysis (b = .068, $p > .05$). In other words, an officer might resolve to report misconduct by colleagues, but such a resolution might not translate into actions. This is an important finding given that survey-based studies of whistleblowing by police officers had hitherto focused exclusively on intentions rather than actions (eg, Long et al 2013; Kutnjak Ivković et al 2022; Wolfe and Piquero 2011).

Moral Features of the Setting

In Situational Action Theory, the moral features of the setting constitute an immediate normative order or social environment of action. For police officers, there is not one normative order but variegated normative orders making competing and, often, conflicting moral demands on them. Consider the case of fictional officer Betty: she works at a local police department with its peculiar culture. But she is also a member of the anti-robbery squad and belongs to associations of women and of minority police officers. Each of these commitments constitute distinct normative orders that might conflict with the formal institutional normative order.[7] That being the case, the demands by the formal law for officers to blow the whistle on unethical colleagues might be constantly under pressure and contestation. Which normative order prevails at any particular space and time is likely unpredictable. Consequently, an important first step in explaining moral actions is information about the kind of normative order in which actions occur. To estimate the moral contexts, I asked the research participants to tell us how often they had known of cases in which fellow officers reported misconduct by colleagues. As previously indicated (see 'Independent Variables'), the officers were presented with 10 cases with a four-point response option that ranged from 0 (never) to 3 (very often). The data for exposure to reporting of each type of misconduct are displayed in Appendix B. In Figure 1 below, we present respondents' mean scores across all the items. These scores were categorised into three distinct ethical settings: *weak* (0.0–0.9); *moderate* (1–1.4); and *strong* (1.5–3).

I found that 45.4 per cent of the officers were policing in a weak ethical setting: that is, policing environments where very little misconduct reporting happens. At the opposite end, I found 19.8 per cent of the officers operated in environments where misconduct reporting was commonplace. I have described such an environment as a strong ethical setting. Between the two poles is located moderate ethical settings in which 34.8 per cent of officers operate: here, misconduct reporting is infrequent. This infrequency suggests uncertainty and unpredictability.

[7] This is further complicated by other moral commitments officers have outside the police department. These might be commitments to family or kin groups, which might require officers sometimes to act in ways that contradict their professional obligations.

The implication is that an officer will need to make a significant time investment in a search for information about the safety of blowing the whistle on unethical actions. There is the risk that officers find such efforts to negotiate the moral context burdensome, becoming more prone to its dictates than act against it.

Figure 1 Moral Settings based on level of exposure to whistleblowing actions

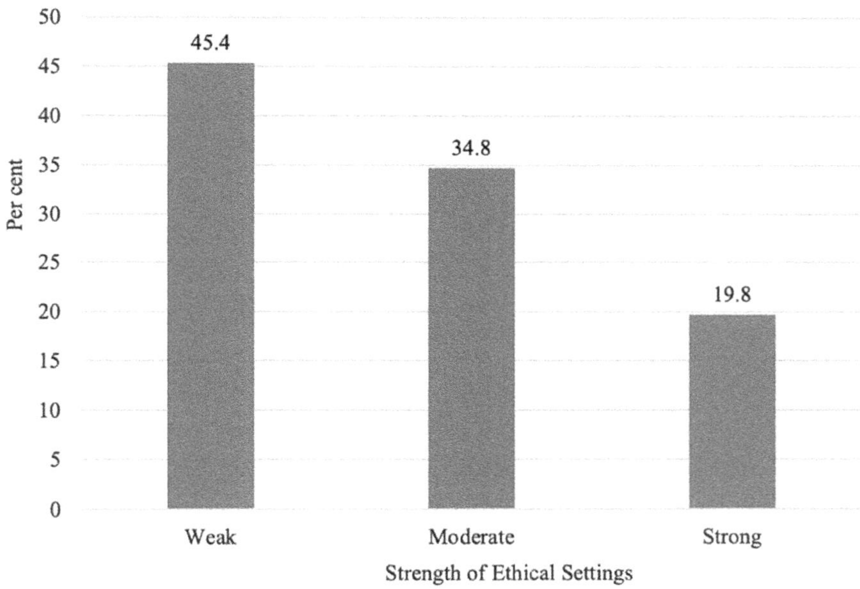

MULTIVARIATE ANALYSES

In this section, I present a series of multivariate regression analyses on misconduct reporting *actions* and *intentions*. This type of analysis can help to establish the unique influence of each of the independent variables on the dependent variable while controlling for other variables included in the analysis. Therefore, when a variable emerges as statistically significant, a researcher can be confident that this is not based on the other variables (Hutcheson and Sofronniou 1999). Table 3 and Table 4 present the standardised correlation coefficients (b), standard errors, and significance levels for each independent variable. Each 'model' is a separate multivariate analysis of certain included variables, showing what is significant when only those variables are included in the model; variables not included are shown with a dash. Variables with asterisks against their corresponding b-values are statistically significant – that is to say, they have some unique influence on the dependent variable. I also report the adjusted R-squared value for each model.[8] Consistent with SAT analytical approaches, z-scores were computed for all the substantive research variables.

Whistleblowing Actions

Table 3, Model I explores the effects of morality on misconduct reporting actions, controlling for gender and length of service. Consistent with SAT propositions, I found that the stronger officers' approval of misconduct reporting, the more likely they were to report misconduct ($b = .180$, $p < .05$). However, the adjusted R-squared value of 4.9 per cent suggests that the explanatory power of morality is very low. In Model II, I examined separately the role of self-control, and I found no evidence that greater self-control was associated with misconduct reporting behaviour. Model III considers, simultaneously, the effects of both morality and self-control: the former's influence persists while the latter continues to show no influence. Next, I combine morality and self-control into an additive measure of propensity (Model IV): the evidence shows propensity is positively associated with misconduct reporting behaviour ($b = .196$, $p < .01$). In other words, as the propensity to report misconduct increased, the likelihood that an officer reported misconduct also increased. This suggests that the influence of propensity on misconduct reporting behaviour may be driven solely by personal morality, with the ability to exercise self-control having a limited role.

Situational Action Theory proposes that people's moral actions can be explained in terms of their exposures to settings that are conducive to such actions. Model V tests this claim by estimating the role of the moral features of the officers' ethical settings. The data showed that the more the research participants were exposed to moral contexts that encouraged misconduct reporting, the more likely they were to report misconduct behaviour by colleagues ($b = .376$, $p < .001$). This is consistent with the SAT proposition that normative contexts influence moral actions. The R-squared values also showed that exposure to pro-reporting settings explained a greater share of the misconduct reporting behaviour of the officers (19.4 per cent: Model V) than propensity did (8.8 per cent: Model IV).

Models VI and VII bring together propensity and exposure variables in the same analysis. The aim was to examine whether they had an influence on misconduct reporting actions that were independent of each other. The data showed that the effects reported earlier for personal morality washed out,

[8] Adjusted R-squared provides information on the explanatory power of regression models; that is to say, how much of a dependent variable a model can explain. Its value ranges from 0.0 to 1.0; a value of 0.3 suggests that a regression model explains 30% of the dependent variable. This means that the larger the value, the stronger the explanatory power of a model.

while self-control continued to show no statistical significance (see Model VI). Exposure, on the other hand, exhibited a dominant influence on misconduct reporting (b = .346, $p < .001$). In Model VII the additive measure of propensity (rather than separate measures of morality and self-control) was used, and it emerged again that exposure was statistically significant (b = .350, $p < .001$), but propensity was not.

Finally, in Model VIII, I explore the SAT claims that moral actions are the outcome of an interaction between propensity and exposure. To test this, I introduced an interaction term between the two variables.[9] However, given that only personal morality demonstrated any effect, but self-control did not, the interaction was limited to personal morality and exposure. As indicated in Table 3, the interaction term was not statistically significant. The inability of the analysis to detect interaction effects might be an artefact of the kind of data used. Testing interaction effects in Situational Action Theory ideally requires data on the space–time convergence of actions and exposure (Wikström, Mann and Hardie 2018). Such data permit researchers to 'locate particular people in particular settings at particular times and tell us whether or not they committed [certain acts] in those particular settings at those particular times' (Wikström, Mann and Hardie 2018: 15). Survey-based data of the kind used in the current study are limited in measuring such convergence; hence the test was not optimal.

Across all the models, there is no evidence that the gender of the officers surveyed affected the act of misconduct reporting. This suggests that misconduct reporting is not gendered. However, 'length of service' becomes (weakly) significant in Models VI–VIII. The more experienced the officer, the more likely they were to report misconduct by their colleagues. Instructively, the influence of length of service emerges when one or other of the 'Propensity' variables is introduced. An exploration of the data revealed a statistically significant association between propensity and length of service ($r = .118$, $p < .05$): the more experienced the officer, the greater the propensity to report misconduct. Given the strong correlation between length of service and rank, the finding might be an artefact of supervisory responsibility. That is, more experienced officers are senior officers with supervisory responsibility, hence they may have a greater feeling of obligation to act when confronted with misconduct by junior officers (see Westmarland and Rowe 2018).

[9] In interaction analysis, one focuses on the joint or simultaneous influence of two or more independent variables on a dependent variable. It, therefore, provides information on whether those independent variables work together to produce an effect. In our current context, an interaction analysis seeks to establish whether propensity and exposure operate jointly to influence whistleblowing actions.

Table 3 OLS Regression Analysis on Whistleblowing Actions

	Model I b (SE)	**Model II b (SE)**	**Model III b (SE)**	**Model IV b (SE)**	**Model V b (SE)**	**Model VI b (SE)**	**Model VII b (SE)**	**Model VIII b (SE)**
Gender	–.113 (.156)	–.135 (.158)	–.129 (.145)	–.138 (.143)	–.131 (.134)	–.121 (.137)	–.123 (.134)	–.116 (.133)
Length of Service	.063 (.009)	.091 (.009)	.134 (.009)	.144 (.009)	.162 (.008)	.142* (.008)	.144* (.008)	.145* (.008)
Morality	.180* (.074)	---	.193* (.074)	---	---	.083 (.073)	---	---
Self-control	---	.133 (.072)	.045 (.071)	---	---	.049 (.067)	---	---
Propensity	---	---	---	.196 ** (.080)	---	---	.108 (.078)	.114 (.077)
Exposure	---	---	---	---	.376*** (.062)	.346*** (.065)	.350*** (.063)	.331*** (.064)
Propensity x Exposure	---	---	---	---	---	---	---	.116 (.060)
F-statistic	4.279**	3.339*	5.552***	7.062***	16.060***	9.991***	12.754***	10.940***
Adjusted R^2	.049	.036	.089	.088	.194	.195	.200	.209
N	189	187	186	188	188	186	188	188

Note: *$p<.05$, **$p<.01$, ***$p<.001$.

The data presented above showed that, in terms of whistleblowing actions, personal morality mattered but not self-control. It also emerged that the personal morality effects were limited and appeared to evaporate once exposure was considered. This evaporation provides prima facie evidence that the moral features of the settings of officers mediate the effects of propensity as measured by personal morality. To investigate this, I conducted a mediation analysis.[10] A mediation analysis examines whether the effects of one variable on another – say, X on Y – depends on a third variable, Z. This 'third variable' is a mediator; it helps researchers to understand why X has an influence on Y (see Baron and Kenny 1986). When applied to the current analysis, it will mean finding out whether the influence of an officer's *personal morality* on misconduct reporting depends on her *exposure* to misconduct reporting by other officers. The results, as displayed in Figure 2, confirm that this is indeed the case: officers who believe it is right to act against misconduct are more likely to do so if they witness, or believe, that other officers do act against misconduct.[11] In other words, personal morality translates into action when the moral features of the settings encourage misconduct reporting.

Figure 2 A Model of Police Whistleblowing Actions

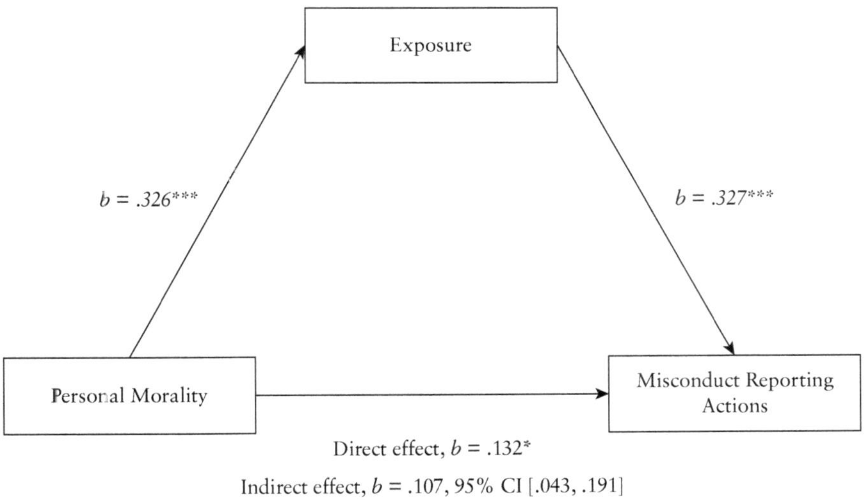

Whistleblowing Intentions

Next, I estimated separate models for misconduct reporting *intentions* using a series of ordinary least squares regression models (Table 4). The rationale

[10] The analysis uses Hayes's PROCESS macro in SPSS.
[11] The results remained unchanged when the combined measure of propensity was used.

was to establish whether Situational Action Theory can help us explain the willingness of officers to report misconduct by colleagues. Model I examined the effects of personal morality while controlling for gender and length of service. The model accounted for 19.4 per cent of the variance in misconduct reporting intentions. It showed that personal morality was a statistically significant predictor of such intentions (b = .334, $p < .001$). That is to say, the more the officers were morally approving of misconduct reporting, the greater their expressions of intent to report misconduct. Model II explored the effects of self-control, and the evidence showed that the stronger the self-control of officers, the greater the intention to report misconduct (b = .334, $p < .001$). The effects of personal morality and self-control persisted when both were considered simultaneously in Model III, implying that their effects on misconduct reporting intentions were independent of each other. In Model IV, personal morality and self-control were combined to create an overall propensity scale; the results showed that the stronger the propensity to report misconduct, the greater the intention to report misconduct (b = .474, $p < .01$). This supports the view of Situational Action Theory that propensity matters for people's intentions to engage in moral actions.

Does exposure to examples of misconduct reporting affect police officers' intentions to act ethically? This is the question answered in Model V. There was evidence that such an exposure does matter: the more officers were exposed to misconduct reporting, the greater their intentions to report misconduct by colleagues (b = .235, $p < .01$). However, unlike the propensity models that accounted for as much as 22 per cent of misconduct reporting intentions, the exposure model explained only 5.3 per cent. This suggests that exposure is a comparatively weaker explanation for officers' ethical intentions.

In Model VI, the potential effects of personal morality, self-control and exposure are considered simultaneously. There was evidence that personal morality and self-control showed statistically significant effects, but the effects reported for exposure diminished. This washing out of the effects of exposure persisted when the combined measure of propensity was used rather than the individual elements. Finally, in Model VIII, the SAT claim of interaction effects between exposure and propensity was tested. Consistent with the findings in Table 3 for reporting actions, there was no evidence that misconduct reporting intentions are the outcome of an exposure-propensity interaction (but see Wikström, Mann and Hardie 2018: 15). A noteworthy finding in this model is that both exposure and propensity proved statistically significant. However, in comparison with Model V, the size of the regression coefficient for exposure was much reduced.

Table 4 OLS Regression Analysis on Whistleblowing Intentions

	Model I b (SE)	**Model II** b (SE)	**Model III** b (SE)	**Model IV** b (SE)	**Model V** b (SE)	**Model VI** b (SE)	**Model VII** b (SE)	**Model VIII** b (SE)
Gender	.007 (.142)	−.050 (.150)	−.008 (.141)	−.012 (.139)	−.033 (.152)	−.006 (.140)	−.006 (.137)	−.012 (.138)
Length of Service	.012 (.009)	.088 (.009)	.012 (.008)	.026 (.008)	.086 (.009)	−.002 (.008)	.006 (.008)	.004 (.008)
Morality	.453*** (.068)	---	.377*** (.072)	---	---	.334*** (.075)	---	---
Self-control	---	.334*** (.069)	.200** (.069)	---	---	.212** (.069)	---	---
Propensity	---	---	---	.474** (.079)	---	---	.447*** (.080)	.446*** (.080)
Exposure	---	---	---	---	.235** (.070)	.119 (.067)	.133 (.065)	.145* (.066)
Propensity x Exposure	---	---	---	---	---	---	---	−.069 (.063)
F-statistic	16.151***	9.100***	14.694***	18.723***	4.513**	12.353***	15.219***	12.411***
Adjusted R^2	.194	.115	.227	.220	.053	.234	.232	.233
N	189	187	187	189	188	186	188	188

Note: *$p<.05$, **$p<.01$, ***$p<.001$.

Given the findings in Models VI–VIII, I examined a conjecture that propensity mediates the influence of exposure on misconduct reporting intentions. Another mediation analysis was, therefore, conducted. The results presented in Figure 3 confirm that the relationship between exposure to misconduct reporting and misconduct reporting intentions is mediated by propensity. In other words, being exposed to misconduct reporting by peers has the effect of inducing among officers a propensity to report misconduct, which, in turn, affects their intentions to act against such conduct.

Figure 3 A Model of Whistleblowing Intentions

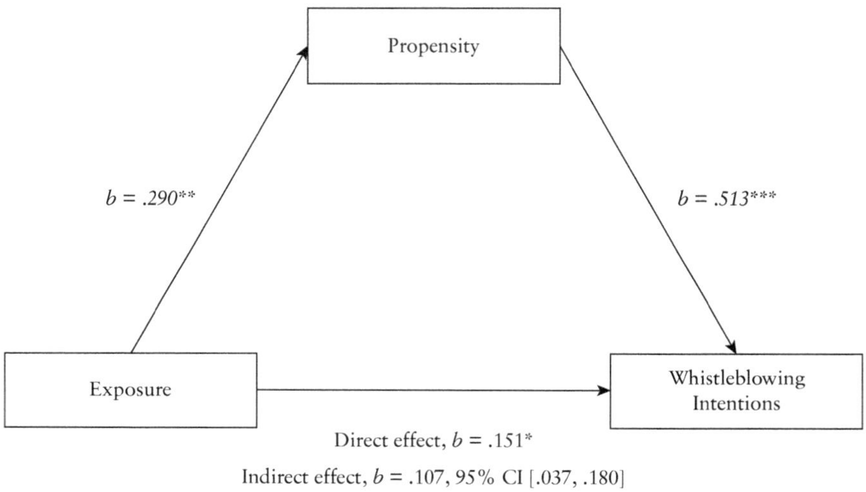

DISCUSSION AND CONCLUSION

Unethical police behaviours are costly. The cost can be estimated in the loss of human lives, the humiliation of citizens and in financial pay-outs by police organisations (Washington Post 2022; Bell 2017). Another aspect of the cost is the damage to confidence in the police and in democratic governance (Desmond, Papachristos and Kirk 2016; Tankebe 2010; Cruz 2015) and in the significant threats to social order through widespread public protests demanding better accountability and better justice for the victims of police misconduct. Preventing these costs requires police officers to blow the whistle on their unethical colleagues. Yet police scholars document that whistleblowing is the exception in policing. However, given the justice costs of unethical policing, criminologists ought to take seriously the task of understanding police whistleblowing behaviours. This was the task for this chapter, and to accomplish it, I sought to apply Situational Action Theory to misconduct reporting actions and intentions by a convenience sample of Ghanaian police officers.

Two sets of findings emerged from the ethical analyses. The first concerns the type of normative order within which the research participants operate, and the prevalence of misconduct reporting actions and intentions. Only one in five of the Ghanaian police officers studied operated in strong ethical environments – defined as those in which misconduct was frequently reported. Most officers worked in weak or moderate ethical settings: they never or only infrequently encountered misconduct reporting. When presented with misconduct vignettes, the research participants imagined themselves most likely to report bribe-taking by officers, and least inclined to report violence against criminal suspects or forcible extraction of confessions from criminal suspects (Table 2). The proportion of the police officers who indicated they had blown the whistle on misconduct ranged from 3.4 per cent of officers in the case of forcible extraction of confession from criminal suspects to 16.2 per cent of officers in the case of refusal to record cases reported to the police (Table 1). Whether these rates are low or high is difficult to establish given the lack of information on the number of misconduct cases the officers might have encountered. However, I also found that the ability to predict acts of whistleblowing in a given misconduct situation from another situation was weak. Whistleblowing appeared random rather than cross-situationally consistent.

How are the variations in the distribution of misconduct reporting behaviours across types of misconduct cases to be explained? The data do not allow any firm answers. However, it is possible to offer some reasoned conjectures. First, injunctions to act ethically can sometimes be 'neutralised' or 'cancelled' by other considerations (Sreenivasan 2013: 301). The consideration may be one of self-interest – a conscious decision to put one's 'desires and preferences ahead of morality' (Price 2006: 28). Within police departments, norms of varying strength can emerge around the reporting of different classes of unethical behaviours. Compliance with such norms may promise officers esteem among colleagues, a social capital they might consider highly beneficial. Contrariwise, the fear of ostracism and other informal sanctions often work to ensure that not all unethical behaviours are equally reportable or reported.

Another reason for the low and random acts of whistleblowing might concern how officers perceive misconduct (Westmarland and Rowe 2018). People's behaviour in a given situation is often variable and unpredictable because it depends on the subjective meanings and interpretations of that situation (Griffin and Ross 1991). Ross and Nisbett (1991/2011: 95) refer to this as an 'actor's construal of the situation'. This subjectivity means actors can sometimes hold 'false moral beliefs' about certain actions (Sreenivasan 2013). In his accounts of ethical failures, Price (2006) argues that power-holders often make two cognitive mistakes: first, mistakes concerning '*what types* of actions are morally permissible or right', or 'why certain kinds of actions are wrong' (Price 2006: 19). Thus, taking bribes from criminal suspects, drunkenness, or refusal to record cases might be viewed as particularly wrong. These behaviours threaten to undermine the police mandate of crime prevention and justice for victims and might even jeopardise the safety of other officers. However, forcible extraction of confessions or violence against criminal suspects might be viewed as a necessary 'dirty means' to achieve the 'good' of 'justice' for victims and society (see Klockars 1980; Westmarland and Rowe 2018); hence, this does not warrant reporting.

The second cognitive mistake identified by Price (2006: 19) relates to the 'moral status of *individuals*, especially to beliefs about their place within the moral community and the extent to which these individuals are subject to the rights and responsibilities that membership implies'. It follows that officers might mistakenly believe that moral obligations regarding due process and respect for the rights of suspects do not apply equally to all criminal suspects. Consequently, the sample of Ghanaian police officers might have held the view that robbery suspects, for example, stood outside the domain of moral commitment.

The second set of findings concerns the applicability of Situational Action Theory to whistleblowing by police officers. I found evidence that such an application is warranted. A key argument of the theory concerns interaction effects between propensity (person) and exposure (situation). The analysis found no evidence of this interaction effect. What did emerge was evidence of a mediation effect. This mediation takes a different form depending on whether the analysis focuses on the ethical actions or the ethical intentions of police officers. In the analysis of *ethical actions*, the evidence suggests a perception-choice process in which the exposure of police officers to pro-whistleblowing settings mediates the effects of their whistleblowing propensity. In other words, the moral features of the setting shape the influence of the ethical dispositions of the officers.

However, where the analyses are focused on the *ethical intentions* of police officers, the causal direction of person (propensity) and situation (exposure) is reversed. Here, propensity holds a greater sway: the misconduct reporting intentions of police officers are shown to be the outcome of a perception-choice process in which reporting propensity partially mediates the effects of exposure to misconduct reporting (*cf* Wikström et al 2012: 11). When I explored the data on reporting actions, it emerged that personal morality, but not self-control, was relevant. For misconduct reporting intentions, both self-control and personal morality proved relevant explanatory variables. Thus, consistent with findings reported by Donner, Maskaly and Thompson (2018), officers with strong self-control imagine themselves acting against unethicality should the opportunity arise. However, and contrary to past research (eg, Long et al 2013), the overall finding is that personal factors swamp situational factors in misconduct reporting intentions.

The evidence presented in this chapter advances understanding of the nature of ethical actions by police officers. The dominant influence of the ethical settings of the surveyed officers on their self-reported actions implies that such moral actions are best conceived as social dilemmas in the sense that they denote a 'situation in which individuals make independent choices in an interdependent situation' (Ostrom 1997: 3). Individual officers must choose how to resolve the transnational ethical problem of misconduct reporting. However, these choices are shaped by what they know other officers are likely to do in such situations. Bicchieri (2017) argues that observing how others behave creates for us expectations about their future likely behaviour and reactions to our actions, which, in turn, shape our decisions. Viewed this way, misconduct reporting is a collective action problem (see Persson, Rothstein and Teorell 2013; Robert and Arnab 2013; Tankebe 2019). Individual police officers might know that reporting misconduct by colleagues is for the collective good of their profession. When reporting leads to action against unethical officers, it will enhance police legitimacy, and the confidence the public have in the police; it can also improve their safety on the job by reducing the resentment and antagonism that misconduct breeds. Yet, they might resile from reporting if they do not trust that others will do so. 'If most officers at my local station don't report misconduct, why should I?' (*cf* Persson, Rothstein and Teorell 2013). Moreover, officers might feel compelled to maintain silence for fear of social ostracism for going against group norms (Wood 1997).

Situational Action Theory is a theory about morality and person–situation interactions. Given this, the findings produced here contribute to some sociological and moral philosophical debates. Within sociology, the debate concerns the relationship between agency and structure in social action. According to Mouzelis (2008), the relationship is not constant but highly variable, both at the level of theory and practice. Sometimes, actors orient themselves to structures in a taken-for-granted manner, regularly following the rules governing their social environments. They do not routinely interrogate the rules, raising questions about their legitimacy, desirability and utility. Police officers, for example, do not ask themselves every day whether they should obey the institutional requirement to wear a uniform. In other cases, actors adopt what Mouzelis calls an orientation of 'distancing strategizing'. That is to say, actors do distance themselves from the rules of their social environments due to a variety of strategic reasons. The distancing can arise from the fact that actors do interact with others and are influenced by the 'unfolding interactive situation' (Mouzelis 2008: 122; see also Crossley 2011). The evidence presented in this chapter is congruent with this view: the Ghanaian police officers owed their relative lack of whistleblowing actions to situational norms. Consequently, the evidence reinforces Crossley's (2011: 1) argument that attempts to understand social life must focus on 'the network of social relations and interactions between actors'.

Within moral philosophy, the findings speak, to some extent, to the situationist critique of virtue ethics. To account for people's actions, virtue ethics assigns primacy to character traits, defined as 'a reliable disposition a person has to behave in certain characteristic ways' (Sreenivasan 2013: 291). People differ in their dispositions and these differences are said to explain differences in their behaviours (Harman 1999). If people possess a certain character trait, they will be expected to act it out in the relevant situation 'even under substantial pressure to moral failure' (Doris 2002: 1). In the context of the current study, a police officer who has the character trait of ethicality will be expected to act ethically when confronted with misconduct opportunities. Situationism questions the empirical basis for virtue ethics, arguing instead that researchers must look to variations in situations rather than dispositions if they seek to explain differences in behaviour (Doris 2002; Harman 1999). According to Sreenivasan (2013: 304), the situationist critique of virtue ethics is double-sided: that '*most subjects lack some cross-situationally consistent character trait*', and that '*situational variables have a powerful effect on behaviour*' (emphasis original). The findings presented in this study lend support to both aspects of the situationist critique: the Ghanaian police officers surveyed showed inconsistency in their whistleblowing actions across the plurality of misconduct situations covered. The whistleblowing actions of the officers were also found to be shaped not by their dispositions but by the moral settings in which they operated. In other words, whatever whistleblowing dispositions officers have, situations appear to have the final say.

It cannot be concluded, as Harman (1999: 316) does, that 'there is no empirical basis for the existence of character traits' (for criticisms of situationism, see Kamtekar (2004) and Sreenivasan (2013)).[12] The data analysed showed the Ghanaian police officers had ethical dispositions, but situational variables eclipsed those ethical dispositions. This raises questions about the strength rather than the existence of character traits. In other words, if fear of ostracism by fellow officers and of a reputation for being a 'snitch' tames character, it only implies a lack of courage to act steadily and to do the right thing consistently.[13] Given this, police training can help to develop and strengthen the kind of character that is not hostage to unethical situational demands. However, training alone is emphatically insufficient; it must be combined with strategies to communicate examples of misconduct reporting by officers and the institutional responses to such reports. By making such information accessible to officers, police supervisors and managers could signal to officers a culture of commitment to ethical policing, and that the police organisation values the reporting of misconduct.

After I submitted the first version of this chapter to the editors, the London Metropolitan Police Service (MPS) released an interim report on its handling of misconduct by officers. The author of the report, Baroness

[12] There is strong criminological evidence to refute the situationist critique. Take, eg, the Peterborough Adolescent Delinquency Study. It is a longitudinal study of a random sample of 716 young people from the ages of 12 to 24 in Peterborough (United Kingdom), interviewing them nine times during that period. The evidence from the study consistently shows that both the criminal propensities of the young people and the moral settings of the situation affect their criminal acts (see Wikström et al 2012). The Peterborough study is the empirical basis for Situational Action Theory, and tests of the theory in other countries have produced findings consistent with its propositions (see Kokkalera, Marshall and Marshall 2020; Schils and Pauwels 2014).

[13] I am grateful to Jonathan Jacobs for this observation.

Casey, was asked to review the MPS misconduct system after the kidnap, rape and murder of Sarah Everard. The interim report focused on institutional responses to whistleblowing by officers and staff. A total of 18,589 allegations against 8,917 officers between April 2013 and March 2022 were reviewed. It was found that it took, on average, 350 days for the MPS to complete investigations into an allegation of misconduct. Officers who were interviewed as part of the review said supervisors often did not want to know about misconduct, hence attempted to talk officers out of blowing the whistle on colleagues; others said that 'the reporting of wrongdoing [had] been a harrowing and totally pointless exercise' (Casey Review 2022: 7). As the Review concluded: 'These experiences reflect a deep mistrust of the misconduct system. Any initiatives which aim to encourage [MPS] officers to report misconduct will continue to be undermined unless the system responds more effectively to those who have come forward' (Casey Review 2022: 7). This is a conclusion that very much aligns with the findings and conclusions of this chapter: without the appropriate institutional signals, officers are unlikely to act on their ethical dispositions by blowing the whistle on colleagues suspected of misconduct.

LIMITATIONS AND DIRECTIONS FOR FUTURE RESEARCH

The present study is not without limitations. First, the data came from a survey of a convenience sample of police officers in one city in Ghana. It is very much an open question as to how far the findings reported can be generalised to the rest of the country. Second, the study uses cross-sectional data to capture people's views and experiences, and their implications for misconduct reporting resolutions and actions. However, propensities and moral settings are not static. There is, therefore, a need for longitudinal studies that track changes in propensities and moral settings, and to specify the corresponding impact on acts of misconduct reporting. Third, a proper test of the interaction effects between propensity and exposure requires the application of the 'space–time budget methodology' developed by Wikström et al (2012). Applying the method will entail collecting data on the specific time officers were in particular settings (eg, on a shift at a police station or out on patrols in a particular community), their duties on that particular shift, the officers on that shift, whether or not officers were exposed to misconduct, and whether or not they reported such misconduct (*cf* Wikström, Mann and Hardie 2018). Police use of body-worn cameras offers an opportunity to collect such unique data on the moral settings of misconduct reporting actions. Future studies that address the issues highlighted above will advance understanding of police whistleblowing behaviours.

REFERENCES

Abbey, R (2000) *Charles Taylor* (Teddington, Acumen).

Afrobarometer (2021) *Ghana Round 8 Summary of Results*, available at: www.afrobarometer.org/publication/summary-results-afrobarometer-round-8-survey-ghana-2019-0/.

Baron, RM and Kenny, DA (1986) 'The Moderator–Mediator Variable Distinction in Social Psychological Research: Conceptual, Strategic, and Statistical Considerations' 51 *Journal of Personality and Social Psychology* 1173.

Bayley, DH (2005) *Changing the Guard: Developing Democratic Police Abroad* (Oxford, Oxford University Press).

Bell, MC (2017) 'Police Reform and the Dismantling of Legal Estrangement' 126 *Yale Law Journal* 2054.

Bicchieri, C (2017) *Norms in the Wild: How to Diagnose, Measure, and Change Social Norms* (Oxford, Oxford University Press).

Boakye, KE and Tankebe, J (2020) *Violent Crime in Ghana: Who is at risk, when and where? Analysis of Police Crime Statistics*, available at: africpgr.org/wp-content/uploads/2020/08/Africpgr-Research-Brief-Series_No-2_August-2020.pdf.

Boateng, FD, Makin, DA, Abess, G and Wu, G (2019) 'Speaking Out: Officers Speaking about Police Misconduct in Ghana' 92 *Police Journal* 21.

Bowling, B, Reiner, R and Sheptycki, J (2019) *The Politics of the Police*, 5th edn (Oxford, Oxford University Press).

Bradford, B and Quinton, P (2014) 'Self-legitimacy, Police Culture and Support for Democratic Policing in an English Constabulary' 54 *British Journal of Criminology* 1023.

Casey Review (2022) 'Interim Report on Misconduct', available at: www.met.police.uk/SysSiteAssets/media/downloads/met/about-us/baroness-casey-review/baroness-casey-review-interim-report-on-misconduct.pdf.

Citinews.com (2018) 'No Evidence 7 'Murdered' Asawase Youth Were Robbers' *Citinews* (19 November 2018), available at: citinewsroom.com/2018/11/no-evidence-7-murdered-asawase-youth-were-robbers-cttee/.

——(2021) '5 Police Officers Detained for Allegedly Extorting GHS 38000 from 2 People' *Citinews* (26 May 2021), available at: citinewsroom.com/2021/05/5-police-officers-detained-for-allegedly-extorting-ghs40000-from-2-people/.

Cohen, J (1988) *Statistical Power Analysis for the Behavioural Sciences* (Hillsdale, Lawrence Erlbaum Associates).

Crossley, N (2011) *Towards Relational Sociology* (Abingdon, Routledge).

Cruz, JM (2015) Police Misconduct and Political Legitimacy in Central America' 47 *Journal of Latin American Studies* 251.

Desmond, M, Papachristos, AV and Kirk, DS (2016) 'Police Violence and Citizen Crime Reporting in the Black Community' 81 *American Sociological Review* 857.

Donner, CM, Maskaly J and Thompson, KN (2018) 'Self-control and the Police Code of Silence: Examining the Unwillingness to Report Fellow Officers' Misbehavior among Multi-Agency Sample of Police Recruits' 56 *Journal of Criminal Justice* 11.

Doris, JM (2002) *Lack of Character: Personality and Moral Behavior* (Cambridge, Cambridge University Press).

Elster, J (2007) *Explaining Social Behavior: More Nuts and Bolts for the Social Sciences* (Cambridge, Cambridge University Press).

Ghana News Agency (2020) 'Police Administration Dismisses 28 Personnel over Misconduct' *Ghana News Agency* (8 September 2020), available at: www.gna.org.gh/1.18675677.

Ghana Police Service (2019) *Police Service Instructions* (Accra, Ghana Publishing Company).

Gottfredson, MR and Hirschi, T (1990) *A General Theory of Crime* (Stanford, CA, Stanford University Press).

Griffin, DW and Ross, L (1991) 'Subjective Construal, Social Inference, and Human Misunderstanding' 24 *Advances in Experimental Social Psychology* 319.

Harman, G (1999) 'Moral Philosophy Meets Social Psychology: Virtue Ethics and the Fundamental Attribution Error' 99 *Proceedings of the Aristotelian Society* 315.

Hirschi, T (1969) *Causes of Delinquency* (Berkeley, CA, University of California Press).

Hirtenlehner, H and Hardie, B (2016) 'On the Conditional Relevance of Controls: An Application of Situational Action Theory to Shoplifting' 37 *Deviant Behavior* 315.

Hutcheson, DG and Sofronniou, N (1999) *The Multivariate Social Scientist: Introductory Statistics Using Generalized Linear Models* (Sage, London).

Jordanoska, A (2018) 'The Social Ecology of White-Collar Crime: Applying Situational Action Theory to White-Collar Offending' 39 *Deviant Behavior* 1427.

Kamtekar, R (2004) 'Situationism and Virtue Ethics on the Content of our Character' 114 *Ethics* 458.

Killingray, D (1991) 'Guarding the Extended Frontier: Policing the Gold Coast, 1865–1913' in DM Anderson and D Killingray (eds), *Policing the Empire: Government, Authority and Control, 1830–1940* (Manchester, Manchester University Press).

Kleinig, J (1996) *The Ethics of Policing* (Cambridge, Cambridge University Press).

Klockars, CB (1980) 'The Dirty Harry Problem' 452 *Annals of the American Academy of Political and Social Science* 33.

Kokkalera, SS, Marshall, IH and Marshall, CE (2020) 'How Exceptional is India? A Test of Situational Action Theory' 15 *Asian Journal of Criminology* 195.

Kutnjak Ivković, S, Haberfeld, M and Peacock, R (2018) 'Decoding the Code of Silence' 29 *Criminal Justice Policy Review* 172.

Kutnjak Ivković, S, Maskály, J, Kule, A and Haberfeld, MM (2022) *Police Code of Silence in Times of Change* (Cham, Springer).

Kwakye-Nuako, CO, Maskály, J, Kutnjak Ivković, S, Afoakwah, R, Aboagye, B and Hammond, PA (2022) 'Do "the Best and the Brightest" of the Ghanaian Police need Further Integrity Education?' in S Kutnjak Ivković, J Maskály, CM Donner, IC Mraović and D Das (eds), *Exploring Contemporary Police Challenges: A Global Perspective* (London, Routledge).

Laurie, P (1970) *Scotland Yard* (New York, Holt, Rinehart and Winston).

Long, MA, Cross, JE, Shelley, TOC and Kutnjak Ivković, S (2013) 'The Normative Order of Reporting Police Misconduct: Examining the Roles of Offense Seriousness, Legitimacy, and Fairness' 76 *Social Psychology Quarterly* 242.

MacCormick, N (2007) *Institutions of Law: An Essay in Legal Theory* (Oxford, Oxford University Press).

McHugh, ML (2018) '*Cramér's V* Coefficient' in BB Frey (ed), *The SAGE Encyclopedia of Educational Research, Measurement, and Evaluation* (Thousand Oaks, CA, SAGE Publications Inc).

Mouzelis, N (2008) *Modern and Postmodern Social Theorising: Bridging the Divide* (Cambridge, Cambridge University Press).

Near, JP and Miceli, MP (1985) 'Organizational Dissidence: The Case of Whistle-blowing' 4 *Journal of Business Ethics* 1.

New York Times (2021) 'Court Vindicates Black Officer Fired for Stopping Colleague's Chokehold' *New York Times* (13 April 2021_, available at: www.nytimes.com/2021/04/13/nyregion/cariol-horne-police-chokehold.html?smid=em-share.

Noppe, J (2018) 'Are all police officers equally triggered? A test of the interaction between moral support for the use of force and exposure to provocation' 28 *Policing & Society* 605.

Ostrom, E (1997) 'A Behavioral Approach to the Rational Choice Theory of Collective Action: Presidential Address, American Political Science Association' 92 *American Political Science Review* 1.

Pauwels, LJ, Svensson, R and Hirtenlehner, H (2018) 'Testing Situational Action Theory: A Narrative Review of Studies Published between 2006 and 2015' 15 *European Journal of Criminology* 32.

Persson, A, Rothstein, B and Teorell, J (2013) 'Why Anticorruption Reforms Fail – Systemic Corruption as a Collective Action Problem' 26 *Governance* 449.

Price, T (2006) *Understanding Ethical Failures in Leadership* (Cambridge, Cambridge University Press).

Robert, I and Arnab, M (2013) 'Is Dishonesty Contagious?' 51 *Economic Inquiry* 722.

Ross, L and Nisbett, RE (1991/2011) *The Person and the Situation: Perspectives of Social Psychology* (London, Pinter & Martin Publishers).

Schils, N and Pauwels, L (2014) 'How Invariant is the Interaction Between Extremist Propensity and Exposure to Extremist Moral Settings in Sub Groups by Gender and Immigrant Background? Testing a Leading Hypothesis of SAT' 7 *Journal of Strategic Security* 27.

Schmitt, N (1996) 'Uses and Abuses of Coefficient Alpha' 8 *Psychological Assessment* 350.

Sreenivasan, G (2013) 'The Situationist Critique of Virtue Ethics' in DC Russell (ed), *The Cambridge Companion to Virtue Ethics* (Cambridge, Cambridge University Press).

Tamanaha, BZ (2001) *A General Jurisprudence of Law and Society* (Oxford, Oxford University Press).

Tankebe, J (2008) 'Colonialism, Legitimation, and Policing in Ghana' 36 *International Journal of Law, Crime and Justice* 67.

——(2013) 'In Search of Moral Recognition? Policing and Eudaemonic Legitimacy in Ghana' 38 *Law & Social Inquiry* 576.

——(2010) 'Public Confidence in the Police: Testing the Effects of Public Experiences of Police Corruption in Ghana' 50 *British Journal of Criminology* 296.

——(2014) 'The Making of "Democracy's Champions": Understanding Police Support for Democracy in Ghana' 14 *Criminology & Criminal Justice* 25.

——(2019) 'Cooperation with the Police Against Corruption: Exploring the Roles of Legitimacy, Deterrence and Collective Action Theories' 59 *British Journal of Criminology* 1390.

Taylor, C (1989) *Sources of the Self: The Making of the Modern Identity* (Cambridge, Cambridge University Press).

Tyler, TR, Callahan, PE and Frost, J (2007) 'Armed, and dangerous (?): Motivating rule adherence among agents of social control' 41 *Law & Society Review* 457.

UNODC (2022) *Corruption in Ghana*, available at: www.unodc.org/documents/corruption/Publications/2022/GHANA_-_Corruption_survey_report_-_20.07.2022.pdf.

Washington Post (2022) 'The Hidden Billion-dollar Cost of Repeated Police Misconduct' *Washington Post* (9 March 2022), available at: www.washingtonpost.com/investigations/interactive/2022/police-misconduct-repeated-settlements/.

Westmarland, L and Rowe, M (2018) 'Police Ethics and Integrity: Can a New Code Overturn the Blue Code?' 28 *Policing & Society* 854.

Wikström, P-OH and Bouhana, N (2017) 'Analyzing Radicalization and Terrorism: A Situational Action Theory' in G LaFree and JD Freilich (eds), *The Handbook of Criminology of Terrorism* (Oxford, Wiley).

Wikström, P-OH, Mann, RP and Hardie, B (2018) 'Young People's Differential Vulnerability to Criminogenic Exposure: Bridging the Gap Between People-and Place-Oriented Approaches in the Study of Crime Causation' 15 *European Journal of Criminology* 10.

Wikström, P-OH, Oberwittler, D, Treiber, KH and Hardie, B (2012) *Breaking Rules: The Social and Situational Dynamics of Young People's Urban Crime* (Oxford, Oxford University Press).

Wikström P-OH and Treiber, KH (2007) 'The Role of Self-control in Crime Causation: Beyond Gottfredson and Hirschi's General Theory of Crime' 4 *European Journal of Criminology* 237.

——(2016) 'Situational Theory: The Importance of Interactions and Action Mechanisms in the Explanation of Crime' in AR Piquero (ed), *The Handbook of Criminological Theory* (Chichester, Wiley).

Wolfe, SE and Piquero, AR (2011) 'Organizational Justice and Police Misconduct' 38 *Criminal Justice and Behavior* 332.

Wood, JRT (1997) *Royal Commission into the New South Wales Police Service, Final Report Volume I: Corruption* (Sydney, Government of the State of New South Wales).

APPENDIX A: SCENARIOS MEASURING WHISTLEBLOWING INTENTIONS

1. Ben is notorious for robberies in your district. Officers have arrested him two times, but in both cases the courts freed him because the evidence against him was weak. Two detectives decide to put a gun in his car, and then arrange for motor traffic officers to stop and search Ben's car. Ben was arrested for illegal possession of a gun. He was convicted and sent to prison. You have information about what the officers did [**Planting of Evidence**].
2. Police officers in your district suspect Max, Dan and Seth of kidnapping. The officers manage to arrest Max, but they did not find Dan and Seth. You are on duty when they brought Max to the station. The officers begin to beat Max so he will confess to the kidnapping and to tell them where they can find Dan and Seth [**Forced confession; assault of a suspect**].
3. It is the third time you have seen James come to your station asking after one of the detectives. James had his laptop stolen and the detectives had arrested a suspect. James comes to the station every week to get information about the status of his case. The detectives always tell him they are

still investigating the case and that he should come back later. One of your colleagues tells you that the detectives took a bribe from the suspect and closed the docket, so James is only wasting his time [**Bribery to close case file**].

4. Beye is arrested for armed robbery. You have information that the officer investigating the case met with Beye's friends and took money from them to make the case a 'foolish case'. How likely is it that you will report the officer for taking bribes to free a suspect? [**Bribery to free suspect**].

APPENDIX B: EXPOSURE TO MISCONDUCT REPORTING BY COLLEAGUES (%)

Does it often happen that some of your colleagues report officers for ...	Never	Sometimes	Often	Very often
Sleeping on duty (*n* = 207)	20.3	63.8	8.7	7.2
Drunkenness (*n* = 206)	16.0	64.6	10.2	9.2
Bribe-taking (*n* = 205)	26.8	57.1	9.3	6.8
Influence-peddling (*n* = 205)	21.0	54.6	18.5	5.9
Violence against suspects (*n* = 205)	24.4	52.7	15.6	7.3
Non-recording of crime (*n* = 206)	18.9	57.8	14.1	9.2
Victim abuse (*n* = 206)	29.1	53.4	11.7	5.8
Nepotism (*n* = 204)	27.5	51.5	12.7	8.3
Unlawful detention (*n* = 204)	20.1	54.4	15.7	9.8
False confessions (*n* = 202)	37.1	42.1	13.4	7.4

4

Morality, Motherhood and (Ex-)Prisoners' Children

CAROLINE LANSKEY, LUCY MARKSON, KAREN SOUZA, SOPHIE ELLIS, FRIEDRICH LÖSEL, AND JENNIFER BARTON-CROSBY*

INTRODUCTION

'Moral problems are problems of human relations' (Gilligan 1982: xix).

MOTHERS OF CHILDREN whose fathers are in prison are frequently beset by hardship, including material and financial constraints as a result of a drop in household income (Braman 2004; Lösel et al 2012), emotional strains linked to the need to take on sole responsibilities for looking after children (Fishman 1990) and social stigma as a result of their association with the father (Condry 2007; Miller 2003). This association can result in mothers' isolation from social networks (Souza et al 2021) and exposure to scrutiny and intervention by agencies of the state (Hairston 2003).

In these challenging circumstances, mothers are frequently faced with questions about what is the *right* thing to do. What, if anything, should they tell their children about the father's offence and prison sentence? How can they protect their children from the potentially stigmatising and hostile gaze of the outside world? To what extent should they try to maintain the children's relationship with the father in prison? In short, how can they ensure their children have a good life despite the varying hardships related to their father's imprisonment? Addressing these questions is a fundamental part of mothering children affected by paternal imprisonment, and while there is much normative guidance published about what mothers in such situations *should* do (eg, Prison Advice and Care Trust undated), there has been little investigation into how

* The FAIR study was funded by the Economic and Social Research Council. Many thanks go to Caitlin McCracken for her help with the coding of the mothers' data and her insightful analytical observations and to Newnham College Cambridge for their financial support of Caitlin's internship.

mothers in these situations navigate such issues in practice, nor a considered attempt to understand the varied reasons for their moral decision-making and practice.

The analysis in this chapter is informed by the theorising of relational sociologists such as Crossley (2011) and Abbott (2020), and in particular by Gilligan's (1982) ethic of care and the work of anthropologists of ethics. Although these approaches do not provide a comprehensive perspective on the topic, each of these strands of theorising offers a helpful perspective on moral action.

Relational sociologists take the sociological lens away from individuals or societies and instead focus it on 'networks of social relations and interactions between actors' (Crossley 2011: 1). They argue that key to understanding people's actions is to know 'the situations in which they find themselves, the others involved and the relations they enjoy with these others' (Crossley 2011: 2). Thus, in order to understand the actions of one person, including their moral actions, it is necessary to reference their relationships with others (Abbott 2020: 180). These relationships are conceptualised as a process of interactions, as too are the moral phenomena embedded within these interactions. Thus, 'a relational approach is able to provide a processual picture of moral action that is sufficiently dynamic to be able to account for the considerable variation and intersubjective emergence of moral practice' (Abbott 2020: 180).

Carol Gilligan pre-empted much of the theorising of relational sociologists in her work, *In a Different Voice* (1982). One of the studies which informed her theoretical argument explored the moral dimensions of women's decisions about whether or not to have an abortion. Gilligan demonstrated how the decisions these women reached were not the result of abstract philosophical reasoning but were born out of the 'messiness of relationally entangled practice' (Abbott 2020: 73). These women spoke 'in a different voice' about the moral thinking underpinning their decisions, focusing on the consequences for the wellbeing of others who would be affected rather than on abstract principles of right and wrong. Gilligan named this an ethic of care. She argued that previous studies of moral reasoning such as those by the psychologist and philosopher of moral development, Lawrence Kohlberg (1969) assumed a single moral perspective: an ethic of justice. This moral perspective focused on rights and rules and was based on principles of equality and reciprocity. In contrast, the moral perspective of the women in Gilligan's research focused on care and responsibility in relationships and was based on a principle of non-violence. Gilligan argued that gender played a role in the adoption of these perspectives and in her research found that men primarily adopted an ethic of justice and women an ethic of care (Gilligan and Attanucci 1988). While there has been critique of Gilligan's gendered analysis of moral reasoning (see eg, Friedman 1987; Hekman 1995) and a distancing from any implicit universalistic assumptions by Gilligan herself (Jorgensen 2007) there is also recognition of the salience of a care-oriented ethic in philosophical and empirical studies (eg, Noddings 1984; Baier 1987; Held 2006; Slote 2007). Indeed, while Kohlberg might not have fully agreed with Gilligan's representation of his thinking, he did acknowledge her alternative set of moral principles and considered they could coexist with his justice principles in his staged theory of moral development (Kohlberg 1986). Gilligan, however, maintained that her ethic of care constituted a different moral paradigm (for a fuller discussion of Gilligan and Kohlberg's perspectives, see Jorgensen 2007). Of particular relevance for this analysis is Baier's (1987) observation that Gilligan's ethic of care is informative for thinking about the moral decisions and actions of parents for whom 'the language of rights' provides insufficient guidance for the parental role. For parents, she argues, of equal importance to the virtue of justice is the 'the virtue, whatever its name, that ensures that each new generation is ... prepared for their adult lives' (Baier 1987: 54–55).

Gilligan (1982) noted that the relationships and interactions that shaped women's decisions were not only the immediate ones with partners or close family members and friends, but also their relationships with their local community and the wider society in which they lived including its norms and judgements. A further important observation from Gilligan's research was that moral decisions were shaped by the contingencies of circumstance. In her abortion study, these included when the choice to have an abortion existed and consideration of the strains a decision would put on a woman's emotional and material resources.

Gilligan's theorising developed out of three interview-based research studies in which participants were asked to reflect on their own decisions and hypothetical scenarios of moral dilemmas. Abbott (2020: 202) identifies such reflection as an important component of moral identity and action:

> [P]eople can and do reflexively engage with their own differentiated, individuated subjectivity in the course of giving direction to their action, and it is likewise true that interpreting one's place in a morally charged intersubjective world necessitates the capacity for evaluative judgements of social life of what is of worth, of what is the best course of action.

However, relational sociologists and anthropologists of ethics (eg, Lambek 2010; Mattingly 2011; Das 2012) argue that moral action is primarily embedded within the practices and routine decisions of everyday life: 'at the level of habituated ethical comportment' (Abbott 2020: 202).[1] For example, Veena Das' anthropological study of women's experiences of violence during the partition of India in 1947 found that the women frequently kept the pain of these experiences to themselves so that their children would not suffer: 'in their everyday

[1] Although some researchers distinguish between the terms 'ethics' and 'morality', in this chapter we follow Mattingly and Throop (2018) and use them interchangeably.

acts of endurance, they protected the children against knowledge they thought would be too hard for them to bear; they allowed life to be lived as best as they knew' (2012: 145). Das' research is interesting because it illustrates how the ordinary routinised moral practices of daily life are not fully explained by habits or tradition, for they can also be shaped by significant life-changing events, whether momentary or ongoing, whose effects persist 'tentacle-like' in the everyday. In order to understand the moral dimension of people's lives, therefore, there is a need

> to provide an explanation of how people come to be able to engage with morality in everyday life in practice on the one hand, while also being alive to the variable factors that mould and shape how such practice is engaged with on the other (Abbott 2020: 200–01).

The insights from these three theoretical strands serve as a useful starting point for thinking about the moral issues arising for mothers when the father of their children is serving or has served a prison sentence. They signal the importance of looking at the interactions which constitute the relationships between the mother and her children, the father, other family members and friends, and wider society. Das' research demonstrates how a significant life event such as paternal imprisonment may shape the practices of the everyday worlds of these mothers and children. Das and Gilligan also identify the relevance of a 'maternal morality' (Gilligan 1982), a moral identity shaped by the relational interactions of motherhood.

DATA AND ANALYSIS

The data for the present analysis come from the Families and Imprisonment Research (FAIR) study. This was a mixed-method prospective longitudinal study which traced the experiences of 54 families in England and Wales who experienced the imprisonment of the father. Ethical approval was received from the University of Cambridge Institute of Criminology's Board of Ethics and the National Research Committee of His Majesty's Prison and Probation Service. The FAIR study built on an earlier study, 'Risk and Protective Factors in the Resettlement of Imprisoned Fathers with their Families' (Lösel et al 2012), which was the first longitudinal study in Europe with a 'whole family approach'. It involved two interviews with mothers, fathers and children from these self-identified families: the first interview took place in the last four months before the father's release from prison; and the second interview was conducted within six months after he had been released. The interviews comprised qualitative open-ended questions and quantitative measures which aimed to capture the detail of individual family members' experiences and to identify similarities and differences in the collective experiences of families, mothers, fathers and children. A specific focus of the second wave was on the men's resettlement and family adaptation. For some results see, for example: Lanskey et al (2016); Lösel et al (2012); Markson et al (2015); and Souza et al (2015).

The FAIR study researchers interviewed members from the families again some six or seven years after the second interviews. This third round of interviews collected additional qualitative data on the families' experiences since the father's release and invited reflection on the longer-term effects of the father's imprisonment in their lives. A total of 36 mothers took part in this third wave and it is from their interview data that the present analysis is drawn. The interviews were held either in their homes or in a local public space such as a cafe or library. The interviews lasted on average between one and two hours and were recorded with the mother's consent. At the time of these interviews the mothers ranged in age from 28 to 54 years and the average age was 37 years old. The mothers were caring for between one and five children (most had two or three children). Ten were still in a relationship with the father and 26 were separated. Of the 26 mothers who were separated, 12 shared parenting responsibilities to varying extents.

As the interview questions did not explicitly address mothers' moral narratives about the father's imprisonment, a twofold analytical strategy drawing on Braun and Clark's (2006) and Gilligan's (1982) approaches to thematic analysis was adopted. First, the interview transcripts were reviewed and coded for references to decisions the mothers had taken and any related reflections which referred directly or indirectly to the rightness or wrongness of these decisions. These included decisions about how and what to tell the children and other people about the father's prison sentence, decisions about the child's contact with the father while he was in prison and afterwards, and responses to the judgements and interventions from others which were linked to their association with the father. These others included members of their wider family, people in their local community, and state agencies such as social services and the police. Second, the researchers coded the mothers' use of terms such as 'duty', 'responsibility', 'fairness', and language that suggested judgement such as 'should' or 'ought to' and the contexts to which these terms were applied. These content and linguistic codes were combined into two central moral themes: the women's identity as a 'good mother' and their aspirations for a 'good life' for their children. Three primary threats were identified in relation to the women's moral identity and aspirations: social stigma, the father's former or ongoing criminal activities, and the uninvited interventions of external agencies.

The findings are illustrated through case study descriptions of three women who took part in the study: Alison, Hope and Donna.[2] These cases are interesting from an ethical perspective because all three women remained in contact with the children's father over the research period. Alison and Donna lived with their partners and their children as a family and Hope and her ex-partner lived apart but actively co-parented their son. Their stories capture in sharp relief a range of moral issues that women in the FAIR study faced. They draw

[2] The names used in this chapter are all pseudonyms in order to protect the anonymity of the research participants.

attention to how the women's association with their (ex)-partner potentially threatened their capacity to act and be seen as a 'good mother' and to establish and maintain a 'good life' for their children. Despite a commonality of ethical orientation – the care of their children and family – the threats the women faced varied. For Alison, it was the informal social stigmatisation associated with her husband's offence which threatened their sons' wellbeing and the security of the family unit. For Hope, it was her ex-partner's former lifestyle which threatened their son's future. And for Donna, it was the active hostility and mistrust by outside agencies, in particular the police, which rendered her and her family vulnerable.

Alison

At the time of the first interview, Alison was 28 years old and described herself as White British. As well as looking after her three sons, she was a professional childminder. She and her husband, Ben, had experienced poverty as children and had worked hard to provide a comfortable environment for their own children to grow up in. They had moved to a relatively affluent residential suburb and had gone to a lot of effort to 'fit in' socially:

> I think that as a family we conduct ourselves so we kinda fit in with most situations, so we don't look like we're earning what we're earning or anything like that, because … it doesn't matter where you're from or what education you've got or anything, if you can – not pretend you're someone else, but handle different scenarios and different situations.

Ben had received a four-year custodial sentence for a drug-related offence. The arrest had been particularly traumatic for the family as the police had raided the house and waited with Ben and the three children for Alison to return home from a shopping trip for christening clothes for the baby. Alison was deeply troubled by Ben's arrest and subsequent imprisonment, fearing that it would have a negative impact on the children. She felt embarrassed by his prison sentence:

> I don't think it's nothing to be proud of, but we was in the situation he'd done what he did, there was reasoning behind why he'd done what he did, but yeah, I just think – live on. We don't have to talk about it.

At the time of Ben's arrest, she told only one close friend about what had happened and kept the news quiet from her children as she did not want them to think badly of him. She told them their father was away at work but took them each week to visit him while he was in a prison. She told others when they asked that she was taking the children to someone's day of work:

> I see mums that are going to work at half 6 in the morning, and I've got my kids in time going on a visit, they'd be like 'oh, where are you going?', 'someone's – day of work' or something like that, because I didn't want them … because everyone does know everyone's business.

Alison's priority was to protect her children from any stigmatising consequences of Ben's imprisonment and to preserve as much as possible the lifestyle they had prior to his conviction. Her fear of social stigmatisation was acute because it would endanger the social position she and Ben had worked so hard to achieve. Without Ben, there had to be some changes to their routines: she was unable to drive so she and the children had to rely on public transport or walk to destinations. She was also concerned that Ben's return home after prison would further jeopardise the family's now precarious financial position: the only source of income was from her work as a childminder and she thought she might not be allowed to continue after his release as inspection agencies might no longer consider the house to be a safe place to look after children.

At the time of the third interview, Ben was at home and suffering from poor physical and mental health. He was not working but volunteered as a sports coach for a local youth group. Alison was no longer a childminder. She worked as a teaching assistant in a school and remained the sole income provider for the family. Ben's imprisonment had never been discussed with the children. It was still a subject that Alison felt uncomfortable about and wanted to avoid others finding out: 'If [Ben's] in the pub and he's had a few, and he's talking, if he gets a little bit loud, I'm like 'they might be listening' – and it's always in my head'.

Life after imprisonment and Ben's health problems continued to be challenging for Alison. She had taken responsibility for maintaining the household, earning an income, looking after their three sons and being a support for her husband during his mental health crises. She had also joined a community watch scheme following an incident where her son was bullied and his bike was stolen. Life was tight financially and she worked hard to live within their means, although Ben's addictive behaviours were difficult:

> He doesn't drink every day, but he is a binge drinker. So he will go out, and then he just doesn't know when to stop. I compare it to the shopping bills. If you didn't spend that, that could have been a week's shopping.

For Alison, family was everything and her life was oriented around keeping the family together. When asked, 'What is the most important to you in your life at the moment?' she replied, 'My family'. She said her valuing of family had come from her own experience of being brought up by her mother:

> So I just think it is important to be together. I think it dates back to when I was brought up, my mum was always there and she just made that extra effort. Just because it's nice to spend quality time, but generally it's me and the boys spending the quality time.

Alison also attributed her personal philosophy of 'keeping going' in spite of difficulties to her childhood experience:

> Just like 'keep going forward, keep going forward'. That's it, get the make up on, you got a smile on, and get on with it. Not always a good thing, can't say I'd recommend it, but that's .... the way I was brought up. My dad left when I was young, so I was kind of brought up where you just get on with it. You've made your bed, now lay in it, get on with it.

Alison's mother had supported her during Ben's imprisonment and afterwards, helping financially and also looking after the children. Since her mother's death a couple of years before the third interview, Alison had had access to very little external support. Although most times she was able to put on a 'brave face', there were occasions when she found it all too much:

> So I'm quite stubborn like that. I don't always wanna talk about things, but when I do, I kinda let it all out ... – the faces ... you take it off and I crumble ... but yeah, I'm a bit stubborn.

Alison's vision of a good life was thus of a strong, thriving and happy family and, like her mother, she devoted all her energies to achieving that: providing practical, emotional and financial care for the children and her husband. After Ben's imprisonment, she took on additional responsibilities at a personal cost in order to maintain the family. These responsibilities included the daily care of her children and her husband, the running of the household, providing the family income, and working to uphold the family's moral standing within the community.

For Alison, Ben's imprisonment presented a threat to the family life that she saw as her core priority – a threat to the children's wellbeing, a threat to the children's relationship with the father, a threat to the stability of the family and a threat to their social standing within their community. Yet, remaining with Ben was also important from her ethical perspective, so she managed these threats by not disclosing his imprisonment to her sons and by sharing the information with very few others. Keeping Ben's imprisonment secret was also possible because the children were all under four and a half years old when he was imprisoned. The opportunity to make that decision would not have been possible if they had been older: 'I think we were quite lucky' cause the boys were so small, God forbid if it was his age (now) ... it would be a whole different scenario, because ... you can't pretend that daddy's at work'.

Alison's moral decision-making aligned directly with an ethic of care, that is, making her decisions in light of the responsibilities for the people she looked after: her children and her husband. But she also spoke of the principle of fairness in relation to her children's life opportunities. She expressed the view that they should not be disadvantaged because of Ben's imprisonment: 'I don't think it's fair on the children, they didn't ask to be in this situation, they didn't ask that we're not earning as much as everybody else, but they should be given equal opportunities'.

In the third interview, Alison reflected on her decision not to tell her sons or staff at their school about Ben's imprisonment. She was conflicted about whether it had been the right decision. She recognised her feelings of embarrassment at the time of his conviction but now felt that staff at the children's school would have been able to show more understanding of any behavioural problems the children presented if they had known:

> I didn't even tell the school, because I was embarrassed, so they didn't know for 19 months, which in hindsight now, and working with children now – really wasn't a good thing … And my kids could have possibly been quite upset in school … but they might just been – 'come on, stop crying, you're being silly now', whereas it could have been a major thing in their life – and the school don't know why. So I think I kind of, I made a bad decision then, but at the time I thought I was doing the right thing.

Alison's changed work circumstances were thus instrumental to the re-evaluation of her earlier moral actions; her change of mind resulted from her experience, working in a school, of seeing how other children were helped with their problems.

In Alison's family, the legacy of Ben's imprisonment remained, as Das (2012) might have described, 'tentacle-like' in their everyday lives, generating moral questions for her about the right thing to do within the context of a cherished, yet now even more fragile, social position. The answers she found were shaped by her values – her deeply felt ethic of care which prioritised her children and her husband and her concern to preserve the family's social status. As Abbott (2020) and Gilligan (1982) posit, Alison's moral dilemmas arose out of her relationships: her husband's situation and circumstances precipitating the moral dilemmas in her relationships with her children, with the school and local community. Alison's decisions were reached with a view as to what would be best for these relationships. Importantly, they were shaped by the possibilities and contingencies of context: not telling her children about their father's imprisonment was possible because they were young. The social distance from neighbours, typical of suburban living, may also have facilitated secret-keeping. Her change of mind about the rightness of that decision had been a consequence of her personal observation of how children in difficult situations were supported rather than stigmatised in school.

Alison's ethic of care was clearly fundamental to her moral decision-making but not to the exclusion of an ethic of justice. The decisions she made were guided both by her deeply held commitment to her family and by a view of what was just for her children. Further, her approach to moral decision-making was shaped by her personal philosophy of taking responsibility and being self-reliant in the face of problems, a philosophy she had acquired from her mother. She carried the burden of responsibility for holding the family together during Ben's imprisonment and afterwards, but the additional responsibilities she took on in order to maintain a good life for her children required significant strength and resolution; and since her mother's death she recognised there were times when she found it difficult to cope.

Hope

Hope was 22 years old at the time of the first interview and described herself as Black British. She was separated from her partner, Ramon, who was in prison serving a three-year sentence for robbery. They had a five-year-old son, Isaac, whom they were co-parenting. Hope saw the three of them very much as a family unit: 'Just because me and his father aren't together doesn't mean that we aren't still a family'. However, she was aware of the challenges of bringing up a son well on her own:

> If his dad was there he'd have both of our dynamics but he doesn't. But I've never been a man. So I don't exactly know how to make someone into one. So I'm like, I'll just try and teach him to be a generally good person, and hope that you translate that into manliness. So that's what I'm working with here!

Hope was close to the rest of her own family and was in frequent contact with them. Her sister did not like her relationship with Ramon but remained supportive and met up with her and Isaac. As a family Hope said they had very much a 'get on and sort problems' out approach to life:

> I mean the family dynamic that I grew up in was very supportive and very strong built. My mum was a single mother. And she made it very very, very clear that … having a disadvantage was no excuse for not doing something. And crying about it ain't gonna help. Cry about it later if you have to but as long as it's done it's done.

At the time of the third interview, Hope reflected on her decisions about her caring priorities after her son was born. She spoke of her dilemma when Ramon was in prison and of the challenges of caring for him and Isaac at the same time. She reflected that at first, when Isaac was a baby, she believed a good partner would keep a son in contact with his imprisoned father: 'And I was like oooh you know, we're a family and you've just got to take your baby to the prison and see the husband'.

However, she became concerned about the effect that the prison environment was having on Isaac. She noted how he had told his nursery school that his Dad worked with the police: 'He obviously knows when we go there there's police presence and everything. And I was like that can't be good for his psyche getting older, so I stopped taking him then'.

She also was upset to see how difficult Isaac found it to leave his father when they visited: 'I just don't like thinking of my baby so distressed. But he was, he was absolutely distraught and I thought to myself I'm not putting him through that again. Never again'. However, she also was concerned for Ramon's wellbeing in prison:

> I was torn between not wanting to give my son the example that that's ok, and not wanting to glorify that lifestyle in front of him. But also not wanting to abandon a person who I had at one point loved. And I still care for him. I don't want him to sit there and go crazy by himself because nobody's caring for him, sending him money, and he turns into some kind of maniac because people abandoned him. I don't want that to happen.

Her resolution to this dilemma was pragmatic. She told Ramon that she would keep in contact with him while he was in prison this time but for any future times he would be on his own until he was released.

Hope's other dilemma related to her son's attitude towards his father's earlier involvement in criminal activities. She had been careful to differentiate this lifestyle from his capacity to be a father. She felt strongly that Ramon was a good father and that Isaac should continue to have a relationship with him:

> His father is his other half and I'm not going to cut him off from that. And I'm not gonna tell him that whatever his father is, is bad, because it's not … I'm just trying to instil in him that your dad isn't bad as a person, he just made really bad decisions once. And now he's trying to make less bad decisions.

Yet, she and Ramon recognised that Ramon's former lifestyle might place Hope and Isaac at risk. They both thought it would be better if she and Isaac moved away from the city they lived in; this was after Hope and Isaac had been stopped in the street one day and threatened by some people who were looking for Ramon. In the six years between the second and third research interview, they had therefore moved to a town about 50 miles away:

> I just kind of concluded that I didn't want to be in that space anymore. Because I was like – people know me as his – as his partner. People know my son as his son. And if people are looking to do that to him God knows what they're looking to do to us … Unbeknownst to my son – obviously he didn't necessarily know the reasoning so it was just like you know – we're going out of [city] because it's countryside and you're freer and there's less chance of you being kidnapped or something.

However, Hope believed that Isaac felt more at home in the city they had left:

> I think he's aware of his … like obviously he's a minority here. And I think he's aware of how – how he feels more represented there than he does here. And I think that might be why he feels more like affiliated to whatever's happening there.

And when they returned to the city to visit family or friends, she noticed his demeanour changed ('The second I step into (city) his trousers go lower, he stops smiling. It's really quite frustrating') and she was worried that he would become involved in the lifestyle his father had been a part of:

> So he's got some friends in (the city) who have boys who dislike them. And these boys – who don't know my son – saw my son with these boys. They were just like 'I dislike them so I dislike you too'. And my son's reaction was to talk to his dad about needing a knife. Obviously his dad told him no, they had that conversation and he nipped that in the bud.

Although she and Ramon were keen to convince Isaac that his father's earlier lifestyle was not something he should aspire to, they realised that the message was not straightforward because Isaac had observed that the time his mother and father were happy together was when his father was involved in criminal activities:

> I can understand it might be a bit confusing for him … So he's like well, it couldn't have been that bad. You guys were in love. That's when you guys were all together and

> happy and stuff. And you know, having babies, that sounds like a good time! When we tell the stories they sound fun. You know – we were teenagers and we did this and we went there and this happened and ha ha ha. But the fact is that at the end of the story, your dad went to jail. And that wasn't fun.

Hope wanted to convince Isaac that his father was trying to make better decisions for Isaac's future wellbeing:

> He's trying to make better decisions so that you can have a better life. But if you make the same mistakes that he made then there's no point in him making these better decisions … if you start making the same bad decisions he made, then nothing's ever gonna get better.

Hope's moral dilemmas, therefore, related to how to address and respond to Ramon's criminal activities and imprisonment in the context of caring for their son. Her moral aspirations were intrinsic to her identity as a mother and could be captured by the question: 'how can I ensure that *my son* leads a good life?' Her resolutions to the dilemmas presented by Ramon's imprisonment and the legacy of his earlier lifestyle were shaped by an ethic of care. After Isaac was born, she realised she could not simultaneously support Ramon in prison and bring Isaac up well, so caring for Isaac took priority over caring for Ramon. Thus, over time, there was a shift in the prioritisation of the subject of her care and what she considered the right action to take.

Hope engaged with her ethical dilemmas in an overtly pragmatic way, reflecting her broader philosophy of life which itself had been shaped by her relationships with her own family. Like Alison, the importance of 'family' was a value that she had gained from her childhood experiences. This value underpinned her ongoing decisions to co-parent with Ramon and to maintain connections between Isaac and her own family.

However, unlike Alison, she did not seem so much concerned about the stigma associated with imprisonment and, in fact, said she had not experienced any such stigmatisation. When asked why, she reflected on how when she was younger, she was with other young people who were in trouble. She also reflected that as a Black woman, she was used to dealing with discrimination in her everyday life:

> Personally for myself I didn't experience anything like that. At least not pertaining to Ramon's part in our life. If it's just generally life then yeah, I deal with it every day. But it's just part of life isn't it?

When comparing Hope and Alison's stories, we also see how their shared ethic to ensure a good life for their children despite their partner's imprisonment played out very differently in part because of the different values they placed on their relationships with the communities with which they were connected. Alison and Ben were seemingly integrated into and accepted by their local community and aspired to live by its norms. Alison saw the biggest threat to her sons' wellbeing as public knowledge of Ben's imprisonment, as this would jeopardise their membership of this community. Being a good parent meant keeping everything *normal*, to 'live on' as before, even if that meant not openly discussing Ben's imprisonment with her sons. Hope's concern for Isaac was not about social stigmatisation, so much as the risk of physical harm and of Isaac getting into trouble himself. She actively sought to distance him from a community she and Ramon had been a part of but which presented risks to his present and future wellbeing. Isaac had some relationships already within this community and Hope needed to alert him to the risks he faced. Keeping silent about Ramon's criminal justice involvement would not have protected Isaac. Being a good parent meant developing a *new normal* for Isaac.

Alison and Hope's stories illustrate the relational embeddedness of moral action. Their different perspectives on telling their children about their father's imprisonment were grounded in what they believed to be right in the context of their wider social relationships as well as what was feasible given the different ages of the children. They also reflected differences in Alison and Hope's conceptualisation of the father's offence. For Alison, Ben's imprisonment was morally tainting, it spoiled his identity (Goffman 1968), and she believed that knowing of his offence would make the children think badly of him. Whereas Hope did not see Ramon's offending as integral to his moral identity so she spoke of him to Isaac as a good father who had made bad decisions.

Donna

Donna was married to Steve, a known member of the Traveller community and they had two sons, Steven and Jamie. She was 31 years old at the time of the first interview and described herself as White British. Since his release from prison, Steve had been in court on various charges and imprisoned for a second time for an assault on Donna. However, they had remained together as a couple throughout the research period. By the time of the third interview, they had moved to a house in a rural location and Donna divided her life between looking after her teenage sons and working part-time in a local supermarket.

Like Hope and Alison, Donna's ethical framework was fundamentally oriented around care. Her aspirations were for a good life for her sons. In response to the question 'What's the most important thing to you in life?' she replied: 'Just the boys … I just want them to be happy'. Donna's orientation towards caring extended beyond the family to friends who also needed help. She described supporting a friend who had just had twins by taking her to all her post-natal appointments: 'I take her to all of her appointments,' cause she's a single mum, bless her … Yeah, I take her to all of her appointments. She's gonna make me and [Steve] godparents to 'em'.

Donna remained in a relationship with Steve throughout the research but challenged his life choices when they were likely to threaten the wellbeing of her sons. When he was first suspected of his offence (possession of an offensive weapon) she argued that he should go to the police station and confess because she had been arrested by the police in connection with the offence and was concerned that their children would be taken away into care:

> He was gonna go and take it to a trial and everything else, but I screamed in his face if you lose me my babies, I will never forgive you … And Jamie was six weeks old … when he got me arrested for that. And, obviously, I've got no criminal record or anything, but yeah, I was, literally, gonna kill him … Because in my mind, if a six-week-old baby goes into care, you're never getting that baby back.

She gave another example of when Steve was in prison serving his three-year prison sentence. He had been based in a prison in a large city but visiting him there with the boys had taken them over four hours. She gave Steve an ultimatum – either he put in for a transfer nearer to their home or she would not visit:

> I said I'm not bringing the boys here again … And he went 'why?' I said it's just taken us four hours to get here … I went you wanna stay here,' cause you know this one, that one, and whatever. Have a wonderful time. I'll see you in seven months. I'm not coming back to this prison … I said if you value your mates more than you do your family, that's fine … I'm not coming back here.

However, for Donna, the main threat to her children's wellbeing and to their family came from local organisations: police, local council, social services, banks and the press. Since her relationship with Steve, she said her interactions with these organisations had frequently been hostile and shaped by mistrust.

When Steve was in prison, she had been accused by the council of over-claiming on benefits. The council would not believe her when she said that her husband was in prison and that the Steven living at home was her son. The council took her to court: 'And the judge went this is ridiculous. Why haven't you taken her word for it? She's telling you you've got her son mixed up with her partner, because they have the same name'. Despite this ruling, the council failed to call off the bailiff:

> There was a knock, knock on the door, I've walked to the side door, I've opened it, and this bloke went yeah, I'm here to levy goods, he said, for £9,000. I went … oh, hold on a second. No, I won this. He went what? I said I won this. I'll just get my papers. He went bang, knocked me sideways into the garage door, he went I'm here to levy goods.

The problem with the council was resolved but the family's harassment by the police became a major issue for her. Since his prison sentence, Steve and the family had been subject to intense scrutiny:

> The second they get a whiff of his name, oh, they centre round him … He'll go from, like, the bottom of the list to the top of the list, and then they try and make a story around him.

One time, when the police were searching for Steve, Donna was arrested and held in the police station. They had accused her of shoplifting. Donna was released without charge after being held at the station for nine hours. During this time, the police had taken her sons out of school and asked them where their father was. Donna made a complaint against the police: 'I found a solicitor … and I said right, I've had enough now. This is harassment, and I won'.

Donna's deepest concern about the police harassment was the effect it was having on her sons. Aside from the incident described above, the family would often experience unannounced police visits day and night. Donna saw how scared her sons were and decided that they needed to move away from the area:

> They would knock on the door where I was before: 'Where is he? What's he doing?' Three, four times a night, right up until 2 o'clock in the morning. 'We need to know where he is'. 'You don't need to know anything. Go away'. But they would terrify the kids. The kids weren't sleeping, and I said 'Right, enough's enough'. So, we moved. So, we moved right out here.

Yet despite leaving the area, Donna described how the family still received unwanted police attention in their new location. One day, Donna's husband rang her when she was on a school run and said that police were searching the house as they were suspected of money laundering and fraud. She said she was too scared to go back to the house to pick up the dogs or to go to the school, so she went to her mother's house and asked her brother to take the children out of school. A follow-on consequence of this police investigation was that her bank account was closed and she had nowhere to pay in the money she was earning from her part-time job. She explained that the bank had told her:

> 'You no longer meet the criteria to bank with us'. 'Well, my criteria hasn't changed in the last 11 years', I said, 'so can you tell me what's changed your end?'… 'We're not in a position to discuss that'. I said, 'well, my criteria, again, has not changed. I'm still working the same job, nothing has changed my end, so now I'm asking you again: what's changed your end?'

Donna had a further poor experience with the police when she had asked for their help with an intruder (an associate of Steve's) who came to the house and stared through the windows to intimidate them. When she went outside, Donna said he began shouting at her and pushed her son, Jamie, who fell and injured his head. Donna called the police; however, upon arrival of the police, she said the man alleged that he had been attacked, and the police refused to arrest the man without arresting the family also. This left her feeling very bitter and with the view the police were not there to protect her children from harm. She said her children had also gained this impression:

> When Jamie got assaulted out there, he even said, 'so the police won't even protect me'. And I went 'what?' And he went, 'so the police won't even protect me against that man because Dad's Dad'.

The family discussions after this incident considered how to protect themselves in future. Steve had told her they should no longer rely on the police to help:

> And Steve went 'next time we'll do it my way'... And I'm, like, 'your way?'... So, me trying to do it the right way, what's the point? ... And I do see his side of it. What is the point?

The continual harassment from outside agencies ('it's just one thing after another') meant that Donna was continually worried about her children ('you're constantly stressing about the kids'). In the face of external hostility, the family turned inward for strength and support. Donna felt that her relationship with Steve had become closer and that they were more resilient as a consequence:

> I just think we've been through that much now with the police never leaving us alone, and everything, it just makes you stronger as a couple ... if anything ... threw us now ... we'd just get on with it and just carry on.

Donna emphasised to her children the importance of honesty in their relationship. She had told their sons of Steve's offence and of any time he was in contact with the police. At the time of his arrest, the papers had reported he had equipment for a robbery in the house. She said to her sons:

> So, then, I'm telling his kids one thing, they're reading something else. Well, this says here ... never believe what a newspaper says, mate, ever ... So, believe your mum ... always believe your mum,' cause I would never lie to you.

The continual battles with outside organisations took their toll on Donna's health. For two days after the court case for money laundering, she said she had remained in bed because she had been physically and mentally exhausted by the experience. Donna reflected on her approach to being a good mother and to giving her sons a good life in light of her own health issues:

> Well, my mum says 'd'you know what the problem is with your family?' I went 'what?' She went 'you've always fixed everything ... You're mum. You fix everything, and they all just go Mum and it's done'.

Looking back over her experiences, she wondered whether she would have had all this trouble if she had not waited for Steve to complete his prison sentence:

> I just wonder what would have happened if I hadn't waited. Would I have had all this shit with the police? ... Would it still be going like this, or would I have been left alone, or would I still have the shit' cause I've got his kids – there's so many questions that go through my head.

Over the six years since the family participated in the FAIR study, Donna reported hostile experiences with the police, banks and the local council. Their actions made her everyday life difficult and in Donna's eyes, demonstrated their lack of belief in her integrity as a citizen. Donna also recognised the power of the police and of social services to coercively break up the family unit. For her the police had become a threat to rather than a protector of her family's wellbeing. In urgent situations which rendered her children vulnerable, she had called on her own mother and brother for support.

Unlike Alison, Donna did not discuss the need to protect her sons from the stigmatising glare of others; similar to Hope, although to a greater extent, hostility from others was seen as part of the family's everyday life. This drew the family closer to each other; the family bonds became stronger in the face of threats from external organisations. Looking inwards, the family enacted its own ethic, placing emphasis on values of honesty, trust and support. Indeed, within the family space, the value Donna placed on honesty was recognised. This was in contrast to the views of external agencies who appeared to mistrust her in light of her association with Steve.

Donna's moral thinking was changed and shaped by her external environment, where so much of what she personally experienced was perceived as unjust and threatening to her primary concern for the present and future wellbeing of her sons. Her view of the right thing to do was rendered unstable as a consequence of these experiences: if the police were not the right people to go to for protection, then who would be? Steve presented her with another option: to let the family address problems on their own in the future. At the time of the third interview, Donna remained ambivalent about what the right course of action would be if her children were placed at risk again – this was a moral dilemma-in-waiting.

Donna's reports of hostility from the police were particularly severe in comparison to the experiences of other mothers in the study and it is possible that this was a result of her connection through Steve to the Traveller community. Traveller participants in Pizani-Williams' (1998) study reported being harassed by the police through frequent stops and searches and verbal abuse from police officers on the streets. A police officer in her study reported that if a Traveller was stopped and questioned and no offence appeared to have been committed, officers were encouraged to 'verbally harass them to provoke a Section 4 assault' (Pizani-Williams 1998: 23). A number of recent studies have also recorded hostile relationships between the police and Gypsy Roma and Traveller (GRT) communities (eg, Cemlyn et al 2009; Coxhead 2007; Mulcahy 2012; Richardson 2007; The Traveller Movement 2018).

Mothers' Collective Experiences

The ethical issues faced by Alison, Hope and Donna and the resolutions they found may be understood in the context of their unique relational experiences of the past and the present, and of their anticipated futures. Yet other mothers in the FAIR study also justified their ethical decisions in terms of what they considered was best to protect the wellbeing of their children and the family.

The concern to protect children from social stigma was expressed by a number of mothers. Similar to Alison, one mother did not want her youngest child to know about the father's criminal conviction because she felt that her ex-partner had changed and that the criminal conviction was a feature of his former life which bore no relevance to the life he was leading now. However, even though his conviction was in the past she recognised the potential for the family to be stigmatised and their family life to be adversely affected:

> We still do loads of things together, and do things with the children, but I think it's hard because I've changed and … I know that he's changed and he's not a criminal any more, but there's a stigma around the whole … and I feel like as much as people like to say there isn't, there is. Even one of my work colleagues, I'll say to him like not to say anything around them … and I 100% don't want my youngest daughter to know.

Two mothers spoke about protecting their children from stigmatisation by other young people. They bought them clothes and shoes so that they would be accepted by their peer group even though this came at a significant financial cost:

> It's my daughter and that's what she needs. She's not going out there to get bullied. You gotta have these certain trainers and certain clothes, you know? And I'm not allowing that not to happen.

> He says 'Oh, you know, my friend's got this pair of trainers, or that pair of trainers'. And I know it's really materialistic, but I don't want him to be looked down on at all. 'Oh, your dad's a heroin addict', d'you know what I mean? Not that they know that, but I do'.

Several mothers, like Donna, feared the coercive intervention of social services when their capacity to be a good mother was questioned. When an intervention happened, it was experienced as demoralising and undermining to the women's identity as a mother: 'I felt so attacked as a mother. Nobody was listening to me. I was under pressure. They didn't understand'.

In the face of external hostility like Donna experienced, mothers would seek the protection of trusted others, neighbours or other family members:

> When she was a baby, the social worker, who was really horrible … was on her way to take her away … So, my auntie said, like, if you're in a different borough, then you're not under her … So, she said move up here … I just got in the car and I just drove up here.' Cause it was either that, or my daughter go, you know.

Alison, Donna and Hope all had an amicable relationship with their children's father but this was not the case for all mothers in the study. Where there had been a break-up, the women reflected on the extent to which their children should have contact with the father. Many women expressed the view that it was part of their responsibility as a mother to allow and facilitate the child(ren)'s contact with their father. These views often arose from an ethic of justice: a sense of what was right for a child:

> Now, if the father's in prison, then why … stop their child from seeing their dad? … I think it's selfish, because I think every child needs their dad, and their parent, and their family in their lives, you know.

> If the children want to see their dad despite what he's done or where he is then that really should be their decision and not yours. That's the advice people gave me. Not to make the decision for those children. That should be their decision.
>
> Yeah. Because, you know, the thing is as well, I want my older son to be able to speak to me about it. I've never said to my older son 'I hate your dad!', because that's for him to make his own decision.

However, when the mothers felt that their children's wellbeing was threatened by the father either physically or psychologically, they took steps to protect them from him and from the negative consequences of his lifestyle. Although Hope's concern that her son would emulate his father's lifestyle was not typical, mothers worried about a range of problems arising from their father's social networks and lifestyle, such as taking drugs and using violence. Some ended the relationship as a result: 'I couldn't possibly stay in that. You have to keep your babies safe don't you?'; 'My children need parents. Need parents that have stability and I feel like if you can't offer my child or my children stability, then you shouldn't be around'.

Other mothers worked to manage their children's expectations about their father: 'I just have to protect them and say, you know if your dad says he's coming he might not come. Or, you know, your dad says he's going to meet you, or give you money, don't rely on that'.

For some women, including Donna and Alison, the burden of living by an ethic of care was hard to bear; doing the right thing by the family required significant moral courage and personal strength. One mother, who was faced with the possibility that her child would be taken into care, described it as an existential battle – a fight to retain her child and their good life together:

> Like, it's so hard … Especially when people like Social Services get involved … it's so easy to give up. I feel like not giving up – fighting – fighting for your lives. Like literally. And … just remembering that, you will make it. It's really hard. It's really hard.

Not all mothers had that strength, and in a society where their reputation as a good mother was vulnerable, they were afraid to admit their own struggles. One mother when asked about whether or not she had mental health problems responded:

> They reckon I have, but I don't want the label … When I lived in the mother and baby … the family unit thing, they kept telling me to go and get all these tests done. I went to Wellbeing Clinic – he asked too many questions, so after a time I went out the door … Most of my friends – well, I say my friends, that I was friends with in there – all got the label, all were on the medication and they all had social services heavily involved, and they were afraid they'd take the kids and I thought 'I don't want that'. So – whatever I've got … I've got to remember I've got the kids, I can't really get too bad anyway. You know, like, really depressed, because I need to be there for them.

Another mother who had not been able to prevent her eldest child being taken into care had described this in terms of her selfishness because she had not considered her child's needs sufficiently:

> And I feel bad,' cause I think to myself I should have thought more of (my daughter). But I was in such a state, and worrying about him, worrying about everything, that to tell you the truth, I was selfish not to think of her.

Common to all these women's narratives was a concern to do what was right for their children; their relationships with their children shaped their ethical decision-making and their conception of a good life. In their concern for the needs, prospects and wellbeing of their children their decisions were responses to a kind of significance that is not reflected in a principle or a calculation, but rather arose from a deeply embedded emotional connection to their children:

> If someone was to take (my son) away from me and he was not to see me ever again, I don't know how he would grow up and be productive and have a happy life … It'd break me in half, if I didn't have him, I wouldn't wanna be here. And I think he'd feel the same.

The above quote illustrates the relational dimension to the moral worlds in which the women in the FAIR study existed. The mothers' ethical concerns aligned with questions about 'how can we have a good life?' or 'how can my children have a good life?' Alongside the deep personal emotional connection to their children, the women also expressed an existential responsibility as a mother: 'They're my children. I mean, yeah. I mean, they didn't ask to be born, did they? So, you know, I guess my … my reason for being at the moment is to bring them up'.

The powerfully felt imperatives of motherhood became heavier for these women as they dealt with the significant challenges relating to the father's imprisonment and as others judged them because of their association with the father. Some women also blamed themselves for the hardships their children faced: 'you feel guilty for the children I think, it's just guilt. Constant guilt for what you think you have created'.

The moral dilemmas some women in the FAIR study experienced were specific to their relational role as mothers with young children. However, in the women's narratives, it was evident that their caring priorities changed over time as new relationships became more important, resulting in a change in their perspectives of what was right. As Hope explained, prior to having a child her focus had been on being a good partner, but when Isaac was born, Ramon's troubles became a lower priority – what became 'right' was to ensure her son's wellbeing. Another mother gave an example of how her care for her own mother took priority as long as the children were young but as they grew older, she had to move to protect them from encountering others who had known their father:

> I don't want (my son) to be going out in the local area as, like, an 18, 19-year-old, and bumping into people who knew (his Dad). That's what I'm quite scared about. So, before that happens, I will move away. Can't do it at the minute' cause mum really wants to be in this area' cause of all the local links, and all that stuff, which is fine.

The temporal perspective on the women's moral practices is illuminating because it illustrates how for these mothers, the hierarchy of important relationships within their ethic of care changed as their relationships changed. It demonstrates the nuanced, contextual and dynamic quality of morality in practice.

CONCLUSION

The analysis of the mothers' narratives from the FAIR study offers new insights into the moral dilemmas generated by paternal imprisonment, and more broadly into moral thinking and action. The father's imprisonment was an event mostly outside the mother's control yet threatened her own moral standing, her identity as a good mother, and her aspirations for the wellbeing of her children.

As Crossley (2011) and Abbott (2020) have argued, the moral issues the women faced were essentially relational, arising out of their relationship as a mother to their children, as a current or former partner of their child(ren)'s father, and shaped by relationships with others external to the family, including state agencies, who could publicly question the mother's moral integrity and relatedly, her capacity to act as a mother. The father's imprisonment presented the mothers with differing threats to their children's wellbeing and safety: threats of social stigmatisation as Alison's story exemplified; threats from police harassment as Donna's story highlighted; and threats arising from the father's lifestyle as in Hope's and Donna's stories. How mothers responded to the threats reflected their own values and personal philosophies and importantly also the personal resources they had to cope with the stresses they encountered. Ethnic relations (as Hope and Donna's stories showed) and class relations (as Alison's story illustrated) play a role here too.

The mothers' narratives illustrate how morality is woven into the fabric of their daily lives. It is grounded in practice, shaping and being shaped by their everyday relational encounters and reflections. Its presence is often unobtrusive, implicit in the practice of the ordinary everyday but it is also actively reflected upon as new experiences and events prompt a review and re-evaluation of past decisions and practices. As Abbott (2020) and Gilligan (1982) identified, morality in practice is thus both situated and dynamic shaped by the contingencies of context and by changing relationships and priorities. It is also embodied; in order to protect the wellbeing of their children in the face of hardships associated with the father's imprisonment the mothers needed to draw on significant physical and emotional strength and courage.

There are interesting comparisons between the findings of this study and those of Cheryl Mattingly's ethnographical study of African American families, in particular mothers and grandmothers, who were caring for children with severe illnesses and disabilities (see Mattingly 2013, 2014). Similar to this study, Mattingly noted how the carers of children in her research 'struggle with and try to make judgments in the ambiguous circumstances of everyday life about how to realise the "best good"' (2013: 5). However, contrastingly, her Aristotelian inspired analysis focused on the conscious process of moral transformation of individual carers. Using the metaphor of a moral laboratory she presented the carers in her study as the 'researchers or experimenters of their own lives' (Mattingly 2013: 6) redefining their ethical identities through the small-scale activities of everyday domestic routines. While some mothers in the FAIR study were concerned to become 'better' mothers than they had been, a conscious effort at personal transformation was not intrinsic to their concern to ensure their children's and family's wellbeing.

Gilligan's (1982) relationally embedded 'ethic of care' captures well the moral perspectives of the women in the FAIR study as their moral dilemmas arising from the father's imprisonment are concerned with the wellbeing of those they were intimately connected to and cared most about. Importantly we can only understand the mothers' moral actions with reference to their relationships to these others. From this relational perspective, the question that concerned the mothers was not the individual Aristotelian one: 'how can I lead a good life?' but a collective one: 'how can we, as a family, lead a good life?' or 'how can my children lead a good life?' This ethic of care was also accompanied in some of the women's narratives with a perspective on what was 'just' and 'right' for their children. Thus as Gilligan and Attanucci (1988) found, two moral orientations – an ethic of care and ethic of justice – could coexist in people's moral thinking. Nevertheless, for the women in the FAIR study an ethic of care was fundamental to their being, it arose out of an existential relational identity: 'I'm a mother, I've gotta make things go right. It's a glue that can't unstick'.

REFERENCES

Abbott, O (2020) *The Self, Relational Sociology and Morality in Practice* (Cham, Palgrave Macmillan).

Baier, AC (1987) 'The Need for More Than Justice' 13 *Canadian Journal of Philosophy Supplementary* 41.

Braman, D (2004) *Doing Time on the Outside: Incarceration and Family Life in Urban America* (Ann Arbor, MI, University of Michigan Press).

Braun, V and Clarke, V (2006) 'Using Thematic Analysis in Psychology' 3 *Qualitative Research in Psychology* 77.

Cemlyn, S, Greenfields, M, Burnett, S, Matthews, Z and Whitwell, C (2009) *Inequalities Experienced by Gypsy and Traveller Communities: A Review* (Manchester, Equality and Human Rights Commission).

Condry, R (2007) *Families Shamed: The Consequences of Crime for Relatives of Serious Offenders* (Collumpton, Willan Publishing).

Coxhead, J (2007) *The Last Bastion of Racism? Gypsies, Travellers and Policing* (Stoke on Trent, Trentham Books).

Crossley, N (2011) *Towards Relational Sociology* (Abingdon, Routledge).

Das, V (2012) 'Ordinary Ethics' in D Fassin (ed), *A Companion to Moral Anthropology* (Chichester, John Wiley & Sons Inc).

Fishman, LT (1990) *Women at the Wall: A Study of Prisoners' Wives Doing Time on the Outside* (Albany, NY, SUNY Press).

Friedman, M (1987) 'Beyond Caring: The De-moralization of Gender' 13 *Canadian Journal of Philosophy Supplementary* 87.

Gilligan, C (1982) *In a Different Voice: Psychological Theory and Women's Development* (Cambridge, MA, Harvard University Press).

Gilligan, C and Attanucci, J (1988) 'Two Moral Orientations: Gender Differences and Similarities' 34 *Merrill-Palmer Quarterly* 223.

Goffman, E (1968) *Stigma: Notes on the Management of Spoiled Identity* (London, Penguin).

Hairston, CF (2003) 'Prisoners and Families: Parenting Issues during Incarceration' in J Travis and M Waul (eds), *Prisoners Once Removed: The Impact of Incarceration and Reentry on Children, Families, and Communities* (Washington DC, The Urban Institute).

Hekman, SJ (1995) *Moral Voices, Moral Selves: Carol Gilligan and Feminist Moral Theory* (University Park, PA, Pennsylvania State University Press).

Held, V (2006) *The Ethics of Care: Personal, Political, and Global* (New York, Oxford University Press).

Jorgensen, G (2007) 'Kohlberg and Gilligan: Duet or Duel?' 35 *Journal of Moral Education* 179.

Kohlberg, L (1969) 'Stage and Sequence: The Cognitive-Developmental Approach to Socialisation' in DA Goslin (ed), *Handbook of Socialisation Theory and Research* (Chicago, IL, Rand McNally).

——(1986) 'A Current Statement on Some Theoretical Issues' in S Modgil and C Modgil (eds), *Lawrence Kohlberg: Consensus and Controversy* (Philadelphia, PA, The Falmer Press).

Lanskey, C, Lösel, F, Markson, L and Souza, K (2016) 'Children's Contact with their Imprisoned Father and the Father–Child Relationship after his Release' 5 *Families, Relationships and Societies* 43.

Lambek, M (2010) *Ordinary Ethics: Anthropology, Language, and Action* (New York, Fordham University Press).

Lösel, F, Pugh, G, Markson, L, Souza, KA and Lanskey, C (2012) *Risk and Protective Factors in the Resettlement of Imprisoned Fathers with their Families* (Milton, Ormiston Children and Families Trust).

Markson, L, Lösel, F, Souza, KA and Lanskey, C (2015) 'Male Prisoners' Family Relationships and Resilience in Resettlement' 15 *Criminology & Criminal Justice* 423.

Mattingly, C (2013) 'Moral Selves and Moral Scenes: Narrative Experiments in Everyday Life' 78 *Ethnos* 301.

——(2014) *Moral Laboratories: Family Peril and the Struggle for a Good Life* (Oakland, CA, University of California Press).

Mattingly, C and Throop, J (2018) 'The Anthropology of Ethics and Morality' 47 *Annual Review of Anthropology* 475.

Miller, RR (2003) 'Various Implications of the "Race to Incarcerate" on Incarcerated African American Men and their Families' in O Harris and RR Miller (eds), *Impacts of Incarceration on the African American Family* (New Jersey, Transaction Publishers).

Mulcahy, A (2012) '"Alright in their own place": Policing and the Spatial Regulation of Irish Travellers' 12 *Criminology & Criminal Justice* 307.

Noddings, N (1984) *Caring: A Feminine Approach to Ethics and Moral Education* (Berkeley, CA, University of California Press).

Pizani-Williams, L (1998) 'Gypsies in the Criminal Justice System – The Forgotten Minority' Cropwood Occasional Paper 23 (Cambridge, University of Cambridge Institute of Criminology).

Prison Advice and Care Trust (undated) *What do I Tell the Kids?*, available at: www.prisonadvice.org.uk/news/what-do-i-tell-the-kids.

Richardson, J (2007) 'Policing Gypsies and Travellers' in M Hayes and T Acton (eds), *Travellers, Gypsies, Roma* (Newcastle, Cambridge Scholars Publishing).

Slote, M (2007) *The Ethics of Care and Empathy* (New York, Routledge).

Souza, K, Lanskey, C, Ellis, S, Lösel, F, Markson, L and Barton–Crosby, J (2021) 'The Mental Health Trajectories of Male Prisoners and their Female (Ex-) Partners from Pre- to Post- Release' 31 *Criminal Behaviour and Mental Health* 399.

Souza, K, Lösel, F, Markson, L and Lanskey, C (2015) 'Pre-Release Expectations and Post-Release Experiences of Prisoners and their (Ex-) Partners' 20 *Legal and Criminal Psychology* 306.

The Traveller Movement (2018) *The preliminary report: policing by consent: understanding and improving relations between Gypsies, Roma, Irish Travellers and the Police* (London, The Traveller Movement).

Part III

Moral Emotions: Shame and Guilt

5

A Plea for Guilt

SOPHIE-GRACE CHAPPELL

INTRODUCTION

JOHN BRAITHWAITE'S DISTINGUISHED research in philosophical criminology has developed a distinction between two ways of shaming, the 'stigmatising' and the 'reintegrative' ways, and argued very plausibly that there is a key place in rehabilitative penology for reintegrative shaming (Braithwaite 1989). Much in Braithwaite's work is impressive and persuasive. Nonetheless, we may well be struck by its stress on shame, and its consequent *lack* of stress on guilt. Whatever happened to guilt?

In this chapter I respond to Braithwaite rather indirectly: not with a 'but' but with an 'and'. My claim is that guilt too is a useful notion for philosophical criminology, and even now still an under-exploited one; so it would be a mistake to react to Braithwaite's influence by neglecting, sidelining, or writing off the role and the significance of guilt. I shall argue this mainly not by reference to criminology itself, but by reference to the philosophical ethics that underlies criminological thinking. In that underlying philosophical ethics also, and to some extent in culture at large, guilt has been decidedly eclipsed. For this eclipse there are various reasons, no doubt interrelated. I will mention six, and say most (in a section of its own) about the sixth.

One historically recent reason lies in the shame-culture/guilt-culture antithesis, nowadays a staple both of academic writing and of less formally restrained speculation. This antithesis owes its currency to Ruth Benedict (1946) in *The Chrysanthemum and the Sword*, her study of the differences in ethical outlook between Japan and her home culture, the United States. Under Benedict's influence, the antithesis has naturally come to be seen as not only between shame-culture and guilt-culture, but also as between shame and guilt themselves.

At the time it came out, the perception of Benedict's book – no doubt she did not intend this – was often effectively racist. It was read (or more likely, just reported) as an exposition of 'why the Japanese aren't like us morally', or even of 'why the Japanese are amoral, and don't have consciences or feel guilt like we do', and hence as an explanation of 'how it was possible for the Japanese to act so appallingly during the Second World War'. Since then, such perceptions have been thoroughly and rightly repudiated: if people want to sharpen their understanding of what counts as 'acting appallingly in war-time', no doubt it is as salutary to look at Hiroshima and Nagasaki as at the Burma Road. Thus the needle has moved to the other end of the dial: where Benedict's shame/guilt antithesis is still accepted, it is often now given the opposite polarity from the original one. Guilt and guilt-culture have become the notions that now look suspect, and shame and shame-culture are talked up as preferable alternatives.

Two earlier sources of this eclipsing of guilt are the great *fin de siècle* theorists of the mind Sigmund Freud and Friedrich Nietzsche, both of whom famously treat guilt as a kind of deformation of consciousness, sometimes useful, but always in danger of becoming pathological and damaging. Both take it as read (rather like David Hume on pride) that a healthy psyche will be strongly self-affirming. Such a psyche will have a very good opinion of itself, and it will have very little time for the kind of neurotic self-laceration and picking at the scabs of the past that (as they see it) is involved in guilt. It will however be highly receptive to notions of honour, prestige and good renown – and therefore to their antonyms, including shame. Guilt, for these two thinkers and their immensely influential heritages, will be something of a dirty word; so today it is entirely normal for the phrase 'guilt feelings' to be used to refer pejoratively to irrational hang-ups that we would do much better simply to shrug off.

Before Freud and Nietzsche, a fourth source is the utilitarian tradition. In chapter 3 of his *Utilitarianism*, John Stuart Mill (1863/1998) portrays conscience (and so guilt, as one key part of the workings of conscience) as a psychological deterrence mechanism, an onboard inhibition-module. Like moral rules and conventions such as blame and punishment, the real function of the reluctances and actual incapacities that conscience and guilt create is instrumental: they are designed to serve the wider and deeper purpose of increasing overall utility, by channelling us dispositionally and behaviourally away from certain kinds of action and reaction. Such a module can be a black box; it doesn't really matter 'what is inside it', provided it serves this conditioning function.[1] Nor then does it ultimately matter, for the utilitarian, whether guilt tracks the truth – though certainly there is very likely to be real utility in *people thinking* that it tracks the truth.

Which people, though? Where on this utilitarian map is the utilitarian himself to be located, given that the utilitarian is the one who understands,

[1] If I have a criticism of Braithwaite's reintegrative-shaming proposal to offer, it is here or hereabouts. Braithwaite too, it seems to me, is more focused on the causal effects of shaming than on the intentional content of utterances or acts of shaming. My focus here is very much on this latter, because I doubt that we can adequately understand either shame or guilt without understanding this intentional content. In particular, this content will make all the difference as to whether shaming turns out to be stigmatising or reintegrative. It is not enough merely to point to the contrast between social inclusion and exclusion. After all, offenders can be stigmatised both by exclusion from relationships and also within those relationships. Indeed, criminology aside, some of the most damaging stigmatisation happens precisely within the context of intimate relationships, as with abusive marriages and toxic parents.

at least *qua* utilitarian, that it doesn't matter whether conscience and guilt track anything real? Via these pressing, and to date unanswered, questions the utilitarian comes to stand in a curiously, and indeed ominously, incoherent relation to the normal practices of moral consciousness, which he apparently both inhabits and participates in like any other citizen (and therefore believes in), and also criticises and evaluates from the theorist's outside (and therefore sees through). His only real reason for taking an interest in 'what's inside the box', in the internal moral psychology of guilt, is to do with its efficacy and reliability as a causal instrument of welfare. For the utilitarian, then, it is not that guilt is devalued *relative to shame*; but it is that the psychic structure, the experiential profile, of guilt is of no importance in itself, provided it plays its role. For the utilitarian, guilt *might as well* be shame – or indeed anything else that does the job.

A fifth source of our contemporary tendency to neglect guilt is that it can seem that shame is less sharply in conflict with determinism than guilt is; it has certainly seemed so to many utilitarians, and also (to come back to *The Chrysanthemum and the Sword*) to many in the Buddhist tradition. With Christianity's relative recession from cultural prominence, both utilitarianism and Buddhism now have considerable popular reach in our society. And both are traditions with a marked deterministic tendency. Consider on the one hand Mill's and Sidgwick's (1907/1981) accounts of causation, both of which presuppose a model of science that has a very nineteenth-century fixity; and on the other the doctrine of *karma*, which is precisely the view that every action is inexorably the result of its causal history in the past, and that anything that I now do will have equally inescapable consequences in the future.

To the determinist shame can seem, as I have just been saying it does to the utilitarian, like a simple instrument of aversion therapy; whereas guilt can seem to be tied up with highly problematic beliefs, rooted in the Christian tradition, about a strong kind of freedom of the will, and also about forgiveness. If I cannot help what I have done, then there seems to be little or no scope for me to feel *guilty* about it; at the very least, cases where I am guilty for my involuntary deeds are not *focal* cases of guilt. But they can still be focal cases of shame. The connections between guilt, forgiveness and a certain kind of absolute responsibility run deep.[2] I shall come back to them, and to the Christian moral psychology that is their historical matrix, at the very end of this chapter.

Sixth and finally, one other writer who has recently argued a highly influential case for shame, and against guilt, is Bernard Williams: a follower of Nietzsche in some senses, but in every sense no follower of the utilitarians. Williams makes his argument in chapter 4 of *Shame and Necessity* (1993); what he says needs some close attention.

[2] To avoid repeating myself, my discussion of these issues here will to some extent presuppose and draw upon things I have written elsewhere, in particular my recent papers 'Moral Conscience Through the Ages' (2016); 'Forgiveness in Classical Greece: Socrates, Plato, Aristotle, and Their Background Culture' (forthcoming), and 'The Cross' (2018); and the much older book *Aristotle and Augustine on Freedom* (Chappell 1995).

BERNARD WILLIAMS ON SHAME AND GUILT

Like all the five other anti-guilt and pro-shame influences discussed so far, the overall tendency of Williams' *Shame and Necessity* is a movement away from Christian moral psychology. Unlike all those five influences except Nietzsche, it is a movement back towards ancient Greek moral psychology. When we extricate ourselves from the influences of the Christian tradition, says Williams (1993: 8), we can come to see how 'the basic ethical conceptions of the Greeks were in many ways more secure than our own'; and then (1993: 12) 'it is beguiling to dream about a history in which it was not true that Christianity, in Nietzsche's words, "robbed us of the harvest of the culture of the ancient world"'.[3]

In the particular case of shame and guilt, Williams' aim seems to be almost completely extirpatory. He does not quite think that we should simply get rid of guilt, and replace it with shame, across the board. But he does think both that there is something deeply 'obscure' about guilt, and also that the possibility of guilt is only intelligible within a wider framework that is created by the possibility of shame. At least some of the crucial moves in his argument are here (Williams 1993: 92–93):

> *What I have done* points in one direction towards what has happened to others, in another direction to what I am. Guilt looks primarily in the first direction … [Where one is guilty] simply of breaking a rule or a resolution, [and] there is no question of wrong to others or of reparation … guilt narrows down suspectly to a desire for punishment. It might then be helpfully replaced by what it should have been in the first place, shame.
>
> Shame looks to what I am … it may be a matter of discovery to the agent, and a difficult discovery, what the source of the shame is, whether it is to be found in the intention, the action, or an outcome … we can fruitfully work to make [shame] more perspicuous, and to understand how a certain action or thought stands to ourselves, to what we are and to what realistically we can want ourselves to be. If we come to understand our shame, we may also better understand our guilt. The structures of shame contain the possibility of controlling and learning from guilt, because they give a conception of one's ethical identity, in relation to which guilt can make sense. Shame can understand guilt, but guilt cannot understand itself.

Here and elsewhere in this chapter, Williams seems to be doing two things at once; two things that are in sharp tension with each other. (As quite often with Williams' elusive and impressionistic, yet elegant and persuasive, writing, it is tempting to adapt to his case a familiar French jibe: *c'est magnifique, mais ce n'est guère un argument*.) First he is pointing to ways in which an account of

[3] Williams (1993: 12), citing Friedrich Nietzsche, *The Twilight of the Idols and the Antichrist* (1888/1968: 60). Nietzsche was writing at a time when the labour of other philologists, particularly other German ones, was making it more than ever apparent how enormously indebted the Western European Renaissance was to Christianity, and in particular to Christian Byzantium and Alexandria, for *preserving* for them 'the harvest of the culture of the ancient world'. No doubt Nietzsche meant to say something outrageously paradoxical. He certainly succeeded.

guilt might be 'obscure',[4] and suggesting that this obscurity is a problem for the whole notion of guilt, and perhaps a reason to jettison it altogether: thus at least some guilt can 'be helpfully replaced by what it should have been in the first place, shame'. But secondly, he is pointing to ways in which an account of guilt might be relieved of obscurity, might indeed be made actually perspicuous, by locating it within the broader framework of an account of shame. So by the end of this quotation guilt can, after all, 'make sense', if and when it is seen in relation to 'a conception of one's ethical identity', as one particular and perhaps special case of what Williams more broadly calls 'the structures of shame'.

If Williams is right on his second claim, then surely he is wrong on his first. If at least some guilt can in fact be freed of obscurity, by locating it within the larger framework of shame, then Williams himself gives us excellent reason to deny that guilt, as such and all of it, should be jettisoned. It then becomes puzzling why Williams thinks (as he apparently does) that he is attacking guilt as such: why he supposes that his argument shows that guilt as such is an unhelpfully obscure Christian inheritance, which we should replace with the more fruitful, pagan-Greek, and perspicuous notion of shame.[5]

The solution to this puzzle, it seems to me, lies in Williams' basic unclarity about the target of his entire argument. Is it Christianity, or is it Kant and 'the morality system'?[6] Given his overall Nietzschean and anti-Christian project in *Shame and Necessity*, and given the care and detail with which Williams expounds Homer, Sophocles and Euripides to lay out his account of pagan-Greek shame, it is very striking how little Williams has to say about the other side: about what account of guilt he takes himself to be opposing. And what he

[4] Elsewhere Williams memorably writes also of the obscurity of *blame*, an obscurity which has much to do with what he takes to be the ultimate obscurity of responsibility and freedom of the will. The obscurities of guilt and blame are clearly connected; we are close here to the connections that I noted earlier with forgiveness and conscience in Christian moral psychology.

[5] On this issue of guilt's obscurity, by the way, an unwary reader of Williams might well end up tempted by the thought – it seems at times to tempt Williams himself – that the pagan Greeks were sunnily free of any similarly obscure guilt-like idea, and that it is only because of Christianity that we are afflicted by such a dark and impenetrable notion. A moment's thought about the Greek tradition should dispel this temptation. Western literature's three greatest explorations of the phenomenology of guilt, and especially blood-guilt – in all its terrible obscurity – are Shakespeare's *Macbeth*, Dostoevsky's *Crime and Punishment* … and Aeschylus's *Choephoroi*. Of the three versions of guilt explored in these masterpieces, it would be hard indeed to make a case that the least obscure of the three is the Aeschylean understanding of *miasma*.

[6] The 'morality system' is a term used by Williams with a special meaning (see especially, Williams 1985/2011: ch 10). It is, he explains, 'a particular variety of ethical thought … distinguished by the special notion of obligation it uses, and by the significance that it gives to it … The philosopher who has given the purest, deepest and most thorough representation of morality is Kant' (1985/2011: 174). He adds that, in this system, 'I may acquire an obligation voluntarily, as when I make a promise … [or] I may be under an obligation through no choice of mine. But, either way, once I am under the obligation, there is no escaping it, and the fact that a given agent would prefer not to be in this system or bound by its rules will not excuse him; nor will blaming him be based on a misunderstanding. Blame is the characteristic reaction of the morality system … [R]emorse or self-reproach or guilt … is the characteristic first-person reaction within the system, and if an agent never felt such sentiments, he would not … be a full moral agent in its terms' (1985/2011: 177).

does say does not begin, unlike his account of shame, from a careful literary and philosophical analysis of one or more of the huge number of available texts from the two thousand years of the Christian tradition that might be taken to display the account of guilt that he wants to target: Augustine's *Confessions*, say, or Ignatius' *Spiritual Exercises*, or Pascal's *Pensées*, or Bunyan's *Pilgrim's Progress* – or almost anything by Luther. He does not in fact begin from *Christian* materials at all; he begins instead from a notably swift and compressed reference to 'the Kantian oppositions' external/internal, heteronomous/autonomous, and egoistic/altruistic (Williams 1993: 77–78). But Kant, though of course he drew deeply on the Christian tradition (and perhaps especially Luther), made it as clear as he possibly could that he was in his ethical thinking not a Christian but a neo-Stoic. (Indeed it is an interesting question where the Stoics fit into Williams' opposition of guilt and shame; but not one that I can get into here.)

What Williams does tell us is that the account that he opposes starts from shame-reactions that we share with the pagan Greeks, and makes 'a special thing' out of those reactions by 'separately recognis[ing] them as guilt' (1993: 91). Again, we hear (1993: 92) that guilt 'is closely related to the conceptions of morality, and to insist on its particular importance is to insist on those conceptions'. (But *which* conceptions?) And that 'the conceptions of modern morality insist at once on the primacy of guilt, its significance in turning us towards victims, and its rational restriction to the voluntary'; 'It is under considerable strain in insisting on all these things at once' (1993: 94). Most importantly of all, Williams says this (1993: 94–95):

> [Guilt] is more isolated than shame is from other elements of one's self-image, the rest of one's desires and needs, and because it leaves out a lot even of one's ethical consciousness ... it cannot by itself help one to understand one's relations to [wronging and damaging that one is guilty of], or to rebuild the self that has done these things and the world in which that self has to live. Only shame can do that, because it embodies conceptions of what one is and of how one is related to others.
>
> If guilt seems to many people morally self-sufficient, it is probably because they have a distinctive and false picture of the moral life, according which the truly moral self is characterless. In this picture I am provided by reason, or perhaps by religious illumination (the picture owes much to Christianity), with a knowledge of the moral law, and I need only the will to obey it. The structures most typical of shame then fall away: what I am, so far as it affects the moral, is already given, and there is only the matter of discerning among temptations and distractions what I ought to do ... In not isolating [in this way] a privileged conception of moral guilt, and in placing under a broader conception of shame the social and psychological structures that were near to what we call guilt, the Greeks, once again, displayed realism, and truthfulness, and a beneficent neglect.

Here too we have a deeply interesting and perceptive attack on *something*. But it is not obvious that it is an attack on *guilt* (as such). Of course, to speak of the truly moral self as 'characterless' is to pick out a historically important phenomenon: the very same phenomenon, I suggest, as Charles Taylor (1989) identifies as 'the punctual self', and Iris Murdoch (1970) as 'the existentialist self'. But important though this phenomenon is historically, and continues to be both psychologically and sociologically, the phenomenon is not proprietary to Christianity. There are non-Christian conceptions of ethics to which a moralised punctual self is central: notably, as just suggested, Kant's and the Stoic conceptions on which Kant drew.[7] There are also – as has been argued at considerable length by three philosophers whom Williams greatly admired, Charles Taylor, Elizabeth Anscombe and Alasdair MacIntyre – Christian conceptions of ethics to which a moralised punctual self is *not* central.

On any conception of ethics that isn't committed to a moralised punctual self, the problems about guilt that Williams identifies may well simply not arise. Since such views needn't be committed to the 'morally self-sufficient' and 'isolated' conception of guilt that Williams describes in the last quotation, it is therefore also open to these views to put guilt back into the kind of explanatory connections that Williams thinks shame has, and specially moral guilt lacks. Guilt too can then 'embody conceptions of what one is and of how one is related to others', and so can also 'help one to understand one's relations' to wronging and damaging that one is guilty of, and 'to rebuild the self that has done these things and the world in which that self has to live'. And this, surely, is the most usual role that guilt actually plays in our actual moral psychology today. As most of us in fact experience guilt, guilt too is a tool of self-understanding, which helps us to understand the interrelations of wrongdoing, self and world just as much as shame does – if not more so.

In this role guilt need not be connected, either, with what Williams is clearly connecting it with in chapter 4 of *Shame and Necessity*: with 'the morality system'. Williams' description of the target of his critique of guilt is, as I have noted, extremely brief and compressed. No doubt this compression comes in large part from the fact that in 1993 Williams had recently described 'the morality system' in much greater detail in *Ethics and the Limits of Philosophy* (1985/2011), and he presupposes that description in his later book. But if anything is obvious to the reader of Williams (as again to any reader of Taylor, Anscombe and MacIntyre), it is that rich and perspicuous ethical thought need have no truck at all with the morality system. And this applies to guilt as much as to any other ethical resource that we might want to keep in play. Guilt is of course connected, as I have already insisted myself, with the notions of conscience, blame, responsibility and forgiveness. That does not even look like meaning that all of these notions can only be alive within the morality system – any more than the notion of shame could only be alive within the Sicilian code of *omertà*. Guilt *can* be connected with a specially moral sense of culpability or indebtedness or deficit. But it can also, and much more fruitfully, be connected with notions like the virtues of pity and justice, the values of vulnerability and equal respect, and

[7] It is also true, of course, that the Stoics were an influence on Christian thought. The full story is a complicated one; but the complications do not undermine the basic point.

with my own sense of myself as someone who is answerable to the standards set by those virtues and values. Guilt then can easily have a role within just the kind of broadly virtue-ethical outlook that might *replace* 'the morality system' – and that Williams himself might want to recommend as a replacement.

Like Williams' own critique of guilt, this line of thought presupposes that we have some kind of grip on the distinction between shame and guilt. For Williams, there is a moralised and extreme form of guilt, which he attacks; but there is also a milder and more plausible form of guilt, which he seems at least partly inclined to rehabilitate as a species of the genus shame. At times he also seems to voice the suspicion that guilt in this milder form cannot ultimately be distinguished at all from shame, or from other things in the vicinity such as 'agent-regret' – his name for what, for example, the blameless lorry-driver feels about the child whom she accidentally runs over. It is cases like the lorry-driver, apparently, that prompt Williams to say, as he does both in *Shame and Necessity* and more than once elsewhere, that it is implausible to try and demarcate *the voluntary* as the scope of guilt.

Here I offer two responses. The first response is that guilt is indeed not always and necessarily felt only about the voluntary. But (to state the obvious) universal necessary-and-sufficient-condition concomitance is not the only way in which two things can be essentially associated. It is perfectly possible to say that guilt is *focally* about the voluntary, about what I have done and could have not done, while also allowing that the sense of the 'could' in question can be highly etiolated, and etiolated without this necessarily meaning that the guilt is felt 'irrationally'.

The second response is that it seems quite mistaken to me for Williams to identify regret with *any* kind of guilt. Regret is something else, something different both from shame and from guilt. The characteristic expression of regret is 'If only', and this utterance can occur in combination with neither shame nor guilt. (I am neither guilty nor ashamed that my parents have both died, but I certainly regret their deaths; that is, I am inclined to think and say 'If only they hadn't died'.)

Regret can also occur in combination with shame or guilt or both. So Williams' lorry-driver may well feel all three of shame, guilt and regret, without that having the slightest tendency to mean that we *cannot tell them apart*. Perhaps her shame will come out when she says 'I didn't mean to, yet I did this awful thing, and *everyone knows it*'; her guilt, in the words '*I have destroyed the life of an innocent child*' (recall the connection that I have just suggested between guilt and the virtues of pity and justice); and her regret in the words 'If only I had come round that corner two minutes earlier or two minutes later'.

It therefore seems to me a serious misstep for Williams to tie together so much of his thinking about shame and guilt with his notion of agent-regret. This latter notion is a useful one, but it is different from both shame and guilt, and it is not helpful to minimise the distinctions between them, as Williams throughout his writings very often tends to.

I also reject Williams' idea that guilt is simply a species of the genus shame. To explain why, I need to develop my own account of the shame/guilt distinction. I give this account in the next section. By the end of that account, it should also be clear why and how guilt can have a positive role in criminologists' thinking about the restitution of offenders; also, why and how guilt is, and remains, a notion that we at any rate are likely to understand best by thinking of it in narrative terms familiar from the Christian tradition. The upshot is that we should not give up on guilt, and that in certain ways guilt is more useful to our society in general, and to the penologist in particular, than shame is.

SHAME AND GUILT IN RATIONAL-EXPLANATORY CONTEXT

Williams' tendency to think that the boundaries between guilt and shame are not as clear-cut as we tend to think has some echoes that are much less plausible than Williams' own version of the thought. In particular, one very unconvincing observation is perplexingly common in some of the recent academic literature, namely that ordinary English speakers often use 'shame' and 'guilt' as synonyms. So far as I can see, ordinary English speakers do no such thing, and it is hard to see how academics could have come to think that they do. Certainly they could not have reached this view by listening to ordinary people. Perhaps they were only listening to each other.

There are at any rate two small justifications for the perplexingly common remark. The first is that, as above, shame and guilt are often attributed (and correctly attributed) to the same people at the same time, so that it can be unclear which of the two a speaker actually intends to pick out. Second, it is not impossible, as Williams suggests in one way and as we shall see again in another, that there may be reactive 'grey areas' *in between* shame and guilt. Also, of course, it doesn't help that a lot of the commonest ways of trying to make out the difference are plainly over-simplified or otherwise inaccurate descriptions of our actual experience; especially when just one of these (say, that shame is 'external', guilt is 'internal') is presented as if it alone might be a full statement of the whole truth about the contrast.

What do we need to say to do better? Well, here as elsewhere, we need to recognise the complication of things. Perhaps the familiar simple contrasts will look more plausible if, instead of insisting on running just one of them as the all-purpose explanation of everything, we try and put them together into a larger-scale but more complex account. That, at any rate, is what I shall try to do here.

As a first step, one may (as Hume would probably put it) look inside one's own breast, and simply report that, as first-personally experienced, shame and guilt *feel* different. For so they do, to me at any rate. I have just said that it is too simple to call shame 'external' and guilt 'internal'; but certainly shame feels closer to the surface of the body. Shame is a cold prickling sensation, associated with a feeling of nausea and a sharp intake of breath; if it is anywhere particular in the body, it is in the (blushing) face and in the rest of the skin, and in the pit of the stomach. Whereas guilt is a dull, anguished, inner throb. (It is an 'inward biting', as is suggested by a word that *is* close to a synonym of guilt, at least in its vividly affective forms, namely 'remorse'.) Like shame, guilt too can be felt in the stomach, but it is also felt in the chest, and in the forehead. (Clutching at one's brow seems to be one of guilt's most typical gestural manifestations; with shame, by contrast, it is hiding one's face.)

On its own, this first step won't get us far enough. While there are certainly typical physical feels and gestures that accompany and display occurrent shame and guilt, there can be shame and guilt *without* these feels. And as with any other emotion, neither shame nor guilt is *only* occurrent – both are dispositional too.

Furthermore, as also with any other emotion, shame and guilt have rational structures. As Philippa Foot (1959) famously argued – and though shame was not one of her examples, its opposite pride was – it is not intelligible to call something an emotion unless we can situate it within a rational-explanatory framework. So, to take another of her examples, by the nature of the concept of fear, fear of X necessarily involves that I should either see X itself as bad and destructive in some way, or believe that something somehow bad and destructive is liable to come from X. And unless these rational connections are there in some form or other, a mere feel, for example, a tearful, panicky fluttering in the stomach, will not count as the emotion of fear at all (though it might count as a feeling of fearfulness). Similarly with pride, the emotion of pride is not merely a feel of happy grandeur that makes you breathe deeper and swell out your chest. To be proud of Y involves thinking first that Y is somehow a good and impressive thing, and secondly that I am in some way connected with Y. Such beliefs can of course be *false*; but unless some such beliefs are present, what we have before us simply is not a case of pride.

How do things go if we try to apply these Foot-type points to the cases of shame and guilt? How are *these* emotions rationally networked? For both shame and guilt, the answer is – as already suggested – quite complex. We can bring out some of the detail by asking some more specific questions, such as the following six.

Q1. What situations evoke shame and guilt? Shame is what you feel when you are *exposed*, literally or metaphorically: when your clothes fall off in public, or your sexual fantasies (be they never so vanilla) are revealed to the world, or when everyone hears about your embezzlement. But guilt is what you feel when you are *convicted* (in a closer to theological than forensic sense): when you come to be aware of the wickedness of your actions, and in particular of their cruelty or their injustice or both.

Thus guilt involves a change in my own view of my actions: I come to think that what I did was morally awful, where before I either thought that my action was all right, or else had just not thought about it. (And here there may indeed be a conceptual puzzle: cp see my 'Forgiveness' paper). By contrast, shame very commonly – though not always – is mainly about a change in others' view of me as a person. I knew all along what I look like naked, about my own really rather unoriginal sexual tastes, about my financial malpractice; and it *may* be (sometimes it is and sometimes it isn't) that I was perfectly unperturbed about these things. What now perturbs me is that *people know*.

Of course this isn't true of all shame: most of us have some habits or tastes that we feel *private* shame about. But with those too, the shame would be painfully amplified if everyone knew that I pick my nose or whatever. Guilt is not usually amplified in this way by publicity. When it comes out about my financial corruption, the revelation adds shame to my guilt (or adds public shame to my private shame). But the revelation does not add to my *guilt* about my embezzlement. It does not affect my *guilt* at all. It may even relieve it somewhat: things may feel slightly 'normalised' when I see that others agree with me in my negative judgement of my own behaviour.

There are also, of course, and very obviously, situations where both shame and guilt are appropriate: as when a politician is publicly revealed to be secretly corrupt, or as when a professor publicly delivers a cruel put-down to a PhD student. It is perhaps in these cases that we are likeliest to get the co-instantiation of guilt and shame that I talked about earlier, and to come closest to cases where it actually is true that the two words are used as synonyms: 'Hang your head in shame' is a tabloid phrase usually applied to public exposés of guilt, not of shamefulness.

A further interesting question here is this. It looks like guilt is a specifically moral emotion, whereas shame is much wider-ranging: it can be felt about moral failures, but it can be felt about other things too. (So at this point, perhaps, guilt *does* look like a species of the genus shame. Perhaps; but bear with me. That is not where we are going to come out.) Now the scope of the moral is usually thought to be *excellence in general*, virtue in life as a whole. So is there, we might ask, any analogue to guilt for more specific and non-moral kinds of excellence? Suppose, for example, that I drop a simple catch in cricket, and drop it because I am not paying attention to the game as I should be (as the role of cricket-player requires me to). Is there an analogue of moral guilt for such cases? The answer seems, fairly clearly, to be 'no'. I may berate myself, and I may wish to do better next time, but the main thing I feel is that I want to sink through the floor, and that (see Q6 below) is a species of shame, not of guilt.

However, this may simply be because cricket is such a minor part of life (at least for most of us). What about larger and more life-central roles, such as one's career: what about wanton failure to do one's job properly as, say, a barrister, or again as a philosophy professor? Won't we get closer to actual guilt, the more these roles become life-central, and therefore judgements about them get closer to whole-of-life judgements such as guilt? Maybe; and maybe not. I don't need to settle this issue here. But certainly, anyone who thinks that there are cases in this area where there *is* a clear analogue of guilt, may also be attracted to the idea that such cases are what I earlier called grey-area cases: they show that the distinction between shame and guilt isn't absolute.

Q2. What is the failing involved in shame and guilt? In shame the thought is that one has failed in dignity, propriety, grace, elegance, self-respect: properties that we might reasonably group together as notions broadly to do with *honour*, or with *kalokagathia*. In guilt it is a failing in *goodness*: as I said in criticising Williams, to feel guilty is to feel that one has lapsed from the standards set by the ideals of the virtues.[8] More gnomically, and very broadly: shame is a response to an *aesthetic* failing, guilt to a *moral* one.[9] Or more gnomically still, and from a different angle: guilt pains the conscience, shame pains self-esteem.

Q3. What do shame and guilt make you feel? As I said above, shame is a cold prickling sensation on the skin and in the pit of the stomach. But guilt is a dull, anguished, inner throb; it too can be felt in the stomach, but it is also felt in the chest, and in the forehead. The paradigm gestures of guilt are clutching one's brow, and pleading with others for restitution and forgiveness; the paradigm gestures of shame are putting one's hands over one's eyes, and hiding from others.

Q4. What are the negative reactions of others, and the shamed or guilty person herself, to someone's perceived shame or guilt? In onlookers, shame induces derision, jeering, mockery and contempt; guilt induces denunciation, judgement and condemnation.

Q5. How do you console someone who feels guilt or shame? When someone is ashamed and we want to console them, we say 'You have nothing to be ashamed of' (meaning: because it wasn't really shameful); or if that doesn't look convincing, 'Well, *I* am not ashamed of you/don't think that you should be ashamed'; or if *that* won't wash, 'This will pass' or 'This isn't a big deal' or 'One day you'll look back on this'.

Consolation for guilt is importantly different, because guilt (and here I agree with Williams) is importantly different from shame in its relation to the voluntary. It is true that, when someone feels guilt, there too we may insist that 'You have nothing to feel guilty about'. And this may be because we don't think that the deed that prompts the guilt really warrants it, because it was not really a bad deed. But we may also have something quite different in mind, for which there

[8] Guilt also often has to do with a sense of damaged *purity*. This is often very evident in the Bible, and in other Judaeo-Christian moral resources. But it would be a mistake to think that there is no such notion in pagan Greek thought. In classical Greek the key notions in this area are *hosiotes* and *eusebeia* – and again *miasma*; with which, for a start, Aeschylus' *Eumenides*, Sophocles' Theban plays, Euripides' *Hippolytus*, and Plato's *Euthyphro* are all deeply concerned.

[9] That this distinction between the broadly moral and the broadly aesthetic is not an absolute or exclusive one is a central thesis of my paper 'Kalou Heneka' (Chappell 2014: ch 7). No indeed; but that is quite different from saying that there is no distinction *at all*.

is only a weak analogue with shame. We may mean that, although the deed was certainly a bad one, *it was not voluntarily done*, and therefore the agent should not feel guilty because the agent was not culpable.

This contrast comes out fairly clearly with Oedipus. It would be perfectly true to say to Oedipus that he has nothing to be *guilty* about, because he didn't mean to kill his father and marry his mother, and did both deeds involuntarily. But it wouldn't be in the least consoling to say that, because Oedipus' anguish is (roughly, in our terms) shame, not guilt, and the shame of what he has done is still there even if these were involuntary deeds (though no doubt it would be worse if they were voluntary).

Similarly with the lead character in another of Sophocles' plays, *Ajax*. It is no good for Tecmessa or whoever to point out to Ajax that he acted under a blinding delusion, imposed on him by Athene, when he made himself ridiculous by killing a flock of sheep instead of the Atreids. Here too, as Williams rightly argues in chapter 3 of *Shame and Necessity*, the same holds: it is the shame of his deed that distresses Ajax, not its guilt or his culpability for it. So it is no consolation to tell Ajax that he acted involuntarily. He knows that, and in this case the involuntariness of his deed does not even mitigate its shamefulness. If he had done it voluntarily that would have been shameful too, of course, but in a different way; and a lesser one – he might then have pleaded the aristocratic right to do whatever the hell he likes, no matter how bizarre. The shame of what he actually does is greater, because it shows him up not as wielding aristocrat's prerogatives, but as *powerless*: befuddled, delusional, a victim of *atê*. It demonstrates how even a great Homeric warrior is helpless in the hands of a goddess like Athene. She *designs* this shame for him, and she *intends* this shame to destroy him. And it does.

Q6. What reparative thoughts and behaviour do guilt and shame prompt? In me my own shame induces a wish to hide, to become invisible, to vanish, to disappear, to see the shameful thing or deed no more. (So it is not for nothing that in Sophocles Ajax and Jocasta kill themselves, and Oedipus blinds himself.) I want this shameful thing not to have happened; I want others not to know that it has happened, or to forget as soon as possible that it has happened. I want it to be *as if this had never been*.

By contrast, what my own guilt induces is a wish to *put things right* and *to be forgiven*. And crucially, neither putting things right nor being forgiven need involve wishing that the bad deed had never happened at all; on the contrary, they typically presuppose and indeed actual *require* the existence of the bad deed.

To bring out what I mean, consider the parable of the Prodigal Son, and in particular its ending (Luke 15: 29–32, Authorised Version):

> [The elder brother] said to his father, Lo, these many years do I serve thee, neither transgressed I at any time thy commandment: and yet thou never gavest me a kid, that I might make merry with my friends: But as soon as this thy son was come, which

> hath devoured thy living with harlots, thou hast killed for him the fatted calf. And [the father] said unto him, Son, thou art ever with me, and all that I have is thine. It was meet that we should make merry, and be glad: for this thy brother was dead, and is alive again; and was lost, and is found.

The elder brother's complaint is that his father is making a great fuss in rejoicing over his wastrel brother, who has finally 'come to himself' as the Authorised Version nicely puts it, repented of his wicked living, and returned to the family home. That is, the elder brother is complaining that his father's forgiveness of the prodigal means that *the prodigal son is not a net loser* by his terrible behaviour. In fact, it is almost as if the father has *rewarded* him for his behaviour. Surely this is unjust? Surely he shouldn't be?

The father, I think – and the author of the parable too – displays a deep wisdom here about guilt and its concomitant thick ethical concepts. The point is that guilt by its nature seeks, not oblivion like shame, but forgiveness. And forgiveness is or can be a step in the narrative that makes things *better than they could have been otherwise* – and in particular, better than they would have been with no original offence. The restored prodigal really is better off than the older brother, and the prodigal's wrongdoing and guilt really is central to the explanation why. The father's forgiveness is redemptive: it transforms the story. But that the prodigal went off the rails is at the heart of the story; indeed, without his aberration, there *is* no story.

We can reach a very similar conclusion by thinking about guilt under the other description that I indicated above, as the desire not to be forgiven, but to put things right. Consider here another Biblical story, the story of Zacchaeus (Luke 19: 5–10):

> And when Jesus came to the place, he looked up, and saw him, and said unto him, Zacchaeus, make haste, and come down; for today I must abide at thy house. And he made haste, and came down, and received him joyfully. And when they saw it, they all murmured, saying, That he was gone to be guest with a man that is a sinner. And Zacchaeus stood, and said unto the Lord; Behold, Lord, the half of my goods I give to the poor; and if I have taken anything from any man by false accusation, I restore him fourfold. And Jesus said unto him, This day is salvation come to this house, forsomuch as he also is a son of Abraham. For the Son of man is come to seek and to save that which was lost.

I have said that guilt by its nature seeks, not oblivion like shame, but to put things right. And putting things right is or can be a step in the narrative that makes things *better than they could have been otherwise* – and in particular, better than they would have been with no original offence. This is literally what happens with Zacchaeus: he gives away half of his fortune, and he explicitly promises to make fourfold restoration of everything he has fleeced from his unfortunate tax-clients (or victims). It is striking that, here as with the parable of the prodigal, there are resentful figures on hand to complain about it when Zacchaeus receives forgiveness. And it is striking too that the form of their complaint is essentially the same. It is that Zacchaeus, who has been such an arrant thief for so long, is going to end up, by way of forgiveness, better off (not richer, but happier – and above all, 'saved') than he would have been if he had never been a thief at all; which seems unfair. For Zacchaeus too, forgiveness is redemptive; and for him too, what forgiveness achieves is not the erasure but the transfiguration of his wrongdoing.

Shame, to say it again, simply seeks the erasure of the shameful. But guilt, in seeking either forgiveness or to put things right or both, seeks not the erasure but the transfiguration of the wrongdoing. Guilt is in the end a richer and more complex notion than shame because it has this remarkable narrative structure, and because where shame is conceptually connected merely to forgetfulness or erasure, guilt is conceptually connected to what we may call *redemption*. And this thought above all is the one that I want to put at the centre of my plea to criminologists to bring guilt back to the centre of their penological thinking.[10]

REFERENCES

Benedict, R (1946) *The Chrysanthemum and the Sword: Patterns of Japanese Culture* (Boston, MA, Houghton Mifflin).

Braithwaite, J (1989) *Crime, Shame and Reintegration* (Cambridge, Cambridge University Press).

Chappell, SG (2016) 'Review of "Moral Conscience Through the Ages"' by R Sorabji 91 *Philosophy* 290.

——(2018) 'The Cross' 26 *International Journal of Philosophical Studies* 478.

——(forthcoming) 'Forgiveness in Classical Greece: Socrates, Plato, Aristotle, and their Background Culture' in G Pettigrove and R Enright (eds), *The Routledge Handbook of the Philosophy and Psychology of Forgiveness* (Abingdon, Routledge).

Chappell, T (1995) *Aristotle and Augustine on Freedom: Two Theories of Freedom, Voluntary Action and Akrasia* (London, Palgrave Macmillan).

——(2014) *Knowing What to Do: Imagination, Virtue, and Platonism in Ethics* (Oxford, Oxford University Press).

Foot, P (1959) 'Moral Beliefs' 59 *Proceedings of the Aristotelian Society* 83; reprinted in P Foot (1978) *Virtues and Vices* (Oxford, Basil Blackwell).

Mill, JS (1863/1998) *Utilitarianism*, ed R Crisp (Oxford, Oxford University Press).

Murdoch, I (1970) *The Sovereignty of Good* (London, Routledge).

Nietzsche, F (1888/1968) *The Twilight of the Idols and the Antichrist* (trans RJ Hollingdale) (Harmondsworth, Penguin Books).

Sidgwick, H (1907/1981) *The Methods of Ethics*, 7th edn (Indianapolis, IN, Hackett Publishing).

Taylor, C (1989) *Sources of the Self: The Making of the Modern Identity* (Cambridge, Cambridge University Press).

Williams, B (1985/2011) *Ethics and the Limits of Philosophy* (Cambridge, MA, Harvard University Press).

——(1993) *Shame and Necessity* (Berkeley, CA, University of California Press).

[10] For helpful discussion I am grateful to Tony Bottoms, Jon Jacobs, Glen Pettigrove and Jake Wojtowicz.

6

Taking the Long View: The Role of Shame and Guilt in Desistance

ALICE IEVINS*

INTRODUCTION

In a recent paper, Anthony Bottoms (2017) outlines a debate among theorists of penal censure who agree that punishment could be justified by its communicative capacity but who disagree about whether punishment should seek to prompt the wrongdoer's repentance. On the one hand, Antony Duff (2001) and John Tasioulas (2007) consider repentance, imagined as serious and pained reflection on the wrongs we have done and the desire to change ourselves so that we do not repeat them, to be an intrinsically appropriate goal of punishment (although there are some significant differences in their respective theses). Andrew von Hirsch (1993, 2003), on the other hand, argues that the liberal state has an insufficiently intimate relationship with its citizens to legitimate it using 'its coercive powers to seek to induce moral sentiments of repentance' (1993: 73). His claim is not that these sentiments are undesirable for individuals to feel, and indeed he argues that it is desirable that blaming punishment 'gives the individual the opportunity to respond in ways that are typical of an agent capable of moral deliberation: to recognise the wrongfulness of the action, feel remorse, [and] make efforts to desist in future' (2003: 408; see also 414–15). However, he is writing within the tradition of liberal political philosophy, and his primary intellectual concern is not with determining what is morally appropriate for the individual but with justifying the practice of state punishment in a liberal state. He therefore argues that making the pursuit of repentance part of the justification of state punishment risks the state becoming invasive as it tries to compel or coerce character change.

* I am grateful to Ben Laws, for talking through different ways of thinking about emotions and for opening my eyes to their importance many years ago. I am also grateful to Tony Bottoms for conversations and readings on these issues over the years, and to him and Jon Jacobs for their insightful comments on earlier drafts of this chapter. Thanks also to the Criminal Jurisprudence and Philosophy group at the University of Cambridge, for a very helpful and stimulating discussion about this chapter.

What penal theorists on both sides of the debate share is a conception of repentance as a condition which involves and may be instigated by painful moral emotions like guilt, shame and remorse (see also Proeve and Tudor 2016: 35). They do not discuss the moral sentiments involved with much precision or consistency, however, nor in a way which takes account of the significant amounts of existing empirical research on their nature, causes and effects. At different points, the theorists involved discuss various 'retractive emotions'[1] being involved in repentance: Tasioulas (2007: 489) talks about guilt and shame as initiators of repentance, Duff (2001: 117) associates it with remorse, von Hirsch connects it to shame and regret (1993: 72), and Bottoms talks about 'self-blame' (2017: 126) and 'deep contrition' (2017: 128). Tasioulas offers the clearest depiction of the process which, in the 'rough temporal order in which [the stages] standardly appear', starts with the wrongdoer being 'assailed by feelings of guilt for his [sic] wrongdoing: these are painful experiences that present his action as wrongful, something for which he is responsible and deserves to be blamed by others and by himself' (2007: 488). It then leads to them coming to a more reasoned judgement of their wrongdoing, confessing and apologising for the wrong, making moral and material reparation, including accepting punishment, and resolving to change their character so that they do not do anything similar again. Tasioulas explicitly states, however, that not all accounts of repentance will be as 'full-blooded' as this account suggests (2007: 491), and that not all stages are required for the process to be named 'repentance'.[2]

In an attempt to resolve the 'repentance' debate, Bottoms (2017, 2021) draws on the Christian tradition to offer a different and less full-blown understanding of repentance as *metanoia*, or 'turning around'. *Metanoia* involves changing one's behaviour, but it does not necessarily involve deep feelings of self-blame and guilt: Bottoms says such feelings are 'not precluded' from *metanoia*, but nor are they its 'dominant motif' (2017: 126). Through this reconceptualisation, he seeks both to allay von Hirsch's concerns about the invasiveness of the state pursuit of repentance, and to incorporate empirical research which suggests that there is a more complex and less causal relationship between the sentiments of repentance and desistance from crime than penal theorists often suggest.

Bottoms' suggestion may address many of von Hirsch's objections to repentance as a goal of state punishment, but viewed from the perspective of moral (rather than political) philosophy, and focusing more on what it is preferable

[1] Proeve and Tudor (2016: 31) suggest that this family of emotions includes (but is not restricted to) 'remorse, guilt, shame, regret, compunction, contrition and repentance'. Explaining the term 'retractive', they say that: '[T]he self experiencing any one of these emotions in some way retracts or withdraws from something which is otherwise seen as belonging to or associated with the self … In experiencing such emotions, the person retreats or resiles from their action or omission or state of being. The common thought is that "I wish I had not done that" or "I wish I was not like that" or a variation of this theme'.

[2] Bottoms (2017: 121) highlights Tasioulas' flexible account of repentance as a key difference between his account of it and the version advocated by Duff.

for the wrongdoer to feel than on what it is appropriate for the state to induce, *metanoia* seems like a less satisfying destination than 'deep' (Bottoms 2017: 118) repentance. Certainly, one drawback of Bottoms' suggestion is the fact that the appeal of the deep conception of repentance advocated by Duff and (to a slightly lesser extent) Tasioulas is normative as well as instrumental. Feelings of guilt and shame about past wrongful actions are considered beneficial not solely because we believe that they contribute to individual moral change (an instrumental question which can be empirically proven or disproven), but because they also show that the wrongdoer shares our evaluation of what happened. This shared evaluation therefore makes it possible for those who have committed serious wrongs to be our moral neighbours again. Bottoms himself (2017: 119–20) alludes to this argument when he fleshes out Duff's underdeveloped account of repentance with Miranda Fricker's paradigmatic account of communicative blame. Fricker imagines this type of blame aiming 'to inspire remorse in the wrongdoer, where remorse is understood as the pained moral perception of the wrong one has done' (2016: 167).[3] One effect of this remorse is 'to prompt a change for the better in the behaviour (inner and outer) of the wrongdoer' (2016: 173); the other is 'an increased alignment of the wrongdoer's moral understanding with that of the blamer' and thus a regenerated 'shared moral consciousness' (2016: 167). Taken together, these two outcomes could constitute repentance, as defined by Duff, and the second, at least, is not at all instrumental. Similarly, Tasioulas describes repentance as a desirable goal of punishment, as it is the mechanism by which 'the wrongdoer re-establishes his [*sic*] standing in relation to [the values that matter to him] by realigning his actions and attitudes with them' (2007: 493). By doing this, repentance also lays the normative and imaginative groundwork for the wrongdoer to be reintegrated with the community that shares these values. The value of repentance, then, is that it entails a deep recognition of the wrong that has been done, and an accompanying desire to change the behaviour. This foundation then makes it possible for the wrongdoer to continue to live in a moral community with the people they have hurt.

The objection which moral philosophers may have to Bottoms' account of *metanoia* – that it advocates a form of change which is too shallow and unfocused for it to repair the moral breach created by the initial crime – is removed if we are able to think of *metanoia* as the first step to a deeper form of repentance – a process which may take years, and which may never be concluded, but which may eventually lead to a shared moral understanding and thus to the possibility of continuing moral relations. Building such an account of 'long repentance' is

[3] Bottoms (2017: 120, fn 53) questions whether the emotion of remorse is as intrinsic to communicative blame as Fricker suggests, arguing that communicative blame could purely entail the pursuit of shared understanding. Fricker (2016: 167) herself supports this suggestion, given her core definition of it as 'a communicative act that reprimands with feeling, in the hope of bringing the wrongdoer to better understand and perhaps correct her behaviour'.

the goal of this chapter, which opens with a discussion of empirical research on shame and guilt, as the retractive emotions about which the most research has been conducted, which criminologists have most often considered to be relevant to processes of desistance, and which penal theorists have discussed in their accounts of repentance. I will argue that these emotions are closely related but that guilt is (often) the form which shame takes after it has been cognitively processed and distanced from the self (Elison 2005). I will then discuss research on the relationship between guilt, shame and desistance from crime, arguing that guilt rarely instigates desistance, and is more likely to emerge *after* a person has undergone an identity change and has already started learning how to live a non-criminal life.[4] I will conclude by arguing that we should think about repentance as a long instead of a deep process, and briefly comment on the difference such a conceptualisation would make to the repentance debate and to penal practice.

SHAME, GUILT AND SHAME-GUILT: BLURRING AND DISTINGUISHING THE RETRACTIVE EMOTIONS

A significant body of empirical research has explored the nature of and distinctions between shame and guilt (for reviews, see Elison 2005; Tangney and Dearing 2002; Tracy and Robins 2016), but despite this there is no clear scholarly consensus about their relationship, nor is there any conceptual clarity about their relationship to other retractive emotions like remorse or regret. For example, even though shame, guilt and remorse are emotions with clear relevance to criminology, some scholars working in the field see them as different terms for the same emotion (Harris 2001, 2011; Farrall and Calverley 2006) and others stress their distinctions (Tangney and Dearing 2002). Some equate guilt and remorse but distinguish them from shame (Harris, Redgrave and Braithwaite 2004; Tangney, Stuewig and Hafez 2011); others see remorse as distinct from both shame and guilt (Bandes 2016); some talk about shame and remorse together and fail to discuss guilt at all (LeBel et al 2008; Von Stokkom 2002); and yet others see all three emotions as related but distinct (Proeve and Tudor 2016).

This conceptual maelstrom could reflect unclear thinking on the part of these scholars, but it could also be telling us something about the murkiness and density of the emotions themselves. Certainly, all emotions are complex – they are affective and embodied, but also involve cognitions and beliefs, and are normally *about* something and often push us to *do* something (Nussbaum 2003; Proeve and Tudor 2016) – and this complexity is therefore unlikely to map clearly onto the labels we give to them. Indeed, the empirical data suggests that people often struggle to find 'consistent, meaningful definitions' (Tangney and

[4] This is, of course, a generalisation, and people can certainly feel deep feelings of guilt immediately after committing wrongful acts.

Dearing 2002: 11) of the emotions of shame and guilt when they are discussed in the abstract, which may account for some of the conceptual confusion in the scholarly literature. Nevertheless, philosophers, psychologists and anthropologists have tried to draw stark dividing lines between shame and guilt, often basing the differentiation either on what the emotion is about (guilt is often assumed to derive from acts we have voluntarily committed, whereas shame is supposed to be directed at who we are) or on the context in which it is felt (guilt is believed to be a private emotion and shame to be a public one; Harris 2001). Were these distinctions to hold true, they would allow relatively firm boundaries to be drawn between the emotions, but there is very little direct empirical evidence supporting either distinction (Tangney and Dearing 2002).

Nevertheless, the empirical data does suggest that, when asked to describe specific experiences of shame and guilt, these experiences differ in theoretically meaningful ways (Tangney and Dearing 2002), supporting the belief that the terms do define two distinct experiences. Guilt is the word we give to the negative feeling we have when we think that we have done something wrong, and when this knowledge troubles us. Its focus is not on ourselves, however, but on our behaviour, and it is empirically correlated with empathy (Von Stokkom 2002), the desire to confess the wrongdoing and change our behaviour (Baumeister, Stillwell and Heatherton 2001), and the desire to repair the harm (Tangney, Stuewig and Hafez 2011). For these reasons it is often seen as the more desirable of the two emotions (Chappell, chapter 5 in this volume), and the one which, on the surface at least, has the most promising relationship to desistance from crime. Certainly, there is research to suggest that guilt but not shame is associated with rule-following behaviour and less violence (Trivedi-Bateman 2019), although it is less clear how this association plays out at the latter stages of a person's criminal career.

Shame, however, is harder to isolate. At its root, it is the word we tend to give to the negative feeling we have when we think we are not the person we want to be. It is often described as a fundamentally social emotion, one associated with how we are seen in the eyes of others, but the empirical support for this association is mixed (Harris, Redgrave and Braithwaite 2004; Tangney and Dearing 2002), perhaps because it is so difficult to differentiate how (we imagine) we are seen by others from how we see ourselves (LeBel et al 2008). Because shame's target is so wide – it is who we are, not what we have done and not a changeable component of our personality – it often constitutes a fundamental threat to our sense of self, and it is often experienced as physical and devastating.[5]

[5] It is therefore distinct from embarrassment, another self-conscious emotion with which it is often conflated, but from which empirical research suggests it should be distinguished (Miller and Tangney 1994; Tangney et al 1996; Harris 2001). Embarrassment tends to be associated with more trivial or even humorous events, which often occur in public. It is also associated with more obvious physiological changes, such as blushing, as well as with smiles and jokes. Shame, however, is associated with deeper-seated flaws which lead us to feel 'immoral' rather than 'awkward' (Tangney et al 1996: 1258), and is more likely to lead to anger and depression.

It is empirically correlated with depression (Nussbaum 2003), distress, psychological problems, substance abuse (Tangney, Stuewig and Hafez 2011), low self-esteem (Velotti et al 2017) and anger (Scheff and Retzinger 2001), as well as with a tendency to externalise blame and avoid taking responsibility (Tangney and Dearing 2002). Theorists have also argued that our struggles to name shame (Lewis 1971) mean that it is often unacknowledged even by the person experiencing it (Scheff and Retzinger 2001), and thus that it is often discharged as anger and violence (Gilligan 2003). For these reasons, it has often been seen as a less constructive emotion than guilt, or even as one which is morally destructive (Chappell, chapter 5 in this volume; although see also Williams 1993).[6]

There are distinctions between the experiences, then, but this does not necessarily mean that they are the binary opposites they are often presented as being. As Elison (2005) argues, the two experiences are normally discussed by emotion researchers as though they belong to the same category and thus as though they are mutually exclusive alternatives to each other, and this framing both results from and leads to conceptual confusion. Instead, Elison suggests that they should be thought of as belonging to different categories. In his view, shame is an affect – a quite fundamental form of emotion – whereas guilt is also a 'socio-legal condition' (Elison 2005: 6) which often becomes associated with an affect, and thus becomes an 'affective-cognitive hybrid' (2005: 9; see also Ortony 1987). In other words, shame is a quite fundamental emotion, whereas guilt has a greater cognitive component and is more likely to be associated with a social or legal state (having done something wrong, or having committed a crime).

This distinction helps to make sense of certain findings on the relationship between shame, guilt and acknowledgement. Nathan Harris used data gathered from over 700 people who had committed drink driving who were randomly assigned to either a court or a restorative justice conference to explore 'the structure of the emotion of shame and the process of shaming' (2001: 94). Through factor analysis, he found three empirically distinct emotions: 'Embarrassment-Exposure', 'Unresolved Shame' and 'Shame-Guilt'. The last of these, which Harris states could have been called 'Shame-Guilt-Remorse' (2001: 117), involved the feeling of having done something wrong and knowing that other people had been hurt, but also of being ashamed of and angry at oneself, and was correlated with higher levels of empathy with victims and lower feelings of hostility. It was more commonly instigated in restorative justice conferences than in courtrooms and was predicted by shaming (ie, other people's

[6] For this reason, some scholars have expressed disquiet about the central role shame seems to play in Braithwaite's (1989) reintegrative shaming theory (see, for instance, Chappell, ch 5 in this volume). This criticism seems to be rooted in confusion between the *process* of shaming and the emotions which it generates. Braithwaite himself briefly suggests that, done reintegratively, shaming could result in the emotions of both guilt and shame (1989: 57), and later empirical research has supported this hypothesis and led Braithwaite to integrate it more deliberately into the theory (Braithwaite and Braithwaite 2001).

expressions of displeasure), but only when it was carried out by respected people and when the shamed person agreed that they had done wrong. It was also associated with feeling reintegrated and not feeling stigmatised. Harris argues that Shame-Guilt marked a significant threat to the individual's identity because it indicated a disjunction between the values they professed to hold and their actions, a disjunction which was highlighted by the disapproval of people whose values they shared. It could only be diminished by somehow realigning behaviours and values, either by changing the value system or by changing the behaviour. Unresolved Shame, however, involved feeling that important issues had not been addressed, was correlated with higher levels of anger and hostility, and was predicted by perceptions of being stigmatised and by believing that the offence was less wrong. Part of what made it so painful and so likely to be discharged with aggression, Harris hypothesises, is that 'being unable to decide whether one has violated ethical norms' (2001: 186), but knowing that other people think that one has, threatens our sense of identity in a way which is difficult to manage.

Harris' argument that shame takes a different form when it is not resolved bears some similarity to the findings of Eliza Ahmed's (2001) study of shame management and its relationship to school bullying among over 1,400 Australian school pupils and their parents, as well as to the work of Scheff and Retzinger (2001) and James Gilligan (2003) into spirals of shame and rage. In her study, Ahmed built on pre-existing research on the importance of shame management to distinguish between Shame Acknowledgement, which involves admitting to feelings of shame and then discharging it by taking responsibility for the wrongdoing and trying to put things right, and Shame Displacement, which involves the shame feelings being discharged as blame of and anger at others. Children who were neither perpetrators nor victims of bullying were able to acknowledge their shame without displacing it, while victims acknowledged their shame and internalised it and perpetrators failed to acknowledge their shame and instead displaced it as bullying behaviours.

These studies have three findings in common, all of which matter to our thinking about the shame and guilt felt by people who commit crime. First, both Ahmed's description of Shame Acknowledgement and (more self-consciously) Harris' of Shame-Guilt, are similar to classic descriptions of guilt, in that they involve recognition of the victim's pain and may propel reparative action.[7] Second, in both cases it is clear that acknowledging the shame – recognising it and taking responsibility for the action that caused it – is what helps it become more like guilt and hinders it from being externalised. There is therefore a cognitive and narrative process involved in managing shame and feeling it as guilt, one which involves actively framing a relationship to the thing causing the emotion; it is this process which

[7] Ahmed herself acknowledges this relationship (2001: 235), and her model of Shame Acknowledgement is positively correlated with Tangney's model of guilt-proneness (Ahmed 2001: 250).

takes the emotion from being pure affect to being a cognitive-affective hybrid, in Elison's (2005) terms. This finding tallies with other empirical research which suggests that the difference between shame and guilt lies in the way the person feeling the emotion appraises responsibility for the event eliciting it (Tracy and Robins 2016).[8] People feel guilty when they attribute responsibility for a failing to internal, unstable and controllable causes, like a temporary failure to control one's temper or an error of judgement – that is, things about themselves that they feel responsible for but to which they do not consider themselves to be reducible. They feel ashamed, on the other hand, when they blame internal, stable and uncontrollable causes, such as stupidity, laziness or weakness – things about themselves which they believe they cannot change and for which they therefore are reluctant to take active responsibility.[9] Third, in both cases, acknowledging the shame (or guilt) is a necessary but not sufficient first step to discharging it, which requires some sort of reparative behaviour, either to the self or to the person harmed. This in turn suggests that the guilt will only be able to be discharged in contexts in which some sort of reparative action is achieved or achievable, reminding us of the relationship between the felt emotion and the circumstances in which it is induced and interpreted. This relationship will be returned to in the concluding section of this chapter, which briefly discusses the ability of different criminal justice interventions to stimulate and structure different emotions.

Taken together, these factors seem to suggest that (acknowledged) shame and guilt are more similar than some accounts might suggest, and that the primary distinction between them and unacknowledged, unresolved or damaging shame is *interpretive*. By itself, unacknowledged shame can be terrifying and is overwhelming. The act of acknowledgement, however, allows the feeling to be objectified and viewed from a third-person perspective. Thus separating the shame from the self makes it easier for it to be reflected on and for its source to be identified. This objectification of the feeling then makes it easier for the person to take responsibility for the behaviour which caused it – if they themselves see that behaviour as wrong – and for the bad feeling to be healthily discharged through reparative action. Seen like this, shame and guilt are not polar opposites, but similar emotions whose differences lie in the ways they have been made sense of.

Thinking about the emotions in this way suggests that an emotion which starts as unacknowledged shame could – over time and in the right conditions – become guilt. This finding in turn encourages us to think about the conditions which might block or facilitate this process of moral sense-making. Harris' (2001) research offers some suggestions: when we are shamed by people whose

[8] It is worth remembering that how someone appraises responsibility to the eliciting event is different from where the responsibility actually lies.

[9] This finding may account for the widespread belief among philosophers, discussed in Chappell (ch 5 in this volume), that guilt is associated with the voluntary.

values we share, when we know we have done wrong, and when we are reintegrated – or in other words, when we have a degree of moral clarity about what we have done, and when our identities and social positions are not overwhelmed or destroyed by our past – it will be easier for us to process our shame into guilt. The nature of the cause of the emotion is also likely to play a role in shaping how we can interpret it. Particularly serious acts of violence, for instance, might be so overwhelming and damaging that they fracture the relationships of those who commit them and lead them to profoundly question their identities, meaning that they spend longer overwhelmed by shame (Williams 1993). Similarly, the way Western culture frames sexuality – as formative of identity (Foucault 1998) – means that we often assume that people who commit acts of sexual violence are particular types of people ('paedophiles' or 'sex offenders'), and this cultural interpretive framework might make it harder for people who commit these crimes to think about what they have done as something for which they take responsibility but which does not define them (Ievins 2023).

Recent research also suggests that the passage of time might play an important role in allowing shame to be processed as guilt, and it is the role played by the passage of time which is the main focus of this chapter. Ben Crewe, Susie Hulley and Serena Wright (2020) recently published a book detailing the experiences of young people given a life sentence for murder in England and Wales. Although not strictly longitudinal, the authors deliberately interviewed and surveyed people in the early, mid and late stages of their sentences, thus offering an insight into how the retractive emotions might take different forms at different times.[10] One of the most striking findings of their project was that people were more likely to admit guilt for their offences as their sentences progressed (only 13 per cent of prisoners in the very early stage considered themselves guilty of murder; 32 per cent in the early stage; around half in the mid to late stage; and about 70 per cent of those who were in prison after the punitive 'tariff' part of their sentence had concluded). In part, this pattern resulted from the disproportionately high number of people convicted under the contentious legal doctrine of joint enterprise in the earlier stages (Hulley, Crewe and Wright 2019), but it also resulted from the increasing ability of prisoners to acknowledge and make sense of their shame as their sentences progressed. Prisoners in the early stages of their sentences, who had recently been convicted of murder and handed shatteringly long terms of imprisonment, were 'overwhelmed' (Crewe, Hulley and Wright 2020: 256) by their situation, and often experienced the intrusive recollections which come with PTSD. In the infrequent cases in which they admitted guilt, their 'self was fissured by the existential crisis and shame

[10] They also asked people to reflect on how their attitudes had shifted during their sentences. They have received an ESRC grant (ref: ES/T005459/1) to conduct follow-up interviews with the people in their original sample, and it will be useful to see what else is learned from a truly longitudinal design.

associated with coming to terms with *being a murderer* and their implications for family members' (Crewe, Hulley and Wright 2020: 254, emphasis original). They often described themselves as having 'lost something of themselves when they took another person's life', an experience which led them to lose trust 'in their moral boundaries and self-definitions' (2020: 257). In a context of such 'deep existential rupture' (Crewe, Hulley and Wright 2020: 284), denial might be a highly adaptable, even functional, response to the shame and 'deep self-loathing' (Wright, Crewe and Hulley 2017: 238) which comes with having caused a death.

Over time, however, 'as the emotional fog of the early years lifted, prisoners found that they had the psychological strength and space' (Crewe, Hulley and Wright 2020: 267) to 'come to terms' with the offence and their responsibility for it. This process involved a 'form of psychological adjustment' which resulted in 'a distinction between actions and selfhood, and a need to honour the past without being swamped by a single episode and its moral implications' (2020: 268). It did not, however, lead prisoners to think about their offence less. In fact, thinking about the offence was rated as a more serious problem by people who were later on in their sentences, and 'most mid- and late-stage prisoners felt morally obligated to work through, and remain conscious of, what they had done' (Crewe, Hulley and Wright 2020: 268), and to use this knowledge to help them to do something better with the remainder of their lives.

Although they use different language, Crewe, Hulley and Wright seem to be describing a shift from a feeling of overwhelming shame at the start of the sentence – which was sometimes warded off with anger, denial and drugtaking (Wright, Crewe and Hulley 2017) – to a more processed and 'intelligible' (Crewe, Hulley and Wright 2020: 277) experience of guilt. It is a transition which seems to have been facilitated by the reflection prompted by imprisonment (see also Kazemian 2019) and further enabled by the passing of the years. Just as Harris (2001) found that it was easier for people to acknowledge their feelings of Shame-Guilt when they were shamed reintegratively and thus were not totally identified with their offence, here the passage of time seems to have allowed people convicted of murder to reflect on their offence as something separate from themselves, allowing guilt to grow out of the seeds of shame and denial. The finding that guilt is something which might emerge gradually is one with implications for the relationship between the retractive emotions and desistance, which this chapter shall go on to discuss.

SHAME, GUILT AND DESISTANCE

Debates among penal theorists about the legitimacy of the state pursuit of repentance rarely take account of the fact that most people who commit crime, even quite persistently, eventually stop doing so (Shapland and Bottoms 2017).[11] Over the last 20 years in particular, a significant amount of criminological research has charted the phenomenon of desistance from crime, and this research has built a detailed account of both why and how people stop committing crimes (Maruna 2001: 26–27). Most of this research has been conducted on desistance among those who previously committed volume crimes – that is, large amounts of (normally) less serious offences – and although there remains significant disagreement among researchers, there is also significant agreement. We know that most people want to stop offending, that the desire does not straightforwardly lead to the reality, that ageing and maturation help, and that both the social context and maintaining a positive sense of identity matter (Shapland and Bottoms 2017). One area in which there is very little consistency, though, is the role that the moral emotions of shame and guilt play in the process. Worse, there are in fact two apparently contradictory ways of thinking about desistance and the retractive emotions: the first sees guilt (although not necessarily shame) as a motivator to desistance, and the second sees both (although particularly shame) as a threat to it.

The idea that guilt for past wrongdoing might propel future behavioural change is consistent both with the implied model of 'deep' repentance which penal theorists like Duff (2001) and Tasioulas (2007) support, and with modern abolitionist thought on the necessity of 'accountability' (Sered 2019) for personal transformation. Certainly, some studies, many quantitative, suggest that there might be a link between guilt and desistance, although they rarely offer a serious account of the mechanism which makes this link work, nor do they use the language of guilt and shame consistently. Leibrich (1996), for instance, interviewed 37 people whom she deemed to be going straight, 19 of whom retrospectively described shame as a motivator. However, her interviewees described private remorse, which she defined as 'the experience of having offending [sic] one's own personal morality' (1996: 287) and which seems reminiscent of Harris' (2001) Shame-Guilt, to be the most important and effective kind of shame. Tangney, Stuewig and Martinez (2014) found that guilt-proneness while people were incarcerated negatively predicted recidivism a year after release; shame-proneness, on the other hand, was not directly linked to recidivism but it may have increased its likelihood via a moderating effect on the externalisation of blame (see also Hosser, Windzio and Greve 2008). LeBel et al (2008) found that regretting the commission of crime was associated with fewer reconvictions, but the experience of shame was not. Similarly, Kazemian (2019), who conducted a qualitative longitudinal study of desistance during long-term imprisonment, found that desisting prisoners were more likely to hold themselves personally responsible for the harms they had caused than those who were not desisting,

[11] Bottoms (2017) is the exception to this.

and they also tended to describe it as important to spend time thinking about the offence. That said, Kazemian thought that excessive feelings of guilt could be damaging to the prospects of long-term prisoners as they may enable 'the maintenance of a negative identity, which may impede the desistance process' (2019: 164).

An alternative camp of desistance researchers, led by Shadd Maruna (2001; Maruna and Copes 2005; Maruna and Mann 2006), contends that guilt and shame threaten the positive sense of self which successful desistance requires. In his 2001 book *Making Good*, Maruna conducted a detailed analysis of narrative interviews with 30 people who were desisting from crime and 20 who were not, and found that maintaining a positive sense of identity was crucial to desistance. He found that desisters did this by telling a 'redemption narrative', a story which 'allows the person to rewrite a shameful past into a necessary prelude to a productive and worthy life' (2001: 87). Such stories often involved high levels of neutralisations, excuses and justifications (as did those of the people who persisted in the offending), and very few of the people he interviewed referred to feelings of guilt or shame. Maruna used this finding to challenge a belief which was then popular in correctional circles: that it is beneficial to encourage offenders to take responsibility for the offences they have committed. If anything, Maruna argued, doing so might expose them to a sort of shame which overwhelmed their identities and trapped them in their pasts. In a cultural context in which admitting responsibility for a past crime is tantamount to admitting to being a particular 'kind of person', or even to being 'irredeemable' (2001: 145), Maruna argued, neutralising past offences with excuses and justifications provides desisting offenders with a way of aligning themselves to conventional morality without outing their past self as fundamentally criminal. As such, he suggested that they might actually be the 'first step in a *softening* process' (2001: 144, emphasis original) away from offending and towards desistance.

Maruna's argument has some empirical support from quantitative data which has failed to find correlations between recidivism and contrition (Romanowski 1988) or expressed remorse (Serin, Mailloux and Hucker 2000; see also Proeve and Tudor 2016). It is also more directly supported by the small amount of existing research on desistance among people convicted of sexual offences, a group whose social identities are particularly stained by their convictions (Ievins 2023). These studies suggest that those who desist from sexual offending are more likely to externalise blame for their offences onto causes like substance abuse and mental health problems (Kras and Blasko 2016) or other situational causes (Farmer, McAlinden and Maruna 2016) than they are to insist that the responsibility was their own. Other research has found that people deemed to pose a high risk of a sexual reoffence who maintain that they are innocent are *less* likely to be reconvicted than those deemed to pose a high risk who accept guilt (Hood et al 2002). Taken together with Maruna's argument, then, there is reason to think that the protective strategies which people follow to stave off negative feelings of shame and guilt may help them in their journey of desistance, at least in contexts in which being known to have committed an offence has a particularly strong effect on our sense of self (see also Maruna and Pali 2020).

There are, then, two contradictory ways of thinking about the retractive emotions' contribution to desistance: one suggests that guilt and shame prompt desistance, and the other suggests that they threaten it. Building on the argument made in the first section of this chapter – that it takes time to process shame into guilt – one way of squaring the circle might be to think about desistance as a process with multiple stages, each of which has different emotional accompaniments. Summarising the findings of desistance researchers, Frank J Porporino (2010) has argued that the process often starts with a moment of dissatisfaction, as a reaction *against* an often unsatisfying and dysfunctional lifestyle. Over time, however, people need to grow *into* a new way of living, and thus in the later stages of desistance, what matters is 'sustaining hope, maintaining a strong sense of self-efficacy, experiencing adaptive shame, and redefining one's sense of self and identity' (Porporino 2010: 73–74). In the earlier phases, shame and guilt would not serve a beneficial purpose to the desister, and if anything might discourage them from taking the tentative first steps away from their offending life. At this stage, then, the forms of neutralisation described by Maruna (2001) may be functional as an alternative to being overwhelmed by shame.

As the process continues, however, people are propelled to reflect on their past as part of the process of identity construction. Barry Vaughan, for instance, theorises that during the final '*dedication*' (2007: 394, emphasis original) phase of desistance, desisters are required to construct a new identity, one which is both more consistent with their desired self and which also makes sense of a past which is 'morally incompatible with whom they wish to be' (2007: 394). This process of sensemaking often takes a narrative form, allowing the narrator to simultaneously display – to themselves and to others – the continuity and distance which exists between them and their past self. One way in which it does this is through the deliberate elicitation of emotions like shame and guilt as 'a device through which harm is acknowledged and yet disavowed' (Vaughan 2007: 399). In other words, Vaughan suggests that guilt and acknowledged shame are the output of narrative self-work which occurs in the later phases of desistance, and which demonstrate and reinforce the distance which the desister has travelled. Acknowledging certain moral sentiments about our past is central to this process, as the emotions allow us to demonstrate – to ourselves as well as to others – that we no longer have the faulty perspective we had in the past. By responding emotionally in the right way, philosopher Peter Goldie argues, we show that we are able to 'look the past in the eye, and respond emotionally as one should' (2003: 313). Earlier in the process, it may be too painful to look at the past in this way, and other responses may be more functional.

This theoretical bone is given empirical meat by the findings of the 'Tracking Progress on Probation' study. This longitudinal study, which was led by Stephen Farrall and colleagues (Farrall 2002; Farrall and Calverley 2006; Farrall et al 2014), involved five 'sweeps' of research interviews with the same sample of probationers in England and Wales, the last two of which analysed the emotional trajectories associated with desistance (although, frustratingly, they deliberately conflated shame and guilt; Farrall and Calverley 2006, note 2: 129).[12] In Sweep Four, Farrall and Calverley (2006) analysed the different emotions experienced by those they deemed to be at different stages of desistance. They found that those who were in the earliest stages often experienced positive emotions and appreciated that they no longer felt the negative feelings of guilt and shame which had come with their offending. Deeper feelings of 'internal disquiet' (Farrall and Calverley 2006: 116) about past actions emerged as the process of desistance continued and became strongest when people were at least two or three years into their desistance journey (albeit sometimes with the occasional relapse). At this stage, people were beginning to see themselves as 'non-offenders', and these feelings of shame and guilt seemed to mark the distance between who they believed themselves to be and who their offending suggested that they had been (or who their relapses suggested that they might still be), and thus perhaps marked their entrance into Vaughan's (2007) dedication phase. A research participant pseudonymised as Justin, for instance, spoke of the shame of being fined for the possession of an unlicensed vehicle several years into his desistance journey:

> Oh it's done my head in. It's nothing to do with the fine it's to do with the amount … the length of time I've been out of trouble to getting something else on my record. It's like I've not stayed away from it, you know what I mean, any more. So now any judge or any policeman or anything like that they'll look at me and say, 'He's not changed, he's just not been caught'. And it's not right, do you know what I mean (Farrall and Calverley 2006: 120).

However, the people who had reached the phase which Farrall and Calverley called 'normalcy' – those whom they deemed to have 'completed the process of desistance' and to be identifiable as 'non-offending members of society' (2006: 124) – spoke about feelings of guilt and shame in the past tense, as emotions they used to have but which were no longer relevant to their securely law-abiding sense of self.

A slightly more complicated picture emerges when we compare this emotional trajectory to that revealed by the interviews conducted at Sweep Five (Farrall et al 2014). As in the earlier sweep, those who were in the later stages of desistance felt very little guilt and shame, largely because they felt such a strong distance from their past selves. In Farrall et al's words, 'their offending has long since been confined to an unfortunate episode of their past, with declining relevance to their current lives' (2014: 208). However, those who were in the

[12] Sweeps 1–3 were conducted between 1997 and 1999, sweep 4 from 2003 to 2004, and sweep 5 from 2010 to 2013.

early stages of desistance reported much higher feelings of shame and guilt than those who were deemed to be in the equivalent stages in Sweep Four between six and nine years earlier. Farrall et al hypothesise that this difference may be because the people in this stage had had much longer offending careers and therefore had more to feel guilty and regretful about (2014: 154). Many of their feelings of guilt also related specifically to the ways they had broken people's trust during earlier relapses, which may also explain why the emotion was experienced earlier. However, it is worth noting that the guilt people felt at Stage Five was experienced 'as a *current pain* rather than an unwanted memory' (2014: 197, emphasis original). This emotional vividness meant that it was often 'an uncomfortable feeling to acknowledge' (Farrall et al 2014: 197) and one which they often struggled to make sense of or identify a root for. In other words, it is possible to hypothesise that they were experiencing a visceral version of shame, one whose power derived from the length of their offending career and their proximity to it, but which had not yet been processed into the more managed forms of shame or guilt which people felt during the later and more consolidatory phases of their desistance.

The picture painted by these two sweeps is extremely complicated and, on the surface at least, self-contradictory. However, looked at alongside Vaughan's (2007) work on the internal narrative of desistance, as well as what we know about the difficulty of acknowledging and managing the retractive emotions and the associated function of staving them off, a tentative pattern emerges.[13] This pattern also reflects that found in Crewe, Hulley and Wright's (2020) account of life-sentenced prisoners' shifting feelings of guilt and shame, although it takes a more complex form in Farrall et al's case: the latter sample contained people desisting from a lifestyle which involved committing many offences, a context in which relapses are common, in which it is difficult to identify the start and end of the desistance process, and in which the source of the guilt and shame is harder to locate in one single event. Nevertheless, there does appear to be a basic structure to the emotional trajectory involved in moving away from crime, whether the crimes in question are volume or serious:[14]

1. *Early and very early stages: as desistance begins, shame risks overwhelming the desister and is sometimes held at bay*

At this early stage of desistance, the shameful past is still very close to the desister, both temporally and in their imagination and that of other people. This proximity means that any acknowledged shame is likely to be overwhelming and

[13] It is worth noting that my interpretation of the Farrall and Calverley (2006) and Farrall et al (2014) data is different from that of Bottoms, who suggests that it shows the 'somewhat unpredictable' (2017: 135) distribution of the sentiments of deep repentance among people desisting from crime. The difference lies in my comparison of this pattern to that found in Crewe, Hulley and Wright (2020), as well as in my differentiation between different types of shame and guilt.

[14] As another example of someone whose emotional journey might follow this trajectory, see the case study of 'John' in Bottoms and Lanskey, ch 8 in this volume. 'Len' offers an example of someone for whom this pattern does not fit.

difficult to process. Many early-stage desisters may struggle to make an account of themselves (Crewe, Hulley and Wright 2020) or to identify and isolate the source of the shame (Farrall et al 2014). Others may successfully ward off the overwhelming feelings of shame with neutralisations and denial (Maruna 2001).

2. *Middle stages: as desistance consolidates, shame is processed into guilt*

As the years pass, a combination between the passage of time and shifting social circumstances may make it easier for people to process and make sense of their shameful feelings about their past. At the same time, the demands of 'rebiographing' (Maruna 2001: 89) push them to reflect on their past and establish an emotionally appropriate relationship to the bad things they have done. The extent to which it is possible or helpful for people to process their shame into guilt will depend on the type and severity of the offence(s) and the extent to which they have been stigmatised and reintegrated (Harris 2001), both of which are likely to affect people's capacity to see their offending as something belonging to a past version of themselves. It will also depend on the availability and effectiveness of neutralisations and denial, which is likely to vary depending on the facts of the case (Vaughan 2007). Allowing the shame to be felt as guilt may be particularly difficult for people convicted of sex offences, as the presumption that the sexual identity persists across time is strong and so levels of stigmatisation are high; in these cases, denial and neutralisations may well be functional for longer (Ievins 2023).

3. *Late stages: once desistance achieved, shame and guilt fade away*

In some cases, people will move so far past their old offending self that shame and guilt will no longer be relevant. They have constructed a new identity and the passage of time makes it much less necessary for them to construct an emotionally regulated link between their new self and their former self. Not all desisters will reach this stage, for similar reasons to those listed above.

This pattern is tentative, and future longitudinal work on desistance should consider the extent to which it holds and whether it applies equally well to those who have committed volume offences as to those who have committed a smaller number of more serious crimes. Nevertheless, I argue that it offers a helpful way of thinking about the apparently contradictory evidence about the relationship between shame, guilt and desistance by suggesting that acknowledging the emotions may be beneficial in the later phases of desistance, but not necessarily earlier on.

Rather than being the prompt to, or cause of, processes of desistance or repentance, as they are described by some desistance researchers (Leibrich 1996) and penal theorists (Tasioulas 2007), feelings of guilt about the offence(s) may actually be both a signal that desistance is in process and a way by which desistance is sustained in its later stages. Indeed, there is reason to believe that denial and neutralisations may be more effective than guilt in nurturing the early phases of desistance, as they are the only way those who have only very recently turned away from crime can keep themselves from being overwhelmed by shame.

As shall be discussed in the concluding section of this chapter, however, these often-functional responses are not always the end of the story. In fact, in some cases they may, counterintuitively, be early steps on the long path to repentance.

CONCLUSION: FROM 'DEEP' TO 'LONG' REPENTANCE

Concluding their description of the emotional trajectories of desistance, Farrall et al (2014: 215) argue that 'the principal lesson to be drawn is that those working with people trying to desist should recognise the need to engender hope first and foremost'. It is hope that makes people believe that another way of living is possible, and hope that makes it possible for them to turn away from their old way of life. On the surface, this model of change comes close to that imagined in Bottoms' (2017, 2021) conception of *metanoia*, but it is inconsistent with that envisaged by those penal theorists who consider deep repentance to be a legitimate goal of punishment, and who consider retractive emotions like shame, guilt and remorse to be central to, and perhaps the triggers of, that process (Duff 2001; Tasioulas 2007). Considered alongside the longitudinal and quasi-longitudinal evidence presented by Farrall and Calverley (2006), Farrall et al (2014) and Crewe, Hulley and Wright (2020), however, it seems that such retractive emotions often emerge as the hoped-for way of life begins to take form, and as desisters are both required and enabled to reflect on their pasts and acknowledge feelings of guilt about what they have done. This finding suggests that a process of repentance which starts as *metanoia* (Bottoms 2017, 2021) might, under the right conditions and over time, lead to the sort of 'deep' repentance considered desirable by Duff and Tasioulas (and, implicitly, by Fricker 2016).

What difference, if any, does thinking of repentance as a 'long' process which might start with something shallow make to the 'repentance debate'? Von Hirsch's (1993, 2003) main objection to the pursuit of deep repentance is that for the state to do so would require it to take an inappropriately close and demanding position relative to its citizens. For von Hirsch, repentance may be an appropriate outcome, but it is a dangerous aim. It was this concern which Bottoms hoped to address with his concept of *metanoia* as a potential aim of punishment, but in addressing von Hirsch's concerns, this concept fails to encapsulate the capacity of 'deep' repentance to enable moral repair by creating a shared understanding of the past events. However, the data presented in this chapter suggests that encouraging people to change their lives in the ways supported by Bottoms' account of *metanoia* might, over time, guide those who commit wrongs to think differently, and more repentantly, about their past. It suggests that it is not necessary for punishment to aim at deep repentance for such repentance to be achieved; instead, it suggests that feelings of shame and guilt about past offending can emerge autonomously in certain conditions, and instead suggests that a potential goal for state intervention (perhaps punishment) would be to aim to create these conditions, or at least to avoid working against them. Thinking about repentance as a potential and desirable outcome of (certain forms of) punishment, rather than a goal of it, thus avoids activating the primary concerns raised by von Hirsch and allows us to reap the moral benefits of repentance occurring without incurring the political costs of pursuing it.

And what difference should the recognition that repentance is a 'long' process make to penal policy? First and foremost, this account supports risk-assessors' and psychologists' growing recognition that offence denial and neutralisations are not necessarily risk factors for further offending, and may in some cases be supportive of change. It therefore suggests that denial and neutralisations should not be reasons to deny people access to rehabilitative opportunities or offending behaviour courses, and also raises questions about the legitimacy of seeing lack of remorse to be relevant to sentencing or for parole decisions (for more details of this complicated debate, see Bandes 2016). Acknowledging the emotional complexity of desistance should also be a reason for rehabilitative opportunities to be responsive to the shifting emotional states of people being punished, and in particular for discussions of offending to be facilitated on a timeline which makes sense to the person being punished (Crewe and Ievins 2021). More concretely, it may also be a reason for restorative justice opportunities to be provided later in people's sentences, or even once their sentences are completed, whenever people are emotionally ready for them.

Thinking about repentance as something which takes place on a long timeline should not, however, be taken as an argument in favour of longer prison sentences, or longer sentences in general, especially given the strong empirical evidence to suggest that imprisonment extends criminal careers (Macleod, Grove and Farrington 2012) and that longer prison sentences tend to increase reoffending (Gendreau, Goggin and Cullen 1999). One of the most important implications of this chapter is that it challenges the widespread belief that that the 'hard treatment' components of punishment provide '*an appropriate psychological setting for feelings of shame and regret*', in the words of von Hirsch (2003: 410, emphasis original), who in turn was paraphrasing Duff. A widespread, and historically significant (Ignatieff 1989; Throness 2008; Warr 2016), justification of punishment in general and imprisonment in particular is that they should seek to induce the sentiments of guilt and shame, which are assumed to be both morally and instrumentally valuable. What this chapter suggests is that it is not helpful to try to force these sentiments and that they are ineffective at initiating personal change. Instead, proper feelings of guilt may be more likely to emerge as a result of a process of desistance and when the person is ready for them. This not a process which is likely to track imprisonment or punishment, and people are as likely to process their guilt after their punishment has been concluded as they are during it – or perhaps even more so, given that reintegration makes such processing easier and stigmatisation makes it harder (Harris 2001), and given that at least some prisons actively stigmatise those they hold (Ievins 2023). If we want to create the conditions for long repentance, we should therefore avoid long punishment.

REFERENCES

Ahmed, E (2001) 'Shame Management: Regulating Bullying' in E Ahmed, N Harris, J Braithwaite and V Braithwaite (eds), *Shame Management Through Reintegration* (Cambridge, Cambridge University Press).
Bandes, SA (2016) 'Remorse and Criminal Justice' 8 *Emotion Review* 14.
Baumeister, RF, Stillwell, AM and Heatherton, TF (2001) 'Interpersonal Aspects of Guilt: Evidence from Narrative Studies' in WG Parrott (ed), *Emotions in Social Psychology: Essential Readings* (Philadelphia, PA, Psychology Press).
Bottoms, AE (2017) 'Penal Censure, Repentance and Desistance' in A du Bois-Pedain and AE Bottoms (eds), *Penal Censure: Engagements Within and Beyond Desert Theory* (Oxford, Hart Publishing).
——(2021) 'Criminal Justice and the Ethics of Jesus' in A Millie (ed), *Criminology and Public Theology: On Hope, Mercy and Restoration* (Bristol, Bristol University Press).
Braithwaite, J (1989) *Crime, Shame and Reintegration* (Cambridge, Cambridge University Press).
Braithwaite, J and Braithwaite, V (2001) 'Shame, Shame Management and Regulation' in E Ahmed, N Harris, J Braithwaite and V Braithwaite (eds), *Shame Management Through Reintegration* (Cambridge, Cambridge University Press).
Crewe, B and Ievins, A (2021) '"Tightness", Recognition and Penal Power' 23 *Punishment & Society* 47.
Crewe, B, Hulley, S and Wright, S (2020) *Life Imprisonment from Young Adulthood: Adaptation, Identity and Time* (London, Palgrave Macmillan).
Duff, RA (2001) *Punishment, Communication, and Community* (Oxford, Oxford University Press).
Elison, J (2005) 'Shame and Guilt: A Hundred Years of Apples and Oranges' 23 *New Ideas in Psychology* 5.
Farmer, M, McAlinden, A-M and Maruna, S (2016) 'Sex Offending and Situational Motivation: Findings from a Qualitative Analysis of Desistance from Sexual Offending' 60 *International Journal of Offender Therapy and Comparative Criminology* 1756.
Farrall, S (2002) *Rethinking What Works with Offenders: Probation, Social Context and Desistance from Crime* (Cullompton, Willan Publishing).
Farrall, S and Calverley, A (2006) *Understanding Desistance from Crime* (Maidenhead, McGraw-Hill Education).
Farrall, S, Hunter, B, Sharpe, G and Calverley, A (2014) *Criminal Careers in Transition: The Social Context of Transition from Crime* (Oxford, Oxford University Press).
Foucault, M (1998) *The Will to Knowledge: The History of Sexuality*, vol I (trans R Hurley) (London, Penguin Books).
Fricker, M (2016) 'What's The Point of Blame? A Paradigm Based Explanation' 50 *Noûs* 165.
Gendreau, P, Goggin, C and Cullen, F (1999) *The Effects of Prison Sentences on Recidivism* (Ottawa, Department of the Solicitor General).
Gilligan, J (2003) 'Shame, Guilt, and Violence' 70 *Social Research* 1149.
Goldie, P (2003) 'One's Remembered Past: Narrative Thinking, Emotion, and the External Perspective' 32 *Philosophical Papers* 301.
Harris, N (2001) 'Shaming and Shame: Regulating Drink-Driving' in E Ahmed, N Harris, J Braithwaite and V Braithwaite (eds), *Shame Management Through Reintegration* (Cambridge, Cambridge University Press).

——(2011) 'Shame, Ethical Identity and Conformity: Lessons from Research on the Psychology of Social Influence' in S Karstedt, I Loader and H Strang (eds), *Emotions, Crime and Justice* (Oxford, Hart Publishing).
Harris, N, Redgrave, L and Braithwaite, J (2004) 'Emotional Dynamics in Restorative Conferences' 8 *Theoretical Criminology* 191.
Hood, R, Shute, S, Feilzer, M and Wilcox, A (2002) 'Sex Offenders Emerging from Long-Term Imprisonment: A Study of their Long-Term Reconviction Rates and of Parole Board Members' Judgements of their Risk' 42 *British Journal of Criminology* 371.
Hosser, D, Windzio, M and Greve, W (2008) 'Guilt and Shame as Predictors of Recidivism: A Longitudinal Study with Young Prisoners' 35 *Criminal Justice and Behavior* 138.
Hulley, S, Crewe, B and Wright, S (2019) 'Making Sense Of "Joint Enterprise" For Murder: Legal Legitimacy or Instrumental Acquiescence?' 59 *British Journal of Criminology* 1328.
Ievins, A (2023) *The Stains of Imprisonment: Moral Communication and Men Convicted of Sex Offenses* (Berkeley, CA, University of California Press).
Ignatieff, M (1989) *A Just Measure of Pain the Penitentiary in the Industrial Revolution 1750–1850* (London, Penguin Books).
Kazemian, L (2019) *Positive Growth and Redemption in Prison: Finding Light Behind Bars and Beyond* (London, Routledge).
Kras, KR and Blasko, BL (2016) 'Pathways to Desistance Among Men Convicted of Sexual Offences: Linking Post Hoc Accounts of Offending Behavior and Outcomes' 60 *International Journal of Offender Therapy and Comparative Criminology* 1738.
LeBel, TP, Burnett, R, Maruna, S and Bushway, S (2008) 'The "Chicken and Egg" Of Subjective and Social Factors in Desistance from Crime' 5 *European Journal of Criminology* 131.
Leibrich, J (1996) 'The Role of Shame in Going Straight: A Study of Former Offenders' in B Galaway and J Hudson (eds), *Restorative Justice: International Perspectives* (Monsey, NY, Criminal Justice Press).
Lewis, HB (1971) *Shame and Guilt in Neurosis* (New York, International Universities Press).
Macleod, JF, Grove, PG and Farrington, DP (2012) *Explaining Criminal Careers: Implications for Justice Policy* (Oxford, Oxford University Press).
Maruna, S (2001) *Making Good: How Ex-Convicts Reform and Rebuild their Lives* (Washington, DC, American Psychological Association).
Maruna, S and Copes, H (2005) 'What Have We Learned from Five Decades of Neutralization Research?' in M Tonry (ed), *Crime and Justice: A Review of Research*, vol XXXII (Chicago, IL, University of Chicago Press).
Maruna, S and Mann, RE (2006) 'A Fundamental Attribution Error? Rethinking Cognitive Distortions' 11 *Legal and Criminological Psychology* 155.
Maruna, S and Pali, B (2020) 'From Victim Blaming to Reintegrative Shaming: The Continuing Relevance of Crime, Shame and Reintegration in The Era Of #MeToo' 3 *International Journal of Restorative Justice* 38.
Miller, RS and Tangney, JP (1994) 'Differentiating Embarrassment and Shame' 13 *Journal of Social and Clinical Psychology* 273.
Nussbaum, MC (2003) *Hiding from Humanity: Disgust, Shame and the Law* (Princeton, NJ, Princeton University Press).

Ortony, A (1987) 'Is Guilt an Emotion?' 1 *Cognition and Emotion* 283.

Porporino, FJ (2010) 'Bringing Sense and Sensitivity to Corrections: From Programmes to "Fix" Offenders to Services to Support Desistance' in J Brayford, FB Cowe and J Deering (eds), *What Else Works? Creative Work with Offenders* (Cullompton, Willan Publishing).

Proeve, M and Tudor, S (2016) *Remorse: Psychological and Jurisprudential Perspectives* (London, Routledge).

Romanowski, KA (1988) 'Crime and Confession: An Analysis of the Relationship between Contrition, Sentence Severity and Recidivism' (unpublished doctoral dissertation, University of Michigan).

Scheff, TJ and Retzinger, SM (2001) *Emotions and Violence: Shame and Rage in Destructive Conflicts* (Lincoln, NE, iUniverse).

Sered, D (2019) *Until We Reckon: Violence, Mass Incarceration, and a Road to Repair* (New York, The Free Press).

Serin, RC, Mailloux, DM and Hucker, S (2000) *The Utility of Clinical and Actuarial Risk Assessments and for Offenders in Pre-release Psychiatric Decision-making* (Ottawa, Correctional Service of Canada).

Shapland, J and Bottoms, A (2017) 'Desistance from Crime and Implications for Offender Rehabilitation' in A Liebling, S Maruna and L McAra (eds), *Oxford Handbook of Criminology*, 6th edn (Oxford, Oxford University Press).

Tangney, JP and Dearing, RL (2002) *Shame and Guilt* (New York, Guilford Press).

Tangney, JP, Miller, RS, Flicker, L and Barlow, DH (1996) 'Are Shame, Guilt and Embarrassment Distinct Emotions?' 70 *Journal of Personality and Social Psychology* 1256.

Tangney, JP, Stuewig, J and Hafez, L (2011) 'Shame, Guilt and Remorse: Implications for Offender Populations' 22 *Journal of Forensic Psychiatry & Psychology* 706.

Tangney, JP, Stuewig, J and Martinez, AG (2014) 'Two Faces of Shame: The Roles of Shame and Guilt in Predicting Recidivism' 25 *Psychological Science* 799.

Tasioulas, J (2007) 'Repentance and the Liberal State' 4 *Ohio State Journal of Criminal Law* 487.

Throness, L (2008) *A Protestant Purgatory: Theological Origins of the Penitentiary Act, 1779* (Aldershot, Ashgate).

Tracy, JL and Robins, RW (2016) 'Appraisal Antecedents of Shame and Guilt: Support for a Theoretical Model' 32 *Personality and Social Psychology Bulletin* 1339.

Trivedi-Bateman, N (2019) 'The Combined Roles of Moral Emotion and Moral Rules in Explaining Acts of Violence Using a Situational Action Theory Perspective' 1 *Journal of Interpersonal Violence* 8715.

Vaughan, B (2007) 'The Internal Narrative of Desistance' 47 *British Journal of Criminology* 390.

Velotti, P, Garofalo, C, Bottazzi, F and Caretti, V (2017) 'Faces of Shame: Implications for Self-Esteem, Emotion Regulation, Aggression, and Well-Being' 151 *Journal of Psychology* 171.

Von Hirsch, A (1993) *Censure and Sanctions* (Oxford, Clarendon Press).

——(2003) 'Punishment, Penance and the State: A Reply to Duff' in D Matravers and J Pike (eds), *Debates in Contemporary Political Philosophy: An Anthology* (London, Routledge).

Von Stokkom, B (2002) 'Moral Emotions in Restorative Justice Conferences: Managing Shame, Designing Empathy' 6 *Theoretical Criminology* 339.

Warr, M (2016) 'Crime and Regret' 8 *Emotion Review* 231.

Williams, B (1993) *Shame and Necessity* (Berkeley, CA, University of California Press).

Wright, S, Crewe, B and Hulley, S (2017) 'Suppression, Denial, Sublimation: Defending Against the Initial Pains of Very Long Life Sentences' 21 *Theoretical Criminology* 225.

Part IV

Desistance from Crime: Analyses in Positive and Critical Morality

7

'Yo, God, What Should I Do?': Striving for Moral Consistency After Prison

RYAN WILLIAMS*

INTRODUCTION

'IN TEACHING THEM about religion, I'm teaching them how to desist'. Shareef, a probation officer in East London working with Muslim 'service users', described desistance as a process involving learning and practice. In contrast, his colleague Mark, advised Muslim men under his supervision to follow the rules prescribed by Islam to desist from crime: 'Islam prohibits alcohol', he would tell men whose offences were precipitated by alcohol. Shareef and Mark's ways of working express two contrasting philosophical positions on ethics and morality that consider how their supervisees can lead law-abiding lives. Shareef conceives of what is often termed ethics as conscious deliberation, choices, learning and practice. This line of enquiry follows a long philosophical tradition of ethical formation in Aristotle and the eleventh-century Muslim theologian Abu Hamid al-Ghazali, who recognised that ethical life is forged through conscious deliberation and 'assiduous practice' (Mahmood 2012: 229). Mark, on the other hand, conceives of morality in terms of simple rule following, and he considers religion to offer a clear 'blueprint' that will inculcate moral behaviours through its rules. His inclination is to think about morality as bound to 'rules, norms, and conventions against which human behaviours are judged good or bad' (Stafford 2010: 188), and this follows a particular philosophical tradition that traces the Kantian genealogy through Durkheim to emphasise social norms and obligation (Dyring, Mattingly and Louw 2017).

*Data collection was supported by the Centre of Islamic Studies, University of Cambridge between 2016 and 2018 under a project titled 'Re-Imagining Citizenship'. I am grateful to each participant for taking the time to share their experiences with me through this research, and to Tony Bottoms and Jonathan Jacobs for their insightful feedback as I prepared this chapter. A preliminary version of this chapter was published in *The Independent* (R Williams 2018b).

Both views are reflected, often implicitly, in criminological theory on desistance. Shareef's emphasis on deliberation and practice has received recent attention in the question, 'can offenders acquire virtue?' (Bottoms and Shapland 2014). Mark's approach reflects assumptions found in social control theory, where morality is located in 'views on what we ought and not ought to do', and where crime is about 'breaches of rules of conduct' (Wikström 2017: 501, 519).

In this chapter, I explore the entanglements between what I shall describe as *ethics* (choice and self-conscious deliberation in everyday life) and *morality systems* (which bind people to rules and norms – the conventions by which human behaviours are judged as good or bad).[1] My aim is not to moderate between philosophical positions on ethics and morality. Instead, with debates around Kant, Durkheim, Aristotle, al-Ghazali and Foucault in the background and with ethnographic accounts of ethics and moralities as a guide, I pay attention to how local, everyday life shows multiple moral and ethical 'logics at work' that are 'intimately entangled' (Fassin 2012: 8). I explore the problem of moral consistency by drawing on the context of Muslims under probation supervision. For the law-breaker seeking reform, and the Muslim seeking to live in conformity with Islamic norms, the problem of moral consistency places analytical attention on subjectivity and agency and opens up investigation into how people desire and strive to conform to a morality system but sometimes fail.

I argue that attention to the problem of moral consistency enables consideration of how people actively and self-consciously strive to bring their behaviours, attitudes and comportments in line with a morality system, and that this has important implications for considering criminal careers and desistance. How do people 'stand back' and deliberate on their own actions and strive to inhabit morality systems, conforming to 'rules' and norms? How do people conform to morality systems, whether these be legal systems or the prescriptions and proscriptions set out by a religion that forms the basis of determining standards for what is right and wrong? How is this process experienced and navigated amidst everyday life circumstances, that, for people released from prison, is often 'obstacle-strewn' (Bottoms and Shapland 2014)?

Analytically, it is imperative to distinguish between moral codes and ethics because they may 'change independently' (Laidlaw 2014: 111). Lived experience often shows a misalignment between what people do and see as good and of value in everyday moments, and the norms and rules of morality systems. The problem of moral consistency also disrupts assumptions about moral and ethical life that suggest that either the law or religion provides a mere 'blueprint' of rules that are readily followed (Giordano et al 2008: 116). This ignores the often

[1] The distinction between the terms 'ethics' and 'morality' is a source of controversy, with much discussion of Bernard Williams' definitions. Williams (1985: ch 10) locates 'ethics' within its Greek roots that relate to character development, and 'morality' within its Latin roots that convey a sense of social expectation (Stafford 2010: 187–88; Keane 2016: 200). For my sociological purposes I link ethics especially to agency and morality systems to structure.

measurable 'gap between the formulation of rules and how they are followed' (Das et al 2014: 7), especially pertinent when considering how people navigate their experiences in everyday life. In other words, existing research on desistance and religion does not account for 'moral failure'. Moral consistency, by contrast, offers an analytical framework that is relevant to studying criminal careers and Muslims after prison as it shows how people strive to align their behaviours to conform with certain social standards and traditions – legal, religious and overlapping.

I address these questions in this chapter by drawing on a sample of Muslim men under probation supervision in East London.[2] I consider the problem of moral consistency through exploring how these men acquired a desire to lead life in an Islamic way and how it was instilled and developed, how Muslims navigated conflicting notions of the good, and how they sought to harmonise contradictions and inconsistencies, sometimes failing and experiencing disappointment. I begin with a discussion of the problem of moral consistency viewed from the vantage point of recent developments in the study of criminal careers and empirical work from the anthropologies of ethics and moralities that have taken religion as the focal point.

THE PROBLEM OF MORAL CONSISTENCY

Morality systems are 'typically easy to see' (Keane 2016: 200; also Laidlaw 2014: 111). It is fairly easy to recognise a 'breach of rules of conduct' when someone breaks the law and the morality systems found in religion are recognisable through the coordinated rules, laws, authorities or rituals that constitute a coherent and consistent whole (Keane 2016: 200). However, morality systems do not guarantee ethical behaviour and assuming that morality systems guarantee coordinated and uniform responses that govern people's lives is 'simply unconvincing' (Keane 2016: 200). The alignment and coordination of moral systems and ethical behaviour is therefore not as obvious as it might initially seem. It is possible to act ethically, for example, in the sense of doing what one sees as right and good, without conforming to the rules of what is morally right: people can behave ethically and immorally at the same time (Stafford 2010).

[2] This chapter draws on fieldwork conducted in 2017 among Muslims under probation supervision in East London that was part of six years of non-consecutive fieldwork in two separate studies in the English criminal justice system. The second study that forms the basis of this chapter included fieldwork in four probation offices and interviews with 18 Muslim men under probation supervision and their probation officers. Participants were recruited through referrals from probation staff and in accordance with data protection procedures over a period of eight months. Interviews were conducted at locations that were convenient for participants, sometimes in probation supervision rooms, overlapping with scheduled probation supervisions, other times at places of work or volunteering, including a mosque, or in 'chicken shops' or cafes of the participant's choosing.

Moral consistency arises as a problem where there is self-conscious reflection on the demands and expectations of a morality system and coordinated efforts that work towards fulfilling a particular model of human flourishing offered by a morality system amidst everyday demands. The problem of moral consistency arises then in the gap between a morality system and behaviour that is filled through self-conscious ethical practices. As I review below, others have described the relationship between morality systems and ethical behaviour as giving rise to 'moral torment' (Robbins 2004) where ethical behaviour does not conform to the edicts of a morality system. Where ethical reasoning and action serve to bring behaviour and sensibilities into alignment within a morality system, this purposeful self-reform has been termed 'piety' where theology serves as the ultimate authority of morality (Keane 2016: 206). The problem of moral consistency has also been described in research on desistance using different terminology and concepts, but sharing the idea of a misalignment between ethical behaviour and a morality system underpinned by socio-legal norms and expectations. Those seeking to desist from crime made 'various', 'active attempts to shape their lives in less criminal ways' (Bottoms and Shapland 2014: 325), highlighting the role of deliberation, judgement and purposeful action in ethical life. I review examples from Christianity, Islam and secular settings that illustrate the problem of moral consistency.

Joel Robbins' ethnography of the Urapmin people in the highlands of Papua New Guinea described an active, enthusiastic conversion of a small group of unmissionised people to Christianity beginning in the 1960s. At the time of Robbins' study in the 1990s, he described the Urapmin people as in a place of 'moral torment', a condition that arose from the contradictions between the ethics embedded in the daily life and sociality of their traditional ways of living and the explicit precepts of their adopted Christianity. These 'contradictions and confusions' (Robbins 2004: 183) between Urapmin indigenous ways of life and Christian ideas led to an 'unsettled state of dual cultural play' and feelings among the Urapmin that they fell 'constantly short of their moral goals', producing a 'conviction of sinfulness that motivates so much of their Christianity' (Robbins 2004: 182–83). This tension arose through their version of Christian morality that was thought of in terms of lawlike dictates and their everyday practices. The examples that Robbins provides include the necessity of maintaining the established pattern of relationships through their everyday ethics of generosity and reciprocity found in their pre-Christian traditional way of life and the post-Christian way of life that demanded establishing new relationships. A similar tension is illustrated in their adoption of apocalyptic ideas that demanded abandonment of this-worldly activities like tending their fields and maintaining communal life and the traditional ethical practices that necessitated maintaining this-worldly activities. Robbins' work illustrates the problem of consistency created in the lawlike dictates and obligations of Christianity as a morality system and the everyday practices that contribute to human flourishing.

To put it plainly, structure and agency were linked, but created tensions that led the Urapmin people to regard themselves indefinitely as sinners.

The problem of moral consistency is also found in Islamic revivalist movements, where moral consistency is achievable through a transformation of comportments, dispositions and habits. Saba Mahmood (2005) and Charles Hirschkind's (2006) influential works raised attention to the deliberative efforts of Muslims in Cairo-based Islamic revivalist movements as they endeavoured to relate to Islamic tradition. Drawing on an understanding of Islamic tradition as practice that involved learning and inculcating ethical practices (Asad 2006: 234), their work portrayed 'ethics in terms of *both* deontology and virtue' (Keane 2016: 205). Mahmood and Hirschkind elevate practice (active, self-conscious behaviours) as the conceptual underpinning for analysing religion rather than beliefs or normative rules and structures, relying upon the Aristotelian origins of *habitus* (through the neo-Aristotelian revival and Foucault's later works on ethics) (see Mahmood 2012). This active and self-conscious attention to ethical self-cultivation contrasts with the concept of *habitus* developed by Bourdieu that suggested a tacit 'instantiation of an ideology or structure' (Mahmood 2012: 225; Klassen 2008; Bender 2012). The mode of enquiry into Islam inspired by Asad, Mahmood and Hirschkind 'has opened for investigation the ways in which individuals in traditions fashion themselves into subjects with certain kinds of desires, sensibilities, and choices' (Moumtaz 2015: 129).

The religious movements in Cairo that Mahmood and Hirschkind investigated show that the aim of piety is to bring daily activities, desires and habits to align with Islamic tradition (see also Keane 2016: 206). Their work helps us to see that Islamic practice is not merely governed by rules or prohibited and proscribed behaviours. Instead, 'moral character is secured' through a 'pedagogical process' that aligns with Islamic tradition (Mahmood 2012: 229). As Mahmood remarks in exploring the significance of *salat* (Islamic prayer): 'I argue that insofar as conventional and rule-governed behaviour cannot be read simply as a social imposition that constrains the self but rather (under certain conditions) as the means by which the self is realised' as a type of 'freedom' through the ritual of salat (Mahmood 2012: 828–29). Hirschkind similarly stressed the significance of cultivating 'moral habits' in relating to religious tradition: 'One of my central arguments in this paper is that anthropologists need to think of religious traditions as founded upon such embodied capacities of gesture, feeling, and speech, rather than in terms of an obedience to rules or belief in doctrine' (Hirschkind 2001: 629, 632). In this view, practice is 'ensconced in a broader set of questions about how one becomes the subject of a certain tradition' (Mahmood 2012: 225). The Cairene men and women in these ethnographies strove actively and self-consciously to lead lives that were consistent with Islamic tradition.

In these examples from Christianity and Islam we see that the relationship of ethics and morality is not simply one of obedience to a tradition, but one of practical judgement and deliberation (see Schielke 2009: 162–63). These activities are ensconced within a 'host of material practices' that are embedded within historically specific ways of life that will 'inevitably produce different results for ethical life than not having them' (Keane 2016: 202). Analytically, Islam represents both a deontological and a virtue-based moral and ethical system. As Fassin explains,

> piety can be a viewed as a religious category but it is also a moral one, or rather, if we consider it not from the perspective of religious morality, which would be imposed on individuals, but from the perspective of ethical subjectivation, which agents would deliberately make their own, it can be regarded as a category of practice (2012: 11).

Is there, then, a secular non-religious equivalent of considering the problem of moral consistency?

In their exploration of how offenders might acquire virtue, I understand Bottoms and Shapland to be saying something quite similar about morality and ethics. The connection is not immediately obvious because their sample of persistent offenders is explicitly not religious and the morality system is framed in relation to the secular legal system in their efforts to live in 'less criminal ways' (Bottoms and Shapland 2014: 325). However, for these persistent offenders from the Sheffield desistance study, there was a 'commitment to change' (Bottoms and Shapland 2014: 320) and, importantly, this included marked, self-conscious efforts of 'making active attempts to shape their lives in less criminal ways' (at 325). The ethical practices that Bottoms and Shapland describe were not linked to religion, though they do offer briefly that 'a small number mentioned Islamic influences' (2014: 332, fn 48). The ordinary ethical practices that they do explore are so ordinary that it is difficult to see their ethical significance. But for Kevin, for instance, having a stable relationship was inscribed as an ethical practice that kept him out of the pub and emotionally invested. Getting and keeping a job, with its own routines, furthered this ethical work on the self. In another example, Len moved in with his mother and exercised restraint (or 'diachronic self-control') by staying home more often to avoid situations that might lead him to engage in acts of crime (Bottoms and Shapland 2014: 324–25). Stable relationships, employment and staying home to keep out of trouble are from the outside unremarkable actions. However, for those 'learning to live a non-criminal life when one has been living a largely criminal life' (Bottoms and Shapland 2014: 326) they were crucial parts of forming habits that were linked to virtue that linked ethics in terms of both deontology (structure) and virtue ethics (agency). In these mundane examples, the structure or rules were societal conventions and norms around employment, relationships and lifestyle activities, and these were not implicit, unconscious practices but instead were recognised as active, explicit objects of awareness.

This self-conscious, active work to bring one's behaviour into alignment with a morality system and its expectations of a non-criminal lifestyle shares perhaps unexpected similarities with the religious lives of the Urapmin people and Cairene Muslims whose efforts and actions strive to conform to historical objects of religious tradition. Each example discussed above, however, shows close links between deontology and virtue. As Keane summarises religious movements:

> [O]n the one hand, each piety movement posits explicit sets of rules, understood as relatively abstract principles that have very general application; and, on the other hand, in practice each movement also fosters the inculcation of certain concrete habits and specific ways of living guided by a vision of the good person (2016: 205).

The 'high' piety of striving to conform to a religious tradition may be seen as dissimilar to the rather 'low bar' of conforming to social standards of law-abiding behaviour for the struggling persistent offender, but as these empirical accounts suggest, they share a perceived gap between moral expectations and ethical behaviour. Self-conscious awareness and behaviours intended to achieve moral consistency serve to make up the difference between who one is and who one wishes to become.

In the following sections I detail the ways in which Muslim men in my study related to the morality system provided by Islamic tradition. I begin by identifying how Islam came to serve as a moral template through brief attention to prison experience and the concepts of 'moral breakdown' and 'ethical affordances' that makes the point that moral systems are not collapsible with the social (Zigon 2007; Dyring, Mattingly and Louw 2017). I then explore three ways that Muslims in my study experience the problem of moral consistency, through harmonising, ambivalence in view of competing 'goods', and lastly, disappointment, speaking to the possibilities and challenges of people's efforts at actively coordinating behaviours and dispositions towards an ethical system.

DESIRING MORAL CONSISTENCY: SELF-REFLECTION AND ETHICAL AFFORDANCES

The sense of obligation to moral systems does not come out of nowhere. People are, of course, socialised into morality systems. But even for those raised as Muslim in my study, Islam did not present an obligatory system of rules. Instead, many described coming to learn about Islam through imprisonment. This aligns with research that has emphasised the significance of practice and learning to Islamic revivalism and piety movements (Mahmood 2005; Hirschkind 2006; Moumtaz 2015) But what is particular about the prison environment and experience in prompting ethical self-reflection? Empirical accounts of religion in prison have often discussed heightened religiosity in prison: 'God is often found behind bars' (Maruna, Wilson and Curran 2006), and the discovery and renewal of Islamic faith is widely chronicled through prison (Calverley 2012; Marranci 2009). But these studies tell us little about how self-conscious reflection, considered so integral to religious practice and ethical life, was prompted by imprisonment. Through a brief discussion of 'moral breakdown' and 'ethical affordances', this section shows that the desire to lead a good Islamic life is not a default position of born-Muslims. Instead desire for moral consistency was cultivated and learned through self-conscious, deliberate actions and attentiveness through a host of material practices that were made salient and available through imprisonment. Islam did not provide a 'blueprint' for moral life that demanded or guaranteed obedience; instead, Muslims cultivated their awareness towards ethical practice.

Interviewees in my study recounted, with hindsight, a comparatively unreflective state before prison. 'I was like a zombie', Wael remarked. Ramzi described a lack of self-knowledge and self-awareness that he thought was partly responsible for his entering prison in the first place: 'I didn't know myself before. My character was all over the place. I would fit myself around people rather than being myself. Trying to fit with others'. Imprisonment intruded sharply into Wael and Ramzi's life, prompting ethical reflection. As Zigon states in describing the concept of moral breakdown: 'The need to consciously consider or reason about what one must do only arises in moments that shake one out of the everydayness of being moral' (2007: 133). Imprisonment seems to be just one of those shaking moments. For the Muslims in my study, this moral breakdown triggered practices that served as part of a pedagogical process that attuned the self towards Islamic tradition. The debate between ethics as conscious action and ethics as unconscious habit and routine is ongoing (Keane 2016; Dyring, Mattingly and Louw 2017). Zigon's characterisation of ethical life through moral breakdown and everydayness illustrates how the desire for moral consistency is provoked and stimulated by intersections between context and agency, and is not socially or culturally predetermined (Dyring, Mattingly and Louw 2017: 23).

For my purposes here, the idea of 'moral breakdown' draws attention towards a shift from unconscious immoral (in the sense of law-breaking) behaviours towards conscious ethical reflection. Jarred by imprisonment, ethical self-reflection was triggered by the peak moments in 'ordinary', everyday life (Mattingly 2014; Keane 2016). Imprisonment was a cataclysmic event that had important implications for ethical life and self-reflection. This may be an obvious point: that prison may trigger self-reflection. However, it is an important point to my argument that helps us to move away from the Durkheimian legacy of thinking about moral systems as 'congruent with the social' (Zigon 2007: 148) – a legacy that produces a view 'in which people move more or less smoothly along the grooves that have been laid out for them' (Keane 2016: 135). For born-Muslims, Islamic culture and morality did not determine the course of the subject's morality, a point I evidence further in discussing moral ambivalence below. Islam did not provide the predetermined 'blueprint' for desistance identified in the literature (Giordano et al 2008: 116). Such a view only upholds long-standing assumptions about Islam as a cohesive morality system or 'culture' that leads it to be construed in 'misleadingly unified, essentialized ways' (Coleman 2013: 254), and erodes understanding of how Muslims actively engage with tradition.

Imprisonment served as the catalyst for self-reflection and it prompted a desire for ethical consistency. Contrary to the fear and scepticism around conversion to Islam and extremism in prison, this self-reflective ethical practice was guided not by 'brainwashing' or coercion, but by a 'non-determined potentiality' (Dyring, Mattingly and Louw 2017) or 'freedom' (Laidlaw 2014; R Williams 2018a), to reflect on how a person might bring their behaviour and sensibilities in alignment with their daily practices, comportment and habits that reflect the morality system of Islamic tradition.[3] Ramzi illustrated this independent self-reflection in connecting to Islamic faith: 'Sometimes [my way of practising Islam] doesn't match with others' [practices] and what I believe internally … Everything I learned about Islam in jail I learned about myself'.

Webb Keane's notion of 'ethical affordances' offers another way of recognising that the desire for moral consistency is not a given, but is induced or afforded opportunity through imprisonment. Ethical affordances recognise conditions that might 'induce reflexivity', the 'opportunities that any experiences might offer as people evaluate themselves, other persons, and their circumstances' (Keane 2016: 31). Prison offered structural and material opportunities that made it easier for Muslims to practise their faith. The prison regime facilitated religious observance through chaplaincy activities, Friday prayer services and provision for religious festivals such as Ramadan. It also catered for religious needs through the regime and provision of material artefacts (eg, reading materials, prayer mats and religious clothing) and access to a prison chaplain. Providing for Islamic faith is part of a broader historical shift in English prisons that responded both to the recognition of religious pluralism (Beckford and Gilliat-Ray 1998) and was considered a necessity given the increase in the numbers of Muslim prisoners, with prison statistics showing a doubling in the number of Muslims between 2006 and 2016 (R Williams 2021a; R Williams and Liebling 2018). These resources and facilities provided the conditions that made practising faith not only possible but regimented and routinised as part of daily and weekly life.

Imprisonment therefore gave prisoners time for faith practice. For Yusef, prison offered him time as a structural opportunity to practise his faith: 'Obviously I know how to read and I know how to pray and all that, but I wasn't practising'. He described how he learned more about Islam in prison than he could outside: 'In these three years, if I'm not going to be here in prison I don't learn this stuff because whatever I would learn on the outside I can't learn it in 20 years'. The prison's support of Islamic practice provided prisoners with a

[3] Recent commentary on conversion to Islam in prisons fails to recognise that piety is actively and wilfully cultivated and it erroneously suggests that Muslims are passive recipients of pre-categorised ideological or theological positions. Rather, I suggest that Islam is related-to against a background of personal, situational and contextual considerations embedded in everyday life. See R Williams (2018a) and Moumtaz (2015) for a description of tradition as the struggle for 'coherence' that is relevant to my argument.

regime or system to coordinate moral behaviour, and this aligned with an ethical potentiality to cultivate a particular vision of an ethical self, to make oneself into a better person through relating to Islamic tradition. As the idea of ethical affordances suggests, coordination of a person's ethical life with a morality system is not guided by 'sheer determinism, on the one hand, or pure self-invention, on the other' (Keane 2016: 31). Islam provided Muslims with a repertoire of ethical practices, and the prison as an institution facilitated the availability of those ethical technologies (R Williams 2018a).

Ethical life involves deliberation, judgement and self-conscious practices that bring behaviour and sensibilities into alignment with a moral system. This does not occur in a vacuum. Prison prompted and resourced these efforts towards moral consistency in Islamic practice, but how closely were Muslims able to bring their behaviour in line with Islam after prison? How did Islamic practice harmonise with journeys towards desisting from crime? The following discussion considers the problem of moral consistency in everyday life through attention to three themes: harmony, ambivalence and disappointment.

HARMONY IN MORAL CONSISTENCY: 'HELPING THE VULNERABLE … GOD LOVES THAT!'

For some Muslims after prison in my study, the problem of moral consistency was achieved through Islamic practice, specifically through charity work that aligned with two of the five pillars of Islam, namely, *zakat* (charity) and the *hajj* (pilgrimage).

For Yusef, the Islamic pilgrimage to Mecca (the *hajj*) served as an important ethical practice within Islamic tradition. He served five years in prison for a 10-year sentence for grievous bodily harm (GBH). Avoiding situations that could spark 'aggro' (aggression), including employment in the restaurant industry where he might be 'provoked', was forefront on his mind. After prison, he was in discussion with his probation officer to seek permission to have his licence conditions relaxed so that he could participate in the *hajj* and to organise and to help lead a group of pilgrims for the journey. This form of social action within his community served to realise what he described as his true 'nature': 'it's probably my nature of giving and giving back and helping others. I mean, I give a lot to charities and I've always done so for quite a while, since I was brought up'.

Completing the *hajj* is incumbent upon able Muslims once in their lives as one of the five pillars of Islam. Yusef had saved his money prior to prison and took his parents on the *hajj*. For Yusef, it represented connection with his family and a 'non-criminal' identity, as his mother would focus on the experience as a focal point for speaking 'proudly' about her son to other family members:

> A lot of people tend to consider to do these kinds of things, these kinds of acts in old age. But my outlook on it was I wanted to try and do it while I was younger. So, I took my parents. I saved up money while I was working and took my parents for

> Hajj. And it was an amazing experience for them. It was a life-changing experience for them (Yusef).

Yusef's desire to give back to his community was grounded in 'transcendence' (Robbins 2016), in an understanding of what God wants. 'I want to actually do some things now, like goodness, like volunteering, helping people out, helping the vulnerable … God loves that!'

Abdul similarly linked pious acts of charity to the normative moral commitments of Islamic tradition. *Zakat* (charity) is one of the five pillars of Islam, those that Muslims are considered obliged to perform. For Abdul, doing Islamic relief work was the best way for him to lead a good Muslim life. Two months out of prison, Abdul described volunteering with aid after the Grenfell Tower fire.[4] His motivation for his charity work was based on Islamic obligation to charity and he further legitimised this activity based on his British identity and his humanity:

> At the time of the fire at Grenfell Tower [I was] part of the support team on the ground … we had about five van-fulls full of clothing, bedding and … we started offloading and loads of people came over and they were like, 'Yeah, it's really good that what you guys are doing'. They started making videos and they said, 'Oh, look, these are Muslims helping us'. We were like, 'Hold on a minute. Yeah, we may be Muslims but we're British as well. We do feel what's going on around us. We're not just here for the Muslim community, we're not strictly here for them. We're here for mankind' (Abdul).

Yusef and Abdul's charity work is consistent with desistance research and the idea of 'generativity' as used by Maruna (2001) – that is, a concern for and commitment to the wellbeing of the next generation, in short, 'giving back' (McNeill and Maruna 2007). This 'giving back' was grounded in the moral and ethical commitments to Islamic tradition.

Through the self-conscious practices of charity and pilgrimage, Islamic morality harmonised behaviours that contributed to desistance from crime. Through these practices of piety and self-conscious, agentive actions aimed at transforming the self into a particular type of Islamic ethical subject, former prisoners were able to bridge the gap between ethical behaviours and the norms and expectations of a morality system. However, as others have recognised (Schielke 2009), moral consistency is fraught with the challenges of everyday life and tensions between multiple 'goods'.

MORAL AMBIVALENCE: 'I CAN'T PRAY INTOXICATED'

After prison, it was harder for some of my interviewees to succeed through conscious deliberation on self-making through Islamic tradition, and they

[4] Grenfell Tower was a 24-storey apartment block in Kensington, London which was completely gutted by fire on 14 June 2017. The fire killed 72 people and all the survivors lost their homes.

instead suffered distraction from competing priorities. Muslim moral and ethical life intersected with everyday life, which contained within it multiple visions of the good. As Samuli Schielke observes among the Muslim men he interviewed in Egypt, there may be many different answers to the question: 'How can I be a good human?' (2009: 165). There may not be a 'clear hierarchy of aims and ideals' that can be resolved through a disciplined habituation of virtues (Schielke 2009: 164). Moral life may be characterised not simply by 'obedience' to religion but of 'practical judgement and deliberation' and against a background of competing and overlapping ethical demands and 'goods' or things of value (Schielke 2009: 162–63).

Yasir describes some tensions between Islamic practices and the day-to-day responsibilities of family and work life after prison:

> If you are outside [prison], if you worship five times a day, then you need to go to work, we need to do certain duties like you have kids, you go out, you've got family, you need to look after them, take them to school, pick them up from school, you need to spend your time with kids and you're busy. You don't have time to read and stuff (Yasir).

There is nothing inconsistent in the attention given to fatherhood and employment and being a 'good Muslim', but Yasir recognises that the ethical practices of Islamic tradition that he rediscovered in prison were impossible to fully actualise after prison given the commitments of everyday life.

For others, like Amadi, coherence between Islamic tradition and everyday life was challenged by clashing visions of the good in life. Amadi expressed a 'buzz' associated with his offending behaviour. There was a value clash between competing conceptions of the good in life, in being a 'civi' (civilian) and hedonistic desires of women, drinking and smoking cannabis. Recently released from a three-year sentence for possession of drugs, he described the conflicts he experienced that characterised his present moment as being pulled in different moral directions:

> Like right now, like I said, I'm praying but there are more distractions now. There are females, girls, drinking. [Females] are the bad ones. They're really distracting. I've been dibbing and dabbing in cannabis. Because you see these little things, like when you're praying it might make you avoid them, like smoking because I can't pray intoxicated (Amadi).

The conflicting notions of the good are clear in Amadi's description where there were competing tensions with Islamic religious life. Intoxication was incompatible with practice; sexual relations were distracting from prayer. Amadi's life history raised the further point of competing goods and interests. After his first arrest, Amadi described how he was ambitious, keen to 'advance in anything to do with a criminal aspect'. He found the pace of the lifestyle thrilling ('a hundred miles an hour'); he earned respect and friends, both representing powerful values in life.

The life history portions of interviews with others underscored this point of the multiple, conflicting demands that people face, particularly through their previous offences and adolescence. Richard described wanting to be a 'have-something' rather than a 'have-not', wanting to achieve the same vision of the good regulated by popular cultural influences and the market economy: 'I've never had and I always wanted something … growing up in all this you're bombarded with energy of clothes, of music, of this and that. You want to be part of that'. Car thefts and shoplifting offered a way to achieve that conception of the good life, redressing economic inequalities he experienced in his community.

The experience of ethical life for youth like Amadi, and for Richard as he reflected on his own adolescence and journey into crime, illustrates competing and compelling voices that speak in different ways about what it means to be a good human being. The voices speaking to what the good life means are multiple and overlapping, internal and external: excitement, respect, a community of peers, an identity, school, romance, parents, material culture (fashion, music) and religion. There may be many different answers to the question: 'How can I be a good human?' There are often competing demands, with no clear hierarchy to help order goods. People's behaviour can sometimes seem erratic, even hypocritical, as they deliberate, evaluate, order and reorder goods. People often do not know what they want or which 'good' is most important to them in the short or long term.

Everyday life presents challenges to moral consistency in Islamic practice, and desistance from crime. Amadi captures these tensions and conflicts within moral and ethical life, and specifically between the normative ethical commitments of Islam and the adrenaline associated with a 'criminal lifestyle':

> I've got my religious aspect where I feel strongly about it, but then there's the other side of me where I'm smoking, drinking, this, that, the criminal lifestyle, it doesn't really work. It doesn't [agree] with the religion. So in answer to your question, at times I feel strongly about my faith and religion because I might feel I'm representing it in the right manner, but then other times, I'm not. [*I: Not quite living up to it?*] A: Exactly. That's why I don't even like to have an appearance of that type of person because people may think it. I pray. Don't get me twisted. I always try to pray. I try to not miss any prayers. So people might think I'm a religious guy. I don't know. I'm not like a high religious guy. These are things you're supposed to be doing anyway. Pray. It's just little simple things I try to keep me grounded. I'd like to say I feel strongly about my faith. Strong about me being a Muslim and whatnot, but sometimes, I don't portray it too well (Amadi).

Amadi was in the process of learning to keep 'grounded' despite moral ambivalence and competing interests. He would ask, 'yo, God, what should I do?' when he was in a position when he might get into trouble and make a bad choice. It is easy to dismiss the criminal lifestyle side of Amadi's life as merely 'un-Islamic' or to consider him to be a not very good Muslim, but this would be to reduce moral life to alignment with rules and miss how integral Amadi's ethical deliberations were to his experience as a Muslim within a wider context of competing interests and answers to the question of how to lead a 'good life'. This striving towards consistency and 'moral failure' may be considered integral to 'faith' for piety movements (Beekers and Kloos 2017). But there is a fine line between 'moral failure' that motivates striving and failure that leads to disappointment.

DISAPPOINTMENT: 'PRAYING FIVE TIMES A DAY … I WISH I COULD'

Active, self-conscious efforts to live morally consistent lives in accordance with an Islamic system was not guaranteed for another reason: self-limitations of mental health and personal circumstances. As summarised above, Robbins (2004) argued that morality systems and ethical practices can come into tension and produce disappointment or 'moral torment'. Islam presented a similar moral reference point for some Muslims after prison: for them, its standards of practice and norms were tragically unrealisable.

Asad was released from a minimum two-year indeterminate sentence (IPP, or an indeterminate sentence in the interests of public protection), for which he ended up spending seven years in prison. For Asad, regularity in Islamic practice of prayer was valued: 'It would make you a good pious person, praying five times a day … I wish I could'. But it was unattainable for him given his descriptions of his material, social and mental health needs. His mind was preoccupied with finding new accommodation in a 'safer neighbourhood', his day-to-day needs, and the requirements of attending probation meetings and liaising with a jobseeker agency to get his CV complete so that he could begin looking for work. He had family support, but he did not want to take 'handouts' from people and wanted to go it alone. It was difficult to see Islamic practice as anything but a luxury or distant ideal.

In view of the unrealisable normative expectations of Islam as a morality system, Asad reframed the tradition from a 'morality system' to recognising that being a Muslim as located in the day to day: 'Being a Muslim is a self-journey. Watching your actions and everything'. The vagueness reflected the uncertainties and inconsistencies of everyday life and perhaps served as a way to buffer his own sense of failure to attain consistency in Islamic practice. Compared with Yusef and Abdul, for whom Islam offered the vibrant prospect for ethical self-cultivation through practices of charity, Islam served as a hazy background and unfulfillable ideal against day-to-day hardships. Asad prioritised his mental health needs and need to find suitable housing and eventual employment. Islamic moral obligations offered little direct solution. Islam was part of a wider 'self-journey' to meet personal, psychological and material need, but it was experienced through his own disappointment in his abilities to achieve moral consistency with Islamic practice. Islam presented a 'high bar' for Asad that contributed to disappointment. For him, the aspiration to bring Islamic obligations together with ethical life were incompatible. At best, he reinterpreted

Islam as an ethical system of consciously 'watching your actions', but he could not rely on himself to achieve consistency in the 'technologies of the self' offered by Islamic tradition through prayer.

CONCLUSION

In addressing the problem of moral consistency, I have wanted to draw analytical attention to how people bring ethical behaviours into alignment with morality systems. Research on desistance and criminal careers would, I suggest, benefit from paying close analytical attention to the often measurable 'gap between the formulation of rules and how they are followed' (Das et al 2014: 7). Separating ethics from morals for analytical purposes offers opportunities for considering the interrelationships between agency and morality systems, a core problem in the study of crime and desistance. Such analysis is crucial for understanding 'moral failure', but also for recognising how people strive to harmonise their actions and values in their everyday lives with the norms, rules and conventions of morality systems against which they are judged as 'good' or 'bad', whether as citizens or Muslims. Separating ethics from morals for analytical purposes and studying their interrelationships raises several productive lines of enquiry: how is the desire for moral consistency initiated? When do people experience a gap between who they are and their actions and who they want to become in relation to socio-legal morality systems or religious traditions? What self-conscious practices serve to bring behaviours and sensibilities into alignment with morality systems? How do people navigate moral failure, for example, through continued striving amidst setback or disappointment? Everyday life shows multiple moral and ethical logics at work that are intimately entangled. Attention to ethics and morality, as considered in this chapter, serves to centre the empirical task in studying criminal careers in describing these entanglements and their implications.

The Muslim men's lives after prison, described in this chapter, have served to illustrate the analytical value in separating ethics from morality. The little consideration given to religion in desistance literature has rather simplistically dissolved religion to a 'blueprint' and ethical life to conformity with that blueprint. Islam does not provide a mere 'blueprint' that guarantees conformity any more than socio-legal norms do, and such a view only contributes to the construction of Islam and Muslims' lives in 'misleadingly unified, essentialized ways' (Coleman 2013: 254). My analysis has shown instead that Muslim men first grew to desire moral consistency through recognising, through imprisonment, a gap between their behaviours and moral standards. Islam provided norms and models for ethical behaviours as a means to fashion themselves into particular kinds of ethical subjects (see R Williams 2021b, for a discussion of the negative consequences of the state's investment in religion in prison for Muslims). The problem of moral consistency highlighted that the desire to live a morally consistent life was by no means a guarantor of living up to the expectations of morality systems after prison where multiple goods and values competed and Islamic practice was difficult. Some men seemed to harmonise ethical practices and Islamic and secular-legal morality systems in 'giving back' through Islamic charity, but others described struggling with moral ambivalence and disappointment.

Returning to Shareef and Mark, the probation officers we met at the beginning of this chapter, we see the interlinking between virtue and deontology. I was initially taken aback with scepticism by the 'sheer determinism' of Islamic morality implicit in Mark invoking Islamic prohibitions to his supervisees. On reconsideration, however, perhaps combining the necessity of adhering to rules with Shareef's insight into Islamic practice in everyday life and its 'bumpiness' offers a way of supporting Muslims in a way that can meaningfully bring their behaviours into alignment with Islamic precepts that cohere with socio-legal norms.

REFERENCES

Asad, T (2006) 'Responses' in C Hirschkind and D Scott (eds), *Powers of the Secular Modern: Talal Asad and His Interlocutors* (Stanford, CA, Stanford University Press).

Beckford, J and Gilliat-Ray, S (1998) *Religion in Prison: Equal Rites in a Multi-Faith Society* (Cambridge, Cambridge University Press).

Beekers, D and Kloos, D (2017) 'Introduction: The Productive Potential of Moral Failure in Lived Islam and Christianity' in D Beekers and D Kloos (eds), *Straying from the Straight Path: How Senses of Failure Invigorate Lived Religion* (Oxford, Berghahn Books).

Bender, C (2012) 'Practicing Religion' in RA Orsi (ed), *Cambridge Companion to Religious Studies* (Cambridge, Cambridge University Press).

Bottoms, A and Shapland, J (2014) 'Can Persistent Offenders Acquire Virtue?' 27 *Studies in Christian Ethics* 318.

Calverley, A (2012) *Cultures of Desistance: Rehabilitation, Reintegration and Ethnic Minorities* (Abingdon, Taylor & Francis).

Coleman, S (2013) 'Afterword: De-exceptionalising Islam' in M Marsden and K Retsikas (eds), *Articulating Islam* (London, Springer).

Das, V, Jackson, MD, Kleinman, A and Singh, B (2014) 'Introduction' in V Das, MD Jackson, A Kleinman and B Singh (eds), *The Ground Between: Anthropologists Engage Philosophy* (Durham, NC, Duke University Press).

Dyring, R, Mattingly, C and Louw, M (2017) 'The Question of "Moral Engines": Introducing a Philosophical Anthropological Dialogue' in C Mattingly, R Dyring, M Louw and T Schwarz Wentzer (eds), *Moral Engines: Exploring the Ethical Drives in Human Life* (Oxford, Berghahn Books).

Fassin, D (2012) *A Companion to Moral Anthropology* (Chichester, John Wiley & Sons Inc).

Giordano, PC, Longmore, MA, Schroeder, RD and Seffrin, PM (2008) 'A Life-Course Perspective on Spirituality and Desistance from Crime' 46 *Criminology* 99.

Hirschkind, C (2001) 'The Ethics of Listening: Cassette-Sermon Audition in Contemporary Egypt' 28 *American Ethnologist* 628.

——(2006) *The Ethical Soundscape: Cassette Sermons and Islamic Counterpublics* (New York, Columbia University Press).

Keane, W (2016) *Ethical Life: Its Natural and Social Histories* (Princeton, NJ, Princeton University Press).

Klassen, PE (2008) 'Practice' in D Morgan (ed), *Key Words in Religion, Media and Culture* (Abingdon, Routledge).

Laidlaw, J (2014) *The Subject of Virtue: An Anthropology of Ethics and Freedom* (Cambridge, Cambridge University Press).

Mahmood, S (2005) *Politics of Piety: The Islamic Revival and the Feminist Subject* (Princeton, NJ, Princeton University Press).

——(2012) 'Ethics and Piety' in D Fassin (ed), *A Companion to Moral Anthropology* (Chichester, John Wiley & Sons Inc).

Marranci, G (2009) *Faith, Ideology and Fear: Muslim Identities Within and Beyond Prisons* (London, Continuum).

Maruna, S (2001) *Making Good: How Ex-Convicts Reform and Rebuild their Lives* (Washington DC, American Psychological Association).

Maruna, S, Wilson, L and Curran, K (2006) 'Why God is Often Found Behind Bars: Prison Conversions and the Crisis of Self-Narrative' 3 *Research in Human Development* 161.

Mattingly, C (2014) *Moral Laboratories: Family Peril and the Struggle for a Good Life* (Oakland, CA, University of California Press).

McNeill, F and Maruna, S (2007) 'Giving Up and Giving Back: Desistance, Generativity and Social Work with Offenders' in G McIvor and P Raynor (eds), *Developments in Social Work with Offenders* (London, Jessica Kingsley Publishers).

Moumtaz, N (2015) 'Refiguring Islam' in S Altorki (ed), *A Companion to the Anthropology of the Middle East* (Chichester, John Wiley & Sons Inc).

Robbins, J (2004) *Becoming Sinners: Christianity and Moral Torment in a Papua New Guinea Society* (Berkeley, CA, University of California Press).

——(2016) 'What is the Matter with Transcendence? On the Place of Religion in the New Anthropology of Ethics' 22 *Journal of the Royal Anthropological Institute* 767.

Schielke, S (2009) 'Ambivalent Commitments: Troubles of Morality, Religiosity and Aspiration among Young Egyptians' 39 *Journal of Religion in Africa* 158.

Stafford, C (2010) 'The Punishment of Ethical Behavior' in M Lambek (ed), *Ordinary Ethics: Anthropology, Language, and Action* (New York, Fordham University Press).

Wikström, POH (2017) 'Character, Circumstances, and the Causes of Crime: Towards an Analytical Criminology' in A Liebling, S Maruna and L McAra (eds), *Oxford Handbook of Criminology*, 6th edn (Oxford, Oxford University Press).

Williams, B (1985) *Ethics and the Limits of Philosophy* (London, Fontana).

Williams, R (2018a) 'Finding Freedom and Rethinking Power: Islamic Piety in English High Security Prisons' 58 *British Journal of Criminology* 3.

——(2018b) 'Muslims and Prison: When Crime Collides with Faith and Morality' *Independent* (27 April 2018), available at: www.independent.co.uk/news/long_reads/muslim-prisoners-crime-islam-faith-moral-life-a8318306.html.

——(2021a) '"The Muslims are Taking Over": The Politics of Space and Geopolitical and National Imaginaries in an English Prison' 44 *Ethnic and Racial Studies* 1779.

——(2021b) 'State of Injury: Liberal Multiculturalism and the Muslim Subject after Prison' 49 *Religion, State & Society* 350.

Williams, R and Liebling, A (2018) 'Faith Provision, Institutional Power and Meaning Among Muslim Prisoners in Two English High Security Prisons' in K Kerley (ed), *Finding Freedom in Confinement: The Role of Religion in Prison Life* (Westport, CT, Praeger).

Zigon, J (2007) 'Moral Breakdown and the Ethical Demand: A Theoretical Framework for an Anthropology of Moralities' 7 *Anthropological Theory* 131.

——(2011) 'A Moral and Ethical Assemblage in Russian Orthodox Drug Rehabilitation' 39 *Ethos* 30.

8

Ethical Aspects of Journeys Towards Desistance by Male Young Adult Recidivists

ANTHONY BOTTOMS AND CAROLINE LANSKEY

THE AIM OF this chapter is to explore the ways in which ethical issues are involved when persistent male young adult offenders attempt to desist from crime – as they often do. The chapter contains four main sections. In the last of these, we consider three case studies of such attempted journeys towards desistance. Before that, the first section outlines, as a background, some principal findings of the study (the Sheffield Desistance Study) within which these men were research subjects. The second and third sections then discuss some key theoretical issues that are relevant to the study of what we shall describe as the 'everyday situated ethics' of desistance journeys.

THE SHEFFIELD DESISTANCE STUDY

The last 20 years have seen an explosion of empirical research into desistance from crime. This has been particularly triggered by the realisation that – as a recent review of the field puts it – although desistance is not universal, nevertheless it is 'the norm, even among those characterised as high-rate, chronic offenders' (Bersani and Doherty 2018: 313). However, research has also suggested that there can be significant differences in the ways in which different types of offenders chart a path towards desistance. Our focus in this chapter is on male persistent offenders, and for this group we may summarise three of the more important research results in the following way:

1. The fastest reduction in the aggregate number of offences committed by such offenders occurs in their early twenties (Laub and Sampson 2003: chapter. 5; Piquero, Farrington and Blumstein 2007: 136), and the final conviction of most such offenders occurs in their late twenties or early thirties (Doherty and Bersani 2018).

2. Most of those who try to desist do so gradually – that is, they usually commit fresh offences as they gradually reduce the frequency of their offending.
3. The factors leading to a successful 'desistance journey' are usually *not* simply the reverse of the factors originally leading to criminality. (This has been described as 'asymmetrical causation': Uggen and Piliavin 1998.) In other words, fresh issues that arise during a desistance journey can be influential, and these need to be understood if desistance is to be adequately explained.

The Sheffield Desistance Study (SDS), the fieldwork for which took place from 2003 to 2007, aimed to explore some of these issues further by conducting a prospective study of recidivist offenders that was focused on the young adult age range (ie, the years when the fastest aggregate reduction in criminality takes place).[1] The research sample was therefore restricted to those born in three consecutive years (1982–84), and the mean age of the sample at the start of the study was 20 years 9 months (range 19–22 years). The study recruited 113 male offenders, of whom most (79 per cent) self-identified as 'White British'. The researchers aimed to interview each SDS respondent four times, at intervals of nine to 12 months, using a mixture of quantitative (checklist) and qualitative questions. The retention rate was good, with 78 per cent completing the fourth interview; also, respondents to the fourth interview were broadly representative of the whole sample.[2]

It is important to understand some key characteristics of the SDS sample, at the time of their recruitment to the study. First, most of the men already had a record of persistent offending. Even at this early age, they had, between them, been convicted of a 'standard list' offence on no fewer than 909 separate occasions[3] – a mean of eight such events per person. (This total actually exceeds the aggregate number of such conviction occasions *by age 40* in the well-known Cambridge Study in Delinquent Development.)[4] A 'conviction occasion' can

[1] The Sheffield Desistance Study was conducted at the University of Sheffield, with Anthony Bottoms and Joanna Shapland as Joint Principal Investigators. It was funded by the UK Economic and Social Research Council as part of a Research Network on 'Social Contexts of Pathways in Crime' (SCoPiC) that was co-ordinated by Per-Olof Wikström (University of Cambridge). For an overview of the main findings of the SDS, see Bottoms and Shapland (2016).

[2] For fuller details of the sample and the way in which it was recruited, see Bottoms and Shapland (2011).

[3] A 'conviction occasion' is a court appearance at which at least one conviction is recorded; it is not uncommon on such occasions for the offender to be convicted of more than one offence, but this is still only a single conviction occasion. The official category of 'standard list offences' includes crimes of violence, sex offences, robbery, theft, burglary, fraud, drugs offences and criminal damage, but it excludes most motoring and administrative offences. In common with most persistent offender samples, most men in the SDS sample had been convicted of a variety of standard list offences. The exception was that, although sexual offence convictions were in principle included, in fact the sample men had no such convictions.

[4] The Cambridge Study of Delinquent Development is a longitudinal study of the criminal careers of a general population sample of 411 males, originally recruited at age eight in a London

however involve being convicted for more than one offence, so the mean number of standard list offences for which the men had been convicted, at the time of their first interview, was 17.6. Turning, secondly, to the SDS men's social backgrounds, 86 per cent had left school with no qualifications, and this naturally made it difficult for them to secure employment, especially as, by the time they left school in the late 1990s, the Sheffield economy had become more service-based, with fewer unskilled jobs available, following the collapse of the local steel industry in the 1980s. Hence, almost 60 per cent of the SDS sample had had no jobs of any kind (even casual jobs) in the year before the first research interview.[5] Both the criminal and the social aspects of the men's life histories therefore had much in common with those of the offenders described in a recent study by David Maguire (2021), which he evocatively titled *Male, Failed, Jailed*. Against that background, any desistance journeys that the men undertook would inevitably be starting from a difficult place.

Quantitatively, 80 per cent of SDS respondents were reconvicted during the period of the research study, but there was a significant reduction in their frequency of conviction during the research period (from an average of 8.6 standard list offences in the year before the first interview, to 2.6 such offences in the period after the third interview, approximately three years later).[6] Two regression analyses were conducted, with the dependent variable being the final offending level as measured, respectively, by official and by self-reported criminality. The structure of the results from the two analyses was very similar.[7] In each, the variables that predicted continuing criminality were measures of:

1. The extent of the respondent's pre-SDS criminal record.
2. The number of 'obstacles to going straight' self-reported by the respondent.
3. Specific factors occurring during the research period (respectively, unemployment in the self-report analysis, and identification with criminal peers in the official crime analysis).

Taken together, these results appear to show that longer criminal records are harder to shake off; that offenders can accurately assess the extent of the challenges that they face in attempting to desist; and that lack of employment and continuing association with peers can constitute real challenges to successful desistance. As we shall see, other aspects of the results from the SDS reinforce the significance of these findings.

borough in the early 1960s. By age 40, 164 of these men had been convicted of a standard list offence, with an aggregate of 686 conviction occasions for such offences (Farrington et al 2006).

[5] In the case of those who were in prison at the time of the first interview, this refers to the year before the prison sentence.

[6] These data are standardised to exclude periods in custody, during which, of course, the men were not at risk of committing offences in the community.

[7] See Bottoms and Shapland (2011: Tables 2.5 and 2.6). Full details of the methodology and results of these analyses will be found in this source.

Yet despite the men's extensive criminality, their values at the start of the study were in some important respects essentially conventional. For example, when asked at first interview what kind of person they would like to become, the principal answers were: 'go straight', 'live a normal life', 'be a good person' and 'be a family man' (Shapland and Bottoms 2011: 262). In addition, a clear majority thought it was 'very important' (37 per cent) or 'quite important' (42 per cent) that people should obey the law (Shapland and Bottoms 2011: 265). It is therefore perhaps not surprising that, at the first interview, 56 per cent said they had 'made a definite decision to try to stop' offending, and a further 37 per cent said they 'would like to stop, but I'm not sure if I can' (Bottoms and Shapland 2011: 57, Table 2.2).

Given the disadvantages of their criminal, educational and (non)-working backgrounds, any desistance journeys that these men tried to undertake would inevitably encounter obstacles. At each research interview, respondents were shown a list of 13 potential 'obstacles to going straight or staying straight' that had been identified in previous research,[8] and asked to say which of these applied to them now. As noted above, the total number of such obstacles mentioned by a respondent was a strong predictor of subsequent offending or otherwise. But the specific obstacles that were the most frequently mentioned were also of great interest: they were 'lack of money', 'opportunity for easy money', 'lack of work' and a 'need for excitement' (Bottoms and Shapland 2011: 61, Table 2.4).[9] These results are worth highlighting, because neither money problems nor the excitement of offending features prominently in the mainstream literature on desistance (although for a partial exception see Giordano, Schroeder and Cernovich 2007).[10]

Bearing in mind some of the above matters (long criminal histories; a wish for normality; significant obstacles to change; a mixed set of values; offending is exciting), Bottoms and Shapland (2016: 109) offered as a 'central conclusion' of the SDS that, for this set of offenders, '*desistance is the process of learning to live a non-criminal life when one has been leading a largely criminal life*' (emphasis original). In an attempt to illustrate some main features of such a process, they sketched a diagram offering a 'heuristic and interactive model of the early stages of desistance' (Bottoms and Shapland 2011: 70).[11] This diagram

[8] This list was adapted from a similar list used in research by Ros Burnett (1992).

[9] It might be thought surprising that 'drug problems' are not among the 'most listed' obstacles. The reason is that only 47 per cent of the sample self-identified as having a significant drug problem at first interview (Bottoms and Shapland 2011: 72, fn 10). Almost all of these men listed drugs as an obstacle to desistance, but 'drug problems' still ranked only sixth among the 13 possible obstacles.

[10] Citing the work of Jack Katz (1988); Giordano et al (2007) refer to the excitement of offending as part of their discussion of the emotional dimensions of desistance. More recent contributions by younger scholars also address these links – see, eg, van Ginneken (2017) on money; Droppelmann (2021) on excitement; and Maguire (2021) on both.

[11] We emphasise that, given the recidivistic character of the sample, what was studied in the SDS was early stages of attempts to desist. There is some evidence that earlier and later stages

attempts to capture some of the unpredictability, or 'zigzag character', of desistance for recidivist offenders, notably by highlighting difficulties (described as 'obstacles, temptations or provocations') that might result in a relapse.[12]

No further interviews with the SDS men have taken place since 2007, but Joanna Shapland (2022) has recently published a paper summarising the men's official criminal records in the 10 years after the end of the SDS fieldwork (2007–17). These data show a high rate of reconviction: all but six of the 111 men who were still alive in 2017 had been reconvicted at least once during the decade. However, and congruently with other studies, the overall rate of offending in the sample continued to decline slowly (Shapland 2022: Figures 2 and 4). Moreover, there were some very substantial 'conviction-free gaps' in the men's records: 85 per cent had at least one two-year gap; 68 per cent had a three-year gap; and 53 per cent (more than half of the sample) had a *four-year* gap (Shapland 2022: 282).[13] These data therefore suggest that, although almost all the men continued to offend, they did so with declining frequency, and in an intermittent fashion that is consistent with the concept of a continuance of 'zigzag journeys towards desistance'.[14]

The moral philosopher Bernard Williams (1985/2006) begins his book *Ethics and the Limits of Philosophy* by reminding readers of Socrates' reported remark that 'what is at stake is far from insignificant: it is how one should live one's life' (Plato 1993: 352d, 40). Centuries later, precisely such a question was being asked in Sheffield by many of the respondents in the SDS – and they were not starting from an advantageous place.

UNDERSTANDING DESISTANCE: STRUCTURE, AGENCY AND RELATIONSHIPS

In this and the next section, we shall consider a number of theoretical issues that are relevant to trying to understand the process of 'learning to live a non-criminal life' when one has previously been a regular offender, with a special focus on ethical aspects of such a process.

of desistance journeys are different in character (Healy 2010; Porporino 2010), and this seems to explain why features identified in Shadd Maruna's (2001) important research on completed desistance (eg, 'redemption scripts' and generativity) were not found in the Sheffield study.

[12] For further discussion of the 'zigzag' character of desistance, and its implications, see Droppelmann (2021).

[13] These 'conviction-free gaps' exclude periods in custody. It is of course possible that some undetected offending occurred during these periods, but the periods themselves are substantially longer than occurred when the men were in their teens. On the importance of conviction-free gaps in lengthy criminal careers, see West (1963). Note also West's finding that for many of the men he studied, these gaps coincided with times when they were living in socially supportive circumstances.

[14] A question that arises from such data concerns why people turn to offending again after substantial crime-free gaps. For a pioneering study of this issue, see Kang and Kruttschnitt (2022).

It is not appropriate in this chapter to offer a full review of the scholarly literature on desistance. However, it is noteworthy that reviews of this literature not infrequently draw a distinction between accounts that place particular emphasis on *personal agency* and those that stress the influence of the *social structures* within which would-be desisters find themselves (for one such recent review, see Bersani and Doherty 2018). This structure/agency distinction is, of course, a staple of traditional social theory, but more recently it has been challenged by *relational sociologists*, who argue that we need to add 'relations' as a third concept in such discussions. It happens that there exist accounts of desistance that have prioritised each of these three concepts (structure; agency; relations), so a useful way in which to orient our theoretical discussion will be to consider the strengths and weaknesses of these three theoretical stances.

A Structural Theory: The Age-Graded Theory of Informal Social Control

The authors of this theory, John Laub and Robert Sampson (2003), developed it from analyses of data from a historical longitudinal study of persistent male juvenile offenders (by Glueck and Glueck 1968), supplemented by Laub and Sampson's own follow-up analysis, which included some qualitative retrospective interviews when the men were aged c 65. The main explanatory emphasis is placed on desistance effects arising from various 'turning points' in the men's lives – in particular, entry into marriages, stable employment and military service. As the title of the theory indicates, the claim is that entering into these new social situations alters the context of 'informal social control' for the person studied; this altered context then leads to fresh normative understandings, and hence to desistance. In their key 2003 volume Laub and Sampson, while acknowledging the existence of human agency, state that 'most offenders desist in response to *structural turning points* that serve as the catalyst for long-term behavioral change … [Hence] the image of "*desistance by default*" best fits the desistance process that we found in our data'. They add that: 'desistance for our subjects was not necessarily a conscious or deliberate process … [and] many men made *a commitment to go straight without even realizing it*' (Laub and Sampson 2003: 278–79, emphases added) when entering the new social context of marriage, employment or the military.

These claims contain important insights, but in our view they are overstated. There is no doubt that attachments such as stable marriages and employment do often generate significant normative change in ex-offenders (see the review of relevant research in Laub, Rowan and Sampson 2019, section II).[15] However, the

[15] Also potentially relevant, although not discussed by Laub et al, is normative attachment to faith communities. On this see, eg, Adam Calverley's (2013) research on desistance among Bangladeshi-origin offenders in the UK; see also Ryan Williams, ch 7 in this volume.

suggestion that 'desistance by default' is a main explanation for desistance has not been supported by most other empirical research studies, including the SDS. Theoretically, also, 'desistance by default' seems to underplay the role of human agency in everyday adult life by suggesting that what the authors describe as 'structural turning points' have a near-automatic effect on those whom they affect. Perhaps the nature of Laub and Sampson's data (retrospective interviews at age 65, discussing a 'turning point' that occurred perhaps decades earlier) has generated an oversimplified view of desistance, glossing over its complexities? Perhaps also the reliance on that data source explains the absence of focus, in the Laub–Sampson study, of the gradual (or 'zigzag') character of desistance among male persistent offenders?

However, a recent defence of the theory, while it contains no formal revisions, presents a somewhat softer, and therefore more persuasive, account (Laub, Rowan and Sampson 2019). The authors rightly claim that there is 'strong statistical evidence of the probabilistic enhancement of desistance' associated with the turning points that they identified. They add that data from their retrospective qualitative interviews suggest that these 'turning points', when they occur, generate new social situations that, to varying degrees:

> (1) 'knife off' the past from the present, (2) … provide both supervision and monitoring as well as new opportunities for social support and growth, (3) … change and structure routine activities, and (4) … provide the opportunity for identity transformation … [Overall, the effect is] to reorder short-term situational inducements to crime and, over time, redirect longer-term commitments to conformity (Laub, Rowan and Sampson 2019: 299).

The final sentence of this extract is of special importance. The authors are claiming that entry into new social contexts has some immediate *situational* effects on a person's daily routines (his or her day is ordered differently), and these changes alter the opportunities and inducements for crime. Subsequently, these situational effects change into 'longer-term commitments to conformity' – that is, *normative pro-social commitments*. Elsewhere, Laub and Sampson (2003: 279) have also suggested that, in time, these longer-term commitments might become *habits*, and (quoting Becker and Murphy 2000: 152) that such 'habits provide an anchor by strengthening the forces making for persistence in behavior'. Thus, the Age-Graded Theory of Social Control valuably suggests that fresh social contexts can generate, over time, *situational* then *normative* and finally *habitual* compliance – that is, a progression through three of the four principal mechanisms of legal compliance identified in the work of Anthony Bottoms (2002, 2019).

An important implication of this part of Laub and Sampson's analysis is that Aristotle's suggestion of a close link between habitual behaviour and human character ('Virtue of character is a result of habituation' – Aristotle 2014: 1103a, 23) seems to have relevance for contemporary desistance studies. But a logical extension to this observation is also crucial to the understanding of desistance: namely, that if a person has become habituated to acting in certain ways, it will probably take time to learn to act in a different manner when similar circumstances arise, so those who have become used to offending will not find it straightforward to change. This point is, in our view, central to understanding the 'zigzag' character of desistance journeys among habitual offenders.

The Laub–Sampson analysis of the importance of social bonds to desistance has been broadly supported in a number of empirical studies. In one of these, based on a study in Catalonia, Cid and Marti (2012) show that it is not only new social contexts that can assist desistance. Rather, this can also occur as a result of fresh meaning and impetus being given to existing social bonds, such as relationships with the would-be desister's family of origin. We shall see that this insight is supported by data from the SDS.

We need finally to add that although Laub and Sampson characterise their theory as focusing in particular on 'structural turning points', they say very little about meso-level and macro-level structures such as economic and political contexts. They are not alone among desistance scholars in this respect, although there have been some attempts to redress this situation (see, eg, Farrall, Bottoms and Shapland 2010; Farrall 2019). Yet some understanding of such wider contexts is essential for a full understanding of the situations faced by men in the SDS. David Maguire has highlighted an important contrast between his study, previously mentioned, and a classic earlier study in the sociology of education, Paul Willis' (1977) *Learning to Labour.* As Maguire (2021: 4) summarises, Willis' study showed 'how schools are crucial sites in the formation and reproduction of versions of working-class masculinities', constructed through 'having a laugh' and rejecting the school's ethos of learning. Post-school, this rejection led, as Willis' subtitle succinctly put it, to the consequence that 'working class kids get working class jobs'. But 30 to 40 years later, in most former industrial cities in England the employment market had been radically transformed, and the great majority of unskilled labouring jobs had disappeared. Hence, while most men studied by Maguire in Hull had school histories similar to those described by Willis, their post-school careers did not involve 'getting working class jobs'; instead, these men experienced persistent unemployment. *Exactly the same was true of SDS respondents*; and this structural issue was then an added burden to those who tried to desist, because not only did they have few if any educational qualifications, they frequently also had no credible employment history.

An Agentic Theory: The Identity Theory of Desistance

This theory, which was originally propounded by Paternoster and Bushway (2009), aims to bring the individual, and his or her agency, much more into focus than does the theorisation of Laub and Sampson. It does so by focusing in particular on the fourth mechanism of legal compliance identified by Bottoms

(2002, 2019), namely compliance that results from *instrumental* or *prudential* choices, influenced by incentives and disincentives.

The introduction of such issues into desistance theorisation is valuable, because – as we shall see in the case histories – would-be desisters do fairly often make instrumental choices of this kind. Moreover, Paternoster and Bushway's (2009) paper introduced some memorable and relevant terms into desistance theory. These include: (i) a would-be desister being motivated by images of his or her future 'feared self' (a disincentive) or 'possible self' (an incentive); and (ii) the suggestion that a turning point in criminal careers comes when an offender feels a 'crystallization of discontent' about his or her current circumstances.

However, the Identity Theory of Desistance (or ITD) takes matters further by explicitly adopting Rational Choice Theory as an overall explanation of desistance journeys.[16] Thus, in a later paper Paternoster et al (2015: 214) argue that offenders first recognise that 'offending is more costly than beneficial', and then

> they make initial moves to change their identity … The feared self provides the first step toward desistance, but to maintain these initial steps, the offender must craft a new, more positive image of what they want to become, 'the possible self'. This newly emerging pro-social identity or possible self then triggers a change in the person's preferences for things like quick and easy money … [toward] more pro-social things like conventional employment.

Notice that this proposed sequence stems from an initial cost–benefit assessment, followed by 'moves to change … identity', followed by 'changes in the person's preferences'. In other words, desistance journeys are seen as a series of *instrumental cost–benefit choices* by the would-be desister, all of which are made by a rational agent, making an individual choice. Hence, according to these authors, 'prosocial opportunities *only arise* and are *only made successful* when there has *first* been an *internal change*… a realization that … they want to change who they are' (Paternoster et al 2015: 218, emphasis added). This claim of course places their theory in a position of sharp disagreement with the Age-Graded Theory of informal Social Control.

In our view, the claims of the ITD, like those of the Age-Graded Theory, are overstated. Empirical studies, including the evidence of the SDS, suggest that while rational choice is certainly present in desistance journeys,[17] it is not as pervasive as this account suggests. In particular, there is significant evidence that pro-social opportunities can arise gradually, as a result of entering into

[16] In a later paper (Paternoster et al 2015), the original thesis is refined by the adoption of Akerlof and Kranton's (2000, 2010) concept of 'identity economics'. However, the authors' conceptualisation of the mechanisms of desistance remains based on rational choice, since Akerlof and Kranton's various writings 'incorporate identity directly into the standard utility maximisation analysis' used by economists (Davis 2021: 2).

[17] See in particular the discussion of 'diachronic self-control' later in this chapter.

positive new relationships *before* people have made any 'initial moves to change their identity'. More broadly, while this is not the place for a full discussion of Rational Choice Theory, we would agree with Margaret Archer (2000: chapter 2) that, theoretically, its individualism and its focus on 'risk discounting and profit-maximising' (at 55) leaves us with an image of human beings that is truncated, and so not recognisable as a total picture. We would, therefore, prefer to set would-be desisters' instrumental choices within broader theoretical frameworks.

A Relational Theory: Desistance as 'Individualised, Reflexive and Relational'

As noted above, in the last quarter-century a number of scholars have argued for the need to add a third concept – that of 'the relation' – to the traditional sociological dualism of 'structure' and 'agency'. In our view, their case is persuasive, although their cause has not been helped by internal debates and division.[18]

A key issue within relational sociology concerns the understanding of the term 'relations'. On this, we follow Crossley (2011: 28) who defines them as 'lived trajectories of iterated interactions'.[19] Developing the point, he argues that:

> A social relation is not an object, akin to a bridge, but rather a shifting state of play within a process of social interaction. To say that two actors are related is to say that they have a history of past and an expectation of future interaction, and that this shapes their current interactions.

In the more plausible versions of relational sociology, the concepts of agency and structure are retained, but both are seen through a relational lens – a matter that, in the present context, is particularly salient as regards agency. A contrary view of agency was taken by Ray Paternoster (2017: 353, fn 4), who argued that it is 'more of an individualistic mental product, and less a social one ... it is important to keep in mind that deliberations, intentions and volitions are acts of the mind' (see also Paternoster et al 2015: 220–25). Of course, Paternoster is right that these things are 'acts of the mind' – but minds are often deeply influenced by the social contexts within which they operate. Relational sociologists therefore rightly argue that agency, while indeed it is something that individuals

[18] These debates can on occasion be vigorous: for some flavour of them, see Powell and Depelteau (2013); Prandini (2015); and Donati and Archer (2015). In the present analysis, we have drawn on insights developed by scholars in different 'camps', but we have done so in ways that are, we hope, theoretically compatible.

[19] For a fuller discussion of this issue see Crossley (2013: 123), where the author proposes 'a positive dialogue' between this conceptualisation of relations and its main alternative, described as 'juxtapositions in a "social space" constituted by the distribution of important social relations (forms of capital)'.

exercise, is shaped not only by social structures and culture, but also – and for some people perhaps especially – by individuals' 'lived trajectories of iterated interactions' with those who are close to them, such as families, close friends and work colleagues.

The relational sociologist Pierpaolo Donati (2011: 130) has, importantly, argued that a relationship 'cannot be reduced to the subjects, even though it can only "come alive" through these subjects'. Thus, while each subject brings to any relationship his or her own agency, the relationship is conceptually sui generis: that is, it has some 'irreducible properties arising from the reciprocal relationship of those involved' (Weaver 2016: 136). This is why most people can remember occasions when, as a result of the social dynamics of a relational situation, they did or said something that they otherwise would not have said or done; the relationship generates its own outcomes. Indeed, criminologists know that people sometimes join in group offending in just such a fashion.

The first major work on desistance to adopt relational sociology as its theoretical framework is Beth Weaver's (2016) in-depth retrospective interview study of a group of six Scottish men, who were in their forties when they were interviewed. In adolescence, these men had been members of a close-knit group ('The Del') who regularly committed crimes together; most did not desist until at least their late twenties. Each man's story is told in separate chapters of Weaver's book, but in her conclusion she binds them together and says that each of the accounts reveals

> a reflexive individual whose ultimate concerns emerge from, are immersed in, respond to and shape their relational worlds …. [T]he individual stories have illustrated the centrality of the relational to the individual and thus to processes of change in a broad sense, and to desistance from crime in particular. Taken together … [they] have revealed an understanding of desistance as a complex, individualised, reflexive and relational process (at 212–13).

Weaver's characterisation of the desistance process as 'individualised, reflexive and relational' is important. Such a process is, she argues, *both* individualised and relational because 'both the individual and the social relation undergo reflexive change in tandem with each other' (at 55). Alongside these concepts she adds that of *reflexivity*, which is a sometimes neglected dimension of agency. Understanding of reflexivity has recently been enhanced by the work of the sociologist Margaret Archer on 'internal conversations'. Archer has insisted that human beings have 'inner as well as outer lives', and that one cannot with integrity 'erect a brick wall between' the outer and the inner (Archer 2000: 317). She has also carried out a pioneering empirical study of these 'internal conversations', relating them to structure and agency (Archer 2003). Her arguments for the importance of internal conversations are compelling, although of course reflexivity/internal conversations must always be seen in a relational context – that is, they take place in light of the subjects' ongoing relationships.

The chapter on 'Harry' in Weaver's (2016: chapter 6) book illustrates her theoretical approach. In his adolescence, Harry was a regular offender with

'The Del' (see above). In the men's early twenties, 'a violent and enduring feud' effectively divided this group into two factions (Weaver 2016: 93). Harry, who chose not to take sides, left the group. He then became immersed in a different and looser group, which was particularly focused around a culture of intense support for a leading Glasgow football (soccer) team; within the norms of Scottish masculine culture, this group 'represented a credible alternative to association with the Del' (Weaver 2016: 133). With others in this new group, Harry continued to acquire convictions for soccer-related violence. Importantly, however, most members of this group, unlike Harry, were employed; moreover, they did not – unlike him – commit property offences. Influenced by this fresh reference group, and more indirectly by the views of his wife,[20] Harry in his late twenties discontinued his property offending, and began – for the first time in his life – to seek employment. In his early thirties, Harry got a job, became a father (a matter of great importance to him), and stopped all offending. Commenting on Harry's case, Weaver notes that he did not (contra the ITD) make any initial 'conscious decision to desist'; rather, his desistance 'gradually surfaced alongside other shifts he initiated in his practices and behaviours' (at 142). But this was also (contra Laub and Sampson's theorisation) not 'desistance by default', nor could his desistance be attributed to a single 'structural turning point'. Rather, he joined a new relational group which – alongside the importance of his marriage – gradually influenced his normative understandings (or 'moral framework'), and he then consciously altered his practices in line with his changing ethical views. Relationships were crucial in developing these changed views and practices.

There is clearly much in this kind of analysis that is potentially fruitful. In particular, a relational focus can readily be integrated with both structural and agentic features of social situations; also, as the case of Harry shows, relationships can influence moral understandings.

When the insights of relational sociology are applied to the data of the SDS, attention particularly focuses on three types of 'lived trajectories of iterated interactions' (Crossley 2011: 28) that – given the age range of sample members during the fieldwork period (roughly, 20–25) – were often of crucial, and also of changing, significance in the men's lives. These relationships are those with girlfriends, with male peers and with families of origin. Romantic attachments with girlfriends, leading to stable partnerships and/or marriage, have become a staple of the literature on desistance among male offenders; but much less attention has been paid to relationships with peers and with parents – and very

[20] Harry's relationship with his wife went back continuously to his late teens. Although she always wanted him to change his behaviour, their relationship was strong even while he was regularly offending, so her love was not conditional on his desistance. But eventually Harry was influenced by his 'concern to maintain the relationship, and to limit the shame' that further offending might cause to his loyal partner (Weaver 2016: 135).

rarely with both. That particular omission – in its full form – has now been challenged both by the SDS (Bottoms and Shapland 2016: 114-15; Shapland and Bottoms 2019) and by Giordano and colleagues (Giordano 2016: 18–20; Copp et al 2020);[21] and the evidence from both sources suggests that how both these types of relationship develop during young adulthood can be crucial to desistance journeys. To understand why this is so, one needs to consider the typical situation of late-adolescent male recidivists who are thinking about trying to desist. They have been regularly offending, which has usually led to severe strains with their families of origin, even where (as is by no means always the case) relationships with those families were previously good. They are also usually unemployed, which means that they have no work colleagues. So, leaving aside girlfriends, their closest current relationships are usually with male 'mates', who they have known for a number of years, and who usually also have criminal records. To illustrate: at the beginning of the SDS research, over three-quarters of the men said that they met with each of their three 'best mates' either every day or every other day; the median length of these relationships was seven years; and 60 per cent or more had committed offences with each of these three mates (Shapland and Bottoms 2019: 33 and Tables 1 and 2). If, in such circumstances, one is serious about desistance, it is likely that one will try to move away from the influence of delinquent friends, and the evidence of the SDS shows exactly such a tendency (Shapland and Bottoms 2019).[22] But SDS data also show that, as desistance journeys are attempted, relationships with families of origin (especially mothers) often improve; and (of course) that girlfriends are frequently important in the men's journeys. Thus, there is often a complex and interactive *relational triangle* of male mates, girlfriends and families of origin running through desistance narratives in this crucial age range, as will be illustrated in the case studies to be considered shortly.

THEORISING EVERYDAY SITUATED ETHICS

The social anthropologist James Laidlaw begins a book that he describes as 'a prospectus for the anthropology of ethics' by reminding his readers that:

> Everywhere human conduct is pervaded by an ethical dimension – by questions of the rightness and wrongness of actions, of what we owe to each other, of the kind of

[21] The importance to desistance of the declining influence of peers had earlier been strongly argued by Warr (2002: ch 5). As previously noted, Cid and Marti (2012) also drew attention to the help given by existing family members, but their sample was of older men (mean age 34).

[22] This is consistent with the general criminological research literature, which shows that the proportion of offences committed in groups is highest in adolescence and declines in the early twenties (see the review by van Mastrigt and Carrington 2019). The same authors further report a 'general tendency for offending groups to be small, homogeneous and transitory' (at 216), which was also true in the SDS (Shapland and Bottoms 2019).

> persons we think we are or aspire to be – so it is an inescapable part of what [social scientists] study (2014: 1).

Such a reminder is necessary, in Laidlaw's view, because anthropology, like other social sciences, has paid too little explicit attention to ethical issues. A similar conclusion as regards criminology is a central theme of this volume, and it applies also to the topic of desistance from crime. In this section, we shall therefore discuss some additional theoretical resources that might help us to develop a better understanding of what we shall call the *everyday situated ethics*[23] that are to be found in the 'zigzag journeys' of recidivist would-be desisters.

Everyday Life: Ethical Issues

The discussion in the previous section suggested that the study of relationships will probably be very relevant to the 'everyday situated ethics' of desistance journeys. A more formal linkage between relational sociology and the emerging 'ethical turn' in sociology has recently been proposed by Owen Abbott (2020), who – in summary – argues that 'morality needs to be considered as something that is *principally* engaged with and enacted in the fuzzy indeterminacy of relationally entangled and intersubjectively emergent practice' (at 181, emphasis added). Or, more fully:

> Our basic practical engagement with the world situates us among others, from whom we take our means of interpreting the world and ourselves. Emotions such as shame at certain actions, or pride in the actions of others, only make sense as phenomena held among other people who shape our facility to interpret and respond to the world around us. Yet, as reflexive actors … we become capable of not simply replicating the moral world of which we are part, but also of construing our own position within it (Abbott 2020: 183).

Abbott here mentions, but does not develop, the role of emotion. But his mention of it reminds us of a point made by Barry Vaughan (2007) in an article on desistance that adopts Margaret Archer's (2000) sociological framework. Vaughan emphasises that Archer's 'internal conversation' is misunderstood if it is seen simply as a cognitive debating forum. This is because

> it is often the case that our emotions provide the first signals about our likely reaction to a situation before we have explicitly started to reflect on [it] … [Emotions] initially indicate that to which we are drawn or shy away from and so provide signals for

[23] We need to distinguish this term from that of 'situation ethics', which is a stance sometimes taken in normative ethics – eg, by some existentialists. For advocates of situation ethics, there are no universal moral rules or rights, and the rightness or wrongness of an act depends upon the situation. By contrast, 'everyday situated ethics' is a descriptive, not a normative, term: its focus is on describing and understanding the ethical aspirations and choices of individuals within the context of their everyday lives.

> reason to decode. [They] provide the initial 'shoving power' (Archer 2000, p 232) to orientate us in a certain way, but the agent often then makes a judgement of worth on whether to assent or not to these initial reactions (Vaughan 2007: 393).

Although the point is not noted either by Vaughan or by Archer, there is a Humean quality to their accounts. In David Hume's philosophy 'passions' (ie, emotions such as hope, fear or disgust) are seen as the primary motivating forces for morality. For him, reason cannot *directly* lead to valid conclusions about morality, but that does not mean that reason plays no part in moral judgements (Millican 2012; Beauchamp 1998: 45–49; also Jonathan Jacobs' chapter in this volume). The case studies that follow will show that both emotions and reasoning are often involved when people try to desist. However, we should not, *pace* Vaughan, see emotions as providing only 'initial shoving power'. For example, in their final research interview some SDS men reported feeling regret for the harm or upset that they had caused to their victims. Such ex post facto moral emotions are likely to be primarily reflective and introspective: they might in time lead to some reappraisals of the self, but this will probably be a gradual process, for which 'shoving power' does not seem to be an apt description.

In their Introduction to this volume, the editors have suggested that important contributions to the project of 'criminology as a moral science' can be made without much in the way of explicit attention to concepts developed by moral philosophers. We agree with this view, but in the context of ethical dimensions of desistance journeys, we have found it helpful to work with the concepts of *moral frameworks*, '*burdened virtue*', '*ground projects*' and *resolutions*.

We begin with Charles Taylor's (1989) concept of a person's *moral framework*. As Ruth Abbey (2000: 34) explains, Taylor believes that 'all individuals have a moral framework, whether they realise it or not'; moreover, in his philosophy moral frameworks 'give shape and meaning to individuals' lives and provide answers, no matter how tacitly, to the existential questions that [Taylor] believes face all individuals about the purpose, conduct and direction of their lives'. It follows that a person's moral framework is an important element within his or her sense of self.

Of special importance in the current context, Taylor's thesis is that, within their moral framework, most people have a bundle of different values and commitments, of varying strength. These might involve, for example, commitments or values arising from family ties or personal friendships, or from political or religious beliefs; and some of these values might be in tension with others. Since it is well known that people often behave differently in different circumstances (eg, for young men, when with their parents, or on the street with their mates), one value within the framework might particularly influence a person's actions in situation A, and another in situation B. Similarly, over time the values and commitments within a person's moral framework might change – either absolutely, or in terms of the priority of different values in his or her life.

The concept of a moral framework is particularly helpful in considering the lives of the SDS men, because – as we have seen – their values at the start of the study were varied and complex. They saw offending as something that they could, in various circumstances, contemplate; it was certainly not an ethical 'no-go area'. However, looking to their longer-term future, most of them did not want to continue as regular offenders – instead, they wanted to 'live a normal life', 'be a good person' and 'be a family man' (Shapland and Bottoms 2011: 262). In other words, their preferred ultimate values were pro-social, but given their recent histories, other values were clearly present in their current moral framework. Over the three to four years of the follow-up, however, the SDS researchers were able to identify shifts in the *priority* of the values of those men who were attempting to desist.[24] More pro-social values came to the fore, usually alongside new relationships or social opportunities, and aided by processes of physiological and psychological maturity (see below on the 'natural order').

How can such shifts in the priority of values be best theorised? In thinking about this question, SDS researchers were drawn to the tradition of *virtue ethics* – a tradition that has been significantly revived within Anglophone moral philosophy since the late 1950s (see generally, Crisp and Slote 1997; Russell 2013). 'Virtue ethics' is a shorthand term used by moral philosophers to describe an approach to normative ethics that 'emphasizes the virtues, or moral character, in contrast to an approach which emphasizes duties or rules (deontology) or one which emphasizes the consequences of actions (utilitarianism)' (Hursthouse 1999: 1). Virtue ethics therefore focuses less on specific moral choices that are made on particular occasions, and more on the overall development of character, or 'the shape of a life'. However, Bottoms and Shapland (2014) were – given the complexity and obstacle-strewn nature of desistance journeys in the SDS – wary of over-idealised accounts within the virtue ethics tradition. They were therefore attracted by Christine Swanton's (2003:19) definition of a virtue as: 'a good quality of character, more specifically a disposition, to respond to, or acknowledge, items within its field in an excellent or good enough way'. Two features of this definition seemed to be helpful in the context of desistance studies: 'first, that a response within a given field that is "good enough" may still count as virtuous; and secondly, that we do not have to look for a fully formed "character" to detect virtue – rather, a "disposition" will suffice' (Bottoms and Shapland 2014: 329–30). These authors then sketched how different dispositions and practices might develop in a journey towards desistance:

> Attempts to desist usually start either with a realisation that one's current situation is far from desirable (a 'push' factor …) or with a glimpse of a more satisfying life (a 'pull' factor …) But this initial step is only the beginning of a process … [I]f they are serious about changing, those who have been deeply involved in crime need to make many adjustments to their way of living … But if desistance is successfully

[24] The SDS researchers have elsewhere expressed their gratitude to the social anthropologist Joel Robbins (Cambridge University) for helping them to see the relevance for the study of desistance of the concept of a 'changing priority of values' as opposed to a 'change in values'.

> accomplished, gradually a different pattern of activities will take shape, which in time will become routine. Often, too, this will be accompanied by changes in the moral evaluation of past behaviour (Bottoms and Shapland 2014: 326).

Elsewhere in this volume, Swanton notes Bottoms and Shapland's contribution, but she argues that virtue ethics *simpliciter* still 'carries an impossible theoretical weight'. She suggests that, to develop a virtue ethics with adequate applicability to the real world, scholars will need to pay greater attention to 'culture, history, burdens, difference of perspective due to, for example, age, roles, gender, and the narrative shape of an individual life in which "projects" have personal significance'. This she describes as a *differentiated* virtue ethics, which takes proper account of relevant social differences. Then, developing the concept of 'burden' from the above list, she suggests that one kind of differentiated virtue can be described as 'burdened virtue', and that 'an agent is burdened in respect of virtue if (i) it is burdensome (very costly, or difficult) to acquire the virtue and/or (ii) it is burdensome (very costly or difficult) to maintain the virtue'. In the case studies below, we shall work with this very helpful proposal.

In the quotation above, Swanton uses the term 'project', and in her chapter she links it to the work of Bernard Williams. In an early paper, Williams spoke of a certain kind of project which he called a 'commitment'; that is, something 'with which one is … deeply and extensively involved and identified' (1973: 116). From this philosophical starting point, the social anthropologist Cheryl Mattingly (2014) utilised the concept (now called a 'ground project') in her study of Californian mothers caring for seriously sick children – a text that is now widely recognised as a major contribution to moral anthropology. Given that 'ground projects' and virtue ethics are closely related concepts, it is not accidental that, in the same volume, Mattingly also advocates 'first person virtue ethics' as a very promising theoretical approach within moral anthropology. We concur with Mattingly that the concept of a ground project has much to offer to social science, although we also – following the logic of Swanton's contributions – consider that it can be fruitfully applied to projects that are not as 'deep' as Mattingly's definition requires.[25]

As noted above, Bottoms and Shapland (2014: 326) have suggested that desistance-related 'ground projects' usually begin either with a 'push factor' or with a 'pull factor'. The case of 'Harry' in Weaver's Scottish study is a good example of a 'pull factor', based on his underlying relationship with his wife and his more public membership of the soccer-loving group of friends. 'Push'-dominated desistance journeys can look very different, and are often generated by what Paternoster and Bushway (2009) have called a 'crystallisation of discontent'. In such situations of significant discontent, one tactic frequently resorted

[25] Mattingly (2014: 12) defines ground projects as 'the kinds of commitments that people find so deep to who they are that they might not care to go on with their lives without them, or would not know themselves if they no longer had them'.

to is to make a *resolution* to change – for example, a resolve to stop offending altogether, or perhaps something less comprehensive but still important, such as a determination to come off drugs.

Ethical understanding of the nature of resolutions has been advanced by the work of the Cambridge philosopher Richard Holton (2003, 2009). Holton (2003: 42) argues that a resolution is 'a special sort of intention', whose 'distinctive feature is that it is supposed to remain firm in the face of the contrary desires that I *expect* to have' (emphasis added). In other words, resolutions are entered into precisely in order to assist the willpower (or 'strength of will') of a person who expects to be tempted to do something that, all things considered, he or she thinks it would be best not to do. For Holton (2003: 39), therefore, the key theoretical issue is not the traditional philosophical question of 'how is weakness of will possible?'; rather, it is 'how do agents succeed in persisting with their resolutions in the face of strong contrary inclinations?', or more succinctly, 'how *strength* of will is possible' (emphasis original).[26] The importance of such a formulation is immediately apparent to anyone who has seriously studied desistance from crime. In the SDS, for example, many respondents said that in certain situations they might very easily be tempted to 'do something stupid' (as they put it). They also knew very well that any resolution to avoid reoffending was not going to be easy to stick to, and that at some stage real willpower was going to be needed.

Strong evidence emerged in the SDS that one tactic in particular was often used by would-be desisters to help them to keep resolutions to change. Drawing on work by the philosopher Jeanette Kennett (2001: chapter 5), SDS researchers described this tactic as 'diachronic self-control' (DSC); that is, self-control that is exercised in advance of an expected event, rather than at the time of the event (ie, it is not 'synchronic').[27] According to Kennett, DSC is a type of action that is open to an individual who believes that she will be tempted or inclined, in some future situation, to do something that, all things considered, she wishes to avoid doing. One way of exercising DSC is then for a person to plan 'her *future circumstances* so as to ensure that the [inclination] cannot be acted upon, or at least to increase the likelihood that it will not be' (at 134, emphasis added). For a would-be desister from crime, the most obvious ways

[26] Holton's crucial move here is to introduce the concept of resolution into the traditional 'weakness of will' debate in philosophy. In the traditional formulation, 'weakness of will' arises when an agent, having decided that X would be the best action in a given circumstance, nevertheless does act Y (ie, a proposed intentional action is replaced by a different intentional action). In Holton's (2003: 42) analysis, however, we are not comparing two actions of similar status, because a resolution is 'a special sort of intention', with the 'distinctive feature' described in the text.

[27] Holton (2003: 55n) notes that there are affinities between 'strength of will' and at least some versions of the concept of 'self-control' in the literature of social science. He restricts his discussion to synchronic situations, but Vierkant (2015) has persuasively argued that diachronic self-control is also correctly seen as a kind of 'strength of will'. For a helpful general discussion of self-control in relation to desistance, see van Ginneken (2017).

to 'plan future circumstances' in this way are: first, to avoid going to certain places where he feels he may be goaded into committing an offence (eg, a pub where violence often occurs); and second, to avoid meeting certain friends, in whose company he fears that he might be drawn into reoffending (eg, because of emotional excitement, or the pressures of group dynamics). DSC is therefore an *instrumental/rational decision*, made in advance by a would-be desister, in order to try to prevent himself – by a *situational tactic* – from committing crimes that he feels he might otherwise be all too likely to commit. Very interestingly, in a representative qualitative sub-sample within the SDS, as many as 14 out of 18 respondents (three-quarters) said that they had at some time adopted tactics of this kind to help them avoid potentially criminogenic situations (Bottoms 2013).

Everyday Life: The Natural and Practical Orders

As Christine Swanton has vividly reminded us, ethical decision-making occurs in *differentiated* real-life contexts. In thinking about real-life contexts, the sociologist Margaret Archer (2000) has also pointed out to social scientists – who naturally tend to focus on social relationships – that human beings must necessarily live in what she calls *the natural and practical orders*. Briefly, the 'natural order' relates to the fact that each human being is an embodied creature, and is subject to the conditions that this entails (eg, we need regular sleep; we cannot bodily be in two places at once). The 'practical order' refers to the fact that all humans need to develop various practical skills and competencies in order to function adequately in the world. The competencies include matters such as turning up on time for appointments with officials, and learning how to live within one's income; the skills can range from the very simple to the advanced, but everyone must develop some skills.

For respondents in the SDS, both the natural and the practical orders were relevant to desistance. As regards the natural order, two main factors were influential. One was that during the research period the average age of the SDS sample increased from nearly 21 to nearly 24. Recent research has shown that the frontal lobe function of the brain 'increases over the course of adolescence … and continues into the late 20s', which has the effect of improving 'various elements of cognition including judgement, consequential thinking, inhibition of impulses and coherent planning' (Royal College of Psychiatrists 2015: para. 1.1). This meant that, although the SDS men's desistance journeys involved many difficulties, they could face up to these difficulties with some improved psychological resources.[28] The second important factor relating to the natural order

[28] This is reflected in some of the interview responses; eg, in response to a question in the final interview about self-perceived changes in thought and behaviour patterns since the beginning of the SDS research, the dominant responses (from 61%) were 'I think before I act now' and 'I think more about the future' (Bottoms 2012: 40).

was drug or alcohol addiction, which can of course create physiological cravings. Statistically, drugs were of special importance: as previously indicated (see n 9 above) at first interview just under half of SDS respondents self-identified as having a drug problem, and later analyses showed that self-reporting drugs as a potential obstacle was a significant predictor of subsequent criminality.[29] Thus, drug addiction, once acquired, has an important (though not necessarily insuperable) role in hindering attempts at desistance.

The practical order was also of great importance within the SDS, and the most obvious manifestation of this was in the field of employment. As noted above, structural changes in the Sheffield economy had by the late 1990s (when the SDS sample left school) resulted in a significant reduction in the availability of unskilled manual jobs. Since the weak school records of most SDS men left them poorly qualified for skilled employment, getting a job was usually a major problem for them. Closely linked to this is the more general issue of money. It remains a puzzle why money has to date been so infrequently discussed in the research literature on desistance, especially in light of the fact that, in the SDS, respondents often pointed out to the researchers that serious attempts at desistance could involve a significant loss of income by comparison with regular property offending. Esther van Ginneken (2017: 251) has also drawn attention to the relevance for desistance journeys of the psychological evidence that 'financial worries lead to poorer decisions and decreased performance on tests of cognitive capacity'.

In the first section of this chapter, we noted that in the SDS at first interview, out of 13 listed obstacles to 'going straight or staying straight', the four most frequently mentioned were (in descending rank order): 'lack of money'; 'opportunity to make easy money'; 'need for excitement or to relieve boredom'; and 'lack of work'. We can now add that the next two were 'having a [criminal] record'; and 'taking drugs'. At the final interview approximately three years later, the proportion of respondents checking each of these items was lower, but exactly the same obstacles again took the top six places (Bottoms and Shapland 2011: 61, Table 2.4).[30] What is especially interesting about these data is that all six of these items refer to problems in either the practical or the natural order. Within the practical order, there are the difficulties of getting work; of coping with little money and with temptations for easy money; and of living with a significant criminal record. Within the natural order, there are the problems of overcoming the emotional excitement of offending, and – for some – the problem of shaking off a drug habit. The predominance, in this list, of issues in the practical and natural orders emphasises the need for academic students of

[29] Interestingly, although the aggregate number of self-reported obstacles was a very strong predictor of subsequent criminality, 'taking drugs' was the only *single* identified 'obstacle to going straight' that significantly predicted future crime (Shapland and Bottoms 2017).

[30] They were also in the same rank order, except that 'lack of work' had moved from fourth to second place.

desistance not to overlook matters of this kind. It also makes the point that the core message of the SDS ('desistance is the process of learning to live a non-criminal life when one has been leading a largely criminal life') is not just a matter of relationships or moral intentions, but of practical changes in patterns of daily life, often in 'obstacle-strewn' contexts (Bottoms and Shapland 2011: 256).

Theorising 'Everyday Situated Ethics'

In this and the previous section, we have explored a number of theoretical resources that might be helpful as we turn to the consideration of some case studies. In the previous section, we found that the traditional sociological concepts of structure and agency, and the more recently developed field of relational sociology, all had value. In this section, we have added to these a number of theoretical approaches developed initially by moral philosophers: affect and rationality; 'moral frameworks'; 'burdened' virtue ethics; 'ground projects'; and resolutions. We have also found helpful Archer's insistence that human beings must live in the natural and practical worlds. With that theoretical background, we can turn finally to some case studies from the SDS.

THREE CASE STUDIES

Because the focus of this chapter is on 'ethical aspects of journeys towards desistance' we have selected for the case studies only men who tried to take some definite steps towards desistance – which not all SDS respondents did.[31] Summary accounts of the three selected cases have been previously reported (Bottoms and Shapland 2014), but they are here considered in much greater detail. Given the data on reoffending in the SDS sample reported by Shapland (2022), it is statistically probable that all three men had one or more further convictions in the period between 2007 and 2017,[32] so these case studies should be read as accounts of serious attempts to desist within a 'zigzag' journey towards desistance.

In considering the case studies, readers are also asked to bear in mind the research methods used in the SDS. The research was not ethnographic, but interview-based. The interviews were wide-ranging in content, but each man was interviewed only four times, at intervals of (usually) nine to 12 months, which means that we cannot present fully continuous narratives of the men's

[31] For a summary of the circumstances of an SDS respondent who did not take such steps, see the case of 'Zed', described in Bottoms and Shapland (2014: 325).

[32] The present authors have no information about offences committed by individual offenders in this later period, as it was a condition of access to the 2007–17 conviction data that such information must remain confidential to Professor Shapland.

lives. To emphasise this point, in the descriptive part of each case study, after some background information we will outline the man's circumstances at three specific points: always the first and final interviews, plus either the second or third interview.

In accordance with standard research practice, all names are pseudonyms, and on occasion a few other small details have been changed in order to prevent identification.

First Case Study: John

Background: The research team first met John in prison when he was serving a six-month sentence. He was 20 years old and had several previous convictions for burglaries and theft, for which he had received community orders and two previous custodial sentences in young offender institutions.

John had grown up with his mother and stepfather on a Sheffield council estate,[33] but he had also spent periods in and out of foster care because of difficult relationships at home. He had had no contact with his birth father since he was six years old, and he did not have a good relationship with his stepfather. He had been closer to his grandfather, who died when he was 12. As regards schooling, at age 12 a poor relationship with his school led to his exclusion from mainstream schooling; he was then sent to a pupil referral unit, but said that he did not attend it after age 13.

First interview: John started offending when he was about 12. Reflecting on why he began, he said: 'It's just what my mates were doing and that. They were all older than me so I just got into it'. As well as the money, offending was 'fun – I've liked it'. However, the reasons he cited for his ongoing offending were different. He said it was mainly to pay for heroin – which he had started using partly to cope with the trauma of an experience of sexual abuse by an adult, and partly because of the 'buzz' of using. He expressed no concerns about his offending or the people he had burgled: 'I don't regret no crimes I've done … not for my victims or nothing'.

Immediately before his current sentence, John had been homeless for five months. His relationship with his mother had been poor, and he had recently burgled her and his stepfather's house, so he was not welcome there. He had found being homeless 'difficult' and had 'blocked it out'. His closest relationships were with his male friends. They were the ones he offended and took drugs with, and they provided him with personal support. He had had a girlfriend,

[33] In England, a 'council estate' is an area of public housing, so called because the dwellings are owned by the local government authority or 'council'. At the time of the SDS research about a quarter of Sheffield households were living on council estates, so this tenure status is not as marginalised as is public housing in some other countries.

but she had eventually ended the relationship because of his drug-taking. They had got on well when they were together, but in John's eyes she had always taken second place to his male friends, and he admitted that he had treated her 'like shit' when his friends were there, because he did not want his friends to think he was a 'muppet'.

Asked at the first interview what were currently the good things in his life, John answered with a single word: 'nowt'.[34] However, when asked who was most important to him, he said 'my family definitely'. He was trying to repair the relationship with his mother by writing to her from prison, but she had not replied, nor had she visited him.

When asked about the longer-term future, John said he would like to have money, a family and to be seen as someone who is 'confident; hardworking; trustworthy; [a] good person to get on with'. When asked about things that might help him to go straight, his initial answer was 'a girlfriend … who was supportive, who I could chat to, who I loved'. He added that he would like a job as a bricklayer, but as he had never yet had a job, he was not sure that he could hold one down. He also was not sure that he could stop offending or drug-taking. Indeed, he felt that he currently had very little control over his life: 'we've all each got our script and we just read from that script. And you've just got to go by that script'. But in the immediate future, his probation officer was going to fix some accommodation for him.

A couple of months after his release from prison, John was convicted for a single offence of commercial burglary, and was given a probation order. In marked contrast to his record in the three years before the first research interview, this was his only reconviction during three years of research follow-up.

Second interview: A year after the first interview, John was now living with a new girlfriend. The couple were expecting a baby, a fact that John said was important for him. He was on a heroin replacement treatment, and said he was feeling better in himself now that he was 'not on drugs any more' (although he was still smoking cannabis). He expressed a greater sense of personal agency and responsibility than in his first interview: 'I have to stand on my own two feet now and think about running my life'. He was also seeing less of the friends he had offended with: 'before I met my girlfriend I was dependent on them, but now it's just someone to talk to really'. His relationship with this second girlfriend was very important to him: 'I can talk to her about anything. I feel confident when I'm around her and she occupies me away from drugs and that'. John's relationship with his mother had also begun to improve in the month or two before this second interview.

John said that he was still doing a few burglaries, but he had sometimes felt uncomfortable about this: 'I've been in some houses and there's been kids' clothes and kids' toys and that and that puts me off a bit'. He now said that he

[34] This is a dialect word, commonly used in the north of England; it means 'nothing'.

wanted to stop offending '*in my head*' but was unsure whether he could achieve it in practice. He thought that to stop offending he would need to 'get a job and stay away from my friends', so it was dispiriting that he had tried to get a job but 'never got any replies back'. He also said that he was 'a bit worried about money', and he was scared of his future if he kept offending, which would mean 'losing everyone'.

Final interview: At his fourth interview, nearly three years after the first, John was still living with his girlfriend and had grown closer to her family. He said that she had had a '*big effect*' on the reduction in his offending, and he could be 'totally himself' with her. Becoming a father had also been very important (the couple's son was now 18 months old). John was now no longer seeing some of his old friends because 'I've stopped robbing and that … stopped carrying drugs and that'; and he now spent four or five evenings a week at home. He had also declined invitations to take part in burglaries, but 'even though I'm trying to stop I have done the odd thing like shoplifting'. Work was still a problem: he had had one job (found for him by the job centre) but nothing since that finished. He attributed this to his lack of qualifications and experience and his criminal record; the situation made him feel 'a bit mad, but I don't worry about it that much'.

More generally, John said that he was more thoughtful now about what he did, unlike in the past: 'I just used to do things without thinking about it first. Now I think more'. He also expressed his regret at the people who had been victims of his burglaries: 'I feel sorry for the people I did it to. And people I've robbed'. His relationship with his mother and the rest of his own family was now stronger: 'They trust me more. They know I'm staying out of trouble'. However, he also said that there were some 'more stressful things' in his life now. He and his girlfriend were having financial difficulties and had got into arrears with their rental payments. This meant that the local council would not prioritise them for a move to better accommodation, even though their current flat had only one bedroom. This was worrying, because he felt a responsibility to provide properly for his son: 'because I've got a child and that'. He felt that if he could get a job, things would definitely be better. But in some ways, he said that he missed the days when he had money (from offending) and was 'not worrying about anything'.

Ethical Dimensions of John's Attempted Desistance

At the time of his first interview, John's offending was a regular part of his lifestyle and was integral to the relationships that he had with his friends. He had found offending exciting and it had also provided him with money to buy drugs. However, in this interview he also expressed an overall dissatisfaction with his life – he had found it hard being homeless, he was unhappy about his poor relationship with his mother and he did not want to be in prison. There were signs (such as his letter-writing to his mother) that he wanted to bring about change;

however, his talk of his life being a 'script' suggested that he felt little capacity to alter its direction. So he did not feel confident that he could stop his offending or drug-taking, or that he would be able to find a job.

But in this same first interview, John also spoke of other values. The social and personal attractions of his lifestyle, and the mates who were integral to it, did not feature in his long-term vision of a 'good life', which included a job, a family of his own and a reputation as 'trustworthy'. A year later, at the time of his second interview, he had taken some steps to realise this 'ground project': with the help of the probation service he had begun to address his heroin addiction, and he was building a life with a new girlfriend. His resolution to come off drugs was reinforced by this new relationship, which not only kept him away from drugs (situational change) but also provided him with emotional and normative support.

John's expressed dissatisfaction with his situation at the first interview (he could identify no good things in it) seemed to provide his primary motivation for change, and was a strong 'push' factor; but more distantly, his aspirations for a different future lifestyle offered at least a sketchy 'pull' factor. In the longer term, however, it was the context arising from his relationship with his girlfriend that proved particularly significant for generating fresh moral action. The habitual moral practices of their family-oriented lifestyle cumulatively and over time led to a change in his routines and a re-prioritisation of values within John's moral framework. For example, unlike his relationship with his previous girlfriend, his relationship with his new girlfriend took precedence over his relationships with his male friends. In his second interview he also spoke about feeling responsibility toward his new family and towards sustaining their life together. The emotional discomfort at seeing children's belongings in houses he burgled at this time is further evidence of his transitioning value hierarchy, and perhaps also of an increased reflexivity in his internal conversation (Archer 2003).

These shifts in John's hierarchy of values brought him closer to his mother and other members of his own family. In his final interview he said that they had greater trust and respect for him, and he felt he could now ask them for help, such as borrowing money. Through the restoration of these relationships John thus gained additional social resources to sustain his new lifestyle. We see here how the ethical, the relational and the practical are intertwined: the family values John now prioritises are ones that his mother and other family members also hold, and this leads to practical support.

However, John's desistance remained tentative. There was a fragility to his transformed value hierarchy, since it was integral to his life with his girlfriend, which was not without its stresses. In the final interview, he said that he and his girlfriend were struggling financially and he recognised that his opportunities to earn money through employment were limited, given his lack of qualifications, minimal work experience and a criminal record. His pursuit of a 'good life' was therefore 'burdened' by the obstacles of the 'practical order' – the structural obstacles to employment and earning money associated with his lack of human and social capital.

If John's relationship with his partner were to break down, his revised value hierarchy would be vulnerable. At the time of the final research interview the attraction of the old carefree lifestyle had not fully dissipated, and if a situation presented itself John said would be still be tempted: 'if I saw something easy that I could get then it would be hard for me to stop'. John's new value hierarchy and associated resolution to desist from crime was therefore situated, linked to the relationships that were most important to him at the time – his girlfriend, son and family of origin – and sustained by the lifestyle they shared together.

Second Case Study: Kevin

Background: The research team first met Kevin when he was on probation, aged nearly 20. Unlike the great majority of the SDS sample, Kevin had not received a custodial sentence when the research team first met him, although he had been convicted three times in the youth court and twice in adult courts. Later, however, Kevin's criminal record worsened, and by the time of the third interview, two years after the first, he had already received three custodial sentences, all for assaults. After this, the research team lost contact with him, so there was an unusually long period of 22 months between the third and fourth interviews.[35] During that period, Kevin began a journey towards desistance.

At the age of four, Kevin was brought to Sheffield by his mother, who had decided to leave her violent husband (Kevin's father). She subsequently formed a partnership with another man, but Kevin reported that the two of them were 'always fighting', and that his stepfather also often shouted at Kevin. At age 14, Kevin was excluded from school after hitting a teacher with a chair; he was sent to a special school where he said that he had few friends because he felt different from the other pupils and truanted a lot. Then, at the age of 16, his mother made him leave home, and soon after that he began offending. His mother kept in some touch with him, and was upset by his offending, but she did not invite him back home. Kevin was deeply hurt by this; in his final interview he commented that: 'if someone's there for you … you don't need to do [crimes] … [but if you're] looking after yourself from a young age and knowing nowt else, you've got no money, so there's nowt else you can do'.

First interview: Kevin was living, as he had been for the past three years, in a small block of single studio flats for under-21s who needed supported housing. Since he had no family support and no job, his male friends were – as in

[35] For most SDS respondents, such a time-lag would not have been possible. It occurred only because Kevin was an early interviewee whose whereabouts were rediscovered right at the end of the fieldwork period.

John's case – of great importance to him. He also had a steady girlfriend, but this relationship was in conflict with his male friendships and his offending: 'if you go somewhere with them, she wants me to go with her … [and] she'll think "he likes them more" … [But] if I don't go with me mates, they don't like me, do they?' Eventually, when Kevin began to receive prison sentences, his girlfriend ended the relationship, which had lasted four years.

Third interview: By the time of this interview, which took place in prison, Kevin's criminality had intensified (see above re his prison sentences for assaults). Drinking was a significant problem for him; his assault convictions were all alcohol related, and he said that he felt very dependent on alcohol. Also, although in the first interview he had self-reported taking cannabis regularly, by this third interview he was dealing in drugs, and for the first time taking cocaine and beginning to feel some drug dependency. Along with the drinking and drug-taking, he had adopted a strongly 'partying' lifestyle: he was spending large amounts on drink, drugs and nights out, financed by his drug dealing and stealing. Overall, therefore, his life had changed significantly since the first interview.

In this third interview, Kevin chose the questionnaire response: 'I would like to stop but I'm not sure if I can'. He added: 'I can say I can now; but on the out I'll need money for stuff, and grafting [stealing] is a quick way'. He also said that, if he stopped offending, his life would be 'happier' but 'less exciting'.

Final interview: In the nearly two years from the third to the fourth interview, Kevin's criminality significantly declined. But this did not happen immediately; indeed, soon after Kevin's release from the sentence that he was serving at the third interview, he was back in prison after a further conviction for assault.

Just before this further sentence, Kevin had begun a relationship with a new girlfriend who was the central figure in Kevin's life during this last period of the research. At the fourth interview, Kevin said: 'I have stopped offending'. He attributed this significant change mainly to his relationship with his girlfriend: 'I'm always with [her] so it's kept me out of trouble'.

Kevin's new relationship had resulted in significant changes in his routine activities. He said he now spent five or six nights a week at home with his girlfriend, whereas before he would have been out most nights. Not only his drinking but also his drug-taking had greatly declined. One reason for this was his concern for his girlfriend's daughter: 'you can't smoke weed in front of the kid'. As to financial overspends, these still occurred, but on a much reduced scale; and when they did, rather than stealing he would borrow from his girlfriend, or from another male friend.

Weekends were also now very different. As Kevin explained:

> We go down to [a seaside town] to see her grandma, [who] lives down there. We stay there for the weekend, come back Sunday night to get babby to the school for Monday … We're always down there normally, cos her nana's poorly … Like she's going blind, we go down and help her out … take her out and that. Like the beach and whether she needs to do her shopping and that.

Kevin said that this more predictable and steady way of life was happier than his previous one, but this 'happiness' didn't mean hedonistic pleasure; indeed, it involved more responsibilities than before. As Kevin put it: '[before], I were just focused on my drinking … [but] I've loads of responsibilities now – keeping out of trouble, looking after our lass and kid, making sure they're alright … [back] then, I didn't have no responsibilities' cos I weren't bothered'.

There were other factors influencing both Kevin's desistance and his different lifestyle. Asked why he had stopped offending, he gave three such reasons. First, he expressed a general feeling, that 'I just wanted … to sort meself out – it's about time to change'. Second, he wanted to avoid what he called 'that horrible life in and out of jail' that he had recently experienced. And finally, he had been given an opportunity to work with his stepfather in the tiling business; Kevin was clear that 'when I sorted myself out with that job with me step-dad, it helped me'. It is important to note that this opportunity arose through a contact with a relative, thus avoiding the difficulties that those with criminal records and no qualifications often experience when looking for work. However, this job would probably not have been offered if Kevin's relationship with his mother had not changed. He described the change by saying that when he was frequently in trouble, his mother would say '"you're like your dad", and so she never wanted to talk to me, thinking I was in his footsteps or summat … So now I'm not [in trouble], she talks to me a bit now'.

What about male friends? In this final research interview, Kevin described how he had now deliberately dropped both of his two main friends from the first interview, because they were still offending. Of his two current best mates one had no criminal record and the other had stopped offending. By contrast with the first interview, there was now no significant tension between his relationships with his girlfriend and his mates. The relationship with his girlfriend had priority, and his two male friends were 'just good lads, good people … [and] they don't get into trouble'.

Ethical Dimensions of Kevin's Attempted Desistance

As with John's story, central to understanding the trajectory of Kevin's desistance, and the related changes in his value hierarchy, are the relationships that had the greatest importance for him. In his first interview, Kevin responded rather generally to the question about his hoped-for future life as simply 'to settle down' However, despite this intention, Kevin's offending increased before it declined. At that first interview, Kevin prioritised his relationships with his mates and his lifestyle of offending with them over others, including his relationship with his girlfriend of the time. Following the break up of that relationship, the values associated with his male friendships became dominant and his offending increased in frequency and severity.

However, as with John, there was a change in Kevin's value hierarchy after he met his new girlfriend and her daughter; indeed, in Kevin's case his readiness to change came about primarily, although not exclusively, because of the 'pull' factor of this relationship. The relationship provided him with opportunities, in small ways, to practise new and valued roles as a partner and stepfather. In the different spaces he encountered through this relationship (his girlfriend's home, the grandmother's home by the sea) he engaged in new caring activities: he picked his girlfriend's daughter up from school and helped to look after her grandmother. He gave up or curtailed activities where there was a value conflict with these new relationships: he did not drink or smoke in front of his girlfriend's daughter and he let his old friendships go. Kevin recognised the increased maturity in his thinking that accompanied this new way of life; he noted that when he was younger all he thought about was drinking but the present was different 'now I don't, I've got other things don't I?' Reflecting from this new emotional context, he noted changes both in his moral thinking ('I think good not bad') and in an altered emotional response to his earlier offending ('sometimes I think I wish I never did it'). Kevin's value hierarchy and associated moral emotions were thus reshaped and reinforced through the everyday interactions generated by new and important relationships in his life. But this was not simply about domestic life: Kevin's altered behaviour had also led to an improved relationship with his mother, which had generated a job and its attendant benefits of income and respectability.

Cheryl Mattingly's concept of 'moral self-making' through the everyday is a helpful way of understanding these changes in Kevin's ethical life. She refers to scenes of action 'in which the "new" is inaugurated, where new experiences are created' (Mattingly 2013: 309). These new experiences can lead to some redefining of the self:

> The re-imagining of oneself, one's family, one's life, is not a private introspective matter, some sort of internal story one tells oneself (though it may be all that too) so much as an active, creative remaking of daily life through the development of just such routines. And in the local morality of the household, it is manifested most vividly, concretely and compellingly in the creation and recreation of domestic routines (Mattingly 2013: 314).

Within the mainstream desistance literature, there is some recognition of these matters in Laub, Rowan and Sampson's (2019: 299) comment that fresh relationships can often 'reorder short-term situational inducements to crime and, over time, redirect longer-term commitments to conformity', including the development of fresh habits. But it is clear from the SDS case studies that such processes are both more complex, and involve greater self-reflection, than is sometimes recognised in the desistance literature.

As a result of his various lifestyle changes, Kevin reported a difference in the way some people related to him. He commented that they used to say '"oh … keep away from him", [but] like now they don't think things like that. They'll talk now, "so you're doing well, aren't you. How long now? Keep it up"'. This social recognition of change was both pleasing and reaffirming to Kevin, who had said in his first interview that he had not liked the label of 'offender'. This reminds us of Aristotle's view that while pleasure can be derived from unethical activities, that does not mean that pleasure itself is bad. Rather, it is 'a good thing when it arises from the proper activities of men (*sic*) in proper moral condition', so a morally well-lived life 'will include pleasure as one of its blessings' (Hutchinson 1995: 212).

However, as with John, Kevin faced constraints and obstacles to sustaining his new lifestyle. He was very aware that his lack of qualifications posed potential future problems in the employment market; he had hoped to get a job in car body repair, but had not done so yet. Another potential constraint was his driving ban, which had now lasted several years. Housing also posed difficulties. He would have liked to get a flat of his own with the council or a housing association, but that was currently impossible because of a complicated debt arising from an earlier tenancy; he was paying this off, but only slowly. The three main things that Kevin himself now identified as obstacles to staying straight were drink, money and the excitement of offending. He said that he still had 'a bit of a problem' with alcohol, and admitted that one of the things that had made it hard to stop was 'not having that money, all that money', as he had done at the height of his offending. Given these various continuing issues, Kevin was clear that moving towards the kind of life he really wanted would be 'hard – very hard, yeah'. Despite the progress made in Kevin's journey between the third and fourth interviews, these structural and personal issues point to a degree of fragility in Kevin's new moral self.

Third Case Study: Len

Background: Len was 22 years at the first interview, when he was on a probation order for handling stolen goods. He had a history of offending from the age of 13, and he had on six occasions been convicted of property offences in adult courts. On one of these occasions, he had been sentenced to 12 months in a young offender institution.

Len had moved to Sheffield with his mother at the age of seven, following the break up of his parents' relationship. They lived in bed and breakfast accommodation and moved frequently until they were given a flat on a council estate. Part of Len's childhood was also spent with grandparents while his mother was working. He did not get on well at school: he was sometimes suspended, and he dropped out at the age of 14. While truanting, he started drinking and taking drugs with friends on the estate. At 16 he received serious injuries from being run over by a car, and he spent some time in hospital. During his adolescence, his relationship with his mother was poor, and he said that she had tried to put him in care. His offending was initially always with friends ('there used to be a big crowd of us on the estate, riding motorbikes and that'); they would plan burglaries together and go out in the middle of the night to do them. Later, however, his offending was linked to funding his heroin habit; he said that recently 'everything's [been] drug-related'.

First interview: Because of continuing tension in his relationship with his mother, for a few months prior to Len's most recent conviction he had been homeless and living on the streets. This had been very difficult ('waking up, trying to find money, trying to find something to eat, stuff like that, day in, day out'); and his main source of support during this period had been his male friends. His two closest mates were 'very important' to him – one would always help him out and 'give me advice'; the other had local respect and was a 'good fighter'. They were the people he would turn to in need: 'if I need support, I call my best mates'.

Len's homelessness had ended when he was caught for the offence for which he was now on probation, because his probation officer had secured a place for him in a good hostel near the city centre. He was very grateful for this, and in his first interview he said that he could now 'think straight ... I don't have to worry about somewhere to live or anything'. In fact, he felt that his life was much improved, because the probation service had also arranged for him to have methadone treatment for his drug addiction, and to attend an IT course.[36] He was unable to work because of health issues arising from his addiction, but was receiving state sickness benefit.

His relationship with his mother was also beginning to improve: 'now I'm not on drugs and that, she sees a change in me and she's given me another chance'. He added that he felt bad about the pain his offending had caused his mum: 'I know I've put her through a lot. She gets upset and cries'. His ex-girlfriend had also been upset by his offending, and their 18-month relationship had broken up because of his drug use. Similar to Kevin, Len did not like the label of 'offender', but he said that he felt no regret for his offences, because 'when you're on drugs you don't care'.

In this first interview Len said he had made a decision to try and stop offending, because he was 'sick of it'. He also cited one of his friend's observations that they were now getting older and needed to 'start living this life and not being like we were when we were younger'. When asked where he would like to be in three years' time he said: 'I'd like to be able to say I've got a really good job in computers, I've got meself a car, a good relationship, a kid, summat like that. Me own flat ... A normal life. And I'd like to be able to say I've not touched no drugs for three years, totally clean'.

Third interview: In this interview, two years later, Len reported seeing much less of his old friends – one had moved away, another had, like him, decided it was time to change. He also described an important new (non-romantic)

[36] Len added: 'If it weren't for this [probation] order, I'd probably still be on the streets ... Yeah, it's helping me a lot'. This was a more positive evaluation of probation than that given by most other SDS respondents.

friendship with Jane, a 40-year-old teacher. He had first met her when he was homeless and she had invited him in for a cup of tea a few times. More recently, they had met weekly while he was at the hostel, and she – like his mother – was actively supporting his attempts to address his addiction and stop offending.

Despite his professed intention to stop, Len self-reported a number of offences in the year between the second and third interviews, although many fewer than in the time before the first interview. He was caught once, when he and a friend went drinking, stole a car and were convicted of taking the car and driving with excess alcohol. (This was his only conviction during the research period.) For these offences, Len received a probation order and a curfew order with electronic tagging; although later, because he missed some probation appointments, the probation was upgraded to a suspended sentence. Commenting on this incident, Len said: 'it's one of them daft things you do'. But his relationship with his mother had been continuing to improve, so they jointly agreed that he would go back to live with her on the outskirts of the city, particularly to 'avoid my old group of friends'. He had refused several friends' invitations to offend again.

Final interview: Len, who was still living at his mother's house, said that he was now completely off both drugs and alcohol. He used to feel dependent on alcohol, but he had stopped drinking six months ago: Jane had been particularly influential in helping him to stop. His offending had also changed 'dramatically' since he returned home. He had completely stopped committing property offences; for a short while he had continued to drive although he was disqualified, but he had stopped doing that six months ago, because he wanted to get a provisional driving licence when his disqualification ended.

Len was now usually spending seven nights a week at home with his mother, with whom he now got on very well. He was still in occasional contact with old friends, but only with those who had stopped offending. Reflecting on why he had stopped offending, he said:

> It got to a point where I had had enough. Drugs, crime and homeless – it was easier to change than carry on. I took one step at a time: it started when I got [the hostel place] and finished when I moved home.

He added that the three best things that had happened to him in the last three years were 'meeting Jane; a better relationship with Mum; and coming home'. But he said he didn't really know how these things happened – they 'just happened'. Similarly, he didn't think much about his past offences – it was best just to 'blank things out' and 'move forward'.

He did, however, feel that his life was now much better. Getting involved with crime had been 'a mistake'. He now took 'more responsibility for the things I do' and felt he was 'more grown up' and 'more like the old me'. Looking to the future, he hoped that his health would continue to improve and – because computing had become an important hobby – he also hoped that he could get a job in computing.

Ethical Dimensions of Len's Attempted Desistance

Len's story differs from those of John and Kevin in that his desistance journey was not influenced by a girlfriend. Despite this significant difference, his case – like theirs – illustrates the importance of relationships in desistance processes.

Len's initial wish to desist arose from the 'push factor' of his dissatisfaction with his offending and addiction lifestyle, culminating in a period of homelessness ('I just got sick of everything'). But he had to start from a difficult place: he had no home, substance addiction, a poor relationship with his mother, and several close friends with criminal records, so his journey – like that of most SDS men – was going to be 'obstacle-strewn'. It was central to his progress that – as he said himself in the final interview – he took it 'one step at a time'.

Key early steps towards desistance were generated by his first probation officer (the hostel place, which provided stability; the methadone treatment, which was a crucial first step away from addiction). His serendipitous friendship with Jane then provided vital support in helping him to hold to his resolution to reduce his dependence on drink and drugs (although he was at that stage continuing to commit some offences). But fundamental to the eventual greater change in Len's lifestyle was his improved relationship with his mother, made possible by these early signs of progress. In his first interview, Len had expressed emotional discomfort that his mother was upset by his offending ('I know I've put her through a lot'), thus recognising that he had some responsibility for their estrangement. It also clearly mattered to him how she felt about him; he later said that his move away from offending was greatly helped when she 'started talking to me again'. Over time, his relationship with her gradually became stronger; and this, together with the setback of his reconviction for taking a car, prompted his crucial move back to her home and away from the temptations of his friends and the city centre.

Their closer contact through living in the same house not only further strengthened their relationship, it also provided additional opportunities for lifestyle change. His new daily routine included going shopping with his mother, contributing to the household bills and giving her advice. As with John and Kevin, Len's altered moral framework was in this way enacted through the routine practices of his new everyday life. After he had moved into his mother's flat, he also reflected that the greater responsibility he was taking for his life was associated with increased maturity.

Rational choice theorists might be tempted to read Len's story through the theoretical lens of the ITD. Some data support this: he did experience a 'crystallisation of discontent' while homeless, and he did make a series of rational choices to further the objectives of his 'ground project' (eg, accepting methadone treatment; gradually weaning himself away from both drugs and alcohol; moving from the town centre to his mother's flat to avoid temptations to offend; discontinuing driving while disqualified to ensure that he could get a provisional licence). These choices provide sequential evidence of Len's *resolution* to change. But there are some significant reasons why the ITD cannot fully explain Len's story. First, his resolution was not always successful: while he was living in the city centre hostel and meeting old friends, both drinking and some property offending continued, and this led to his further conviction. As Holton (2003: 39) points out, 'it is all too easy to see how an earlier resolution could be overcome by ... a subsequent desire ... the interesting question [is] ... how *strength* of will' can be maintained (emphasis original). The ITD does not discuss failures of this sort, but given the strong evidence of the zig-zag character of desistance for many who attempt it, any adequate account needs to be able to explain such setbacks. Second, Len's resolutions, although clearly his own choices, were crucially supported by his relationships with Jane and then with his mother. In Len's case, therefore, the answer to Holton's question about 'how strength of will can be maintained' is to be found primarily in these relationships, and in what flowed from them. The authors of the ITD seem wary of anything 'social' that might detract from their insistence that 'one's identity motivates action because it is the focus of preferences ... [and] *identity [is] more individualistic than social*' (Paternoster et al 2015: 223, emphasis added). But all of us, including would-be desisters, make agentic choices that are genuinely our own, yet are influenced by our situation and our relationships; and like Len, many of us are glad to acknowledge such influences. Thus agency, structure and relationships are always in play interactively, and a pure 'individualism' is a mirage (Crossley 2011: chapter 2).

We should note also that, within these three case studies, Len's move out of town to live with his mother was the most important example of the exercise of 'diachronic self-control' (see earlier discussion). This move had a dual significance: it was, first, a situational means to support Len's resolution to desist; and, second, it provided a symbolic expression of desistance that increased the practical and conceptual distance between Len and his former friends and their collective offending lifestyle.

When we have occasionally used Len's case in seminar presentations, some audience members have expressed concern at Len's self-imposed life constraints in pursuit of desistance (eg, by staying at home almost every evening). We therefore need to say that Len himself did not see matters in this way. He thought that his relationship with his mother was now excellent – a marked change from the situation three years previously. Moreover, in response to the question in the final interview 'how would you *like* to see yourself living in say 18 months time?', he answered that he would like to be 'still at home', with a job in computers and perhaps a new relationship with a girlfriend ('we'll see what happens'). For him, therefore, his current situation was the right one, offering the possibility of moving on in various directions: for him, it was simply not as constrained a life as it seemed to our seminar participants.

CONCLUSION

In the first section of this chapter, we provided a summary of the main findings of the Sheffield Desistance Study (SDS), a three-year prospective study of the lives of more than a hundred young adult male recidivists. We emphasised the extent of the men's prior offending, their poor educational and work histories, and the obstacles that they knew they would have to face if they tried to 'go straight'. We also showed, however, that most of them wanted to change, and that despite their offending they held some significant conventional values.

In the second and third sections, we explored a range of theoretical resources, drawn not only from the research literature on desistance, but also from theoretical sociology and from moral philosophy. We will not here repeat the conclusions of these sections; rather, we will focus on how some of these theoretical resources have been found relevant in the case studies.

Relationships have emerged as of central importance in our analysis. We were drawn to this topic by two studies in particular: first, Beth Weaver's (2016) pioneering linkage of relational sociology to the study of desistance in her fascinating Scottish empirical study; and second, Owen Abbott's (2020) theoretical monograph on the relevance of relational sociology to the study of 'morality in practice'. These sources have proved very fruitful, because collectively the life narratives of John, Kevin and Len show how these men's ethical lives were, to a significant extent, situated, enacted in everyday routines and shaped by the relationships that were important to them. The changes in their 'everyday situated ethics' were integral to their attempted desistance, and our study has confirmed Weaver's (2016: 213) conclusion that desistance is 'a complex, individualised, reflexive and relational process'. The analysis has also drawn attention to a complex *relational triangle* of girlfriends, male 'mates' and families of origin that often seems crucial when young adult male offenders try to desist.

Not surprisingly in the light of previous criminological studies of persistent offenders, many SDS sample members had histories of social disadvantage. Thus John's, Kevin's and Len's descriptions of their early lives included many unwelcome experiences such as family break-ups and conflict, alienating experiences of school, and (in John's case) sexual victimisation. Their schooling difficulties also led to a lack of qualifications and thus – in Sheffield's now largely post-industrial economy – to persistent unemployment; accordingly, the lives of all three men shared many characteristics with the subjects studied by David Maguire (2021) in his aptly titled book *Male, Failed, Jailed*. Like Maguire's subjects, all three men had also found support in male friendship groups.[37]

[37] As its subtitle indicates, Maguire's book adopts a version of masculinity theory as its primary theoretical lens. Masculinity theory might well also be helpful in explaining the adolescent lives of many SDS men, but as it was not part of the theoretical focus of the Sheffield study, we cannot comment further here.

At the beginning of the SDS fieldwork, their moral frameworks were in significant ways aligned with the lifestyle of offending, drug-taking and drinking that they had developed with their mates, which they found exciting as well as sometimes instrumental to practical and emotional survival.

Yet none of these men aspired to maintain this lifestyle in the longer term. It had brought with it some real personal hardships (eg, family tensions, imprisonment, homelessness), and each of them had a vision of a non-offending life in the future. Those visions variously included matters such as an intimate partnership, good family relationships, a reasonable job, a home of their own, and a reputation as 'trustworthy'. Thus, like Socrates in the *Republic*, they found themselves asking 'how one should live one's life?'; and it is for this reason that the tradition of virtue ethics seems relevant to the study of desistance. However, for these men the road to a different life was never going to be straightforward. For a start, many of the values that underpinned their current lifestyle were incompatible with the values that underpinned the relationships and normatively conventional life that they aspired to; and as they initiated changes in their lives and relationships, the clash of values sometimes generated emotional discomfort (finding children's toys in houses that they burgled; being labelled an 'offender'; recognising that people they cared about were upset by continued offending). Of course, the transition to a more legally compliant lifestyle would, in time, reduce such clashes of values; but it would also require overcoming some very significant obstacles. In view of this, Christine Swanton (in this volume) rightly insists that desistance-focused virtue-ethical journeys must be understood through the concept of 'burdened virtue' – and indeed this concept has clear resonance in each of the case studies.

Where the path to a different lifestyle is 'burdened', supportive relationships can often play a decisive role in assisting change. This is seen in the case studies: through their loving sharing of a new home and lifestyle and a place to live, Kevin and John's girlfriends and Len's mother each provided the practical opportunity and the emotional support for the men to distance themselves from old friends and to develop a new ethical life and routines. Over time, the new moral framework arising from their everyday actions and interactions became more normatively embedded, as hypothesised in the Age-Graded Theory of Informal Social Control. It also became visible to others, which in turn generated new supportive relationships which further strengthened their altered ethical way of life. As seen particularly in Len's case, supportive relationships also made it easier for the men to maintain the *strength of will* that was needed when resolutions to stop offending or to stay off drugs seemed to be under threat from contrary desires in a specific situation.

Precisely because supportive relationships can be so vital in maintaining change, desistance journeys can be vulnerable when those relationships themselves face stresses. More generally, the case studies suggest that the smaller and more fragile is the network of relationships that sustains the revised value hierarchy of the men's changed lifestyle, the less secure that lifestyle change is likely to be.

Taken together, the case studies therefore provide helpful insights into the moral trajectories of the desistance process. In addition to relationships, the following points are of relevance in this regard.

First, the case studies show how John, Kevin and Len, even while they were still involved in offending, already held some values that were compatible with a non-offending life (see further Shapland and Bottoms 2011). There was therefore no 'epiphany' or decisive 'turning point' in their ethical life, but rather a gradual transition as a preferred lifestyle and set of relationships became possible: a change in the priority of values rather than a change of values. This change in priorities can take place in small and subtle ways, as Kevin's case particularly illustrates; this confirms Mattingly's (2017: 311) insight that 'small scale activities and situations … create conditions for the emergence of new virtues'. In addition, there was no clear sequential order to the change in the men's value hierarchies. Rather, values changed in priority as the desistance-related 'push and pull' factors that were generated in the men's everyday lives accumulated and combined 'simultaneously and as mutually reinforcing facets of the change process' (Giordano 2016: 15).

Second, the case studies draw attention to the men's moral agency and resolution: relationships matter, but so does agency and will. All the men developed, in one way or another a desistance-related 'ground project' (Mattingly 2014) to move away from crime. A ground project, seriously undertaken by people facing an 'obstacle-strewn' and 'burdened' path, will take time to achieve, and will require a number of steps, including some resolutions. Keeping those resolutions will require, as Holton (2003, 2009) has valuably shown, strength of will. Maintaining such strength will certainly be assisted by supportive relationships, but in the end it is a matter for the would-be desister himself. Diachronic self-control (thinking ahead and taking steps to avoid failures in resolution) is an obvious tactic to employ in such a situation, which is no doubt why it was so often used by SDS respondents (Bottoms 2013). But when thinking about will and agency we must always, as both Swanton (in this volume) and the relational sociologists remind us, pay attention to the context within which it is exercised. It is also clear from the case studies that both emotion and rationality play their part in agentic decisions.

Third, while the focus in the case studies is upon the personal and social lives of the respondents, it is important to note that in two of the cases (John and Len) there were very helpful moves by the probation service to assist progress by arranging accommodation and heroin replacement treatment. This raises the question whether more could be done by official agencies to help the ethical transitions of those in the midst of 'zigzag desistance journeys' by providing additional social capital and relational support. This is clearly an important issue, but it cannot be further discussed here.

To conclude, we return once again to the comment by Bottoms and Shapland (2016: 109) that, for recidivist offenders, 'desistance is the process of learning to live a non-criminal life when one has been leading a largely criminal life'. This chapter has tried to provide a fuller discussion than before of the ethical aspects of desistance journeys by recidivist offenders; yet this comment remains as the bedrock of our analysis. But it is certainly not the end of the matter, for when one tries to explain in detail how people try to make such a change, and what difficulties they may face in the process, what a wealth of issues (practical, psychological, sociological and philosophical) is uncovered![38]

REFERENCES

Abbey, R (2000) *Charles Taylor* (Teddington, Acumen).

Abbott, O (2020) *The Self, Relational Sociology and Morality in Practice* (Cham, Palgrave Macmillan).

Akerlof, GA and Kranton, RE (2000) 'Economics and Identity' 115 *Quarterly Journal of Economics* 715.

——(2010) *Identity Economics* (Princeton, NJ, Princeton University Press).

Archer, MS (2000) *Being Human: The Problem of Agency* (Cambridge, Cambridge University Press).

——(2003) *Structure, Agency and the Internal Conversation* (Cambridge, Cambridge University Press).

Aristotle (2014) *Nicomachean Ethics*, rev edn (trans and ed R Crisp) (Cambridge, Cambridge University Press).

Beauchamp, TL (1998) 'Editor's Introduction' in D Hume, *An Enquiry into the Principles of Morals* (Oxford, Oxford University Press).

Becker, GS and Murphy, KM (2000) *Social Economics: Market Behavior in a Social Environment* (Cambridge, MA, Harvard University Press).

Bersani, BE and Doherty, EE (2018) 'Desistance from Offending in the Twenty-First Century' 1 *Annual Review of Criminology* 311.

Bottoms, AE (2002) 'Morality, Crime, Compliance and Public Policy' in AE Bottoms and M Tonry (eds), *Ideology, Crime and Criminal Justice: A Symposium in Honour of Sir Leon Radzinowicz* (Cullompton, Willan Publishing).

——(2012) 'Active Maturation: Why Crime Falls in Early Adulthood' 2 *Eurovista: Probation and Community Justice* 39.

——(2013) 'Learning from Odysseus: Self-Applied Situational Crime Prevention as an Aid to Compliance' in P Ugwudike and P Raynor (eds), *What Works in Offender Compliance? International Perspectives and Evidence-Based Practice* (Basingstoke, Palgrave Macmillan).

——(2019) 'Understanding Compliance with Laws and Regulations: A Mechanism-Based Approach' in M Krambia-Kapardis (ed), *Financial Compliance: Issues, Concerns and Future Directions* (Cham, Palgrave Macmillan).

[38] We are most grateful to Jonathan Jacobs for his constructive comments as this chapter has been developed.

Bottoms AE and Shapland, J (2011) 'Steps towards Desistance among Male Young Adult Recidivists' in S Farrall, M Hough, S Maruna and R Sparks (eds), *Escape Routes: Contemporary Perspectives on Life after Punishment* (London, Routledge).

——(2014) 'Can Persistent Offenders Acquire Virtue?' 27 *Studies in Christian Ethics* 318.

——(2016) 'Learning to Desist in Early Adulthood: The Sheffield Desistance Study' in J Shapland, S Farrall and AE Bottoms (eds), *Global Perspectives on Desistance* (London, Routledge).

Burnett, R (1992) *The Dynamics of Recidivism* (Oxford, Oxford University Centre for Criminological Research).

Calverley, A (2013) *Cultures of Desistance: Rehabilitation, Reintegration and Ethnic Minorities* (London, Routledge).

Cid, J and Marti, J (2012) 'Turning Points and Returning Points: Understanding the Role of Family Ties in the Process of Desistance' 9 *European Journal of Criminology* 603.

Copp, JE, Giordano, PC, Longmore, MA and Manning, WD (2020) 'Desisting from Crime during the Transition to Adulthood: The Influence of Parents, Peers and Shifts in Identity' 57 *Journal of Research in Crime and Delinquency* 294.

Crisp, R and Slote, M (eds) (1997) *Virtue Ethics* (Oxford, Oxford University Press).

Crossley, N (2011) *Towards Relational Sociology* (Abingdon, Routledge).

——(2013) 'Interactions, Juxtapositions and Tastes: Conceptualizing "Relations" in Relational Sociology' in C Powell and F Depelteau (eds), *Conceptualizing Relational Sociology: Ontological and Theoretical Issues* (New York, Palgrave Macmillan).

Davis, JB (2021) 'The Status of the Concept of Identity in Economics' 50 *Forum for Social Economics* 1.

Doherty, EE and Bersani, BE (2018) 'Mapping the Age of Official Desistance for Adult Offenders: Implications for Research and Policy' 4 *Journal of Developmental and Life-Course Criminology* 516.

Donati, P (2011) *Relational Sociology: A New Paradigm for the Social Sciences* (London, Routledge).

Donati, P and Archer, MS (2015) *The Relational Subject* (Cambridge, Cambridge University Press).

Droppelmann, C (2021) *Transitions Out of Crime: New Approaches on Desistance in Late Adolescence* (London, Routledge).

Farrall, S (2019) 'The Architecture of Desistance: Exploring the Structural Sources of Desistance and Rehabilitation' in S Farrall (ed), *The Architecture of Desistance* (London, Routledge).

Farrall, S, Bottoms, AE and Shapland, J (2010) 'Social Structures and Desistance from Crime' 7 *European Journal of Criminology* 546.

Farrington, DP, Coid, JW, Harnett, I, Jolliffe, D, Soteriou, N, Turner, R and West, DJ (2006) *Criminal Careers up to Age 50 and Life Success up to Age 48*, Home Office Research Study No 299 (London, Home Office).

Giordano, PC (2016) 'Mechanisms Underlying the Desistance Process: Reflections on "A Theory of Cognitive Transformation"' in J Shapland, S Farrall and AE Bottoms (eds), *Global Perspectives on Desistance* (London, Routledge).

Giordano, PC, Schroeder, R and Cernovich, S (2007) 'Emotions and Crime over the Life Course: A Neo-Meadian Perspective on Criminal Continuity and Change' 112 *American Journal of Sociology* 1603.

Glueck, S and Glueck, E (1968) *Delinquents and Nondelinquents in Perspective* (Cambridge, MA, Harvard University Press).

Healy, D (2010) 'Betwixt and Between: The Role of Psychosocial Factors in the Early Stages of Desistance' 47 *Journal of Research in Crime and Delinquency* 419.

Holton, R (2003) 'How is Strength of Will Possible?' in S Stroud and C Tappolet (eds), *Weakness of Will and Practical Irrationality* (Oxford, Clarendon Press).

——(2009) *Willing, Wanting, Waiting* (Oxford, Oxford University Press).

Hursthouse, R (1999) *On Virtue Ethics* (Oxford, Oxford University Press).

Hutchinson, DS (1995) 'Ethics' in J Barnes (ed), *The Cambridge Companion to Aristotle* (Cambridge, Cambridge University Press).

Kang, T and Kruttschnitt, C (2022) 'Can Persistent Offenders Help Us Understand Desistance from Crime?' 8 *Journal of Developmental and Life-Course Criminology* 209.

Katz, J (1988) *Seductions of Crime: Moral and Sensual Attractions in Doing Evil* (New York, Basic Books).

Kennett, J (2001) *Agency and Responsibility: A Common-Sense Moral Psychology* (Oxford, Clarendon Press).

Laidlaw, J (2014) *The Subject of Virtue: An Anthropology of Ethics and Freedom* (Cambridge, Cambridge University Press).

Laub, JH, Rowan, ZR and Sampson, RJ (2019) 'The Age-Graded Theory of Informal Social Control' in DP Farrington, L Kazemian and AR Piquero (eds), *The Oxford Handbook of Developmental and Life-Course Criminology* (Oxford, Oxford University Press).

Laub, JH and Sampson, RJ (2003) *Shared Beginnings, Divergent Lives: Delinquent Boys to Age 70* (Cambridge, MA, Harvard University Press).

Maguire, D (2021) *Male, Failed, Jailed: Masculinities and 'Revolving Door' Imprisonment in the UK* (Cham, Palgrave Macmillan).

Maruna, S (2001) *Making Good: How Ex-Convicts Reform and Rebuild their Lives* (Washington, DC, American Psychological Association).

Mattingly, C (2013) 'Moral Selves and Moral Scenes: Narrative Experiments in Everyday Life' 78 *Ethnos* 301.

——(2014) *Moral Laboratories: Family Peril and the Struggle for a Good Life* (Oakland, CA, University of California Press).

——(2017) 'Moral (and other) Laboratories and the Semantic Impertinence of Metaphor: An Afterword' 41 *Culture, Medicine and Psychiatry* 309.

Millican, P (2012) 'Hume' in T Angier (ed), *Ethics: The Key Thinkers* (London, Bloomsbury Academic).

Paternoster, R (2017) 'Happenings, Acts and Actions: Articulating the Meaning and Implications of Human Agency for Criminology' 3 *Journal of Developmental and Life-Course Criminology* 350.

Paternoster, R, Bachman, R, Bushway, S, Kerrison, E and O'Connell, D (2015) 'Human Agency and Explanations of Criminal Desistance' 1 *Journal of Developmental and Life-Course Criminology* 209.

Paternoster, R and Bushway, S (2009) 'Desistance and the "Feared Self": Toward an Identity Theory of Desistance' 99 *Journal of Criminal Law and Criminology* 1103.

Piquero, A, Farrington, DP and Blumstein, A (2007) *Key Issues in Criminal Career Research: New Analyses of the Cambridge Study in Delinquent Development* (Cambridge, Cambridge University Press).

Plato (1993) *Republic* (trans and ed R Waterfield) (Oxford, Oxford University Press).

Porporino, FJ (2010) 'Bringing Sense and Sensitivity to Corrections: From Programmes to "Fix" Offenders to Services to Support Desistance' in J Brayford, F Cowe and

J Deering (eds), *What Else Works? Creative Work with Offenders* (Cullompton, Willan Publishing).

Powell, C and Depelteau, F (eds) (2013) *Conceptualizing Relational Sociology: Ontological and Theoretical Issues* (New York, Palgrave Macmillan).

Prandini, R (2015) 'Relational Sociology: A Well-Defined Sociological Paradigm or a Challenging "Relational Turn" in Sociology?' 25 *International Review of Sociology* 1.

Royal College of Psychiatrists (2015) Written Evidence to the House of Commons Justice Committee, available at: The treatment of young adults in the criminal justice system (parliament.uk) 76.

Russell, DC (ed) (2013) *The Cambridge Companion to Virtue Ethics* (Cambridge, Cambridge University Press).

Shapland, J (2022) 'Once Convicted? The Long-Term Pathways to Desistance' 61 *Howard Journal of Crime and Justice* 271.

Shapland, J and Bottoms, AE (2011) 'Reflections on Social Values, Offending and Desistance among Young Adult Recidivists' 13 *Punishment & Society* 256.

——(2017) 'Offending and Offence Patterns in the Early Stages of Desistance: A Study of Young Adults in England' in A Blokland and V van der Geest (eds), *The Routledge International Handbook of Life-Course Criminology* (London, Routledge).

——(2019) 'Disengaging from Peers in the Process of Desistance' in H-J Albrecht, M Walsh and E Wienhausen-Knezevic (eds), *Desistance Processes Among Young Offenders Following Judicial Interventions* (Berlin, Duncker & Humblot).

Swanton, C (2003) *Virtue Ethics: A Pluralistic View* (Oxford, Oxford University Press).

Taylor, C (1989) *Sources of the Self: The Making of the Modern Identity* (Cambridge, Cambridge University Press).

Uggen, C and Piliavin, I (1998) 'Asymmetrical Causation and Criminal Desistance' 88 *Journal of Criminal Law and Criminology* 1399.

Van Ginneken, EF (2017) 'Constrained Agency: The Role of Self-Control in the Process of Desistance' in EL Hart and EF van Ginneken (eds), *New Perspectives on Desistance: Theoretical and Empirical Developments* (London, Palgrave Macmillan).

Van Mastrigt, SB and Carrington, P (2019) 'Co-Offending' in DP Farrington, L Kazemian and AR Piquero (eds), *The Oxford Handbook of Developmental and Life-Course Criminology* (Oxford, Oxford University Press).

Vaughan, B (2007) 'The Internal Narrative of Desistance' 47 *British Journal of Criminology* 390.

Vierkant, T (2015) 'Is Willpower Just Another Way of Tying Oneself to the Mast?' 6 *Review of Philosophy and Psychology* 779.

Warr, M (2002) *Companions in Crime: The Social Aspects of Criminal Conduct* (Cambridge, Cambridge University Press).

Weaver, B (2016) *Offending and Desistance: The Importance of Social Relations* (London, Routledge).

West, DJ (1963) *The Habitual Prisoner* (London, Routledge).

Williams, B (1973) 'A Critique of Utilitarianism' in JJC Smart and B Williams, *Utilitarianism: For and Against* (Cambridge, Cambridge University Press).

——(1985/2006) *Ethics and the Limits of Philosophy*, with commentary by AW Moore (London, Routledge) (originally published by Fontana 1985).

Willis, P (1977) *Learning to Labour: How Working Class Kids Get Working Class Jobs* (Farnborough, Saxon House).

9

Living Non-Criminal Lives: What Role for the State?

MATT MATRAVERS*

INTRODUCTION

The aim of this chapter is to address the question of what kinds of reasons the state might have to help its citizens to live non-criminal lives. On first reading, this may seem an odd question to ask given that the answer might seem obvious, but I hope over the course of the chapter to show that it is not. This is because there are various and different *kinds* of considerations that are relevant. In part, this is a matter of the stage in the criminal justice process on which one chooses to focus (ie, at criminalisation, enforcement, trial, punishment, or post-punishment), but it is also because the reasons appeal to very different concerns: criminal justice policy and expenditure, welfare policies, our obligations to fellow citizens, and so on.

The chapter moves between these, but it progresses from questions of the policies that might help citizens to live non-criminal lives to reasons to provid individual support to those who have offended in the past and who are trying 'desist'. Thus, the first section considers two different kinds of policy conce the design of state institutions (including, but not limited to, institution

* I am grateful to the following for their help in developing the ideas in this chapter: Bottoms, Jacob Bronsther, Antje du Bois-Pedain, William Bülow O'Nils, John Charve Duff, Stephen Galoob, Jonathan Jacobs, Nicola Lacey, Sandra Marshall, Andrew Sime Weale and Lucia Zedner. I benefited hugely from the opportunity to discuss earlier Political Turn(s) in Criminal Law Theory Seminar, the Surrey Centre for Law and P the University of Surrey, and the Colloquium of the Institute for Law, Politics and University College, London. My thanks to the organisers for the invitations and to pants (sadly, I cannot remember the source of every comment but on each occas great deal). I am also grateful to the Leverhulme Trust for a Major Research Fe MRF-2020-090) that enabled me to work on this chapter. Discussions with Helen J who I am fortunate to work with on the project, contributed enormously to th ally. In addition, she located background materials and factual information to of the more empirical claims made in the chapter. I have not thanked her in eac agreement).

criminal justice), and the use of cost–benefit analyses to evaluate particular interventions. The second section then looks at supporting those who have offended and possible reasons that go beyond cost–benefit considerations to provide that support. The argument here rests on general claims to welfare and on the idea that the state ought not to make the situation of those who have offended worse. The third section examines the possible grounds of these reasons, and in so doing develops and enriches the understanding of the duty of the state (and of each of us) to help all of us – including those who have offended – to live non-criminal lives.

The point of the chapter is less to determine answers to specific questions – 'what precise reason do we have to do *x* and how weighty is it in relation to the conflicting reason to do *y*?' – than it is to indicate the kinds of arguments that need to be made to answer such questions. As Bernard Williams (2005: 77) reminds us, 'the reasons that go into political decisions and arguments that bear on them may be of various kinds'. Amongst the kinds considered in this chapter are reasons of political philosophy and of empirical criminology. The chapter is thus an exercise in 'critical morality' as it is understood by Bottoms and Jacobs in the Introduction to this book. Although it does not aspire to provide detailed and specific policy recommendations, the arguments in the chapter are ·ot merely abstract. Rather, they draw on empirical evidence precisely in order ·reflect critically on policies and practices in criminal justice. As an exercise in ·ical philosophy, the chapter emphasises the political dimension inherent in ·ology as a 'moral science' (*cf* Loader and Sparks 2022).

·e beginning, it is worth making two preliminary remarks. The first ·he distinctive (and stipulative) way in which I am using the term 'state', · in relation to 'its reasons'. In asking what reasons the state might ·ean is the reasons we have as members of the state to endorse (or ·nents of the criminal justice system. And by that, what I mean is ·be identified as part of a defensible theory of liberal criminal · do not deny the importance of 'the state' as an institution, ·is with what Antony Duff calls 'rational reconstruction', ·empt to give a defensible account of existing practice ·ho object to this use of 'the state's reasons', can instead ·ons do we have as citizens rationally to endorse *x* or ·our criminal justice system?'.[1]

·three assumptions: the argument applies to the · 2005: 8), by which I mean to societies roughly ·rthern European welfare states (the position ·r); these states are 'roughly just', or at least

·ould not be seen as one "we" devise to prevent ·h free citizens could devise to regulate their

not sufficiently unjust, so that sufficient bonds of reciprocity hold; there is a legitimate (albeit contested) role for the regulation of society by criminal law including the threat, and use, of penal hard treatment (ie, a 'non-abolitionist' assumption). Moreover, where those who have been punished appear in the discussion that follows, I assume that their punishment was appropriate. These assumptions are briefly discussed at the end of the chapter, but for the moment should be taken *ad arguendum*.

PUBLIC POLICY AND LIVING NON-CRIMINAL LIVES

This section takes up two principal ways in which general public policy considerations might intersect with the question of living non-criminal lives. These speak to broad questions of design, and to specific issues around policy interventions, respectively.

Questions of Design

As we shall see in the next subsection, public policy considerations with respect to helping people live non-criminal lives are often deployed in fairly straightforward cost–benefit ways to argue for or against some particular law, regulation, policy or intervention. However, we can also think more radically about broad questions of the design of state institutions including, but not limited to, the criminal justice system. To see this, consider the following series of events modelled on a recent case in England.

A is driving home from work at about 40 mph on a road where the speed limit is 30 mph. He passes through a set of traffic lights as they change from green to amber. Tragically, at the same time, *B*, a young woman whom *A* cannot easily see because of roadside furniture, and who is listening to music through her headphones, crosses the road without stopping. She does so anticipating that the red pedestrian light is about to change to green. By the time *A* can see *B* it is too late, and *B* is killed.

The results of this tragic accident are terrible: in particular, *B* is dead, and her family and friends are bereaved. In such circumstances, it is often difficult to think empathetically of *A*, but of course we should do so (not '*instead* of' but 'in *addition* to' *B*). He is traumatised, his psychological health deeply impaired, and his life, and that of his family, are about to be radically upended by a conviction for causing death by dangerous driving and his incarceration.[2]

[2] The example is drawn from *R v Youssaf* [2021] EWCA Crim 1094. Reviewing the sentence, the Court of Appeal noted a psychiatric report that recorded Mr Youssaf's 'mental trauma' and the 'profound adverse impact' of having caused his victim's death. There are further details that perhaps

A's and *B*'s behaviour was regulated by colour-coded road signals with which they were familiar. Let us assume (not implausibly) that *A* would not have driven through a light that had been red for some time, and of course had he not driven through the amber light, the outcome would have been different. Assume the same with respect to *B*. She would not have crossed the road without checking had it not been for the change to the road traffic light that made her anticipate the change to the pedestrian light, and of course had she waited for the red pedestrian light to change to green, she would not have been killed.

Now, amongst many other things, we can ask what reasons we have to align these signals in different ways. To simplify things, imagine that because of technological constraints there are only three options: the gap between the traffic signal turning red and the pedestrian signal turning green (and vice versa) could be one second, 15 seconds, or 30 seconds. Which should we choose, and more particularly, to what kinds of reasons should we appeal when making that decision?

It might be tempting to think that the primary (or, only) considerations in this decision are the safety of drivers and pedestrians, and traffic efficiency. On the one hand, a gap of one second seems inadequate from a safety perspective. It is predictable that some proportion of both drivers and pedestrians will 'jump' the lights for various reasons and a single second does not seem sufficient to protect both.[3] On the other hand, a gap of 30 seconds is likely to be inefficient given that both drivers and pedestrians wish to make progress and given the need to align traffic signals along routes to ensure as far as possible that traffic flows smoothly. Moreover, a gap as long as 30 seconds may 'delegitimise' the system in the eyes of those who use it and make them less inclined to moderate their behaviour in accordance with the traffic signals.

However, the example points us to another kind of reason: that of avoiding not just accidents and death whilst ensuring efficient traffic flows, but also avoiding criminal conviction. I suspect every reader of this chapter who drives a car has at one time or another driven through an amber/red traffic light (just as everyone has crossed a road on foot 'against' a pedestrian red light). In Andrew von Hirsch's terms, we are in general neither angels nor brutes, but flawed and prone to (moral and other) errors.[4] We have strong reasons to design criminal

explain the conviction for the more serious crime of causing death by dangerous driving rather than the less serious 'causing death by careless driving'. Specifically, Mr Youssaf had been using his phone prior to the accident – although not at the time of the accident – and he irresponsibly left the scene of the crime initially thinking to avoid being caught (although he did later voluntarily go to the police).

[3] That said, as Albert Weale pointed out to me, the law sets general expectations of reliable behaviour (it is not unique in doing that, but it explains why, as in this example, using legal regulation is apt). Given that it does this, it is possible that a gap of one second will set up a general expectation among motorists that they should be careful when approaching traffic lights, thus rendering the gap safe.

[4] 'Persons are assumed to be moral agents, capable of taking seriously the message conveyed through the sanction, that the conduct is reprehensible. They are fallible, nevertheless, and thus face

justice systems in light of that; that is, in ways that make it more likely that we will live non-criminal lives.

I think this argument has wide application. For example, it might speak both in favour of, and against, aspects of criminalisation. On the one hand, I have argued elsewhere that the 'fallible human' argument provides *one* way in which we might try to make sense of some aspects of 'preventive justice'. A rule prohibiting possession of a knife above a certain length may restrict freedom, but it might also help some people – for example, young men in pressured situations – from making catastrophic choices that ruin theirs, and others', lives (Matravers 2013).[5] On the other hand, we also have reasons to think carefully about the ways in which criminal law and procedures might put people 'on the wrong path'. The criminalisation of some drugs, for example, together with the rigid enforcement of those rules, may put someone on a path of criminality that could have been avoided by non-criminal regulation and/or by diversion from criminal justice into some other mechanisms of redress.[6]

Similarly, consider two very standard 'rule of law' requirements: first, that the state must only enact (in this case, criminal) legal rules with which it is possible to comply (a 'crime' of being more than two centimetres tall is not one any human being can avoid committing); and second, that having enacted rules, the state must tell those governed by them what the rules are in advance (imagine that the state changed the legal speed limits on its roads on an hourly basis, failed to inform the population of the change, and applied the rules retrospectively).

These requirements can, and should, be understood as flowing from what is needed if the state is to engage in the justified punishment of transgressors. It is unfair to convict and punish someone for something with which it was impossible for them to comply or for transgression of a rule that it was not possible for them to know. However, these rules can *also* be understood as flowing from the reasons we have to design criminal justice institutions in ways that help us (make it less likely that we will fail) to live non-criminal lives. Moreover, this understanding may have more of a role in less clear-cut cases such as in instances of complex laws that may be either or both hard to follow and to understand.[7]

temptation … The account would make no sense were human beings much better or worse: an angel would require no appeals to prudence, and a brute could not be appealed to through censure' (von Hirsch 1993: 13).

[5] One might worry that this argument would allow not only extensive criminalisation, but other methods by which the state could attempt to 'disable' people from committing future crimes (what Albert Weale, who put this objection to me, calls the 'Clockwork Orange' problem). However, as we shall see below, the account advanced in this chapter also provides good reasons to reduce the use of criminal law and other state powers.

[6] *cf* Jacobs (2020: 252): 'legislatures have created a great deal of crime via criminalization, which, in many cases, is indicative of a failure of imagination more than an urgent social need'.

[7] One way in which we might respond to some of the inevitable complexity of some areas of criminal law is by giving citizens 'the benefit of the doubt' when it comes to first offences or offences that are complicated or unclear. This might be, for example, by use of police discretion at the enforcement stage or in the use of conditional discharges or suspended sentences at conviction (on which see Bottoms 1981: 19–20). I am grateful to Helen Brown Coverdale for this suggestion.

Finally, the reasons we have to design criminal justice institutions to help us to live non-criminal lives extend also to non-criminal justice institutions. The argument here intersects with Situational Action Theory (SAT). SAT focuses on the 'person, place and situation'. As Per-Olof Wikström puts it (2019: 260–61), 'people do as they do because of who they are and the circumstances in which they take part'. My point here is that we have reason to work on both 'situations' and on 'persons' not only to reduce crime but to reduce the possibility of our being criminals. For example, the state must ensure that its citizens get (some degree of) moral and social education (Jacobs 2020: §1.3). If we have not had the chance to learn how to navigate the social world (or have not been in a position to take advantage of such an opportunity),[8] then we have not had a fair opportunity to avoid failing to do so adequately. (Note, this is not a claim about reduced culpability – although it could be – but about our reasons to design institutions in certain ways given our interests in living non-criminal lives.) Again, that is not the only, or even the main, argument for trying to ensure that children are properly raised, but it is *an* argument that they should be, and it is one that can extend to other institutions including those of the welfare state (although that is not something pursued here).[9]

Public Policy and Cost–Benefit

The focus of the discussion above is on issues of institutional design, but – as noted at the start of this section – this is not the usual way in which instrumental reasons of public policy figure in discussions of criminal justice. More ordinarily, they feature in a traditional cost–benefit sense. Consider the following three passages: first from a national newspaper article by one of the UK's leading forensic psychiatrists; second from a press release from the UK government quoting the country's then Deputy Prime Minister (and Lord Chancellor and Justice Secretary) Dominic Raab; third from the then President of the National Sheriffs' Association in the United States commenting on a Bill to allow limited federal medical aid to be given to incarcerated individuals around the time of their release:

> Treating younger people effectively in prison makes it less likely that they will return in later life. And given the costs of keeping someone incarcerated (around £40,000 per year), providing therapy is time and money well spent … We all want the world to be a safer place. I suggest the pressing question about the treatment of violent offenders is not 'Why bother?' but 'Can we afford not to?' (Adshead 2021).

[8] Brown Coverdale (2018: 125), considers a number of ways in which a person may fail to learn (eg, lack of opportunity, it being the wrong time, and the subject being unwilling).

[9] It is instructive to think of the conversations that some African American parents have with their (male) children about how to avoid trouble with the police. At an individual level, *given policing practices in some places*, it is of course rational to teach one's child how to avoid getting arrested (or worse). But, all that shows is how corrupted policing has become in those places. The issue ought to be how we design criminal justice institutions and practices – and other institutions and practices including education – to help all of us (who are neither angels nor brutes) to live non-criminal lives.

> Giving an ex-offender a second chance can be win win for them and their employer. Business owners have told me that ex-offenders are among the most reliable and motivated workers in their team – they have a desire to prove themselves trustworthy and they have something to lose. It's a win for society too – ex-offender [sic] with jobs are paying their taxes and are significantly more likely to turn their backs on crime (Ministry of Justice 2021).

> In the long run this will reduce recidivism and therefore ease budgetary burdens from the jail system. Our taxpayers deserve that (Cottle 2021).

Despite their different roles, all three of the quoted individuals express two powerful instrumental arguments for state intervention that might enable (in this case) ex-offenders to live non-criminal lives.[10] First, it decreases recidivism and so reduces the overall costs of the prison system. Second, it reduces the risks of future offending and so makes the world a safer place. In addition, Raab argues that businesses can gain from reliable workers 'with something to lose', and that employed ex-offenders are not only less likely to reoffend, and so cost money, but will contribute to the state in tax income.[11]

Instrumental reasons such as those given above are common, and there is perhaps not much for a philosopher to say about the policies they recommend. As Brian Barry once remarked, 'adherence to utilitarianism makes for very boring political philosophy, because once the goal has been postulated … everything else is a matter of arguing about the most efficacious means to that end' (1990: 35). Moreover, they seem commonsensical (it does indeed make sense to try to ensure that ex-offenders do not go on to reoffend and do go on to productive – even tax-paying – lives), but whether therapy and/or encouraging businesses to employ ex-offenders and/or providing Medicaid are the most effective means is something for experts in those fields and not for political and penal philosophers.

That said, it is worth commenting on the place of such reasons in the overall argument. On the one hand, there is something instrumentally self-defeating – not to say, infuriating – about a system that seems in so many aspects of its operations to include policies and practices that reliably produce poor outcomes. To invoke an example that is discussed further below, consider the description given by the criminologist Shadd Maruna of how prisoners are released:

> You're released in the middle of the night … you're on a bus to the inner city where you are dropped off with your fifty quid *which is exactly enough money to score, not enough money to pay for a week's rent* (2021: 47:15, emphasis added).[12]

[10] Like many penal theorists and criminologists, the term 'ex-offender' makes me uncomfortable as it seems to define people by their past criminal acts. I continue to use it only in the absence of an appropriate widely used alternative.

[11] It is worth noting that although Raab initially says employing ex-offenders is a 'win win' for *them* and their employers, when he unpacks this the 'winners' in his eyes seem to be the employers and tax payers. This feature of standard cost–benefit analysis – indifference to the distribution of benefits and burdens – is discussed below.

[12] The prison discharge grant for people serving over 14 days was £46 from 1995 to 2021, when it was raised to £76 and rebranded as a 'one-off subsistence payment'. It is supposed to cover the period until the person's benefit application is approved. Current government guidance suggests that takes around five weeks.

As Adshead might say, 'can we afford not to change' such a practice, and in that sense criminal justice policies and practices are rightly subject to criticism based on instrumental, outcome related, criteria.

On the other hand, thinking of these kinds of instrumental reasons as amongst the range of relevant reasons for government action need not commit us to the view that it is *only* generalised costs and benefits that matter, or to full-blown utilitarianism. Utilitarianism is a distinctive doctrine that combines two elements: a claim about the good (welfare, happiness, preference satisfaction, or whatever); and a claim about maximisation (that we ought to maximise the good either in our actions or in the rules we adopt). Its favouring of maximisation and indifference to the distribution of the good – what Rawls famously noted as its inability to respect the separateness of persons (1971: 191) – is what gives rise to familiar criticisms such as that utilitarianism would endorse sacrificing one for the many, punishing the innocent, and so on.[13] However, one can endorse outcomes as mattering, without endorsing the claim that they are the only things that matter or that good outcomes ought generally to be maximised whatever the costs to particular individuals.

Even so, and admitting that the extremes of utilitarian public policy can be avoided, it is nevertheless worth noting the ways in which even a limited instrumentalism can have implications for how issues are characterised. As others have noted, instrumental arguments linking rehabilitation to reducing recidivism and/or the costs of punishment can subtly shift the focus from the offender to the wider public (and to the wider public as potential victims): it is the needs of the community as tax payers and as potential victims, rather than the needs of the offender, that take centre stage. As Gwen Robinson put it in 2008 (with reference to David Garland's work):

> [I]t is no longer offenders themselves who are seen as the main beneficiaries of rehabilitative interventions, but rather communities and potential victims. As Garland (2001: 176) notes, in a context which has seen the revival of 'less eligibility' concerns and the rise of the victim to 'centre stage', rehabilitative interventions can only be justified to the extent that they are compatible with the interests of these (other) stakeholders. Correctional staff 'now emphasise that "rehabilitation" is necessary for the protection of the public. It is future victims who are now "rescued" by rehabilitative work, rather than the offenders themselves' (Garland 1997: 6) (Robinson 2008: 432).[14]

Thus, Barry is right that political and penal philosophers are not the experts when it comes to questions of what policies will lead to the best outcomes.

[13] For an important argument that the very features of utilitarianism that make it unsuitable as a form of personal morality are features that make it apt for political morality, see Goodin (1995); Matravers (1997).

[14] For further discussion, and an 'updating' of Robinson's important paper, see Bottoms (2021).

Nevertheless, they can still usefully point out the dangers that come when the focus shifts to general outcomes such as recidivism rates and costs. Such things *do* matter, but they are not the *only* things that matter.

PERSON-BASED REASONS

The preceding section has discussed policies that might be implemented to help people in general to live non-criminal lives. This section, by contrast, is concerned with arguments focused on those persons who have offended and been punished (more specifically, those who are trying to desist from offending), and their prospects for living non-criminal lives. Again, it might be thought that this is an odd question to pose because it seems obvious that the state has person-based reasons to support those it has punished to live non-criminal lives. In articles such as that by Adshead cited earlier, there is a sense that in addition to the economic sense it makes to rehabilitate offenders, it is something that is *owed* to them as a matter of compassion or justice (Adshead makes passing reference to both). However, the argument is not made out, and it seems to me not at all obvious. That is, *assuming* that those who have been punished have been justifiably burdened through a just sentence, why should it be the case that the state *owes* them something with respect to, say, their attempts to live non-criminal lives beyond that which it makes sense for the state to offer for instrumental reasons?[15]

The focus, as noted above, is on ex-offenders and their prospects. It is not strictly only on 'desistance', but to frame the discussion consider a (would-be) desister; that is, someone with a history of offending whose rate of offending is decelerating as he tries to turn his life around and move from a life engaged in criminality to a non-offending life. Our questions are, what would help such a person, does the state have reasons of a different kind from the public policy ones considered above to provide that help, and if so, what are those reasons?

What would help such people is a complex, and individual, matter, but is in part captured by the subtitle to Frank Porporino's (2010) paper, 'Bringing Sense and Sensitivity to Corrections: From Programmes to "Fix" Offenders to Services to Support Desistance'. The importance of moving from 'fixing' to 'supporting' stems from what Anthony Bottoms calls 'arguably the most important single finding of desistance research', which is 'asymmetrical causation'. What is meant by asymmetrical causation is that

> the factors that explain someone's desistance from crime are often not the reverse of the factors that explained why he or she began offending ... Desistance is accordingly

[15] *cf* Yankah (2020: 76), 'what does a liberal democracy owe to even those citizens it rightfully punishes?' Yankah's answer is examined briefly below.

> associated with both enhanced *human capital* and enhanced *social capital* (Bottoms 2021: 91, emphasis original).

The importance of this finding is, in part, that it points towards the need to focus on the future – on the support would-be desisters need to succeed – as distinct from (or, at least, in addition to) rehabilitative attempts to address past offending behaviour. Bottoms identifies, as amongst the most significant elements of such support: working *with* offenders; an individualised programme of support; help in developing human capital and in accessing social capital; the recognition that desistance is gradual and sporadic and that support is needed to manage lapses constructively (Bottoms 2021).[16]

These things are very expensive. Working with offenders in individualised ways requires investment in trained supervisors. Enhancing human capital, by which is meant 'the knowledge, skills, and health that people accumulate throughout their lives, enabling them to realize their potential as productive members of society' (World Bank undated) requires, for example, education and training, and offenders tend to start from a low baseline. Enhancing social capital – that is, valuable 'connections within and among social networks' (OECD 2010) – requires would-be desisters to be helped to develop valuable networks through, for example, employment, social clubs and organisations, and family, and again offenders tend to start from a low baseline at least when it comes to *valuable* social networks.

In this section, we are not concerned with what 'cost–benefit' reasons might apply. It might be cheaper in the long run to assist in desistance, but our question is whether, and if so why, we have reason(s) to do so independent of generic costs and benefits. In what follows, I consider two arguments. In the next subsection, I examine arguments from a general obligation to ameliorate suffering (and one potential counter-argument to that). In the subsection that follows, I consider a duty not to make things worse that is discussed in relation to sentencing and then to modes of punishment (specifically incarceration). These arguments are not mutually exclusive; all I think contribute something and not all of them will apply (equally) to all would-be desisters.

The Argument from Amelioration and the Objection from Choice

Recall, our questions are what would help and what reasons there are for the state to provide that help. What would help are the things outlined by Bottoms

[16] *cf* Shapland (2022: 1, citations omitted): 'Desistance is a process requiring both the agency of the offender (a decision to desist) and appropriate social support to allow desistance and to maintain desistance. That social support and social context requires accommodation, a legitimate means of acquiring income, and, preferably, prosocial partners, friends and family to maintain the desire'.

above and include, for example, assisting the would-be desister with resources to facilitate his desistance.[17]

Perhaps the most straightforward reason to provide that help is that, at least in modern welfare states, the state has an obligation to help its citizens to live adequate lives and to ameliorate their sufferings where possible and at least to some degree. Thus, states provide unemployment insurance, pensions, housing, some degree of health care, and so on. What grounds this obligation is considered in the next section.

There are numerous theories, and empirical instances, of such states and they vary widely,[18] but for simplicity (and perhaps least controversially) assume a state with at least the obligation to ensure that its citizens have 'sufficient' (ie, a guaranteed minimum floor of wellbeing below which citizens ought not to fall).[19] So, for example, if a person suffers from a setback such as an accident that renders her unable to work, then she is not left to starve but receives state support.

Such support, although it might be fairly basic depending on the welfare state in question, will help the (would-be) desister. Perhaps that is better put in the negative: the absence of adequate resources will make desisting considerably harder. This is implicit in the quotation from Maruna above. Not having enough money for rent (and just enough for drugs) presents a considerable barrier to

[17] The Senate in the US state of Hawaii has recently introduced a Bill (that is unlikely to pass) 'to establish a pilot program to provide up to one year of guaranteed income to people who are economically coerced or trapped into the sex trade, including sex trafficking victims, and who are seeking to exit the sex trade'. Prostitution is illegal in Hawaii. The Bill thus sets out to provide resources to make exiting the trade possible for those who wish to do so, but who cannot for want of those resources. See: www.capitol.hawaii.gov/session2022/bills/SB3347_.pdf I am grateful to Michelle Madden Dempsey for directing me to this.

[18] In what is sometimes called 'the Western world', perhaps the most marked contrast is between the social democratic understanding of the state characteristic of Northern European countries and the more 'classically liberal' one that has endured in the US. As Jonathan Jacobs remarked to me (private communication), during the last 100–120 years, there have been numerous developments in liberal democracies through which the state has come to have increasing social responsibilities: safety net; social security; low interest loans for various groups; support for university-level education, etc. In the US, the welfarist responsibilities of the state have not changed the liberal understanding of the state that many people still hold onto; that is, that the state should largely stay out of people's lives. In the US, there remain many 'classical' liberals (or at least strong supporters of the free market and less-rather-than-more government). Granted, in many cases they are just out to protect their own assets but there is a very large constituency of small business owners, contractors, entrepreneurs who genuinely want people to be able to make it on their own, who believe that with effort one can do that, and they do not want to be swamped with regulation, administrative law and taxation. In the UK and in other European countries, there is a more social-democratic political culture. That is, the state is recognised as having a significant, essential role in promoting various social aims and, by and large, that is regarded as a basic, accepted responsibility of the state. These differences will be significant for the argument that follows in that the 'content' of what is owed will vary depending one's stance on the above.

[19] For an overview of sufficientarian theory, see Shields (2020). Of course, even this minimal state will exceed what can be justified on some forms of libertarian theories: see, eg, Nozick (1974).

turning one's life around. Yet, a recent 'draft' document produced by the UK Ministry of Justice, and distributed to prisons, included advice about accommodation for those about to be released, the following 'practical tips' for those who may end up homeless: 'Sometimes you can find shelter from abandoned buildings … there might also be bridges' and that 'you can put newspaper between layers of clothing to keep warm'. In addition, 'if you can find cardboard, you can put this under you, between the cold ground to provide a bit of cushion and warmth' (Shaw 2022).[20]

The admission by the Ministry of Justice that homelessness is a distinct possibility for former prisoners – and a reality for around one in eight[21] – is not only an instrumental failure of criminal justice policy (in that it is likely to lead to further crime and further costs of punishment), but failure of welfare policy in delivering, as a matter of what is owed to all citizens, a minimally adequate standard of living. And, whilst a minimally adequate standard of living might not be sufficient to enable people to live non-criminal lives, it may well be close to necessary.

The argument that the state has an obligation of the kind described above is subject to one counter-argument. In the example used to introduce the idea, the person unable to work was rendered so by an accident. This, it might be argued, makes that case and the case of the would-be desister disanalogous.

The philosophical form of this argument rests on a distinction between 'chance' and 'choice' neatly summarised by Barry (1991: 142):

> A just society is one whose institutions honour two principles of distribution. One is a principle of compensation. It says that the institutions of a society should operate in such a way as to counteract the effects of good or bad fortune. The other principle is one of personal responsibility. It says that social arrangements should be such that people finish up with the outcomes of their voluntary acts.

This is an intuitively appealing argument. We do distinguish – at least in the first instance – between the machinist made redundant by new technology and the wastrel whose boss finally fires him after he has chosen many times to remain in bed rather than to arrive at work on time. Arguably, or so the objection would go, those who have committed offences fall on the 'choice' side of this critical divide and so are not, or are at least less, entitled to support.[22]

One response would be to reject the chance/choice distinction and the 'luck egalitarian' arguments that go with it.[23] After all, in a functioning welfare state

[20] The status of this document is contested. Although it had been circulated to prisons, presumably with a view to it being given to those about to be released, when Shaw approached the Ministry of Justice, they denied that it was the final version and insisted that it was a draft.

[21] 'Less than half (48%) of people released from prison between 2020 and 2021 had settled accommodation on release. Around one in eight (12%) were homeless or sleeping rough' (Halliday 2022: 56).

[22] Moore (1997: 86) seems to endorse something like this view.

[23] 'Luck egalitarianism' is an umbrella term for theories that hold that justice should be sensitive to chance and choice. Chance – or, on some accounts, 'brute' bad luck – ought not be allowed to

we do not leave even the wastrel to starve. However, that comes with both a philosophical and a 'political' cost. Philosophically, while the distinction between chance and choice might not be as foundational to 'a just society' as is suggested in the quotation from Barry,[24] the idea of responsibility is central to liberalism, and it would be reckless to disregard it entirely.[25] Politically, the idea of individual responsibility is a powerful weapon often wielded by those on the Right and it would be a mistake to cede it as uniquely to be deployed by them.[26]

Fortunately, there is no reason to discard the idea of responsibility, or the idea that the distinction between chance and choice often matters, to see that it does not matter in this instance. Even if we grant that those who commit offences do so by choice, the consequences of those choices are properly captured by the criminal law and in sentencing provisions. That someone's destitution is a consequence of their punishment is not a choice made by him, but by the society in which he lives. Accordingly, responsibility lies with the state and not with the would-be desister.[27]

Of course, this is a simplification. A person's condition will depend not simply on his having been punished, but on a multiplicity of factors including decisions the person makes in response to having been punished. This is not the place to consider how and when personal responsibility should determine outcomes, but it is worth noting that there are good reasons to think that not all 'choices' are equally relevant to justice. For many people – including many would-be desisters – choices are radically limited and the circumstances in which they are made are hardly sufficient to warrant there being the grounds for holding the person fully liable to all the consequences (for discussion, see Matravers 2007).[28] Moreover, as we shall see in the next subsection, there may be reasons to think that many forms of punishment leave the would-be desister worse off when it comes to reshaping her life.

disadvantage some relative to others, but inequalities that arise through choice – 'option luck' or the exercise of personal responsibility – can be permitted. For a useful summary, see Knight (2013), and for discussion of the chance/choice distinction in relation to both distributive justice and punishment, see Matravers (2007).

[24] Barry himself moved away from the chance/choice distinction in his later work. See, eg, Barry (2005).

[25] Unless, of course, one is a responsibility sceptic. See, eg, Pereboom (2013) and Caruso (2021).

[26] Reacting to Ronald Dworkin's formulation of luck egalitarianism, the Marxist philosopher GA Cohen (1989: 933) commented that it incorporated 'the most powerful idea in the arsenal of the anti-egalitarian right: the idea of choice and responsibility'.

[27] A different way to think of it might be that it is 'shared'. See, eg, Lacey (2016) and Ristroph (2011).

[28] As William Bülow O'Nils pointed out to me (and I am grateful to him for the references), it is also the case that 'incarceration of a parent in childhood leads to a significant increase in teen crime and significant decreases in educational attainment and adult employment' (Dobbie et al 2019: 2). See also Murray and Farrington (2008: 135): 'we conclude that parental imprisonment is a strong risk factor (and possible cause) for a range of adverse outcomes for children, including antisocial behavior, offending, mental health problems, drug abuse, school failure, and unemployment'. So, those making the 'choice' may well have been significantly disadvantaged by parental incarceration in their early lives.

One argument, then, that the state has reasons to support persons in living non-criminal lives is parasitic on the general claim that the state has reasons to ameliorate suffering and to support its citizens in living (minimally) decent lives. Such an argument does not depend on the fact that the would-be desister has been punished. That is, what the state owes to the would-be desister is just what it owes to all citizens.

Is there anything the state owes specifically in virtue of having punished the person? The arguments in the next subsection suggest that there is, even if it is only that the punishment of persons ought not to make it *harder* for them to live non-criminal lives.

Not Making Things Worse

Many of our current criminal justice practices impede rather than enhance the chances of would-be desisters from successfully living non-criminal lives. This subsection focuses on two different ways in which this is true, and on the duties to respond in the first case by changing what we intentionally do and in the second by 'compensating' for what we have often unintentionally, but foreseeably, done.

Sentencing

For some proportionality theorists, each crime has a proportional punishment and the place of any given crime within the sequence of a criminal career makes no difference. In short, the severity of the sentence is to match the seriousness of the particular offence irrespective of whether it is the person's first or fiftieth appearance in court. However, for most penal theorists and in most jurisdictions, sentences are adjusted depending on whether they come first ('first offenders') or later ('repeat offenders') in a potential sequence. There are two main competing justifying accounts of this. One allows that we are all granted a certain leeway for initial mistakes but that if we repeat these, then we progressively lose this (so-called 'progressive loss of mitigation'), and after three occasions it is lost altogether. The other holds that each repeat offence demonstrates disregard for what has come before and so merits an 'enhanced' sentence.[29]

This is not the place to survey the complex literature surrounding the sentencing of repeat offenders. However, whatever the subtleties and nuances of one's favoured account, the focus is on culpability. If the sentence imposed

[29] For an overview of the debate, see Roberts and von Hirsch (2010). For a more recent critique, see Roberts and Frase (2019). In a recent paper Christopher Lewis (2021) has argued for 'a recidivist sentencing discount' (I am grateful to Stephen Galoob for the pointer). However, his argument is not based on desistance but on background injustice and the collateral effects of punishment.

is progressively more severe (or 'less mitigated') as the sequence of offences unfolds, it is because our evaluation of the offender's culpability changes. In short, his culpability increases (or his mitigation decreases) as he commits additional offences.

This is a common thought. Any parent, for example, will be familiar with refrains like 'I warned you', 'I told you last time', and 'Despite what happened last time, you've gone and done it again'. The underlying idea seems to be that there is something almost arrogant in the offender's refusing to acknowledge the lessons of the past, and in refusing to try to learn from them. But that thought seems not to survive in the case of someone trying to stop, but not succeeding all at once; that is, of someone *decelerating* in the way described in the desistance literature. Genuinely trying to stop is hardly an instance of demonstrating arrogant disregard for the lessons of the past. If that is right, then any 'mechanical' application of increased sentences for repeat offenders will not do justice to the complexities of changes in culpability. Moreover, given the effects of punishment described below, more severe sentences may make it harder for the would-be desister to succeed in desisting.

We might also consider ways in which the state may fail even when trying not to make things worse. Consider the following example, which is loosely based on a real case.[30] A man leaves the army. His relationship with his wife is in trouble and he starts drinking and soon becomes dependent on alcohol. His wife divorces him, and he loses custody of his two children. This makes his drinking worse. Following an incident, he is charged with possession of an offensive weapon and driving with excess alcohol. He is found guilty. Aware of the drawbacks of punishing the man, the judge defers the sentence to give him a chance to stop drinking and to engage with the probation service. However, he does not take this chance and misses several appointments with his probation officer in each case because he is drunk. Brought to court for sentencing, he receives a custodial sentence.

Now, let us imagine that there are no alcohol recovery services in the man's area and the waiting list for mental health treatment is more than a year. Moreover, although he has a probation officer, swingeing cuts to that service mean that he is just one of many on that officer's list and receives only a brief phone call and text messages giving the times and places for the appointments.

In prison – described in court as 'maybe the best place for him to dry out' – similar funding cuts mean that he is kept in his cell for most of the day and the therapy sessions on alcohol recovery and dealing with addiction are cancelled.

[30] See: www.lancs.live/news/lancashire-news/end-line-alcoholic-preston-dad-20599352. I have drawn on this case, and on some quotations from the report of it, but I have also added details (particularly in the second paragraph). Since the point is just to give an illustrative example, I could have adopted an entirely hypothetical case, so the added details do not damage the point being made.

In addition, the poor pay of prison officers and the general lack of monitoring because of staff shortages, mean that he has access to alcohol and other recreational drugs such as 'spice' that are either made as 'hooch' from materials in the prison or are smuggled in. He leaves prison with his alcohol addiction enhanced, additional drug problems, and his prospects of living a non-criminal life diminished, and he goes on to reoffend. This is despite the fact that his pre-sentence report had stated that '*all* [he] wants to do is to get his own home, be in full-time work and stop drinking'.

There are multiple failures here, not just missed opportunities. The state cannot demand of someone something that cannot, or can only with great and unusual difficulty, be done. Moreover, if the state offers an implicit or explicit 'bargain' – do this, take these courses, learn these skills, etc, and it will favourably affect the outcome for you of the criminal justice processes in which you are involved – then there is an obligation on the state to provide the opportunities required.

In both these examples (ie, the 'recidivist sentencing premium' and 'the lack of services' situation), the state makes it more difficult for the would-be desister to succeed. That is, the state's interventions make things worse without justification.[31] Having an obligation not to make things worse is, of course, weaker than having an obligation to make things better, but the former can nevertheless do some work. It can also, as we shall see next, ground a more positive obligation loosely modelled on the idea of compensation.

Punishment

Punishment is meant to be 'of an offender for an offence' (*cf* Hart 2008). If we focus on incarceration, the idea is that the offender receives a sentence the severity of which is proportionate to the seriousness of the offence.[32] The punishment consists in the loss of liberty and all that goes with that. In reality, imprisonment not only affects the offender but also, for example, her family and dependents. It breaks social bonds, and literally and figuratively isolates the offender from certain support networks.[33]

[31] Similar claims could be made about many 'collateral' effects of punishment such as requirements to disclose conviction or arrest records. On collateral sanctions, see Hoskins (2019). As Shadd Maruna puts it (2011: 5, citations omitted), 'except for a very fortunate few who have their offenses formally forgiven through pardons or other legal means, individuals with felony records can remain permanently stigmatized, excluded from employment, educational and social opportunities, on the grounds of something they did many years or decades earlier. The resulting cycle of stigma and recidivism is predictable and tragic'.

[32] For some critical questions around proportionality, see the essays collected in Tonry (2020) and du Bois-Pedain and Bottoms (2018).

[33] Fergus McNeill (2016: 76) proposes a similar argument for the state's duty to rehabilitate based on the claim that punishment should not extend beyond the legal sanction imposed by the court.

In addition, prison itself sometimes – perhaps often – has predictable harmful side-effects. As summarised by Dore-Horgan (2022: 6, footnotes omitted):

> Imprisonment can precipitate a decline in people's ability to interact socially. It can compromise people's capacity to make decisions for themselves, can have a brutalising influence, and can bring about a decline in brain functions connected to self-regulation. Additionally, and most obviously, imprisonment can be traumatising for those subjected to it, precipitating an increase in negative emotions and a deterioration in mental health – something which might, in turn (though the evidence on this is mixed), place these individuals at a higher risk of recidivism and repeat incarceration.

Not all prisons are the same and some will do less harm than others,[34] but for now and even in relatively just states, some prisons predictably worsen or harm many of those they incarcerate and, as Jonathan Jacobs has argued (2016: 8), the state has *at least* an obligation not to do that:

> While a liberal polity should not require specific virtues of its members or enforce some specific conception of how to live, it is also antithetical to the principles of a liberal polity for it to *worsen or harm* members in known, regular and avoidable ways. Current forms of incarceration often have such effects (emphasis original).

Many of these forms of harm, and the criminogenic nature of many prisons, mean that some of those who have been incarcerated will find it *more* difficult than otherwise to live non-criminal lives on release.[35] That is, 'their chances of refraining from crime [are] diminished through punishment' (Dore-Horgan 2022: 7).

In the sentencing of repeat offenders, in the failure to put in place the means to achieve routes out of the criminal justice system even when these are mandated by that system, and in using forms of punishment that worsen or harm those punished, the state inhibits desistance. In the first instance, it should try not to do so. It should revise repeat offender sentencing guidelines, ensure the availability of support for those it tries to divert from punishment, and it should use methods of punishment that are less harmful. Even then, though, many of those punished – particularly those who have been incarcerated – will *in virtue of that* find it harder than they would otherwise to live non-criminal lives.

[34] For work on what makes (and does not make) a good prison, see Liebling with Arnold (2004). For a more detailed account of the effects of imprisonment, see Morgan et al (2019).

[35] Moreover, in addition to the points made about the state making it more difficult for those who have been incarcerated to re-establish themselves (because of poor transition planning and/or collateral sanctions), some forms of incarceration that, eg, involve little more than 'a fixed schedule that is the same day after day' with 'few occasions for deciding anything of consequence' will make 'going from institutionalized life to life in civil society … a bewildering and very difficult step' Jacobs (2020: 187). *cf* du Bois-Pedain (discussing Fichte): 'offenders cannot be prepared for a responsible life in freedom through an experience of animal-like captivity in which their ability to lead a self-directed life is dulled instead of furthered' (2017: 212).

Insofar as this consequence is not part of the justified punishment imposed by the state, but a predictable side effect, the state has an obligation in some way to make up, to compensate, for this harm.[36] Providing resources, for example to help a would-be desister to rebuild valuable lost human and social capital might be one way to do that. That is, the state should not return the punished person to society with less chance of living a non-criminal life than he would have had in the absence of state punishment.

GROUNDING AND EXTENDING THE STATE'S OBLIGATIONS TO WOULD-BE DESISTERS (AND OTHERS)

So far, I have considered arguments from the state's duties to ameliorate suffering; not to make things worse; and to compensate when it predictably, but unintentionally, does make things worse. This section examines possible theoretical foundations for these duties. I consider two possible approaches. The first – a rights-based approach grounded either in a form of moral realism or in commonly accepted human rights norms – is discussed relatively briefly. The second – that depends on an idea of 'justice as reciprocity' – is unpacked at greater length with a view to understanding how it might provide the foundations for a positive non-instrumental obligation to support fellow citizens, including but not limited to would-be desisters, in living non-criminal lives. In providing these foundations, it endeavours to develop and enrich the arguments offered above.

Dignity and Rights

One form of argument appeals to human dignity and to ideas with a family resemblance to dignity such as the inalienable worth of each person, the injunction to treat persons always as ends in themselves and not as a means only, and so on. The philosophical tradition here is long and the contemporary developments in these ideas are nuanced and complex.[37]

The advantage of such an approach ought immediately to be apparent. At the very least, it can underpin the argument not to make things worse. No one committed to human dignity could, for example, condone the psychological damage done to those in long-term solitary confinement as described by Jacobs,

[36] *cf* Rotman (1994: 297): 'If imprisonment itself is the punishment, the unchecked harmful effects of incarceration on the mental and social health of the inmate represent illegal additional punishment'.

[37] See, eg, Beitz (2013). For an interesting recent use of 'humanity' in this tradition, which includes further reflections on the harms done by incarceration, see Bronsther (2020).

or the practices of Sheriff Joe Arpaio who boasted that he spent more on the food for the prison dogs than on that for the prisoners.[38] For those working in this tradition, it can of course do more, and appeals to human dignity underpin substantive claims about what is, and what is not, permissible across many areas of moral and political discourse.

Dignity is also a powerful driver in discourses around human rights and public law. For example, in an important case, the European Court of Human Rights has held that it is a violation of human dignity to imprison a person without giving that person the chance to 'regain' his freedom at some point, and that in order to satisfy that demand the state must offer 'genuine and tangible' opportunities to prisoners to rehabilitate themselves.[39] In this case, the right to rehabilitation is established as a means to realise a more important right, which is to be treated with dignity, which itself is taken to require that those imprisoned for extended periods have the chance to demonstrate that they have changed and so may safely re-join society.

Similarly, in Germany, the idea of 'resocialisation' provides a critical, if not precise, benchmark for sentencing and for the treatment of offenders both during and after imprisonment. Analysing the German Federal Constitutional Court's reasoning, Sonja Meijer (2017: 153) identifies two sources for the 'principle of resocialisation', the first of which is 'respect for human dignity: individuals have a right to dignity and a right to develop their personality freely (Articles 1 and 2 Basic Law)'.

Such an idea recognisably sits beneath a number of rights-based accounts that have tried to address the question of what the state owes to those it has rightfully punished. Insofar as they locate the source of the reasons in something intrinsic in the person, they speak to the kind of account we are seeking. In what follows, I briefly consider three such accounts before outlining my reasons for scepticism and setting the basis for an account that is, I believe, to be preferred.

[38] Joe Arpaio: 'It costs more to feed our police dogs than our inmates. The dogs never committed a crime and they're working for a living', as cited in Attwood (2010: 7).

[39] *Murray v The Netherlands* [GC], no 10511/10, ECHR 2016, Judgment of 26 April 2016 (para 101). In this context, the Court held that it would be incompatible with human dignity – which lay at the very essence of the European Convention system – forcefully to deprive a person of his freedom without striving towards his rehabilitation and providing him with the chance to regain that freedom at some future date (ibid, § 113). It went on to note that there was now clear support in European and international law for the principle that all prisoners, including those serving life sentences, be offered the possibility of rehabilitation and the prospect of release if that rehabilitation was achieved (ibid, § 114). While the Convention does not guarantee, as such, a right to rehabilitation, and while Art 3 cannot be construed as imposing on the authorities an absolute duty to provide prisoners with rehabilitation or reintegration programmes and activities, such as courses or counselling, it does require the authorities to give life prisoners a chance, however remote, to some day regain their freedom. For that chance to be genuine and tangible, the authorities must also give life prisoners a real opportunity to rehabilitate themselves; *Harakchiev and Tolumov v Bulgaria* [2014] ECHR 8 (para 264). For further discussion, see Ashworth and Zedner (2019: §§VII–VIII); Spano (2016); Lippke (2017).

In a recent paper, Kimberlee Brownlee has developed a right to hope, and what she calls 'a hope standard for punishment' that includes a right to the possibility of a 'future after punishment worth hoping for' (2021: 598).[40] From this standard, Brownlee generates specific and demanding conditions for morally justified punishment that are relevant to the issues pursued in this chapter. In particular, she argues for 'experiences upon release [that] must give him [an ex-offender] good enough support that he can re-establish himself in society' (2021: 603); 'being able to hold some legitimate position within society, including employment appropriate to one's skills or … the option to compete on equal terms with others for such positions' (at 604); and 'a meaningful option to return to the positions he held before his offence' where that would not be inappropriate (at 604).

In a similar vein, albeit located in a different political theory, Ekow Yankah has argued that reintegration is a political right and that

> [f]urther, reintegration is more than simply a right to be left alone after one has been punished, more than having paid their debt to society. It garners an active duty on the part of the state to return the punished to their role as a functioning citizen (2020: 80).

Finally, Antje du Bois-Pedain argues that:

> Punishment does not merely mark out the punishee's actions as wrong and blames him for engaging in this wrongful act. It also defines how both punishee and punisher will move forward from here. The penal agent lays down the terms of his or her future co-existence with the offender in a shared social world. Because this is punishment's central social function, there is a reintegrative momentum inherent in punishment … If we break the law, terms of atonement must always be offered to us (2017: 203, 215).[41]

Yankah and du Bois-Pedain locate their arguments in the claim that the offender is a continuing member of a community of what the former calls 'civic equals' (Yankah 2020: 83). Moreover, like Brownlee, they think the rights inherent in being a civic equal ensure a right to reintegration, which at least in Yankah's case, gives rise to duties on the state that resemble those articulated by Brownlee:

> A right to reintegration must address the full range of ordinary activity necessary to fully participate in civic society. In particular, addressing an ex-offender's ability to participate as an ordinary member of the modern economy is essential as to reintegration. For practical, psychological, and symbolic reasons, employment is considered essential for full membership in modern American society (Yankah 2020: 103).

[40] For a US perspective on hope, see Ristroph (2010).

[41] *cf* Duff (2001: 149): 'imprisonment must not be *mere* exclusion. It must itself, even while excluding the offender from normal community, be a way of reconciling him with the community'.

The goal of being a society that provides a future after punishment worth hoping for, or at least a meaningful reintegration, is an admirable one (and one, I should make clear, I fully share). However, philosophically one might wonder what grounds such a right and how it can be made to do so much work. Brownlee herself, although she discusses why hope is valuable (2021: 604), begins with courts' recognition of hope, but does not discuss what foundations it might have or explain how she moves from a recognition of a right to hope, and hope's value, to its being a necessary condition of a justified system of punishment. Yankah and du Bois-Pedain locate the rights they endorse in the constitutional arrangements of civic republicanism and a liberal condition of equal freedom, respectively, but these arrangements draw on a more fundamental but ungrounded commitment to the intrinsic equal value of every person.

One possibility is that there is no further available grounding of ideas such as human dignity or the intrinsic equal value of every person. Rather, these are principles that, as John Rawls puts it (1987: 6), are 'latent in the public political culture of a democratic society', and/or are assumed and developed in the jurisprudence of international and constitutional courts. However, the problem, at least for those who are unpersuaded by incantations of words such as dignity, hope, equality and freedom, is that such injunctions have the status of commands whose origins and justifications are opaque. Thou shalt not steal, thou shalt not murder, thou shalt treat others with dignity, and according to one contemporary realist, thou shalt not play Beethoven's late quartets in an elevator (Scanlon 1998: 100).

Moreover, having been deployed, one might be suspicious when they then generate policies that unfailingly suit the political commitments of the author using them. So, an ungrounded right to hope becomes a right to a future worth hoping for that in turn becomes a right to a future with employment appropriate to one's skills, and so on. Perhaps these things are true, and some of course have the status of legal commands, but they stand in need of a grounding that goes beyond that we hold them to be self-evident (not least because many people clearly do not) or that they happen to be shared as 'latent' by people like us, and that is suitable for what David Gauthier (1988: 385) calls our 'post-anthropomorphic, post-theocentric, post-Nietzschean world'.

The next subsection offers an account of social cooperation as grounded only in the willingness of participants to engage with one another under agreed rules. Although it necessarily operates at a high level of abstraction, the argument is that such an account can give us reasons to endorse the limited criminal justice system described earlier as well as a system of punishment that entitles those punished to have a genuine opportunity to re-engage with the community after they have completed their sentences.

Justice as Reciprocity

I said above that Meijer identifies two sources for the 'principle of resocialisation' in the German Federal Constitutional Court's reasoning. The first was the principle of human dignity, discussed above. The second, she writes, is

> founded on the notion that social reintegration is the end towards which the penal system should strive, in accordance with the constitutional principle of the 'social state' (*Sozialstaatsprinzip*, Article 20 (3) Basic law). This notion of the 'social state' implies that the state has a constitutional obligation to assist 'those groups in the community who, because of personal weakness or shortcomings, incapacity or social disadvantage, have been adversely affected in their social development; prisoners and ex-prisoners belong to this group. Not least, resocialization serves to protect society itself – after all, it is in the interests of society that offenders do not re-offend' (Meijer 2017: 153).

With the exception of the last sentence, which I will in any case put to one side as an instrumental argument, this is a general argument for state support for the disadvantaged amongst whom 'prisoners and ex-prisoners' are to be counted. It thus resembles the argument from amelioration discussed above. In this subsection, I sketch another way of understanding the state as a certain kind of community – a 'social state'[42] – that in turn explains how we might think of the obligations we owe one another to assist people in living non-criminal lives.

The argument in this section conceives of punishment not as a bolt-on to community to ensure that wrongdoers receive their 'just deserts' from us, or if not from us potentially from God,[43] but as a constitutive element of community. Liberal societies are fragile human achievements.[44] Their origins and the ways in which they are understood by their members are many and various, but these are not my concern here. Rather, what is of concern is how a liberal society might be rationally reconstructed and that reconstruction offered as an attractive way to live together in political societies.

I have argued elsewhere (Matravers 2000) that each of us has self-interested reasons to participate with others in society conceived as 'a co-operative endeavour for mutual advantage', but that this in itself is insufficient. What is additionally needed is a commitment to live together with others in a certain way; one that recognises the claims others make for themselves as agents. Rules, to which sanctions for non-compliance are attached, help constitute the community, and punishment acts both as a censuring mechanism for those that fail to

[42] I am not claiming that the argument in this section underpins the particular meaning given to the idea of a *Sozialstaatsprinzip* in contemporary Germany.

[43] In *Punishment and the Moral Emotions*, Jeffrie Murphy (2012: 81) writes of Michael Moore that 'if he believed in God, he would not be so concerned to organize secular systems of criminal law around retributive values'.

[44] For an account of liberalism, on which I have drawn here, see Charvet (2019).

live up to their commitment and as an 'assurance' to others that their co-operation is not an invitation to free-riders to exploit them.

Even if this account of the nature of liberal societies is rejected, there should be enough that is familiar in the account of punishment for most penal theorists to find something with which they can agree. State punishment is a social and political construction that, in its ideal form, censures and sanctions those who wrongfully violate certain public rules to achieve ends that include crime reduction, assurance for those who cooperate, and the reassertion of the value of both the particular rule and the rule-based system of which it is a part.

Described at this high level of abstraction, it might seem unlikely that such an account can generate answers to considerably 'downstream' questions of criminal justice practice. However, this not the case. The account cannot, of course, determine which particular programme or techniques ought to be deployed but it can, I believe, underpin the arguments in favour of there being a positive obligation on the part of the state to assist would-be desisters in living non-criminal lives.

Exclusion and Non-Exclusion

A society constituted by a reciprocal commitment of its members is one that is justified in excluding from its ranks those who steadfastly refuse that commitment. For example, Rawls (2005) excludes those who are 'unreasonable' in his account of political liberalism, and Barry (1995) allows that there may be cases in which the only viable option for liberals is to 'fight with cudgels'.[45] However, this is a last resort. Liberalism is designed to solve the problem of 'how to live together given that we have different ideas of how to live' (Barry 1995: 77), and it ought to be able to appeal to the self-interest of non-liberals given that it offers a second-best for all who would impose their beliefs on others (for such people, living in a liberal society is vastly more attractive than living in a non-liberal society organised around any belief system other than their own).

Confronted by political instability, then, the liberal state has reason to try to appeal to the self-interest of those who oppose it. Nevertheless, as Rawls and Barry acknowledge, there may be cases in which such appeals fail. In such cases, exclusion – and possibly violence – may be the only option. However, this is *not* an accurate description of most of those who commit offences. Such people are co-operators who have, as it were, erred. Moreover, as noted at the start of this chapter, we know that we are not perfect or always able to resist the temptation to engage in criminal behaviour, and the consequences of criminal conviction both for ourselves and for those around us are often very serious. In agreeing

[45] The cover of Barry's book is Francisco Goya's 'Fight with Cudgels'. When I asked Barry about his choice (I was his research assistant on the book) he explained that it depicted the alternative to cooperation under just rules.

(rationally reconstructing the rationale for) the system of punishment, then, we have reason to endorse a system that censures, but that is also minimal, and that offers the opportunity to reaffirm one's commitment and to reintegrate into the cooperative venture that is liberal society.

On such an account, the system of punishment is part of what makes the community possible, but each of us has reason to endorse it only to the degree that it is necessary, and in light of our own vulnerabilities and weaknesses. Being held criminally responsible – where appropriate – is in part recognition of one's status as a participant in the community and undertaking one's punishment is a route back to full status. As Duff (2006: 111) puts it:

> [B]eing treated as a citizen is not just a matter of being held criminally responsible: it is a matter of being included, of being allowed to share, in the benefits as well as the burdens of citizenship; of being allowed – indeed encouraged and helped – to take part in the political life of the community, to share in its material and social goods, to benefit from its welfare, educational and medical provisions, and so on.

For this to be substantive, and not just formal, the state must provide assistance to those who would otherwise not be able to realise the goods Duff lists so that they are able to do so. That group will not be limited to those the state has punished, but for reasons we have seen, many of those who have been punished will be amongst them. For these people, the state – and citizens as fellow participants in the political community – must honour the claim that punishment resets the relation between the offender and the community and must at least do what it can to enable the person to live successfully once more as a cooperative member for mutual advantage.[46]

On this account, a liberal society is one underpinned by *mutual* advantage. Each person has reason to endorse her commitment to live together on the agreed terms only if others in the agreement do the same, and only if by doing so that person advances her self-interest. How this is to be understood is complex, and the degree to which actual societies are governed by rules that could be the outcome of such rational engagement will differ; that is, societies will be more or less just.

There are two implications of this that are relevant to the arguments of this chapter. First, we can refine and enhance the argument from amelioration and the response to the objection to it. Think of the benefits of social cooperation as occurring unevenly across the course of citizens' lives. Someone who has 'missed out' on the benefits of social cooperation early in life might reasonably expect to benefit later. This may well apply to many offenders who have suffered from

[46] Of course, although to varying degrees, this is not how many ex-offenders are treated. Rather, as Jacobs (2020: 191) puts it, they are in some cases 'regarded as having diminished standing for life and as "belonging" to a distinct population distinct from society overall'. There is an important discussion to be had about the extent of the duties of fellow citizens – as well as street level bureaucrats – to assist ex-offenders in living non-criminal lives.

unjust material disadvantage in early life. That is, to the degree that they have not been able to share in the 'benefits of citizenship', they have an extra claim in being able to do so later; for example, by being positively supported in gaining the social and human capital needed to desist.[47]

Second, there will be societies that are sufficiently unjust as not to be instances of reciprocity at all. In such circumstances, those who are excluded from the benefits of social cooperation – or who receive substantially less than their fair share of such benefits – cannot reasonably endorse their own commitment to participate under the rules. There are serious and difficult issues in identifying the appropriate baseline and 'trigger', but we cannot exclude the possibility that a society such as the contemporary United States that systematically distributes the benefits of social cooperation in ways that fail to acknowledge some of its members, itself undermines the terms of agreement and the reasons those members have to cooperate.[48] Of course, for those members there may remain compelling prudential reasons to obey the law, and to seek its protections when available, but these reasons are only prudential.

Similarly, the state – and those who benefit from injustice – have prudential reasons to correct course; those who are excluded can be dangerous. In time, cooperation for prudential reasons may transform into genuine social cooperation but that depends on the wills of those involved and, in particular, of those with power.

CONCLUSION

This chapter set out to ask what kinds of reasons the state has to help its citizens to live non-criminal lives. In one sense, the answer is that it has many such reasons. The state has reason to design institutions to help all of us in living non-criminal lives. It also has reason to engage in 'evidence-based policy'. However, in doing so, it needs to be alert to the dangers that come with aggregating costs and benefits without concern for their distribution.

With respect to its other reasons, the picture is more complex. Nevertheless, I hope to have shown that the state has reason to support its citizens (at least)

[47] I am grateful to Jacob Bronsther for pressing this point.

[48] As I say, there are serious difficulties in identifying the appropriate baseline. Moreover, as Albert Weale has pointed out to me, on the one hand, the US does have contributory social security pensions, free education, a degree of public health care, and so on (on this, see Marmor, Mashaw and Harvey 1990). On the other, the interaction of penal policy and distributive injustice is such as to make me doubt that at least two of the assumptions of this chapter hold for the US. First, that the society is bound by reciprocity. Second, that the punishments of many of those who are punished are appropriate (criminogenic social inequalities that are the responsibility of the state render this assumption suspect). For a compelling account of the situation of poor Black Americans and of the implications of injustice for their obligations to obey the law, see Shelby (2016). For discussion of Shelby's work, see Kelly (2022); Mills (2022); Yankah (2022), and the reply in Shelby (2022). For an overview of the relationship of issues of penal and social justice, see Matravers (forthcoming).

to live adequate lives and to ameliorate their suffering. In addition, it should not unjustifiably impede its citizens in living non-criminal lives, and it should compensate when it does so.

These reasons could be grounded in something like human dignity or the right to hope. I think that is inapt, and I have offered an alternative account of a community of reciprocity. As members of such a community, we have reasons to endorse efficient and parsimonious criminal justice institutions, including institutions of punishment. Our awareness of our own fallibilities, and of chance and happenstance, also give us reasons to endorse institutions that will support us in living non-criminal lives, and that will allow for a genuine chance of reintegration for those of us who fail in that endeavour.

REFERENCES

A Bill for an Act 2022 (SB No 3347). Hawaii: The Senate, available at: www.capitol.hawaii.gov/session2022/bills/SB3347_.pdf.

Adshead, Gwen (2021) 'Why We Should be Giving Therapy to Violent Offenders' *Guardian* (12 July 2021), available at: www.theguardian.com/commentisfree/2021/jul/12/therapy-violent-offenders-forensic-psychiatrist-prisoners.

Ashworth, A and Zedner, L (2019) 'Some Dilemmas of Indeterminate Sentences: Risk and Uncertainty, Dignity and Hope' in JW de Keijser, JV Roberts and J Ryberg (eds), *Predictive Sentencing: Normative and Empirical Perspectives* (Oxford, Hart Publishing).

Attwood, S (2010) *Hard Time: A Brit in America's Toughest Jail* (Edinburgh, Mainstream).

Barry, B (1990) 'Political Argument After Twenty-Five Years' in B Barry, *Political Argument: A Reissue with a New Introduction* (Berkeley, CA, University of California Press).

——(1991) 'Chance, Choice, and Justice' in B Barry, *Liberty and Justice: Essays in Political Theory 2* (Oxford, Clarendon Press).

——(1995) *Justice as Impartiality* (Oxford, Clarendon Press).

——(2005) *Why Social Justice Matters* (Cambridge, Polity).

Beitz, CR (2013) 'Human Dignity in the Theory of Human Rights: Nothing But a Phrase?' 41 *Philosophy & Public Affairs* 259.

Bottoms, AE (1981) 'The Suspended Sentence in England, 1967–1978' 21 *British Journal of Criminology* 1.

——(2021) 'Desistance Research and Penal Policy' in T Daems and S Pleysier (eds), *Criminology and Democratic Politics* (Abingdon, Routledge).

Bronsther, J (2020) 'Long-Term Incarceration and the Moral Limits of Punishment' 41 *Cardozo Law Review* 2369.

Brown Coverdale, H (2018) 'Punishment and Welfare: Defending Offender's Inclusion as Subjects of State Care' 12 *Ethics and Social Welfare* 117.

Brownlee, K (2021) 'Punishment and Precious Emotions: A Hope Standard for Punishment' 41 *Oxford Journal of Legal Studies* 589.

Caruso, GD (2021) *Rejecting Retributivism: Free Will, Punishment, and Criminal Justice* (Cambridge, Cambridge University Press).

Charvet, J (2019) *Liberalism: The Basics* (Abingdon, Routledge).

Cohen, GA (1989) 'On the Currency of Egalitarian Justice' 99 *Ethics* 906.
Cottle, Michelle (2021) 'This Bill Could Save the Lives of Formerly Incarcerated People' *New York Times* (20 December 2021), available at: www.nytimes.com/2021/12/20/opinion/medicaid-reentry-act.html.
Dobbie W, Gronqvist, H, Niknami, S, Palme, M and Priks, M (2019) 'The Intergenerational Effects of Parental Incarceration' HKS Faculty Research Working Paper Series RWP19-031.
Dore-Horgan, E (2022) 'Do Criminal Offenders Have a Right to Neurorehabilitation?' *Criminal Law and Philosophy*.
Du Bois-Pedain, A (2017) 'Punishment as an Inclusionary Practice' in A du Bois-Pedain, M Ulväng and P Asp (eds), *Criminal Law and the Authority of the State* (Oxford, Hart Publishing).
Du Bois-Pedain, A and Bottoms, AE (eds) (2018) *Penal Censure: Engagements Within and Beyond Desert Theory* (Oxford, Hart Publishing).
Duff, RA (2001) *Punishment, Communication, and Community* (Oxford, Oxford University Press).
——(2006) 'Answering for Crime' 106 *Proceedings of the Aristotelian Society* 87.
——(2018) *The Realm of Criminal Law* (Oxford, Oxford University Press).
Fenton, Amy (2021) '"End of the line" for alcoholic dad who lost custody battle' *LancsLive* (14 May 2021), available at: www.lancs.live/news/lancashire-news/end-line-alcoholic-preston-dad-20599352.
Gauthier, D (1988) 'Moral Artifice' 18 *Canadian Journal of Philosophy* 385.
Goodin, RE (1995) *Utilitarianism as a Public Philosophy* (Cambridge, Cambridge University Press).
Halliday, M (2022) *Bromley Briefings Prison Factfile* (London, Prison Reform Trust).
Harakchiev and Tolumov v Bulgaria [2014] ECHR 8.
Hart, HLA (2008) 'Prolegomenon to the Principles of Punishment' in HLA Hart, *Punishment and Responsibility: Essays in the Philosophy of Law* (Oxford, Oxford University Press).
Hoskins, Z (2019) *Beyond Punishment? A Normative Account of the Collateral Legal Consequences of Conviction* (New York, Oxford University Press).
Jacobs, J (2016) 'From Bad to Worse: Crime, Incarceration and the Self-Wounding of Society' in S Farrall, B Goldson, I Loader and A Dockley (eds), *Justice and Penal Reform: Re-shaping the Penal Landscape* (Abingdon, Routledge).
——(2020) *The Liberal State and Criminal Sanction: Seeking Justice and Civility* (New York, Oxford University Press).
Kelly, EI (2022) 'The Ethics of Law's Authority: On Tommie Shelby's, *Dark Ghettos: Injustice, Dissent, and Reform*' 16 *Criminal Law and Philosophy* 1.
Knight, C (2013) 'Luck Egalitarianism' 8 *Philosophy Compass* 924.
Lacey, N (2016) 'Socializing the Subject of Criminal Law: Criminal Responsibility and the Purposes of Criminalization' 99 *Marquette Law Review* 541.
Lewis, C (2021) 'The Paradox of Recidivism' 70 *Emory Law Journal* 1209.
Liebling, A and Arnold, H (2004) *Prisons and their Moral Performance: A Study of Values, Quality, and Prison Life* (Oxford, Oxford University Press).
Lippke, RL (2017) 'Irreducible Life Sentences and Human Dignity: Some Neglected and Difficult Issues' 17 *Human Rights Law Review* 383.
Loader, I and Sparks, R (2022) 'Reasonable Hopes: Social Theory, Critique, and Reconstruction in Contemporary Criminology' in A Liebling, J Shapland, R Sparks

and J Tankebe (eds), *Crime, Justice, and Social Order: Essays in Honour of AE Bottoms* (Oxford, Clarendon Press).
Marmor, TR, Mashaw, J and Harvey, PL (1990) *America's Misunderstood Welfare State: Persistent Myths, Enduring Realities* (New York, Basic Books).
Maruna, S (2011) 'Reentry as a Rite of Passage' 13 *Punishment & Society* 3.
——(2021) *The Locked Up Living Podcast* [Desistance or Desistence?] (23 June 2021), available at: lockeduplivng.podbean.com/e/desistance-or-desistence-shadd-maruna-explains-the-term-and-implications-for-progression-in-criminal-policy-planning/.
Matravers, M (1997) 'Robert E Goodin, *Utilitarianism as a Public Philosophy*, Cambridge, Cambridge University Press, 1995' 9 *Utilitas* 261.
——(2000) *Justice and Punishment: The Rationale of Coercion* (Oxford, Oxford University Press).
——(2007) *Responsibility and Justice* (Cambridge, Polity Press).
——(2013) 'On Preventive Justice' in A Ashworth, L Zedner and P Tomlin (eds), *Prevention and the Limits of the Criminal Law* (Oxford, Oxford University Press).
——(forthcoming) 'Punishment and Social Injustice' in J Ryberg (ed), *The Oxford Handbook of Punishment Theory and Philosophy* (Oxford, Oxford University Press).
McNeill, F (2016) 'What Good is Punishment?' in S Farrall, B Goldson, I Loader and A Dockley (eds), *Justice and Penal Reform: Re-shaping the Penal Landscape* (Abingdon, Routledge).
Meijer, S (2017) 'Rehabilitation as a Positive Obligation' 25 *European Journal of Crime, Criminal Law and Criminal Justice* 145.
Mills, CW (2022) 'Dark Mores: Some Comments on Tommie Shelby's *Dark Ghettos: Injustice, Dissent, and Reform*' 16 *Criminal Law and Philosophy* 29.
Ministry of Justice (2021) *Giving an Ex-Offender a Second Chance Can Be a Win-Win for Business, says Deputy Prime Minister* (London, Crown Copyright).
Moore, M (1997) *Placing Blame: A General Theory of the Criminal Law* (Oxford, Oxford University Press).
Morgan, RD, Van Horn, S, MacLean, N, Hunter, J and Bauer, R (2019) 'The Effects of Imprisonment' in DLL Polaschek, A Day and CR Hollin (eds), *The Wiley International Handbook of Correctional Psychology* (Newark, NJ, John Wiley & Sons).
Murphy, JG (2012) *Punishment and the Moral Emotions: Essays in Law, Morality, and Religion* (New York, Oxford University Press).
Murray, J and Farrington, D (2008) 'The Effects of Parental Imprisonment on Children' 37 *Crime and Justice* 133.
Murray v The Netherlands [GC] no 10511/10, ECHR 2016.
Nozick, R (1974) *Anarchy, State and Utopia* (New York, Basic Books).
OECD (2010) *Social Capital, Human Capital and Health: What is the Evidence?* (Paris, OECD).
Pereboom, D (2013) 'Free Will Skepticism and Criminal Punishment' in T Nadelhoffer (ed), *The Future of Punishment* (Oxford, Oxford University Press).
Porporino, FJ (2010) 'Bringing Sense and Sensitivity to Corrections: From Programmes to "Fix" Offenders to Services to Support Desistance' in J Brayford, F Cowe and J Deering (eds), *What Else Works? Creative Work with Offenders* (Cullompton, Willan).
Rawls, J (1971) *A Theory of Justice* (Cambridge, MA, Harvard University Press).
——(1987) 'The Idea of an Overlapping Consensus' 7 *Oxford Journal of Legal Studies* 1.
——(2005) *Political Liberalism: Expanded Edition* (New York, Columbia University Press).

Ristroph, A (2010) 'Hope, Imprisonment, and the Constitution' 23 *Federal Sentencing Reporter* 75.

——(2011) 'Responsibility for the Criminal Law' in RA Duff and S Green (eds), *Philosophical Foundations of the Criminal Law* (New York, Oxford University Press).

Roberts, JV and Frase R (2019) *Paying for the Past: The Case Against Prior Record Sentence Enhancements* (Oxford, Oxford University Press).

Roberts, JV and von Hirsch, A (2010) *Previous Convictions at Sentencing: Theoretical and Applied Perspectives* (Oxford, Hart Publishing).

Robinson, G (2008) 'Late-Modern Rehabilitation: The Evolution of a Penal Strategy' 10 *Punishment & Society* 429.

Rotman, E (1994) 'Beyond Punishment' in A Duff and D Garland (eds), *A Reader on Punishment* (Oxford, Oxford University Press).

R v Youssaf [2021] EWCA Crim 1094.

Scanlon, TM (1998) *What We Owe to Each Other* (Cambridge, MA, Harvard University Press).

Shapland, J (2022) 'Once Convicted? The Long-Term Pathways to Desistance' 61 *Howard Journal of Crime and Justice* 271.

Shaw, Danny (2022) 'Street Talk' *Danny Shaw* (4 March 2022), available at: www.dannyshaw.net/post/street-talk.

Shelby, T (2016) *Dark Ghettos: Injustice, Dissent, and Reform* (Cambridge, Belknap Press).

——(2022) 'Dark Times, Black Light: A Reply to Yankah, Kelly, and Mills' 16 *Criminal Law and Philosophy* 45.

Shields, L (2020) 'Sufficientarianism' 15 *Philosophy Compass* e12704.

Spano, R (2016) 'Deprivation of Liberty and Human Dignity in the Case-Law of the European Court of Human Rights' 4 *Bergen Journal of Criminal Law and Criminal Justice* 150.

Tonry, M (ed) (2020) *Of One-Eyed and Toothless Miscreants: Making the Punishment Fit the Crime?* (New York, Oxford University Press).

Von Hirsch, A (1993) *Censure and Sanctions* (Oxford, Clarendon Press).

Wikström, P-O (2019) 'Situational Action Theory: A General, Dynamic and Mechanism-Based Theory of Crime and its Causes' in MD Krohn, N Hendrix, G Penly Hall and AJ Lizotte (eds), *Handbook on Crime and Deviance* (Cham, Springer International Publishing).

Williams, B (2005) *In the Beginning Was the Deed: Realism and Moralism in Political Argument*, ed G Hawthorn (Princeton, NJ, Princeton University Press).

World Bank (undated) *Human Capital Project*, available at: www.worldbank.org/en/publication/human-capital.

Yankah, EN (2020) 'The Right to Reintegration' 23 *New Criminal Law Review* 74.

——(2022) 'Whose Burden to Bear? Privilege, Lawbreaking and Race' 16 *Criminal Law and Philosophy* 13.

Subject Index

[Note: References such as '178–79' indicate (not necessarily continuous) discussion of a topic across a range of pages].

Name Index

[Most, but not all, names listed are of cited authors. Authors of cited single-author and dual-author works are included, but for multi-authored works only the first author is listed. In accordance with publishers' guidelines, chapter-authors' citations to their own works are not included]